ZEW Economic Studies

Publication Series of the Centre for European Economic Research (ZEW), Mannheim, Germany

ZEW Economic Studies

Further volumes of this series can be found at our homepage:
springeronline.com/series/4041

Vol. 11: K.L. Brockmann, M. Stronzik (Eds.)
Flexible Mechanisms for an Efficient Climate Policy
Cost Saving Policies and Business Opportunities
2000. VIII, 130 pp. ISBN 3-7908-1314-1

Vol. 12: W. Smolny
Endogenous Innovations and Knowledge Spillovers
A Theoretical and Empirical Analysis
2000. VIII, 277 pp. ISBN 3-7908-1320-6

Vol. 13: M. Lechner, F. Pfeiffer (Eds.)
Econometric Evaluation of Labour Market Policies
2001. X, 242 pp. ISBN 3-7908-1372-9

Vol. 14: M. Beise
Lead Markets
Country-Specific Success Factors of the Global Diffusion of Innovations
2001. XVI, 305 pp. ISBN 3-7908-1430-X

Vol. 15: O.H. Jacobs, C. Spengel
Effective Tax Burden in Europe
Current Situation, Past Developments and Simulations of Reforms
2002. X, 131 pp. ISBN 3-7908-1470-9

Vol. 16: U. Kaiser
Innovation, Employment, and Firm Performance in the German Service Sector
2002. X, 164 pp. ISBN 3-7908-1481-4

Vol. 17: J. Köke
Corporate Governance in Germany
An Empirical Investigation
2002. VIII, 184 pp. ISBN 3-7908-1511-X

Vol. 18: E. Wolf
What Hampers Part-Time Work?
An Empirical Analysis of Wages, Hours Restrictions and Employment from a Dutch-German Perspective
2003. X, 174 pp. ISBN 3-7908-0006-6

Vol. 19: P. Cecchini et al. (Eds.)
The Incomplete European Market for Financial Services
2003. XII, 255 pp. ISBN 3-7908-0013-9

Vol. 20: C. Böhringer, A. Löschel (Eds.)
Empirical Modeling of the Economy and the Environment
2003. VI, 326 pp. ISBN 3-7908-0078-3

Vol. 21: K. Rennings, T. Zwick (Eds.)
Employment Impacts of Cleaner Production
2003. VIII, 322 pp. ISBN 3-7908-0093-7

Vol. 22: O. Bürgel, A. Fier, G. Licht, G. Murray
The Internationalisation of Young High-Tech Firms
An Empirical Analysis in Germany and the United Kingdom
2003. XII, 291 pp. ISBN 3-7908-0120-8

Vol. 23: F. Hüfner
Foreign Exchange Intervention as a Monetary Policy Instrument
Evidence for Inflation Targeting Countries
2004. X, 175 pp. ISBN 3-7908-0128-3

Vol. 24: E. Lüders
Economic Foundation of Asset Price Processes
2004. XII, 121 pp. ISBN 3-7908-0149-6

Vol. 25: F. Reize
Leaving Unemployment for Self-Employment
An Empirical Study
2004. XII, 241 pp. ISBN 3-7908-0168-2

Vol. 26: Ch. Böhringer, A. Löschel (Eds.)
Climate Change Policy and Global Trade
2004. VIII, 381 pp. ISBN 3-7908-0171-2

Vol. 28: L. Lammersen, R. Schwager
The Effective Tax Burden of Companies in European Regions
2005. XI, 251 pp. ISBN 3-7908-1562-4

Vol. 29: Ch. Elschner, R. Schwager
The Effective Tax Burden on Highly Qualified Employees
2005. VIII, 123 pp. ISBN 3-7908-1568-3

Vol. 30: Ch. Lauer
Education and Labour Market Outcomes
2005, X, 286 pp. ISBN 3-7908-1569-1

Klaus Jacob · Marian Beise · Jürgen Blazejczak
Dietmar Edler · Rüdiger Haum · Martin Jänicke
Thomas Löw · Ulrich Petschow · Klaus Rennings

Lead Markets for Environmental Innovations

With 52 Figures
and 20 Tables

Physica-Verlag
A Springer Company

ZEW
Zentrum für Europäische
Wirtschaftsforschung GmbH
Centre for European
Economic Research

Series Editor
Prof. Dr. Dr. h.c. mult. Wolfgang Franz

Authors
Dr. Klaus Jacob
Professor Dr. Martin Jänicke
Freie Universität Berlin
Environmental Policy Research Centre
Ihnestraße 22
14195 Berlin

Dr. Marian Beise
Kobe University
Research Institute for Economics
and Business Administration
2-1 Rokkodai, Nada-ku
Kobe-shi 657-8501
Japan

Professor Dr. Jürgen Blazejczak
University of
Applied Sciences Merseburg (FH)
Geusaer Straße
06217 Merseburg

Dr. Dietmar Edler
German Institute
for Economic Research (DIW)
Königin-Luise-Straße 5
14195 Berlin

Rüdiger Haum
Dipl.-Kfm. Thomas Löw
Dipl.-Vw. Ulrich Petschow
Institute for
Ecological Economy Research (IÖW)
Potsdamer Straße 105
10785 Berlin

Dr. Klaus Rennings
Centre for
European Economic Research (ZEW)
L7,1
68161 Mannheim

Cataloging-in-Publication Data
Library of Congress Control Number: 2005922602

ISBN 3-7908-0164-X Physica-Verlag Heidelberg New York

Physica-Verlag is a part of Springer Science+Business Media

springeronline.com

Printed in Germany

Cover design: Erich Dichiser, ZEW, Mannheim

SPIN 10981283 43/3153-5 4 3 2 1 0 – Printed on acid-free paper

Preface

Some countries are earlier than others in the development and introduction of environmental innovations. If other countries follow their examples and adopt their innovation design as well, these countries can be analysed as lead markets. In this book, contributions from innovation economics, environmental economics, and policy sciences are reviewed to explain the leadership of such countries. In case studies on environmental innovations such as photovoltaic cells, fuel cells, chlorine-free paper bleaching, diesel particulate filters, social responsible investments and others the lead markets are identified and factors that determine their advance are analysed. Often, the leadership in technological development is accompanied by a leadership in environmental policy. There is a parallel diffusion of environmental technologies and policies. Based on the theoretical considerations and the case studies, policy recommendations for R&D policies, environmental and industrial policies are derived to support the development of lead markets for environmental innovations.

This book is the result of a joint research project under the title “Policy Framework for the Development of International Markets for Innovations of a Sustainable Economy – from Pilot Markets to Lead Markets (LEAD)”. The authors are grateful for the funding provided by the German Federal Ministry of Research and Education (grant number 07RIW1A).

Table of Contents

1 Introduction

1.1 The Notion of Lead Markets

There are considerable differences in the rate of adaptation of environmental innovations among the different countries. Some countries are earlier in adopting innovation, and the penetration of markets is more encompassing than in others. If these innovations are adopted subsequently without great changes in other countries, the countries where the first market introduction took place, can be viewed as *lead markets*. The concept of lead markets has been developed and fruitfully applied for any type of technological innovations. Examples for lead markets for non-environmental innovations are the mobile phones that were introduced in Finland, the fax in Japan or the internet in the USA (Beise, 2001). The lead market is not necessarily the country where the technology was actually invented. These markets have the characteristic that product or process innovations that are designed to meet local demand preferences and conditions can be introduced in other geographic markets as well and successfully commercialised without many modifications. A lead market is the core of the world market where local users are early adopters of an innovation on international scale (Beise, 1999). This definition focuses on two characteristics of lead markets. Firstly, they are pioneering countries in the development and – more important – the marketing of innovations. Secondly, innovations that arise in these markets subsequently diffuse worldwide. Both phenomena call for analysis and explanation.

At first glance, lead markets are countries with the following features (Meyer-Krahmer, 1999):

- High per capita income,
- Demanding, innovative buyers and high quality standards,
- Problems creating pressure for change and innovation,
- Flexible regulation and innovation-friendly basic conditions for producers and users,
- Product standards acknowledged in other countries.

These factors hint to the fact that there are many different economic and policy factors that contribute to the emergence of such markets. Our study systematises the different factors that can be found in different streams of literature. Our approach is largely explorative, since no encompassing explanation has been developed for the emergence of lead markets for environmental innovations so far. Based on this study we develop recommendations for policy strategies that are able to stimulate the emergence of lead markets.

Our studies are dealing with lead markets for environmental innovations. It can be expected that the above mentioned factors are characteristic of lead markets for *environmental* technologies as well, but that there are also additional factors at work here, arising from the particular context in which environmental innovations are developed, both at the national and international level.

The history of environmental protection is rich in examples for lead markets: It encompasses the legally enforced introduction of catalytic converters for automobiles in the United States, desulphurization technologies in Japan, the Danish support for wind energy or the CFC free refrigerator in Germany. Another impressive example is the global diffusion of chlorine-free paper, from the political activities by Greenpeace and the EPA in the United States, by way of the introduction of chlorine-free paper whitener in Scandinavian countries and various Greenpeace campaigns in Germany and Austria, right through to effective political market intervention in Southeast Asian countries like Thailand (Mol and Sonnenfeld, 2000, see chapter 4.4 for a more detailed analysis). The latter case shows that political action that stimulates internationally successful innovations is not limited to governmental agencies only, but that this function at least regarding the process of setting environmental objectives may also be taken over by environmentalists.

Lead markets can be represented by the rate of market penetration in the different countries. The diffusion starts earlier and the market penetration is typically more complete than in other countries. An example is the catalytic converter for cars (see for more detailed discussion: chapter 4.5):

Fig. 1. Share of passenger cars equipped with catalytic converter in %

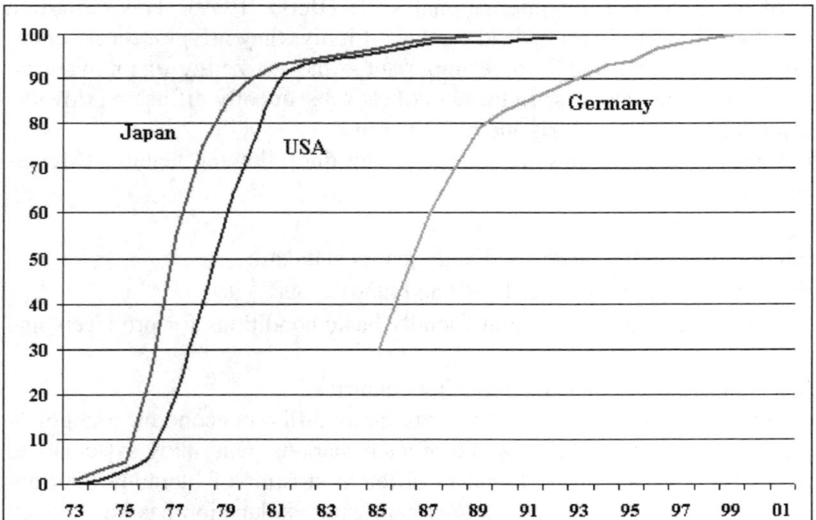

California became the pacesetter for air quality and automobile emission standards from the 1960s on. U.S. congress took over these far-reaching standards in

1970 that were not to be met with existing technologies. That was for the first time a purposeful technology forcing. However, the short period of time to meet the standards did not allow the development of a new engine design. Therefore, the catalytic converter became the dominant technical strategy to reduce emissions. The U.S. regulations were adopted by several countries with automobile industry. In particular Japan adopted early the US regulations, in order to adapt its own car industry to global markets and to enhance its competitiveness.

While the U.S. standards were postponed and lowered due to successful lobbying of the U.S. car industry, the Japanese government maintained the earlier objectives. In Europe, the regulations favouring a catalytic converter had been adopted in 1985, and among the European countries Germany took over the leading role, mainly due to its export oriented automobile industry.

What are the determinants that cause the differences in the introduction of innovations? What are the characteristics of the leading countries? Is there room for manoeuvre for a purposeful establishment of lead markets for environmental innovations?

From our case studies as well as previous studies we can infer that technical *environmental* innovations have to be largely ascribed to governmental (or NGO) activities. Environmental innovations are not only stimulated by the higher environmental standards of consumers in a country as compared with those in other countries, but also by special promotional measures, or by political intervention in the market (Klemmer et al., 1999; Jänicke et al., 2000). If the technologies cause additional costs without improving the benefits for the users as for the case of end of pipe measures, regulatory interventions are even indispensable for innovation and diffusion. But also in cases of integrated technologies, with additional advantages in efficiency, policy measures are often necessary to stimulate innovations and to support their diffusion. The underinvestment in environmental innovation can be explained by the double externality of R&D efforts made in environmental technologies: Alongside the spillover effects that can be observed for any R&D activities, efforts in *environmental* technologies do result in improvements of the environment which again is a public good. Therefore an underinvestment in environmental innovations can be expected (Rennings, 2000).

Environmental innovations do have another characteristic that is in favour of their international diffusion: They provide marketable solutions to environmental problems that are usually encountered worldwide, or at least in many countries. Thus, technological solutions to environmental problems inherently lend themselves to adoption in international or global markets.

The regional differences in adoption and diffusion of innovations cannot be explained with the specifics of environmental innovations. For this purpose, the framework conditions and political strategies in the leading countries have to be analysed. The dependence of environmental technologies on regulatory measures leads to the question to what extent national environmental policies to stimulate lead markets remain possible and effective in the context of globalisation. Our theoretical and empirical investigations, however, reveal that there is considerable room for manoeuvre for national actors. Typically, policy innovations arise in a national framework rather than being imposed by an international regime. Innovative policies do diffuse very much like technological innovations. The process of diffusion is determined by the capacities of the innovating countries to develop environmental policies, by the type of innovation and the underlying problem, and by activities of international actors that often look for best practices on the national level and stimulate their diffusion (Tews et al., 2003, see chapter 2.2 for a more detailed discussion).

There is a close inter-linkage in the innovation and diffusion of environmental policies on the one hand and the innovation and diffusion of technologies on the other hand. The interplay between the diffusion of environmental policy measures and environmental technology can take a wide variety of possible sequences as depicted in the following graph.

Fig. 2. Stage model of the diffusion of environmental innovation

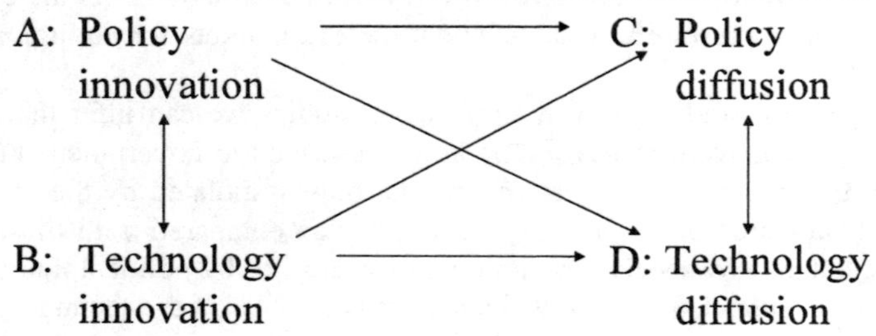

Policy induced diffusion
Technology forcing (A⇒B⇒C⇒D): e.g. US-car emission standards (1970)
Political initiative (A⇒B⇒D⇒C): e.g. Cadmium substitutes
Political dominance (A⇒C⇒B⇒D): no example yet?

Technology induced diffusion
Technological initiative (B⇒A⇒C⇒D): e.g. wind energy
Technological dominance (B⇒A⇒D⇒C): e.g. CHP technologies
Autonomous diffusion (B⇒D): e.g. Incremental improvements of energy efficiency

Source: Jänicke (2000).

Theoretically, it is possible to distinguish between the following diffusion scenarios, depending on the factors leading to the political and technological innovations:

- *Technology forcing* (A⇒B⇒C⇒D): A national environmental policy innovation in one country forces a technological innovation which diffuses if the policy innovation also diffuses (e.g.: catalytic converter technology in cars).
- *Technological initiative* (B⇒A⇒C⇒D): An existing environmental technology induces a political innovation the diffusion of which in turn encourages the diffusion of the technology (e.g.: wind energy in Denmark).
- *Political initiative* (A⇒B⇒D⇒C): A national environmental policy leads to technological innovations the diffusion of which in turn encourages diffusion of the policy innovation (e.g.: cadmium substitute).

- *Technological dominance* (B⇒A⇒D⇒C): An innovation in environmental technology is successfully diffused and as a result receives political support both nationally and internationally (e.g.: combined heat and power in industry).
- *Political dominance* (A⇒C⇒B⇒D): The innovation in environmental policy is successfully diffused before a corresponding technology is available (this scenario is symptomatically very rare in ecological modernisation).
- *Autonomous technological development* (B⇒D): An innovation in environmental technology is successfully diffused without political intervention; this case, beyond incrementally increasing energy efficiency in companies, seems to be rather rare.

The different patterns of innovation and diffusion can be distinguished regarding the degree of difficulty of the underlying political strategies. On the one hand, a policy measure will meet resistance of the target groups in particular in those cases where a technology that is able to fulfil the required standards has yet not been developed and an international example for comparable policy measures is missing (technology forcing). On the other hand, policy measures that primarily aim at a support for the diffusion of developed technologies may still meet the resistance of the affected industries if they prefer to use their previous technologies for a longer period of time. However, these policies are easier to be enforced if the related technologies have proved their technological and their economic feasibility. This is particularly true if there are international examples for such policy measures. These examples are often used to legitimise planned policies. In this way, technological innovations provide additional options for policymakers.

By this logic of different degrees of difficulty of policy interventions, a technology forcing can be observed only rarely (e.g. Californian exhaust gas standards, to a lesser degree also the European standards for automobiles). Environmental policy up to now, has had its merits in the support of the diffusion of developed innovations (Conrad, 1998; Jacob, 1999).

For the choice of policy instruments it can be concluded, that in those cases where no innovator exists yet, distributive measures e.g. R&D funding are easier to be implemented. For policies that aim at a diffusion of existing technologies regulative measures are likely to be more efficient and effective. The opposite extreme of technology forcing – the autonomous emergence and diffusion of innovations in environmental technology – is the exception rather than the rule and such developments usually yield only limited incremental increases in efficiency.

The mechanism of international diffusion of policy innovations is favourable for the creation of lead markets for environmental innovations. On the one hand, the convergence of standards and regulations implies – in the case of technology-based policies – a widening of the market for technologies. On the other hand, the availability of technical solutions makes the diffusion of the corresponding policy innovation more likely.

Technologies with advantages beyond environmental relief (e.g. cost reductions or users' higher willingness to pay) are more likely than end-of-pipe (EOP) technologies to be successful abroad, even in the absence of policy diffusion. There is evidence, however, that EOP technologies, in combination with supporting regulation, diffuse in a very similar manner. Often technologies address environmental problems of an international nature, i.e. problems that are on the international agenda or at least occur in various regions of the world.

However, the emergence of lead markets is not a matter of the introduction of a single policy instrument and the successful stimulation of innovations cannot be explained by focusing on policy instruments only, but the political will and favourable framework conditions are decisive. In addition to an innovation oriented environmental policy it is favourable for the emergence of lead markets if the countries have attained the image of a pioneer in environmental policy making. Furthermore, lead markets emerge more often in countries that have accumulated a high level of technological competences in their industries.

We expect these mechanisms to have a considerable potential for an encompassing ecological modernisation. Ideally, lead markets affect competition in other market regions, trigger appropriate responses and adaptations, and thereby promote the international diffusion of the new technology. Thus, lead markets may fulfil a range of functions. From an *international* perspective, they provide marketable solutions to global environmental problems. Lead markets in high-income countries are able to raise the necessary funds for the development of innovations. This may help new technologies through their teething troubles. In demonstrating both technical and political feasibility, they stimulate other countries and enterprises to adopt their pioneering standards.

From a *national* perspective, ambitious standards or support mechanisms may create a first-mover advantage for domestic industries. Furthermore, ambitious policy measures can attract internationally mobile capital for the development and marketing of environmental innovations. Finally, economic advantages legitimate the national policymakers, and a demanding policy provides them with an attractive role in the global arena.

1.2 Studying Lead Markets

There is no single disciplinary approach that is able to analyse and to explain the emergence of lead markets. For our analysis we draw on several approaches that contribute to the understanding of the phenomenon. In chapter 2 the core ideas and methods of the disciplines that contribute to our analysis are depicted. The concept of lead market has been developed by innovation economics. The core question of innovation economics is how innovations are selected and what are the determinants of their success and failure. We are focusing on the country specific determinants that contribute to success and failure of a certain innovation and on the question how these factors influence the selection of innovations that are adopted in other countries as well. Many of these factors are influenced by policies, and in the case of environmental innovations political measures are often even indispensable for their success. Therefore, policy analysis constitutes the second pillar of our theoretical framework. We are particularly concerned with the question why and how the diffusion of policies takes place from one country to another, because this mechanism creates market opportunities in other countries. Environmental economics contributes to the question to what extent countries may gain economic advantages in setting stricter environmental standards than others. Recent game theoretical approaches shed some light on a consistent explanation for this phenomenon for which many empirical examples have been shown. Finally, management science contributes to the analysis by explaining the behaviour of firms. We analyse what characteristics of a firm must be taken into account, in particular if there are only few companies that compete in a certain market segment in order to explain, why some step ahead and why certain markets are chosen for the introduction of their innovations.

All of the distinct theoretical approaches, defined by their methodologies and their respective subjects of research as described above, contribute to the analysis of this phenomenon. In section 2 the contributions of the various theoretical approaches are described in more detail. We conclude the first part of this study with the development of an integrated model for the analysis of lead markets that is based on the above mentioned approaches.

Within this framework for analysis, we study historical cases of innovation and diffusion based on an analysis of the literature. In total 12 innovations are analysed in this part of the study. Our studies comprise energy technologies (biomass CHPs, wind energy), innovations for automobiles (technologies for fuel efficient cars, catalytic converters for cars), substitutes for hazardous chemicals (CFCs in refrigerators, cadmium in paints, phosphates in detergents), innovations in the paper production (chlorine-free/reduced bleaching, black liquor gasification), and organisational/institutional innovations (EMAS, leasing of solvents, return systems for waste). For this study we have selected those cases for which lead markets are well documented in the literature.

The second part of our empirical studies comprises cases of emerging technologies. We apply the lead market model to innovations for which it is not yet decided where the leading countries are. Our examples are photovoltaic, fuel cells for mobile and stationary applications, technologies for the reduction of diesel emissions, technologies for the substitution of paper as well as technologies for the recycling of paper, paints with a reduced content of solvents and as another example for an institutional innovation, social responsible investments. For each of the cases we analyse the regulatory framework and the activities of companies in those countries which are the most likely candidates for becoming a lead market. From these studies we derive policy recommendations for strategies that advance the emergence of lead markets.

Due to the explorative character of the study, we dismiss a narrow selection criterion for the analysis. Instead we aim at covering a broad set of different technologies, from a great variety of sectors in various countries and with different degrees of maturity. While some of the technologies are still in the stage of development, in other cases it is mainly the process of policy diffusion that is of primary concern. Table 1 gives an overview of the characteristics of the innovations studied.

Table 1. Characteristics of the innovations ●: directly/fully applicable; ○: indirectly/partly applicable.

	Fuel cells stationary	Fuel cells mobile	Substitution of paper	Recycling of paper	Low solvent paints	Photovoltaic	Social responsible investment	Diesel emission reduction	Biomass CHP	Catalytic converter	CFC substitutes	Phosphate substitutes	EMAS	Wind energy	Cadmium in paints	Technologies for fuel efficient cars	Chlorine-free /reduced paper	Black liquor gasification	Leasing of solvents	Return systems for waste
Sector																				
Automobiles	○	●						●		●					○	●				
Energy	●	○				●			●					●						
Chemicals	○	○			●						●	●			●				●	
Paper			●	●													●	●		
Fin. services							●													
Waste man.																			○	●
Maturity of Innovation																				
Development	●	●	●			●														
Market intr.								●	●							●				
Policy diff.				●	●		●							●					●	●
Complete										●	●	●			●		●			
Underlying problem																				
Climate ch.	●	●				●			●					●		●		●		
Em. to water												●					●			
Waste reduction/cleaning															●				●	●
Em. to air		●			●			●		●	●									
Regions																				
Europe	○	○	○	●	●	●	●	●	●		●	●		●	●	●	●		●	●
USA	●	●	●		●					●	●	○								
Japan	●	○	●			●				●										

The study concludes with a generalisation of our findings regarding the opportunities for political strategies that are favourable for the creation of lead markets. There is a great variety of starting points in the different sectors of policy making. There is no single "lead market instrument" that is able to foster all the conditions required for the successful stimulation of innovations that are adopted also in other countries. What is required is a comprehensive strategy that encompasses all the stages of the innovation process from invention to diffusion. A coordinated approach of innovation policy, environmental policy and industrial policy is required to successfully stimulate lead markets for environmental innovations.

2 Theoretical Approaches

2.1 Lessons from Innovation Economics

The main question the lead market theory must address is why countries follow a lead market in adopting an innovation, even if these markets have previously favoured different environmental innovation approaches or designs. An innovation design is a technical specification of an innovation idea. An environmental problem can be solved by a variety of innovation designs. Different countries usually prefer different innovation designs for a given problem, as the initial market contexts pose different technical requirements. Not only strong needs and the demand for a particular innovation, but also the ability to transfer specific national innovations or preferences to other countries are prerequisites for a lead market. A variety of lead effects are responsible for this internationalisation of an innovation design. The lead or leverage effect is the mechanism by which a design adopted by the lead market spreads to lag markets, supersedes initially preferred alternative designs in these markets, and becomes the globally dominant design. There are several factors that can explain this internationalisation pattern. Basically, lower prices and the certainty of the benefit of an innovation design can compensate for internationally varying market conditions. Secondly, an international trend that is most advanced in the lead market brings about an internationalisation of needs (or preferences), and thus the adoption of innovations which respond to these needs by more and more countries. Beise (2001) has reviewed these and other explanations of the lead market phenomenon. On the basis of his results, a system of five groups of lead advantages of a country has been derived:

1. Price advantage. National conditions that result either in relative price decreases of a nationally preferred innovation design compared to designs preferred in other countries, or in the anticipation of international factor price changes.
2. Demand advantage. National conditions that result in the anticipation of the benefits of an innovation design emerging at a global level.
3. Transfer advantage. National conditions which increase the perceived benefit of a nationally preferred innovation design for users in other countries, or by which national demand conditions are actively transferred abroad.
4. Export advantage. National conditions that support the inclusion of foreign demand preferences in nationally preferred innovation designs.
5. Market structure advantage. National conditions that increase the level of competition between domestic companies and facilitate low market entry barriers for new ones.

Demand Advantage

National demand advantage results from local conditions which facilitate the anticipation of the benefit of nationally preferred innovation designs in foreign markets. This mechanism allows the internationalisation of innovation designs and is dependent on a global trend in which specific innovations become increasingly beneficial or preferable to most countries. This trend can be, for example, a demographic trend, an environmental trend, or simply an increase in per capita income. A trend can also mean a time lead in building up infrastructure complementary to the innovation. Lead markets are at the forefront of the international trend. Various factors can put users in a country at the forefront of a trend: high income, as in the case of Vernon's (1966) product life cycle; a national context that foreshadows global environmental changes; an advanced accumulation of collateral assets, such as infrastructure. When other countries catch up, they demand the innovation already in use in the country at the forefront of the trend.

Price Advantage

Countries may gain a price advantage if the relative price of the nationally preferred innovation design decreases, so that differences in demand preference to foreign countries can be compensated. This price mechanism is the centrepiece of Levitt's (1983) globalisation hypothesis, in which the consumers in foreign markets "capitulate" to the attraction of lower prices and abandon their initial selection of goods. Price reductions are mainly due to cost reductions based on static and dynamic economies of scale. The two nation-specific factors of economies of scale are market size and market growth. Another price advantage emerges from anticipatory factor prices; the lead market demands innovations induced by factor price changes which later occur worldwide. A factor that is more expensive in the lead market than in other countries, e.g. petrol, induces innovations causing the factor to be used less, e.g. more fuel-efficient cars. When the factor becomes expensive in other countries as well, the same innovations are adopted in these lag countries. In such a case, the lead-market country anticipates a worldwide price trend. The same price advantage results from price changes of goods complementary to the innovation design.

Export Advantage

National conditions that support the inclusion of foreign demand preferences in nationally preferred innovation designs constitute a national export advantage. One can derive three factors of a national export advantage: domestic demand that is sensitive to the problems and needs of foreign countries; long-time export experience of domestic companies; and the similarity of local market conditions to foreign market conditions. Firstly, even if a country is not at the forefront of a global trend in terms of domestic environmental issues, domestic users may be more sensitive to global problems and needs than potential adopters in countries where the problem is more advanced. This sensitivity of demand can provide incentives for domestic companies to adopt a global perspective and increase their ability to meet global problems ahead of companies in other countries. For instance, consumers in a given country may be sensitive to the effects of worldwide climatic change, even if their domestic environment is not as seriously affected as that of other countries.

Secondly, firms in a given country have an advantage over foreign competitors if their innovations can be exported more easily. Innovations can be exported more easily if (1) the environmental and market conditions of foreign countries are similar to the market for which the innovation was designed, and (2) a design includes features that make it suitable for a variety of contexts. The reduction in the variety of nation-specific designs is faster, because it is easier for a country to turn to a foreign design if the loss of benefit is small. Dekimpe et al. (1998) support the hypothesis already proposed by Vernon (1979) that the higher the similarity of cultural, social and economic factors between two countries, the greater the likelihood that an innovation design adopted by one of two countries will be adopted by the other country as well. Companies can gain an export advantage if knowledge of the benefit of innovations to users in foreign countries is applied in the design of their innovations. Knowledge of foreign market conditions enables an innovator to design his innovations to fit the local as well as foreign markets by incorporating additional features. With such "dual-use" or "robust" innovation designs, a company can catch up with foreign firms' innovations in their home markets at an early stage, so as to pre-empt the international competition for nation-specific technologies. A country's context, including its users, suppliers and national institutions, can support or pressure companies to design innovations which can be exported. Small countries' firms are often pressured into developing innovations for both domestic and foreign environments, because the domestic market is too small to justify the necessary R&D investment.

Transfer Advantage

When users in a given country adopt an innovation design, this can increase the perceived benefit of the design among users in further countries, thus influencing their adoption decisions. The perceived benefit increases when information on the usability of the innovation design is made available. Information about the innovation not only raises awareness of the innovation design, but also reduces uncertainty surrounding new products and processes. A country can have a transfer advantage if its market context supports increases in the perceived benefit of a nationally preferred innovation design for users in foreign countries. Diffusion theory suggests that the international diffusion of durable goods depends on the intensity of communication between two countries (Takada and Jain, 1991). The lead market could therefore be the country that has the strongest communication ties with other countries. Lead countries are those that are generally watched by many other countries, for instance countries that are intensively covered by mass media or whose lifestyles are often present in television series and motion pictures. In the international innovation diffusion context, the "demonstration effect" (Mansfield, 1968) becomes an international "lead effect" (Kalish et al., 1995). Potential adopters in a second country observe the success of the innovation in the first market earlier than the success of innovations adopted in other, not so keenly watched countries. The reputation and sophistication of a user can be a signal for the quality of an innovation design. As Porter (1990a) pointed out, it is not only the quantity, but also the *quality* of the home demand that determines the international competitive advantage of a nation. Therefore, even a small country with a small market size can achieve a competitive advantage in certain segments. The quality of home demand can be interpreted as information on the specification of an innovation, based on the users' competence, know-how and prior experience with related products or processes.

International network externalities constitute a further transfer advantage. The Internet has gained international appeal because it connects all countries in a standardised transmission protocol. The preference for a design can likewise be actively transferred abroad. A country transfers demand for innovation design abroad through multinational companies, using the innovation in their foreign subsidiaries.

Market Structure Advantage

Innovations may be adopted internationally simply because, among all alternatives, they are the most beneficial to most countries. The reason users in one country adopt an innovation before users in other countries is sometimes that the market pushes local companies to innovate, making the innovation available earlier in that country. Faster development and more market-oriented innovations can be supported by competition. From Posner (1961) to Dosi et al. (1990), the degree of competition and entrepreneurial effort in the domestic market has been described as one of the main determinants of international patterns of innovations. Even in the case of Japan, Sakakibara and Porter (2001) found that the higher the domestic competition, the bigger the country's export success. Firstly, buyers tend to be more demanding when the producers face competition than when they are tightly regulated or hold a monopoly (Porter, 1990a). Secondly, competing companies are more strongly pressured to follow those who have already adopted a new technology (Mansfield, 1968: 144). Thirdly, and perhaps most importantly, more innovation designs are tested in a competitive market than in a monopolised market. As a result, a competitive market is more appropriate for finding a design that is not only the best within the domestic environment, but in all national environments. Fierce domestic competition facilitates the tapping of an internationally homogeneous latent consumer demand for innovations.

2.2 Lessons from Policy Analysis

The research project LEAD focuses on regional differences regarding the diffusion of environmental innovations. As a rule, both the innovation as well as the diffusion of such innovations is stimulated and supported by policy measures. On this background the conditions for national pioneering policies have to be analysed. Under which circumstances are countries adapting policy measures that exceed the level of regulation of other countries? Furthermore, if the diffusion of technologies depends on the adaptation of policies in other countries, it has to be analysed secondly, under which circumstances countries do implement policy measures that spread internationally. In the following, the state of the art in policy sciences regarding both questions is compiled.

Conditions for a Pioneering Role of Countries

It is subject of controversial debate, which influence the internationalisation of markets and the worldwide mobility of goods, humans and capital have on the scope for action of modern, democratic states. Some argue that the nation state is under considerable pressure to modify its national systems of taxation and regulation in order to avoid the exodus of capital and the movement of enterprises: This may force nation states to lower environmental standards because they affect the competitiveness of many industries adversely (so called "race to the bottom") (Green and Griffith, 2002; deVries, 2001; Hardt and Negri, 2000; Cerny, 1999; Strange, 1998).

A second argument stresses the limitations of the nation states' autonomy of action that arise both from the norms of international regimes and regional confederations of countries such as the EU or NAFTA as well as the appearance of new actors such as multinational enterprises and nongovernmental organisations and the fact that nation states lack the competence to solve many environmental problems because of their global nature (Koehn and Rosenau, 2002; Nye and Donahue, 2000; Held and et al., 1999; Haas and et al., 1993).

It is widely believed by politicians that unilateral action in the context of economic globalisation becomes less likely not only in case of trans-boundary problems, but also for all environmental problems if they bear additional costs. This implies that there is the danger of a "regulatory chill" (Hoberg, 2001: 213) independent of the real existence of adverse impacts on competitiveness of more far reaching unilateral environmental regulations: If politicians and voters are convinced that regulatory measures affect the competitiveness adversely, this argument can be utilised from the target group of a policy to make credible threats. (Hay and Rosamond, 2002; Hoberg, 2001; World Trade Organisation, 1999: 5). In this case, innovative environmental policy measures will not be adopted.

From this point of view, promising solutions to the problem are mainly dependent on whether the international community of nations will agree on binding law and create the institutional framework for a new governance structure on the international level that is able to enforce these agreements (Young, 2002; Esty, 1999; Keohane and Martin, 1995). A more optimistic view perceives the appearance of new actors such as nongovernmental organisations or scientific networks, the rapid growth of the body of international law and organisations, and the emergence of new forms of regulation such as public-private partnerships, as the rise of a first outline of a governance beyond the nation states (Park, 2002; Knill and Lehmkuhl, 2002; Auer, 2000; Zürn, 1998). Under certain circumstances, norms are even developed in bilateral negotiations between private actors without including governmental actors at all (Jacob and Jörgens, 2001).

A more sceptical position argues that in general, international bargaining processes do generate insufficient results because of the disparate structure of interests and an unclear hierarchy for decision making (Suranovic, 2002). However, both lines of argument postulate a declining importance of the role of nation states.

The results of comparative empirical research are contradicting the often postulated assumption of an extensive loss of national capacities in environmental policies. Despite of the political and economic globalisation, some countries still carry on with an ambitious environmental policy beyond the regulatory level set by international agreements. Even the global scale of many environmental problems, such as climate change, ozone depletion of the loss of biodiversity that cannot be solved by unilateral action, does not lead to a ceasing of ambitious policies. Likewise the frequently feared general lowering of environmental standards to improve the economic competitiveness cannot be observed empirically yet (Weidner and Jänicke, 2002, Lafferty and Meadowcraft, 2000, Desai, 2002, Wheeler, 2001, Liefferink and Andersen, 1998).

Despite all critical forecasts, nation states seem to keep their central role in the international development of environmental policy, both in the model of horizontal diffusion and country by country learning as well as in the model of furthering international regimes (Volkery and Jacob, 2003, see also SRU, 2002). Looking at the basic environmental policy innovations during the past 30 years reveals processes of innovation and diffusion: Environmental policy innovations of certain countries do spread either voluntarily from one country to another by learning and adaptation or they are taken over and further developed by international agreements (Tews et al., 2003, Binder, 2002; Busch and Jörgens, 2003). The emergence of many international agreements can be traced back to the initiatives of single countries or groups of countries that also influenced their figuration without meeting great resistance by other countries (see Young, 2002, Underdal, 1998).

Although the importance of pioneering behaviour for the further development of international environmental policy is generally acknowledged in the literature, there are partially oppositional assumptions about its prerequisites and the extent to which these prerequisites can be expected to change. Furthermore there is no consensus about the conceptualisation of the phenomena (Volkery and Jacob, 2003, with other references). The empirically oriented research on pioneering countries is based mainly on comparative country case studies (e.g. Jänicke and Weidner, 1997, Weidner and Jänicke, 2002, Anderson and Liefferink, 1997, Lafferty and Meadowcraft, 2000, Desai, 2002). Regarding the international diffusion of single instruments a research project[1] by the Environmental Policy Research Centre has been finished only recently. As part of this project, the spreading curves of 22 laws, instruments and institutions for 45 countries have been ascertained. The results of the project underline once more the importance of pioneers in environmental policy. It remains open, however, which factors are supporting countries in developing and adopting environmental policy innovations. Several distinct approaches of policy sciences, law and economics deliver contributions for single aspects of this question. In the following, the different ap-

[1] "Die Diffusion umweltpolitischer Innovationen als Aspekt der Globalisierung von Umweltpolitik".

proaches will be outlined to what extent they contribute to an explanation of pioneering behaviour in environmental policy.

It can be expected that a high *capacity for environmental policy* is needed, both for policy innovation and the adoption of innovations (see Jänicke and Weidner, 1997; Weidner and Jänicke, 2002, with more references). The OECD defines it broadly as "a society's ability to identify and solve environmental problems" (OECD, 1994: 8). While the terms capacity and capacity building were used previously by numerous institutions such as UNEP, FAO, World Bank, OECD, and others in connection with less developed countries only, they have now been fruitfully extended to industrialised countries as well. They refer to the structural preconditions for successful environmental policies and encompass the collective actors (esp. environmental institutions and organisations). The structural preconditions refer to (a) the institutional set-up (e.g. open and effectively integrated political institutions, administrative competence), (b) the system of creation, transfer and application of knowledge and (c) the economic-technical basis.

Scholars of law and policy science who focus on international regimes deliver contributions regarding the extension and limitation of possibilities for national pioneering strategies. An extension is given for example if the internationally agreed objectives legitimise the enforcement of ambitious but disputed measures on the national level. Likewise, the requirements of international regime may lead to an extension of national institutional capacities which then form the basis for further reaching measures (more comprehensive see: Jacobson-Brown and Weiss, 1998).

Innovative policies are frequently supported by international organisations that were founded in the context of the formation of international regimes. By spreading information about best practice, even weak organisations which are merely provide an international arena rather than being international actors (Underdal, 2001) do have a chance for effective action. For example the OECD is continuously evaluating, comparing and benchmarking national policies and by this successfully supporting a convergence in policymaking without having any formal legitimacy of its own.

Limitations of the national possibilities for action are frequently arising at the interface of environmental law and international trade law (Altemöller, 1998). The world trade regime limits the possibilities for countries to enact product or process standards that lead to restrictions of imports. An immediate limitation is given, however, only regarding product standards. Standards regarding the production processes are affected by trade liberalisation only if production sites may be dislocated, or if a border adjustment is planned for imported goods. The purpose of the international trade law is mainly to secure the enactment of policies avoiding limitations of competition but is not to consider other protection objectives. Thereby, contradictions between the different domains of law can be avoided and national pioneering behaviour remains in principle possible (Kelemen, 2001).

Further limitations for national pioneering behaviour may be caused by the guidelines of regional free trade agreements such as NAFTA, MERCOSUR or ASEAN. A special case in this respect is the EU. For the achievement of the European Single Market the Member States transferred far-reaching competences to the European level. But the European competition law does not lead to a general pressure on the member stated to lower their environmental standards. Meanwhile, it has been shown that for product standards the opposite is true. Restrictions are given regarding subsidies that are offered because of environmental objectives (instead of several others: Scharpf, 1999, with more references).

On this background an analysis of the national opportunities has to differentiate between the different levels and areas of action, instruments and their impacts (see among others Miles B. et al., 2000, Haas, 2002, Young, 2002, Mitchell, 1994).

The anticipation of economic advantages of pioneering behaviour in environmental policy can be seen as another determinant. Advantages for the competitiveness may arise from an early and strict regulation (see section 2.3 for a more detailed discussion). Quantitative analysis reveal a high statistical correlation between the competitiveness and strictness of environmental regulation (Schwab et al., 2003; Esty and Porter, 2000; Europäische Umweltagentur, 2001) or between eco-efficiency and competitiveness (Sturm et al., 2000). The causal direction between these variables remains ambiguous: Technological innovations may be induced by environmental policies that again improve the competitiveness. However, the opposite direction is possible too: Technical innovations may be a resource for the advancement of environmental policy, and regulators frequently take up the capabilities of technologies in their standard setting, thereby contributing to their diffusion (Jänicke and Jacob, 2002; Jacob, 1999). Furthermore, the empirical analysis of innovation oriented environmental policy reveals that innovation effects cannot be attributed to a single policy instrument, but that policy style and actors configuration are self-contained influencing factors (Jänicke et al., 2000). By this, additional potentials for action arise from the arrangement of policy processes.

Conditions for the Diffusion of Environmental Policy Innovations

Recent comparative research on the spread of environmental policy among countries reveals an international convergence in the development of national policy patterns (Kern et al., 2000; Kern, 2000; Jörgens, 1996; Tews et al., 2003). Standard solutions in pioneer countries diffuse worldwide, thus causing a substantial convergence in policy formulation at national level – irrespective of extremely different capacities for action. Unlike in the 1970s, when for example the USA or Japan had a major innovative function in global environmental policy, nowadays innovations in environmental policy emerge often in small EU countries that are tightly integrated in the global market (Jänicke, 1998).

The – reformed – institutional fabric of the EU seems comparatively favourable, both for innovations and for their diffusion (Héritier et al., 1994). The EU must firstly, at least in principle, accept a "high level of protection" in Member States; it must secondly seek to harmonise innovations in environmental policy, implemented at national state level. Pioneer countries, for their part, often have an interest in anchoring their policy innovations within the EU framework in order to thus minimise their subsequent need to adapt to European policy. It is also often a matter of "Europeanising" certain national pioneer measures, favouring the particular country's domestic industry. Policy diffusion within the EU, however, takes place not only by way of EU harmonisation, but also from country to country. In the latter case the policy innovation in question will often need first to be introduced by one of the more influential EU countries before it achieves the necessary wide-spread impact. For example, the CO2/energy tax was already introduced in the Netherlands and the Scandinavian countries in the early 1990s – but the system did not receive the decisive push towards European diffusion until the red-green coalition government in Germany adopted it in 1998. Up to now, the CO2 tax is an example of "horizontal" diffusion (Tews, 2002). The recent establishment as a European measure has yet no influence on the national adoption.

The diffusion of innovations in environmental policy thus takes place both directly from one country to another, i.e. by way of imitative policy learning or "lesson drawing" (Rose, 1993) and by way of international institutions (e.g. international regime), organisations (OECD, UNEP, World Bank, Greenpeace), or expert-networks (e.g. the International Network of Green Planners). It is striking how rapidly many innovations in environmental policy are diffused. Environment ministries have, in a period of less than 30 years, clearly asserted their position in the industrialised countries. Environmental plans, as defined under "Agenda 21", just ten years after the Rio Conference (1992), are adopted almost worldwide – though in extremely disparate quality. However, in other cases (e.g. soil protection legislation) the diffusion rate is clearly curbed by the difficulty of solving the underlying problems.

The process of innovation and diffusion depends on the *type of policy innovation* and on the *type of the underlying problem*. In general, technology based policies will diffuse faster than policies aiming at structural change. In addition, policies supporting marketable technologies, e.g. by improvements in efficiency, are more likely to diffuse than those policies requesting for example EOP technologies. Pioneering national environmental policy is more likely to diffuse, if it refers to environmental problems which are highly visible and which are on the international agenda, e.g. climate change. Policy innovations, which are able to assert themselves by their nature are likely to diffuse more rapidly. Distributive instruments (e.g. subsidies) or informational instruments are more likely to diffuse than regulatory instruments (e.g. command and control) or re-distributive policies.

Initially, there is a variety of policy instruments that can be applied for the different environmental issues. The different regulatory designs may be even in competition among each other. For example to support renewable energies, some countries introduced feed-in regulations while others chose quoting models (Busch, 2003). Energy taxes were introduced in some countries on primary energy, while in others on secondary energy. The SO2 policy in the USA is based to a large degree on emission trading, while in the Member States of the EU command and control measures for the approval procedures dominate. Which of the instrument becomes internationally dominant does not depend solely on the properties of the respective policy innovation or on possible transfer activities of a country or an international organisation, but also to a large degree on properties of the countries that introduce the respective policy instrument.

For an analysis of the factors that determine the leading position of a country in the development of environmental policy innovations the hypotheses on lead markets for technical innovations can be utilised. (Beise, 2001; Jänicke and Jacob, 2002; Beise et al., 2003). This research looks for properties of countries to explain why technologies are introduced earlier in these countries than in others that are later adopted by other countries without major changes in their design. Part of the identified lead factors (price advantages, demand advantages, export advantages, transfer advantages, and market structure advantages) can be immediately applied as hypotheses for the international diffusion of environmental policy innovations. By a recursion on competing models of policy innovations, firstly, the factors for a pioneering role of countries should be identified. Secondly, if theses factors are weaker than in other countries or if they are lacking at all, they should be able to explain a failure in the international diffusion of policy innovations from a given country. Thirdly, in a dynamic perspective, a decline in these factors should explain also the decline in the demand for policy innovations from a country if this cannot be ascribed to the innovation capacity of a country thereby leading to a loss of its pioneering role. In the following, the hypotheses from the economic lead market research are drafted (see section 2.1 for a more detailed discussion) and an attempt will be made to transfer the different factors to the analysis of political systems.

Demand Advantages

For this category of factors, the focus is on regional differences regarding the advantages that arise from the application of a technology. Variations exist regarding the demand for quality standards or the leading position of a country with respect to an international trend.

A transfer to policy innovations may imply that a country that has a high environmental problem pressure will develop earlier and more far-reaching environmental standards. However, such a pressure is not sufficient to introduce environmental policies. Only if there is a perception of environmental problems and if there is a capacity to solve these problems political initiatives are triggered.

The demand for environmental standards in a country is therefore also determined by the degree of environmental awareness, the existence and strength of environmental interest groups and by the administrative capacities, i.e. the relative strength of environmental administrations in the government.

Analogous to the hypotheses from innovation economics, the international diffusion of policy innovations may be furthered by the existence of a global trend in favour of a regulation in a certain policy domain. These trends may be reinforced by international organisations.

Export Advantages

According to another hypothesis of economic research on lead markets those countries obtain advantages in export that consider also preferences in other countries. Such a consideration may be expected if the demand is met by multinational enterprises, or if the customers of a country have preferences also regarding global problems (e.g. working conditions in other countries, animal protection, or environmental degradation in other countries). Another factor for export advantages is seen in similarities of preferences. A disadvantage is a monopolistic demand for technologies.

Analogous to this group of factors export advantages for policy innovations can be expected if environmental actors or consumers are considering environmental problems in other countries as well. Examples can be found in nature and animal protection or in climate protection. This does not only influence their consuming behaviour but it also legitimises policies in this regard. Unlike demand advantages it is not only the domestic environmental problems that may be more pressuring (or higher visible) than in other countries, and this category focuses on international or foreign environmental problems.

Another export advantage can be occasionally observed if multinational enterprises are affected by environmental policy measures. Frequently, they are influencing the policy process and in cases they developed suitable substitutes for harmful technologies, they support the international harmonisation of standards because the diffusion of environmental standards leads to an extension of their markets.

Transfer Advantages

According to innovation economics, a country has transfer advantages if the application of a technology reduces the risks of adoption for other customers by demonstrating the feasibility, or if the users are internationally mobile. Furthermore, network externalities or complementary goods may cause transfer advantages.

These types of variables change the focus: While for the other hypotheses the focus is mainly on the innovating country, the transfer advantages focus on the advantages for the potential adopters that arise from the pioneering behaviour. Also in the case of policy innovations a risk reduction for potential imitators can be observed. Pioneering countries demonstrate the political, technical and economic practicability of their policy measures. With a reference on the successful example national actors in countries that are potential adopters, legitimate similar demands.

The international mobility of users has its counterpart in the membership and presence of national political actors in international organisations and networks.

Market Structure Advantages

Lead market advantages can be expected in countries with a degree of competition, because in those countries several different technical innovations may be given a trial and a particular high pressure in favour of cost reduction can be expected.

Transferred to policy measures a regulatory competition can be observed best in federal structures. The multilevel political system of the EU or the USA allows such a competition because of the relative high autonomy of its members. This competition apparently depends on the issue at stake and may lead even to a lowering of standards. Other federal systems where the different levels depend on the mutual consent for the introduction of policy measures, may lead to blockades in the political process rather than stimulating competition.

Advantages in Prices and Costs

According to the economic lead market model a country will have a leading position in the introduction of *technologies* if there are advantages regarding prices and costs of a new technology. These advantages may arise from a particular large market, from a rapid growth of the market or by earlier anticipation of changes in factor costs, e.g. a rise in energy prices.

For this type of variables, it is most difficult to derive hypotheses for the development of policy innovations that diffuse internationally. Those countries may have cost advantages that stress efficiency criteria in the selection process of policy instruments. The environmental policies of industrialised countries show considerable differences in this respect. The consideration of efficiency criteria is institutionalised in a varying degree. For example, cost-benefit analysis is a standard and central procedure in the policy process in the USA, while e.g. in Germany the effectiveness of environmental policy seems to be more important. This variation is, however not random, but it is based on differences in regulatory traditions and the core values of political actors. This limits the diffusion of environmental policy instruments that do not fit in these path dependencies.

To conclude, there is a considerable potential for national pioneering strategies that are in turn an important factor for the emergence of lead markets for environmental technologies. Economic globalisation and the emergence of international regimes are shifting the opportunities for influencing the international developments in different directions, but it cannot be assumed that there is a general decline. Furthermore, the question which countries and which policy innovations are successfully diffusing globally against competing countries and innovations has not been answered yet. The transfer of the economic lead markets model to policy innovations is merely a starting point for further research and requires empirical validation.

2.3 Pioneering Policy from the Perspective of Environmental Economics

Relevant Areas of Environmental Economics

Two closely related areas of environmental economics seem particularly relevant for the questions addressed in the present study:

- the investigation of incentives for firms created by instruments of environmental policy for the (generation and) adoption of environmental innovations (dynamic incentives; induced innovation); *the relevance of this discussion originates from the hypothesis that an early adoption may establish a lead market position of a country;*
- the study of incentives for environmental policy makers to choose progressive environmental regulation in view of non-optimising behaviour of firms (innovation offsets) or in view of advantages on international markets (strategic en-

vironmental policy). Progressive regulation is defined as regulation which is either early or strict in excess of the optimal level or in excess of the level in other countries; *this question is of importance as it may shed some light on the question why countries pursue a pioneering environmental policy which is one of the possible prerequisites for creating a lead market.*

Dynamic Incentives, Induced Innovation

Environmental regulation generally creates incentives for firms to innovate and thus induces innovation. The ranking of such dynamic incentives, i.e. the cost savings in case of an innovation, generated by different instruments of environmental policy has been extensively studied in theoretical and empirical investigations. Even in simple *theoretical models* of perfect competition no general superiority of economic instruments such as taxes and tradable permit can be established (Feess, 1998). Crucial among the conditions that determine the ranking of different policy instruments with respect to their dynamic incentives is the behaviour of other firms with respect to the innovation (*do they independently adopt or not adopt or do they follow the innovator)* and of the environmental agency with respect to a tightening of standards (*does it tighten environmental standards when the innovation is feasible or when the innovation has taken place or does it leave standards unaltered)*.

Game-theoretic models of imperfect competition take into account strategic interdependencies between firms with respect to innovation as well as output and between firms and the regulatory agency. The extension of these models to several nations leads to the realm of strategic environmental policy (see below). The result of simple models is confirmed: The ranking of different policy instruments is highly sensitive to even small changes in the assumptions (Feess, 1998). There seems to be a range of situations, however, where market-based instruments create stronger incentives for the diffusion of environmental technologies (Jaffe et al., 2002). Only under quite special conditions of strategic interdependencies between firms and regulatory agencies disincentives to innovate may arise.

Theoretical models have also been studied to determine if the incentives to innovate for firms originating from environmental policy result in the socially optimal amount of innovative activity (Feess, 1998). Under perfect competition and monopoly, innovation incentives are generally too low. Under the more realistic case of oligopolistic competition an indirect, strategic innovation incentive may arise from interdependent output decisions *as the innovation of one firm lowers its costs, thus leading to a higher output. In Cournot competition the second firm will then supply a lower output; this creates a positive strategic innovation incentive for the first firm* leading to an overinvestment in R&D. Strategic interdependencies with respect to innovation activities may result in either under- or overinvestment in R&D as well: If spillover effects exist firms have an incentive to free-ride; there will be underinvestment in R&D. Patent races, on the other hand, will generally create incentives to over-innovate.

Incentives to innovate resulting from environmental policy may thus create over- as well as underinvestment in R&D. As a result, a mix of environmental and innovation policy instruments can be expected to be superior to a single instrument. However, a general justification for subsidising innovations cannot be taken for granted even if they are intended to reduce environmental pressure but has to be established on a case-by-case basis.

The design of optimal environmental and R&D-policies is further complicated if – realistically – individual firms obtain different cost savings from given innovative activities while the regulatory agency cannot observe these differences (Carraro and Siniscalco, 1992). *In such cases of asymmetric innovation only second best solutions (i.e. a minimisation of welfare losses) can be hoped for.* Similarly, the design of an efficient environmental policy is more challenging if it induces innovation. Generally, environmental innovation lowers avoidance costs and thus leads to higher optimal environmental standards; environmental policy should thus be tightened. However, environmental innovation may crowd out innovation in the wider economy if the supply of R&D capacities is inelastic, for example. Again, this calls for a well balanced policy mix. Time lags between innovation and cost reductions as in the case of learning by doing alter the time pattern of avoidance costs (*they make later avoidance cheaper relative to current efforts*); in such cases environmental standards should be tightened gradually in line with decreasing costs.

Theoretical models of the kind referred to above have been criticised because they ignore important aspects of the innovation process (Kemp et al., 1994) such as different types (process, product) and ranges (radical, incremental) of innovations, the availability of a multitude of technological solutions, varieties of clean technologies and phases of the innovation process. While some of these aspects have been incorporated in theoretical models (e.g. Löschel, 2002), others – studied more extensively in the realm of innovation economics (see above) – have been studied in *empirical investigations*. Generally the available evidence – which mainly relates to energy efficient and end-of-pipe technologies – seems to support the view that market based instruments have stronger positive effects on invention, innovation and diffusion of environmental technologies (Jaffe et al., 2002).

Innovation Offsets and Strategic Environmental Policy

A pioneering environmental policy of a country may be favourable for reaching a lead market position for environmental technologies. It is therefore of interest to understand why countries may want to be pioneers with respect to their environmental policy regulations.

From the perspective of environmental economics a pioneering environmental policy is understood to set standards in excess of their efficient level or the level chosen in other countries. This seems to imply a cost to society and thus requires explanation. To give a rationale for a pioneering environmental policy is the core of the Porter hypothesis, which became prominent in the 1990s and is supported by case studies (Porter, 1990b, Porter and van der Linde, 1995b). It states that environmental regulation does – regularly – not reduce the profits of firms.

Looked at from the perspective of evolutionary economics, the search of firms for new solutions is not correctly characterised as optimising behaviour. Rather it is to be described as local search guided by bounded rationality. In this case strict environmental regulation may create incentives to pursue opportunities to innovate otherwise not realised; resulting cost savings may then offset or even more than offset the cost of compliance. While traditional economic models can produce this kind of results as second best outcomes in principal-agent constellations under asymmetric information (Holmström and Tirole, 1987), the empirical importance of such innovation offsets is debated (Palmer et al., 1995).

The Porter hypothesis also refers to the prospect that pioneering environmental policies can be successful in increasing the share of domestic companies in international markets and thus increase national employment and income (Stähler, 1998)[2].

Modern game theory founded environmental economics building on the strategic trade literature supports the view that strict environmental policy implemented in advance of other countries – even while increasing costs to regulated companies – can improve the competitiveness of domestic enterprises under certain conditions (Ecchia and Mariotti, 1994; Feess and Muehlheusser, 2002 (emphasising the profits of suppliers of environmental technologies as a justification for a pioneering environmental policy); Feess and Taistra, 2001; Scholz and Stähler, 1999; Taistra, 2000; Ulph, 1996; Ulph and Ulph, 1996). [3] Different mechanisms are suggested as being responsible for this.

Firstly, strict environmental policy can incite companies operating on oligopolistic international markets to behave more aggressively by supporting them to make credible commitments to expand their market share. Foreign firms – if not supported by their governments – may then reduce their production in order to avoid having to accept lower prices.

Secondly, if economies of scale exist for suppliers due to learning, or for users of environmental technologies due to network effects, and the environmental policy diffuses to foreign countries, domestic firms can gain market shares. It is important that foreign environmental policy neither follows too early, i.e. before economies of scale have become effective, nor too late, in which case domestic enterprises will bear higher costs than their foreign competitors over an extended period. Companies manufacturing environmental products are more likely to improve their competitiveness if foreign environmental policy is strict and foreign demand for environmental technology reacts strongly. For domestic users of environmental technology it is essential that foreign demand for their products does not strongly react to prices.

Thirdly, if innovation offset exists, i.e. if the cost of compliance is offset or more than offset by cost savings through innovation, the environmental policy stimulating such innovation creates a cost advantage relative to foreign competitors, but only as long as environmental policy abroad does not follow.

---

2 The market share of domestic companies in international markets is an indicator of sectoral competitiveness. It does not necessarily imply an increased competitiveness of the overall economy. Using this indicator corresponds to the view of strategic environmental policy as a form of industrial policy. See Scholz and Stähler, 1999.

3 Under some conditions maximisation of national welfare requires eco-dumping instead of a pioneering environmental policy (Barrett, 1994).

Fourthly, greater willingness to pay for environmentally sound process technology or goods produced by means of environmentally friendly technologies may lead to increased competitiveness for suppliers of such technologies.

The conditions under which the Porter hypothesis holds in theoretical models are rather restrictive. Besides being dependent on demand created by regulation, beneficial effects for domestic companies arise only if

- there are barriers to market entry,
- solely domestic firms and governments have the option to behave strategically, and countermeasures are not taken in other countries,
- enterprises do no relocate,
- there are no spill-overs and intellectual property rights are respected.
- For multinational enterprises the concept of strategic environmental policy may not be appropriate at all.

Conclusions

- Generally, environmental policy induces innovation.
- An unanimous ranking of environmental policy instruments with respect to their dynamic incentives cannot be established. There is some evidence suggesting that sometimes market-based instruments create stronger incentives for the diffusion of environmental innovation.
- Environmental policy may induce under- as well as overinvestment in R&D; this calls for a mix of environmental and innovation policy instruments; a justification for subsidising R&D in environmental technologies has to be established on a case-by-case basis, however.
- If the behaviour of firms is characterised by bounded rationality or if principal agent problems are present, strict environmental standards even in excess of their optimal level need not increase the cost of firms as compliance costs may be offset by cost savings due to innovation.
- Pioneering environmental policies can under certain – rather restrictive – conditions increase the share of domestic companies in international markets and may increase national employment and income.

2.4 Companies and Strategic Management

To explain the emergence of innovations and their international diffusion, it is not enough to examine country-specific factors or properties of an industrial sector alone, when only few companies compete internationally. The characteristics of firms must additionally be taken into account. Two approaches from management sciences which explain the strategic management of companies may be utilised in this context: on the one side, Porter's strategic positioning school and, on the other, the resource-based view (from static to more dynamic views). Strategic positioning builds on theories of industrial organisation, whereas the resource-based view builds on several research traditions, including, for example, evolutionary theories. Furthermore, the resource-based view may be interpreted as one part of a traditional SWOT analysis (strengths and weaknesses) and the strategic positioning school as representing the other part (opportunities and threats) (Spanos and Spyros, 2001; Rugman and Verbeke, 1998). The following hypotheses build on these traditions, as well as on some lessons of the case studies.

1. The strategic choices of a company take into account its positioning within a market, as well as the development of capabilities of the firm in a dynamic context.
2. With regard to the environment, the strategic choices of companies must take into account the environmental policy of the home base, the national environmental policies of other countries and of the international arena, and the action of other societal and supranational actors in a dynamic framework.
3. Companies therefore must decide either to develop "green" capabilities to comply with policy or, in the case of non-enforcement, not to react. The specific environmental policy and institutional context must be considered in this decision. Therefore, a general rule may not exist. The following matrix shows some possible interdependencies.

Fig. 3. Corporate strategy with national and international environmental pressures

		Resource Based Response to National Environmental Pressure	
		Weak	Strong
Resource-based response to international environmental pressure	Strong	1. International based capabilities	3. National and international capabilities
	Weak	2. Compliance but no capabilities	4. National based capabilities

Source: Rugman and Verbeke (1998).

When analysing lead markets, the following aspects of companies' strategic management have to be considered:

- From a dynamic perspective, the creation of a lead market might start in quadrant 4 with the development of nationally based capabilities and then – with the diffusion of environmental policies – move to quadrant 3, where national and international markets and capabilities are created.
- Environmental policy is not independent of company action. National environmental policymakers usually take into account the position of the firms in their country when negotiating international environmental agreements or the development of supranational environmental policy, e.g. in the European Union.
- Further differentiation is necessary with regard to environmental innovations created in a pilot market. Is this development mainly driven by market forces, as suggested by the lead market theory, or by regulatory measures? In both cases, the strategic situation of firms must be taken into account.

- Multinational enterprises with production locations in various countries must comply with different policy patterns and societal behaviour, and must react to these different challenges. They must make strategic choices; they have the possibility of learning from the varying circumstances, creating special corporate capabilities and thus playing an important role in the diffusion of technological as well as organisational innovations, and may further create "green" corporate capabilities. It must be taken into account that the context of "green" innovations (especially the creation of a lead market) might not be the place of production. One main reason for this is the transferability of innovations between contexts, especially by multinational companies.

3 Towards an Integrated Model of the Lead Market for Environmental Innovations

The emergence of lead markets for environmental innovations cannot be explained by a single disciplinary approach. All of the distinct theoretical approaches, defined by their methodologies and their respective subjects of research as described above, contribute to the analysis of this phenomenon. In this paper we attempt to integrate the approaches in a multi-level analytical framework (Fig. 4).

The framework, however, is not a deterministic one. The factors which can influence lead markets for environmental innovations, as derived from the theoretical discussion above, are expected to be positively correlated with the emergence of a lead market. The statistical validation is not examined in this paper. Instead, we report the results of several case studies to illustrate the national factors responsible for the international diffusion of the environmental innovations analysed.

This new model of the international diffusion of environmental innovations should explain the internationalisation of environmental innovations compared to national adoption without international diffusion. We utilise the lead market factors as the main explanatory factors for the internationalisation process.[4] The reason for this is that international diffusion, in contrast to national diffusion, cannot be directly explained by policies, but only by economic or political reasoning, as no actor or policy has the power to pressure all companies worldwide to adopt an innovation. The theory integration is accomplished by integrating the additional arguments for environmental innovations into the lead market factors (policy diffusion, Porter effect) and modelling the impact of actors and policies on the lead market factors.

The policy level consists of actors and policies. It comprises a range of different national and international actors. It includes governmental and economic actors, as well as NGOs and their respective international organisations. The role of multinational companies in the international diffusion of environmental innovations by the various means described above is located at this level. All actors, their interests, their specific resources, and their corresponding strategies form a policy pattern (Blazejczak et al., 1999). This encompasses instrumentation (such as emissions control legislation, tax regimes, subsidies for specific technologies, etc.), policy style, and the configuration of the involved actors. Our case studies, which

---

4 The stage model in figure 3 is a complementary taxonomy that includes the sequence of policy and innovation diffusion but is not explanatory.

we describe below, confirm the need to look beyond single policy instruments and to consider the framework in which the policy measures are applied.

The elements of the policy level can have a direct influence on the willingness of a country to adopt innovations. This relationship is marked with (1) in Fig. 4. Our analysis of the relationship between a policy pattern and the willingness to innovate builds on the results of a preceding research project (Klemmer et al., 1999). The Klemmer project focuses on the likelihood that innovations occur at the national level. Yet it does not elaborate under which circumstances an international diffusion of innovations occurs. The traditional impact of policies on the adoption of innovations in a country (1) is not sufficient to account for the distinction between lead markets and idiosyncratic innovation markets that adopt innovations not adopted by other countries. This can be achieved only by the inclusion of the lead market factors. Our further analysis should reveal to what extent policy patterns and actors have an influence on the internationalisation factors of environmental innovations (marked as (2) in Fig. 4).

The internationalisation factors constitute the second level of the model. We argue that the environmental policy-specific arguments can in principle be assigned to the five lead market factors elaborated in innovation economics and described in section 2.1. The analysis within innovation economics has focused on the relationship between the lead market factors and the potential of a country to lead the adoption of a specific innovation design internationally (marked as (3) in Fig. 4). These factors are likely to improve the chances for an innovation to diffuse internationally (marked as (4) in Fig. 4). To apply the model for environmental innovations, the lead market factors are adapted to the specific context of environmental innovations. The fact that policies diffuse between nation states or are harmonised in international organisations provides an additional strong factor in favour of the internationalisation of environmental innovations. Policy diffusion internationalises other innovations as well, such as pharmaceuticals or product safety improvements. The traditional lead market model integrates the arguments for international policy diffusion as a transfer advantage (Beise, 2001: 102). The regulatory context of countries seen as pacesetters in the development of environmental policy is often transferred to other countries that are risk-averse. Such a pacesetter position may be gained either through innovativeness or through an important role in international organisations. In environmental innovations, policy diffusion plays such a prominent role that we add it as an extra internationalisation factor.

The market structure advantage, which describes competition as the most important factor in pushing innovations, is interpreted in the context of environmental innovations as the "Porter effect". The Porter effect is the main argument in environmental economics to explain why, in the absence of policy diffusion, national regulation leads to global innovations. The main idea of the market structure advantage is that there are innovation opportunities hidden in the technological opportunity space and that market forces push companies to discover those opportunities. The greater the competition, the more likely it is that companies will discover profitable innovation opportunities. Porter and van der Linde, (1995a) argue that environmental innovations can also be profitable, but that, due to complacency, companies often do not pursue them. Environmental innovations, however, are driven less by competition than by regulatory means. To denote these differences, we refer to the market structure advantage as the Porter effect. The open question is what kinds of regulations can push companies to develop innovations that are profitable in foreign countries as well as in the domestic market.

Fig. 4. Framework for analysing the international diffusion of environmental innovations

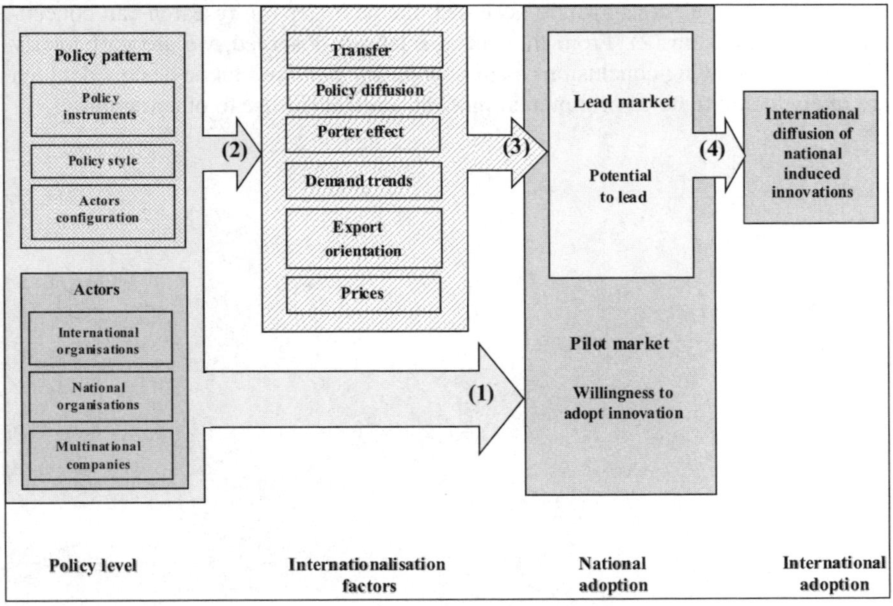

The internationalisation mechanisms are based on country-specific attributes. They can, however, be influenced by various political and public actors and policies. For example, a tax regime can actively change factor prices for energy, pushing a country to the forefront of an international factor cost trend. Multinational companies can have a large impact on the international transfer of innovations and policy diffusion; international organisations can spur policy diffusion, which contributes to the lead effect. The framework illustrated in Fig. 4 can be used to analyse the impact of policies on the lead market role of countries in environmentally responsive industries. It complements the traditional relationship between the policy level and the national adoption of innovations. The determinants of the lead market role of a country are modelled as a function of its lead market factors (relationship 3 in Fig. 4). The lead market factors themselves are determined by the policy level (relationship 2).

The framework can be used to analyse the effects of policies and actors on the adoption and international diffusion of innovations. Its advantage over former studies of environmental regulation is that it makes a clear distinction between national and international adoption. With the help of the lead market concept of the international diffusion of innovations, this distinction can be theoretically substantiated. The original concept put the reasons for the international success of innovations down to theoretical attributes of countries. The traditional policy analysis focused on the effect of policies and styles on national innovation development and adoption. Our reformulation within the framework of environmental innovations emphasises the role of policies and actors for the internationalisation of innovations. Relationships (1), (3) and (4) are not only validated by theoretical reasoning, but supported by a rich literature, as well as by the results of our case studies. If these relationships are accepted, the next steps in research can concentrate on relationship (2). From the causal relations observed, we are particularly interested in drawing conclusions as to how policy patterns can be designed which are likely to stimulate environmental innovations that diffuse to other countries.

4 Case Studies of Lead Markets from Literature Studies

From these distinct theoretical perspectives, altogether 13 cases of environmental technologies and organisational innovations in the literature were explored with regard to the pioneering and lead markets where they started from. The selection criteria for the case studies were mainly pragmatic. The cases had to be well documented in the literature, they had to represent marketable environmental innovations, and a wide variety of sectors and countries had to be included. The case studies followed a common questionnaire asking for: (1) a description of the innovation design, the lead market, the regulatory measures taken in the pioneering country, and the actors involved; (2) an analysis of the lead market factors of the *country*; (3) the lead market factors of the *innovation*; and (4) the lead market factors of the *policies* supporting innovation and diffusion. In the following, a summary is presented of those case studies in which the phenomena of lead markets are most obvious.

4.1 Fuel-Efficient Passenger Cars

Fuel efficiency is one means of reducing harmful or greenhouse gas emissions. Fuel-efficient passenger cars consume less fuel per 100 km or achieve high mileage per gallon. Vehicle fuel efficiency can be achieved with diesel or gasoline direct injection combustion engines or by combining a gasoline engine and electric motor (hybrid cars). In Germany, the most fuel-efficient cars are known as "3-Liter-Autos", which means that they consume less than 4 litres per 100 km. In the 1990s this was a realistic goal for most car manufacturers bearing in mind European driving habits and design preferences, and supportive policies such as favourable tax treatment were introduced as a result. By the end of the 1990s several German car models met this low consumption target.

Modern fuel-efficient passenger cars use a bundle of technologies designed to reduce a vehicle's fuel consumption. The most effective fuel-saving technologies are the use of low-weight materials, making car bodies more aerodynamic, and optimising the combustion process. Technical developments have tended to focus on the latter strategy, partly because it is the most efficient of the three, and partly because it conforms with market preferences. In fact, cars have become even heavier over time and body design has to meet safety, as well as aesthetic criteria (Franke, 1998). High-pressure direct injection – high-pressure injection or common-rail injection systems – proved to be the most successful engine technology during the 1990s. High-pressure injection improves combustion, reduces the emission of exhaust gases and, at the same time, improves the performance, notably the acceleration, of cars. It became the standard system for diesel engines in the 1990s (Fig. 5). Modern injection systems have been developed by several car companies in Europe and Japan. Germany was the lead market, however. The USA and Japan, where diesel-powered engines have a much lower market share and are regarded in a less favourable light, lagged behind in terms of this technical change (Petersen and Diaz-Bone, 1998).

Fig. 5. International diffusion of diesel-high-pressure injection

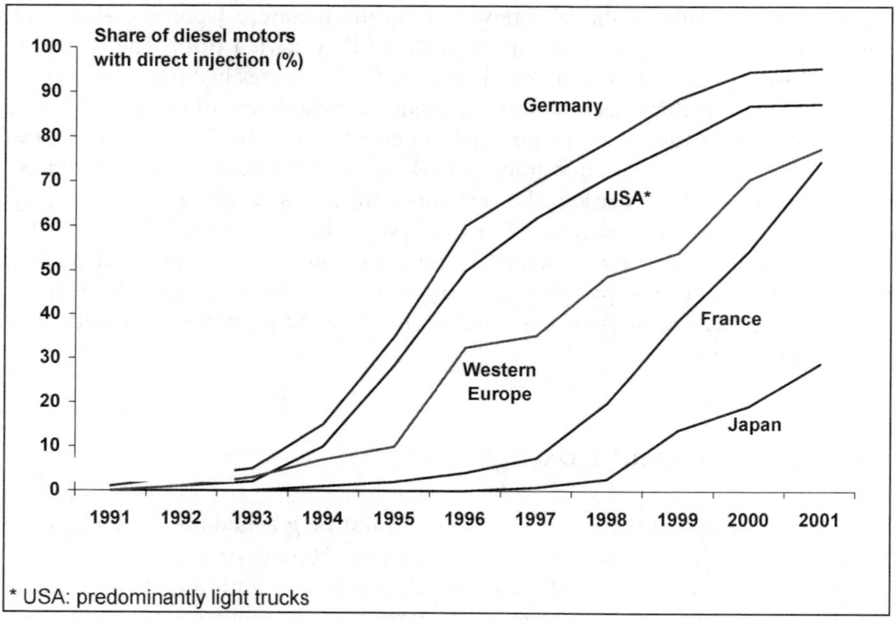

Sources: ZEW, Bosch.

There are relatively few policy instruments in the car industry that directly stipulate the fuel consumption of cars. The US was alone in 1975 in introducing a fuel economy rule (CAFE) for new cars which requires every company which sells cars in the US to achieve a maximum of the average consumption of all cars sold in one year of 8.77 litre per 100 km. This rule has so far not been adopted in other countries. In Europe, in particular, a voluntary fleet consumption reduction plan by the European Automobile Manufacturers Association prevented fuel economy objectives finding their way into legislation. However, one of the reasons why this regulation has not been copied internationally is that it has proved to be rather ineffective because of the loopholes it contains. Not only have car firms violated the rules and been willing to pay the related fines, the market share of SUVs (sport utility vehicles) – which were allowed a much higher mileage limit (11.63 litres per 100 km) – has grown continuously. SUVs now account for more than 50% of all sales and consume 41% of gasoline used. Although loopholes do not invalidate a regulation per se, low effectiveness will hamper the international adoption of a regulation regardless of the reasons for its ineffectiveness (Dolowitz and March, 1996).

On the other hand, the US successfully leads the way in terms of legislation aimed at reducing pollutants (see section 1). The stringent provisions of the Clean Air Act can only be achieved by fitting vehicles with catalytic converters. As the US Clean Air Act was adopted internationally, the catalytic converter followed in its wake. The effectiveness of the legislation, America's – and especially California's – reputation for seriously tackling the negative effects of traffic, as well as the weight of the US market resulted in the same regulations being adopted in most other countries as well. The US context did, of course, place more weight on the reduction of pollutants than on achieving greater fuel efficiency. While Europe is also striving to reduce pollutants, it is more interested – and has been more successful – in increasing fuel efficiency than the US or Japan. This lead-lag constellation, and the specific context of Europe, induced specific innovations such as diesel technology. Diesel engines have become increasingly popular in Europe as diesel engines are more fuel-efficient than gasoline engines, even when taking into account the higher energy density of diesel (International Energy Agency, 2003a). Currently, the arbitrary limit of three litres of fuel per 100 km is easily achieved at efficient cost with diesel technology. The diesel engine, however, was at odds with environmental preferences in the US as NO_x emissions of diesel engines are up to three times higher than those of comparable gasoline engines. The context of national regulation therefore shapes the engines preferred by manufacturers as they seek to dovetail domestic market and statutory requirements as economically as possible.

Pollution-cutting innovations were successful internationally owing to the international diffusion of the relevant US legislation. Why, however, were the fuel-efficiency innovations adopted in Europe even more successful internationally, even though the relevant fuel-efficiency regulations were not adopted internationally? Europe has the highest fuel prices in the world. As a result, fuel-efficient innovations will have the greatest economic impact in Europe. At the same time, while worldwide gasoline prices are slowly rising, local differences – and especially between some European states and the US – are still so large that fuel-efficiency is not in itself enough to persuade US users to adopt the relevant innovations. The only innovations to be diffused internationally have been those which reduce fuel consumption and, simultaneously, enhance other popular vehicle attributes as reflected by demand trends. Another global trend is at work. Over time cars have become more luxurious, more powerful and heavier. Fuel-efficient technologies are needed in order to prevent increases in consumption levels. As well as their fuel efficiency features, high-pressure direct injection has significantly improved diesel engines which previously suffered from low acceleration performance. The main reason for the international success of this technology was neither fuel-efficiency legislation nor any other environmental factors which might make fuel-consumption more economical. Fuel efficiency technologies enjoy international success if they are compatible with demand preferences in major markets. Small or microcompact cars are successful in Japan or parts of Europe – they probably never will be in large countries such as the US. High-pressure injection is not only used in 3-litre cars, but in all other types of cars as well, including large luxury vehicles, and diesel engines are likely to become more successful worldwide.

This explains why several innovations that only optimised environmental criteria, but did not place high priority on meeting other consumer demands such as driving power, have failed. A good example is the Golf Ecomatic, developed by Volkswagen and launched on the market in 1993. The Golf Ecomatic switched the engine off automatically when it was not in use, e.g. at red traffic lights, and started the engine again when a gear was used. This technology leads to a substantial 20-25% reduction in fuel consumption, especially in urban traffic. Although the innovation won several environmental awards, only 3,000 vehicles were sold in total on the market (Petersen and Diaz-Bone, 1998). The positioning of the car and the sluggish driving behaviour of the Golf Ecomatic, combined with the high price tag, failed to attract buyers (Hoffmann, 2002) despite high fuel prices. At the same time, a Golf equipped with a high-pressure-injection diesel engine, which was not only fuel-efficient but also offered increased driving-power, was very successful. The most fuel-efficient new model, the Lupo TDI, was positioned as a high-tech model and sold better than the Golf Ecomatic even though it came at an equally high price.

4.2 Wind Energy

The world market for renewable energies and especially wind energy has grown rapidly in recent decades, boosted by the oil crises and subsequent discussion of the environmental impact of fossil fuels. The developing international market is dominated by the small Nordic country of Denmark. Denmark is the pioneer country for wind-generated electric power. Although Germany has the largest installed wind energy capacity in the world, the use of wind energy as a share of total wind potential is still smaller in Germany than in Denmark. Fig. 6 shows the penetration rate of wind energy use in different countries and identifies Denmark as the lead market. Germany follows closely, while other countries are developing wind energy with a considerable lag. The penetration rate has been measured as the percentage of exploitation of on-shore wind potential. We have also used other possible indicators, such as wind energy as a share of total electricity production. The results are the same.

Fig. 6. International diffusion of wind energy

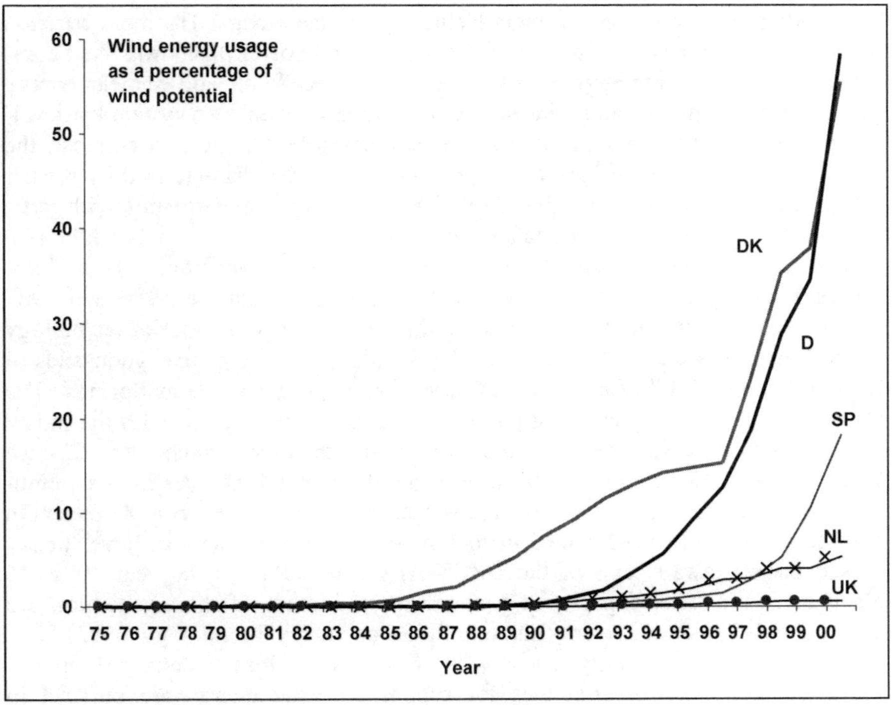

Sources: OECD, 2002a, Lehmann and Reetz, 1995.

Thanks to its leading role in the use of wind energy, Denmark is the world's largest exporter of wind turbine generators. A comparison of the import and export markets of both countries reveals that Germany exports only a small part of its wind turbines to other countries (BTM Consult, 2002). While Denmark's wind industry is geared to the world market, the German wind industry relies more on domestic demand and regulation (Denmark: 81% exports, 19% imports; Germany: 10% exports, 90% imports).

The technical development of windmills has a long history in Denmark. As early as 1918, 120 Danish energy utilities were operating windmills, typically of 20 to 35 kW, and were providing 3% of total electricity production in Denmark. The so-called "Danish Concept" is traditionally characterised by three rotor blades. Direct current generator plants have been replaced since the 1950s by generators which produce alternating current (modern types of these generators are asynchronous generators). The third typical feature of current modern wind energy converters was also developed prior to the oil crisis – today's converting systems are now equipped with pitch or active stall regulations. Both deploy different techniques for increased flexibility in response to changing wind forces.

While wind energy was originally regarded as too expensive to compete with fossil fuels, the situation changed during the oil crisis. Several countries began installing big 1 megawatt plus wind power plants such as the GROWIAN wind turbine in Germany. These failed in technological terms, however, due to premature scaling-up based on insufficient technological knowledge. The main criterion for the technological development of such large wind power plants was their compatibility with existing systems of large, centralised fossil and nuclear energy plants. Energy utilities had no incentives to undermine their own system by developing a decentralised alternative system of renewable energies. In contrast, the technological trajectory of wind energy in Denmark was characterised by greater variety and flexibility (Heymann, 1995). Although some experiments with large wind power plants were undertaken, the industrial and economic breakthrough was achieved by the continuous improvement of smaller converters. The 55 kilowatt generation of wind turbine generators developed between 1980 and 1981 realised cost reductions of about 50%. In the 1980s a large number of technology support programs were set up all over the world, e.g. in California. Thousands of Danish Micon 55 kilowatt wind turbines were exported to Palm Springs. The Danish producers enjoyed a first mover advantage having started with the industrial production of wind turbines five years earlier than their competitors (Danish Wind Industry Association, 2002). Since the 1980s wind turbines have continuously grown in size. The diameter of new rotor blades increased from 23 meters in 1990 to 44 meters in 1993 and 63 meters in 1997. Modern generators have already passed the megawatt class of the GROWIAN generation. In the year 2000, 15 plants had an installed capacity of 2 megawatts and more. Offshore generators are planned with 3 to 5 megawatts (Institute for Solar Energy Technology, 2002).

Policies for wind energy usage vary considerably from country to country. Three distinct types of strategies for supporting wind energy are pursued in Europe (Langraf and Kellner, 2000; Haas, 2001; BTM Consult, 2002):

- Renewable energy feed-in tariffs (REFITs),
- Bidding systems,
- Tradable permit systems for renewables.

Some countries have implemented systems with additional incentives, such as tax reductions or specific depreciation privileges for renewable energies.

Renewable energy feed-in tariffs (REFITs) have been implemented in Germany, Denmark, Spain, Italy and Austria. They were used temporarily in Ireland (until 1994) and the Netherlands (until 1995) and have also been introduced in France recently (in 2001). Denmark switched to a quota system in 2000. The REFITs system introduces fixed prices for green electricity which have to be paid by energy utilities to producers of renewable energy. Thus, in practice the system subsidises wind energy. The REFITs system is however contentious as it conflicts with the current trend towards liberalised energy markets. The main advantage of the system is the low risk for investors which has led to considerable investments in wind energy parks in countries with REFITs systems. On the other hand, fixed prices remove competitive pressure on producers to reduce costs, and wind energy is therefore likely to be more expensive than it would be in a more competitive market environment.

Bidding systems have been implemented in the United Kingdom and in Ireland (since 1995). They were also used temporarily in France (until 2001). Competition among electricity producers is created by calls for tender from an agency representing the government. Energy utilities have the obligation to buy a fixed amount of renewable energy per year from different sources. The quantity is defined by the authority, and suppliers with the lowest price are awarded contracts to produce it. Energy utilities are compensated for additional costs by a national tax on energy paid by all energy consumers. The bidding system leads to high competitive pressure, low costs and prices. In 1997, average wind energy prices in Germany were twice as high as in the United Kingdom. In the bidding system, only the best wind locations have any chance at all of succeeding, while prices under the REFITs system are higher because they are based on estimates of average wind energy costs. Bidding systems do, however, pose a high risk for investors, a risk which is reinforced by the application process which is often characterised as expensive, time-consuming and bureaucratic. A further problem is the lack of continuity caused by frequent changes in bidding conditions. As a result, a substantial wind industry has not been established in any of the countries running bidding systems.

To date, a system of green tradable permits for renewable energies has only been introduced in the Netherlands. Denmark switched from the REFITs system to a system of quotas in 2000 with the aim of making quotas tradable. Tradable permits combine the efficiency gains of bidding systems with the advantages of REFITs systems (achieving environmental goals by means of fixed targets for the development of renewable energies). The state defines quotas for renewable energies and issues certificates to firms producing the kind of green energy required. Certificates can be traded on the market. Energy utilities are obliged to hold a certain percentage of renewable energy in their portfolio, i.e. they must decide whether to buy a certain number of certificates for renewables on the market or to produce green electricity themselves.

Substantial differences can be identified where regulation systems are related to the development of a national wind industry (Haas, 2001). A wind industry tends to develop rapidly in countries with a REFITs system, such as in Denmark, Germany, Italy, Austria and Spain, as well as – until 1994 and 1995 respectively – in Ireland and the Netherlands. In countries with bidding systems wind energy use has developed very slowly, despite the available wind resources. In France, the United Kingdom and Ireland, the wind industry is poorly developed even though these countries have coastal regions with high wind potentials.

Finally, it is too early at this stage to evaluate the impact a system of tradable green electricity permits will have on the wind industry. Its success is likely to depend crucially on the design of the trading system and the underlying quota system. The European Commission has formulated the ambitious goal of doubling the share of renewable energy within 10 years – i.e. by 2010 (Jung, 2002). If the system of tradable quotas is geared to ambitious goals like this, it may inject considerable dynamic into the development of the wind industry and wind energy technologies. If the quotas are less ambitious, the development of the wind industry may stall. Denmark experienced just such a slowdown in 2001 after switching from the REFITs system to the quota system. In 2001, only 117 MW of new wind capacity were installed in Denmark, compared with 802 MW in Spain and 2,659 MW in Germany (BTM Consult, 2002).

4.3 Substitutes for CFCs in Domestic Refrigerators

CFCs are chemicals used as, among other applications, coolants in refrigerators and blowing agents for insulating foam. In the late 1970s they came under the suspicion of damaging the ozone layer. This led to the steady development of an international regime aiming to phase out and replace these substances. There are three primary substitutes available: 1) partially chlorinated HCFCs, 2) non-chlorinated HFCs, with HFC 134a as the most prominent chemical, and 3) natural gases such as butane or propane (HCs).

The first class of chemicals, partially chlorinated HCFCs, have a small remaining ozone depletion potential (ODP) and are therefore considered to be a viable alternative only for a transitional period. In the long term, amendments to the ozone regime require the phasing out of these chemicals as well. The second option, HFCs, was favoured by the chemical industries in both the US and, initially, Europe. This class of chemicals has been known since the 1950s. Considerable research efforts have been undertaken and advances in production technologies made under threat of regulation and, especially in the US, the fear of expensive skin cancer liability cases. The US-based corporation DuPont has been a leader in this area. The driving force for the search for substitutes was the early commitment of the company to stop production, should the suspected damaging potential of CFCs be confirmed. The company's search for alternatives is reflected in the rising expenditures for R&D in this field (Grundmann, 1999: 254) and the large share of related patents held by the company (Oberthür, 1997: 93). The US was also the first country to prohibit the use of CFCs as propellants. Taken in 1977, this measure gave momentum to the search for an alternative for other applications as well.

The prospect of a technically and economically feasible alternative for CFCs accelerated the negotiations of the global regulations laid down in the Montreal Protocol of 1986. DuPont supported global regulation of CFCs from 1986 on, while European manufacturers such as Hoechst opposed it, since European producers lagged behind in the development of substitutes. But the European position changed gradually from the mid-1980s onwards. As a result, the world production of CFCs has declined steadily.

Whereas the US favoured the second class of substitutes, HFCs, the third alternative, HCs, became dominant in Europe. While HFCs do not harm the ozone layer, they do hold considerable global warming potential, and are therefore criticised by environmentalists. At the beginning of the 1990s, Greenpeace Germany initiated the development of a refrigerator which employed hydrocarbons (HCs) as coolants and blowing agents. The major refrigerator manufacturers initially resisted this technology due to the combustibility of the gases. However, shortly after a small producer, in collaboration with a university institute, developed a prototype which met safety standards and Greenpeace started a public campaign in support of this company, the major German manufacturers adopted this technology (e.g. Lohbeck, 1999). German manufacturers converted to HC technology at their foreign production sites as well. Bosch-Siemens, for example, now produces on an HC basis in all of its subsidiaries. Electrolux switched to HC technology for the European market. Meanwhile, this technology has also been adopted by low-cost producers such as the Italian manufacturer Candy, which switched in 1999. Other manufacturers that have converted to HC technology are based in countries as diverse as Sweden, Denmark, France, Japan, Turkey, India, China and Cuba.

Currently, all three refrigerator coolant alternatives are on the market: CFCs are still produced in developing countries such as China and India; HFCs have gained a large market share in North America, Japan and Southern Europe; and HCs have become the dominant chemical for refrigerators for domestic use in Northern Europe. In Germany, the market share of HC technology is reported to have already reached 100% (World Bank et al., 1996). In Japan HFC has become the predominant technology for refrigerants, but HC is utilised as well. As of 2000, approximately 40% of blowing agents used in refrigerator production were based on HFCs, while 60% utilised HC (Arthur D. Little, 2002a). The jury is still out as to whether one of these two alternatives will become globally dominant, but HC has strong potential to become the global choice.

There is a lack of current data on the market penetration of HC technology. Its diffusion between 1992 and 1996 in Germany and Europe as a whole, the countries leading the international development, is shown in the following graph. It should be noted, however, that the German data is included in that of Europe. There are many signs that HC market penetration in other countries has also advanced considerably by now, and that a diffusion is taking place, particularly to less-developed countries (e.g. World Bank et al., 1996).

Fig. 7. Market share of HC refrigerators

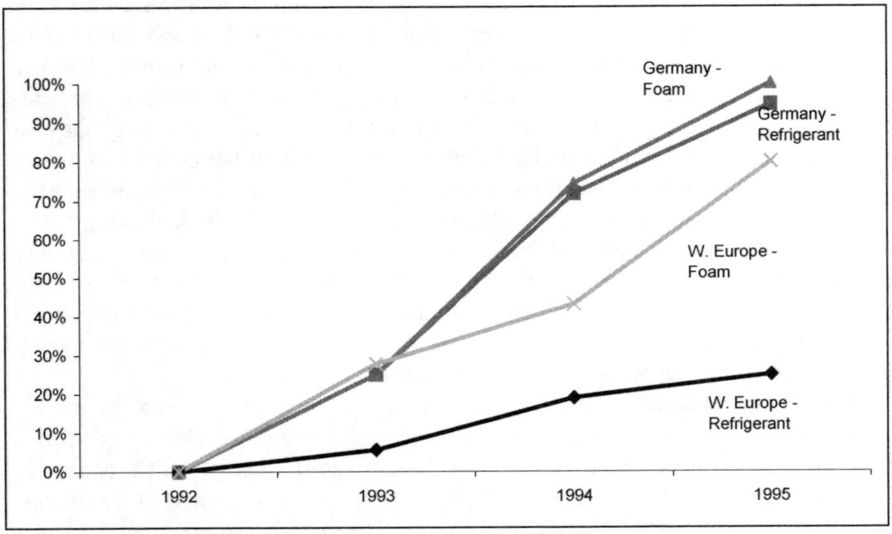

Source: Authors' calculations based on data and estimates of Sicars, 1995.

In the mid-1990s, HC technology had made few inroads outside of Western Europe. Minor applications were reported from Eastern Europe, Japan, China and

Oceania, whereas most producers in Central and South America, Africa and Asia continued to use CFCs (UNEP, 1998). In recent years, however, the share of HC-based refrigerators has grown significantly. According to a Greenpeace study, in 2000 there were more than 55 million HC refrigerators in operation worldwide (Maté, n.d.). This represents a share of roughly 10%. Lohbeck estimated the 1999 worldwide production to be about 15 million units annually, and the market share to be around 20% (Lohbeck, 1999).

A considerable increase is owed to a conversion made by large Chinese manufacturers. It is reported that two Chinese manufacturers (Kelon and Haier) have almost completely switched their annual production of 2.5 million units to HC technology. This gives China the largest share of HC technology outside Europe (Lohbeck, 1999). The conversion in China was supported by the German and Swiss governmental development agencies, by Greenpeace, and by the German manufacturer Liebherr.

Other German development assistance projects were started in India to develop a plant based on HC technology which was planned to be finished in the late 1990s (Sicars, 1999). Campaigning by Greenpeace and Friends of the Earth also took place in African countries and in Australia. The Swiss/German development projects were supported by the World Bank and were part of the "Multilateral Fund" (MF) that was set up in the framework of the Montreal Protocol to finance conversion to CFC-free technologies. Countries in the South are particularly interested in HC technology, because there are no licence fees to be paid as there are for the patented HFC technologies.

Despite the early lead in the conversion from CFCs, in the US the HC campaigning has not been successful. A recent study comparing the HFC and HC technologies argues that the US producers are unlikely to adopt this technology because US manufacturers are concerned that even a small risk of accidents due to the flammability of HCs may result in large financial claims and product liability insurance cost could increase significantly (Arthur D. Little, 2002a). The predominant type of refrigerator in the US is not only considerably larger, but also has an automatic rather than manual defrost system, which would lead to higher safety requirements if HC technology were applied. Furthermore, it is more difficult to meet the mandatory energy-efficiency standards with HC technology. The same study argues that the overall contribution of HFCs to global warming is only of minor importance as compared to CO2. This view of important barriers in the US market is countered by other authors, mainly based on the European experience, with almost no accidents, improvements in energy efficiency, and a switch to automatic defrost as well (see overview in Lorentzen, 1995).

Despite Greenpeace's campaign in favour of HC technologies and the above-mentioned government projects to support their adoption in developing countries, there are few countries with policies that discourage the use of HFCs or favour HC. Although HFCs are affected by the Kyoto Protocol due to their global warming potential (GWP), specific policies are rare. The Danish Environmental Protection Agency published a plan to phase out their use, along with that of other fluorinated gases, by 2006. French climate change strategy covers HFCs and proposes voluntary agreements for their reduction, as well as an extension of the planned CO2 tax in accordance with their GWP. The UK draft climate change programme states as a general principle that HFCs should be avoided wherever acceptable alternatives are available. The Netherlands specifies a reduction target of 23%. In other countries (Germany, Belgium, Austria), subnational regulations are in place to reduce the use of HFCs. Ecolabels are planned in Austria, and are implemented for refrigerators in Germany (Anderson, 2000).

The main driver for innovation in the lead country, Germany, has been the campaigning by Greenpeace. Their activities have also been important for the diffusion of HC technology in Europe and in developing countries. This diffusion was promoted by development aid projects sponsored by the Multilateral Fund, and by the adoption of this technology by German producers in their foreign subsidiaries as well as at home. It is too early to tell whether this technology will be adopted in the US as well, but European experience and NGO activities in the US make this conversion more likely.

4.4 Chlorine-Reduced Pulp Production

In the process of producing pulp from woodchips one major problem is to reduce the lignin content of the pulp as much as possible (delignification). This has an immediate impact on the pulp quality. The brightness of the resulting paper (or cardboard) depends on the percentage to which the lignin parts have been separated. At the same time, the strength of the pulp should not be reduced. By far the largest amount of the lignin content is separated out during the so-called cooking, a thermo-chemical step in the pulp production process. The lignin content is further reduced in an additional step called bleaching.

Up to the 1980s, the production of pulp was (predominantly) based on the use of elementary chlorine in bleaching. In the mid-1980s it became known that the use of elementary chlorine leads to the generation of environmentally highly problematic chlorine compounds, such as dioxin.

When the dangers of organochlorines came on the agenda – which can only be reduced through in-process technologies – Scandinavian mills were best able to adopt these technologies, as they were not locked in to secondary waste water treatment facilities. Additionally, their experience in developing in-process technologies to reduce overall waste streams put Scandinavian suppliers of pulp production technologies in a favourable position to respond to the demand for equipment to reduce chlorinated organic emissions.

The improvement in the competitiveness of Scandinavian suppliers has not been detected in analyses of trade data, however (Scholz and Stähler, 1999). One possible interpretation offered by the authors is that in the pulp and paper industry the diffusion of innovations occurs via imitation rather than through purchasing of equipment. It can also be argued, however, that trade data on equipment for pulp and paper production thus far investigated are too aggregated to detect improvements in individual segments of the equipment market.

Several technologies with the potential to reduce chlorinated organic emissions have been developed and are applied in large-scale production facilities.

- In the technology for *extended delignification,* additional lignin removal is achieved by lengthening the cooking process. Pulping chemicals, which are largely recovered, are used here as functional substitutes for bleaching chemicals, which have to be disposed of. The technology was developed in Sweden by the research institute STFI and commercialised by Kamyr/Kvaerner (Sweden) for the – more common – continuous cooking processes and by Beloit (US) and Sunds Defibrator (Sweden) for the – usually older – batch processes. Retrofitting existing plants is possible in most cases, but involves high capital costs. The process results in reduced operating costs compared to conventional processes.
- *Oxygen delignification* technology uses an additional oxygen reactor between the pulping and bleaching step, to remove additional lignin in an alkaline environment. This technology can be integrated with extended delignification in one process line. Kamyr/Kvaerner (Sweden) and Sunds Defibrator (Sweden) developed and manufactured much of the technology. It is also characterised by high capital costs and reduced operating costs. Although retrofitting is possible, the introduction of the technology is more profitable when used in building up new capacity. One disadvantage is a reduction in pulp quality due to strength degradation. The supply of cheap oxygen in Japan encouraged diffusion of oxygen delignification in that country. In the US, the advantage of reduced levels of BOD (biological oxygen demand), which is connected with this technology, could not be exploited, as most facilities were already equipped with biological treatment systems (due to former strict regulation of water emissions).
- *Ozone delignification* technology uses ozone as bleaching agent. Ozone has to be produced on-site, which accounts for a significant part of total capital cost. The process results in very low emissions, because all effluent can be recycled. It was developed by the pulp and paper company Union Camp (US) to meet regulatory demands under specific natural conditions for its Franklin mill. The technology was marketed in a joint venture with Sunds Defibrator (Sweden). Its installation requires high capital costs and results in reduced operating costs, especially for softwoods. Integrated with oxygen and/or extended delignification upstream, the technology allows the production of TCF (totally chlorine free) pulp.
- The *substitution of chlorine dioxide for chlorine* at a higher rate is a proven technology to reduce the formation of chlorinated organics. The technology is comparatively cheap and easy to retrofit. It results in moderately increased operating costs, because chlorine dioxide is more expensive than chlorine. Chlorine dioxide must be produced on-site. The problem of generating by-products in excess of plant needs has been reduced by new solutions. Installation in the US is driven by increasingly strict regulation. The highly corrosive chlorine compounds limit the potential for effluent recycling and conflict with the long-term prospect of a zero-emission or eco-cyclic pulp mill.

The complete substitution of chlorine dioxide for elementary chlorine results in elementary chlorine-free, or ECF pulp. A combination of technologies for extended cooking, oxygen and/or ozone delignification is the basis for producing totally chlorine-free, or TCF pulp. The first TCF pulp was produced in Sweden in 1990 by a small producer. Large-volume producers soon followed suit.

The diffusion of pulp production technologies can be described by looking at the production volumes of pulp differentiated by chlorine use in production. In the US, diffusion started only in 1990, but has increased steadily since then. As can be seen in Fig. 8, the diffusion of chlorine-reduced technologies started much earlier in Scandinavia and had already reached 100% of production by the mid-nineties. The role of Scandinavia as lead market for chlorine-reduced pulp production is underpinned by these data.

With regard to the distinction of ECF and TCF pulp, it is obvious that TCF plays a significant role in Scandinavia but not in the US. The share of TCF pulp did not increase from 1995 even in Scandinavia. The early diffusion of TCF was supported to a large extent by Greenpeace campaigns which resulted in strong demand for chlorine-free paper in Europe, especially in Germany (indirect demand effect). Since these campaigns levelled off, incentives for a further diffusion of TCF have seemed to be missing.

Fig. 8. International diffusion of ECF and TCF pulp (location of production)

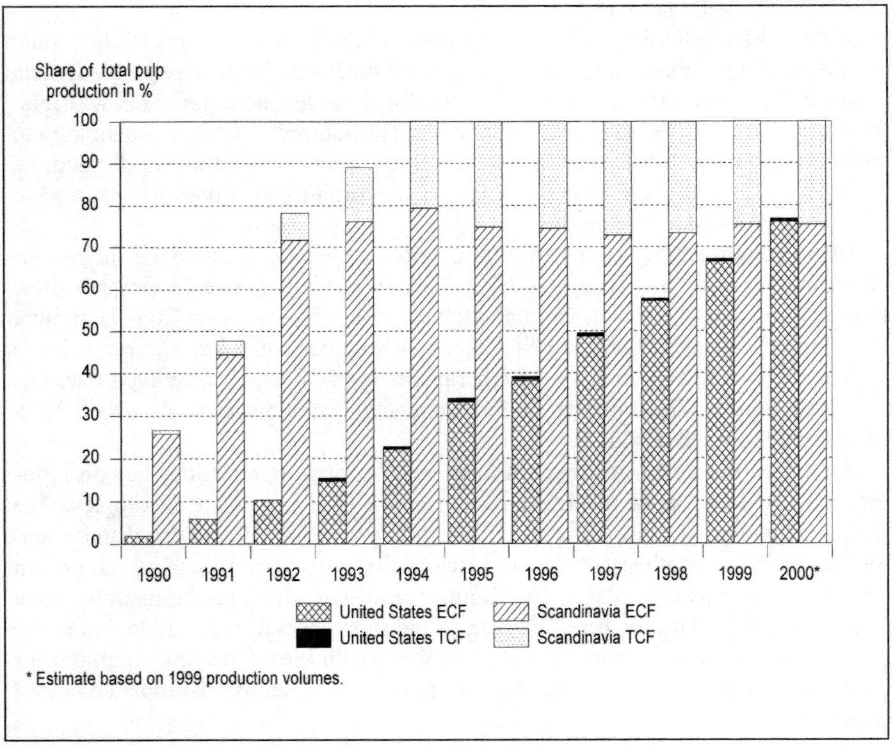

Source: Alliance for Environmental Technology (http://www.aet.org/aet_trends_2000.html)

In the 1970s the US led environmental regulation of the pulp and paper industry. Regulation required that manufacturers adopt BAT (best available technologies) to avoid the release of conventional pollutants, such as suspended solids and oxygen-demanding organic materials. These requirements could only be met by the installation of primary and secondary waste water treatment facilities, which was very costly.

In Scandinavia, specifically in Sweden, requirements with respect to conventional pollutants came later and were more lenient. Compared to the US, few mills were required to install secondary treatment of effluents. This was due to the high assimilative capacity for conventional pollutants of the large bodies of water into which mills discharged in Sweden. It was possible to meet the Swedish requirements through in-process modifications, which reduced overall waste streams. Swedish environmental regulations are shaped by the country's participation in international agreements, such as the Helsinki Convention (Baltic Sea Convention) signed in 1974.

Once secondary treatment was installed, the benefits of TCF processes such as oxygen and ozone bleaching were reduced to avoid the release of chlorinated organics; the additional benefits of reduced conventional pollutants – through lower waste loads, which emerged out of the possibility of recycling chlorine-free waste streams – did not pay off.

In the mid-1980s, the release of organochlorines became a concern that could be addressed only through process changes. At that time, Scandinavian equipment suppliers had won a strong market position for these technologies. This was reinforced by the long period (more than a decade), required to bring a technology to commercialisation in this field, while US firms were required to rapidly address the problem of organochlorines. In addition, US producers of pulp were forced to make a second major investment.

The development of in-process modifications to reduce or eliminate the release of organochlorines was promoted by NGOs. In particular, Greenpeace put pressure on publishing houses in Germany to use paper manufactured from TCF pulp. This had repercussions for their Scandinavian suppliers of paper and pulp. Some early movers were able to capture higher prices for TCF paper. One impact was an increased spread of information on environmental problems, as well as their solutions throughout the world.

In the US, the threat of litigation from water sports organisations had an influence on the decision of manufacturers to adopt ECF pulping technologies. The further diffusion of chlorine-reduced technologies to newly industrialised countries, namely in Southeast Asia, was financially supported by aid agencies. An important role was also played by leading consulting firms, predominantly based in Scandinavia, who advocated the use of the most advanced technologies in the build-up of new production capacities in these countries. The few suppliers for these technologies act worldwide and are interested in selling the most advanced solutions.

The case of ECF/TCF pulp production demonstrates the advantages of regulations which encourage a reduction of the entire waste stream, thus curbing the release of yet unrecognised problem materials.

The result of this case study is inconsistent with the hypothesis that moving ahead with stricter regulation will invariably promote international competitiveness. Rather, it becomes obvious that the flexibility of the Scandinavian regulations was responsible for the good starting position of suppliers in these countries when the release of organochlorines was recognised as a problem of pulp production.

The importance of flexibility of environmental regulations has not been investigated in theoretical environmental economics models yet.

4.5 Introduction of the Catalytic Converter for Cars

In the 1950s automobile exhaust emissions were identified as a main source of smog. This led to the adoption of air quality and auto emissions standards in California in 1959, imposing requirements for the reduction of HC by 80% and CO by 60% by 1966. Through this and later legislation, California established itself as the pacesetter for US policy.

At the federal level, the Clean Air Act was passed in 1970, calling for a reduction of 90% in HC and CO within five years, and in NO_x within six years. These ambitious standards were set against the backdrop of a presidential campaign which saw the candidates (Nixon and Muskie) competing in the field of environmental policy.

This was the first time that Congress had set environmental targets, which were meant to be technology forcing, since the car manufacturers claimed there was no existing emissions control technology able to meet the new standards. The automobile industry, however, was not convinced that the standards would be enforced in the long term. Indeed, the EPA delayed their implementation until 1978, while in the 1977 amendments to the Clean Air Act, Congress again relaxed standards for NO_x.

The automotive industry in the US might be characterised as an oligopoly, as it effectively avoids price as well as non-price competition. In the 1970s, after the oil price shock, the sector came under heavy pressure by Japanese and European imports.

The requirements for emissions control were a new challenge for this industry. There were different strategies available to meet these standards: (i) modifications of engines and control systems, as well as emission control devices and (ii) the investigation of alternative power trains for automobiles. US automakers cooperated in investigating technologies they considered likely to be successful. Cooperation in this area began as early as 1954. It continued until it was finally prohibited in 1969 as the result of a lawsuit brought by environmentalists arguing that the industry denied public access to technological findings concerning emission controls.

Another case of (international) cooperation, the Inter-Industry Emissions Control Program (IIEC), was initiated at the beginning of the 1960s. This body included Ford, several oil companies, and import manufacturers such as VW and Toyota. GM and Chrysler did not participate because of the antitrust law.

R&D efforts regarding the catalytic converter began at the end of the 1950s at GM. At the same time, efforts were made in the development of alternative power train technologies, in particular electric, petrol, electric hybrids, as well as Stirling, steam power, fuel cell and gas turbine systems. In 1967 the Department of Commerce reviewed these alternative engines, concluding that they had not been adequately studied and there was a need for further research.

More strenuous efforts in research on the catalytic converter did not start until the end of the 1960s. GM established a task force in 1969 which was asked to evaluate the potential of catalytic converters for automobiles. This task force of high-ranking individuals indicates that the problem of emissions control had become a priority within the strategy of GM.

The catalytic converter became the dominant technical strategy to reduce emissions for two main reasons. Firstly, it did not affect basic engine design[5], and secondly, it could be abandoned if there were a change in the law by Congress.

The market for catalytic converters for mobile sources did not exist before the enactment of the US regulation. Catalytic converters for stationary sources were produced by a small number of companies, all of which were present on the American market at this time. Three firms in particular achieved success in developing and marketing catalytic converters for mobile sources: the British-based company Johnson Matthey, and two American companies, Engelhard and Corning. Both of the US companies entered this field only after the passage of the Clean Air Act in 1970. The suppliers who were active and successful on the US market at the beginning of the 1970s are still the dominant producers worldwide today. In 1998 Engelhard (US) controlled 30% of the world market, Johnson Matthey (UK) 25%, Degussa-Hüls (Germany) 17%, and Delphi Automotive Systems (US) 15%. Along with NGK (Japan), Corning remains the major supplier of carrier materials for catalytic converters.

The Japanese automotive industry focused early on the US emissions regulations. While Japanese automakers modified their export models as early as 1963 to meet the emissions standards set by New York and California, they did not comply with their own government's request in 1963 to build domestic models with lower emissions. In 1971 the Japanese government adopted the emissions standards of the 1970 Clean Air Act, setting a target date of 1975 for full compliance. A policy supporting unleaded gasoline had been adopted in 1970, motivated equally by industrial policy ("benefit of trade") on the one hand, and the need to address domestic environmental problems on the other.

---

5 Although the catalytic converter is usually considered as an add-on device, it cannot function alone, but must be incorporated as a component in an overall emissions control system which requires unleaded gasoline, a change in the design of existing technology as for example electronic engine control technology, and engines with lowered compression ratios and upgraded valve seats. Therefore the catalytic converter technology is not a simple add-on technology – instead there was a need for technological adaptation and in this context occurred network effects.

A range of technical solutions to meet these standards were developed, such as catalytic converters, improved combustion control technology (lean burn combustion, the compound vortex combustion chamber or CVCC, and stratified combustion), as well as the incineration of toxic emissions by thermal reactors. However, in order to meet the NO_x standards and adapt to global markets, the Japanese government chose the 3-way catalytic converter as its preferred strategy in 1978.

Even when the US relaxed its air quality standards against the background of the energy crisis and the difficulty of the automobile industry in complying with the legislation, Japan maintained a strict pro-environment policy, mainly because of successful lobbying and lawsuits brought by some cities in their fight against air pollution. A report on the technical feasibility of catalytic converters supported the EPA's decision to put the standards into force in 1978 with little delay. Compared to the US car market (big three), the automobile industry in Japan was much more competitive.

With regard to regulatory style, there has been a much more co-operative structure between industry and government in Japan compared to the situation in the USA. The government supported the introduction of tax incentives for low-emissions cars.

The European emissions standards were mainly driven by concerns about European harmonisation. Companies that exported to the US (such as Mercedes, Saab and Volvo) had to meet the US standards and had incentives to promote their adoption in Europe. Sweden had adopted the American standards in 1976, with other countries following in 1985.

The development of more stringent regulations in Europe was rooted in the German regulation limiting the lead-content of petrol (1978) and in the debate on acid rain (Waldsterben) in 1983. This led to regulatory initiatives of the German government at the European level.

However, the German manufacturers were divided. On one side were the exporting producers who had experience with catalytic converters, and on the other the manufacturers producing mainly for the European market. Ironically, it was the subsidiaries of two American producers, Opel and Ford, who were least prepared to introduce the catalytic converter.

The 1984 European Commission proposal for emissions standards did not stipulate any specific technology. The issue divided the member states into two opposing groups. Countries without automobile industries, such as Denmark and the Netherlands, joined Germany, home both of major car exporters to the US and of Bosch, the main supplier of electronic automotive equipment. The opposing camp, which included France and the United Kingdom, focused its efforts mainly on the development of clean engines. French car manufacturers, especially, argued that there should not be a decision in support of the BAT – which at this time was the catalytic converter – but rather that time should be left to develop alternative technologies.

Finally, the European Community adopted a directive in June 1985 which imposed different emissions standards according to engine type. As a result, unleaded petrol became available throughout the EU and high-powered cars had to be equipped with 3-way catalytic converters. This standard was later tightened such that low-powered cars also had to be equipped with 3-way catalytic converters from 1993 onwards. According to some commentators, some German automakers were able to achieve a temporary competitive advantage over the French car industry.

Driven by the environmental problems mainly in the cities of developing countries, the diffusion of the catalytic converter is still in progress, as, for example, in India or China. International institutions such as the World Bank, along with various organisations, are important supporters of the diffusion.

4.6 Substitutes for Phosphates in Detergents

The eutrophication of waters that is caused by emissions of phosphates triggered environmental policy activities in the late 1960s in the USA and in the 1970s also in Germany. The main sources of phosphates are wastewater from industry and households, emissions from agriculture and the use in detergents. Industrialisation and the sharp rise in the consumption of detergents since the 1950s aggravated the situation in most western industrialised countries. The problem can be tackled in principle by the construction or refitting of wastewater treatment plants with a tertiary sewage treatment, or by a substitution of phosphates in detergents. Initially, the environmental policy initiatives focused only on the option of substitutes in detergents, because of the high costs for waste water treatment plants. It was only in Sweden where the latter option was chosen already in the 1970s.

Some US States prohibited the use of phosphate starting in the early 1970s with Indiana being first in 1970. Also in this year the Canadian government limited the maximum content of phosphates to 8.7% which was later reduced to 2.2% (Hartje, 1985: 19). There was no generally accepted substitute available at this time, therefore many other regulatory initiatives in US States were not successful. The debate on the harmfulness of phosphates led to R&D activities to identify possible substitutes. Mainly two competing substitutes were developed, from which NTA (Nitrilotriacetic acid) was introduced to the US and the Canadian market first. But soon the health authorities in the USA uttered the suspicion of cancerogenic effects and NTA was taken from the market again (Nösler, 1974). Furthermore, the Environmental Protection Agency (EPA) expressed fears that the use of NTA might mobilise heavy metals such as cadmium and mercury from sediments. Against this background the market penetration of NTA was hindered in the USA and it was used on a large scale only in Canada.

In Germany a policy on phosphates emerged in the 1970s. In 1971 an expert hearing was conducted by the federal government. Representatives of the industry and chemists favoured initially the construction or refitting of waste water treatment following the Swedish example, but this was refused by the Länder because of the cost burden (Hartje, 1985: 20). In 1975 the Detergents Law was enacted that provided the possibility for the authorities to limit the content of phosphates if suitable substitutes are available.

Also in Germany the association of chemists recommended not to use NTA as a substitute. The possibilities of biodegradation, the potential to mobilise heavy metals remained to be unsolved and therefore problems for waste water treatment and the extraction of drinking water could be expected (NTA-Koordinierungsgruppe, 1984: 8). Even when Zeolites were developed as a suitable substitute encompassing research activities were conducted, because the industry didn't want to give up NTA as a second option. Furthermore, several voluntary agreements were made to limit the use of NTA until the ecological risks would be assessed (Jacob, 1999). Comparable public debates took place in the Netherlands, Switzerland and Scandinavia (Berth, 1984).

Against the background of these national and international activities German companies started to develop another substitute from the 1970s on. The oligopolistic market structure with 3-4 main producers of detergents was in favour of stimulating a competition on the development of a suitable substitute. Henkel was little ahead of its competitor Procter and Gamble in patenting Zeolite A as a possible substitute for phosphates (Rohe, 1988). The regulatory activities in the USA furthered the R&D activities in Germany (Hartje, 1985; Nork, 1992: 265). Furthermore the rising prices for natural phosphates gave additional incentives, in particular the sharp escalation in 1973. The research activities can be read from the patenting figures for the different substitutes:

Fig. 9. Patent registrations for substitutes for phosphates in Germany 1971-1983

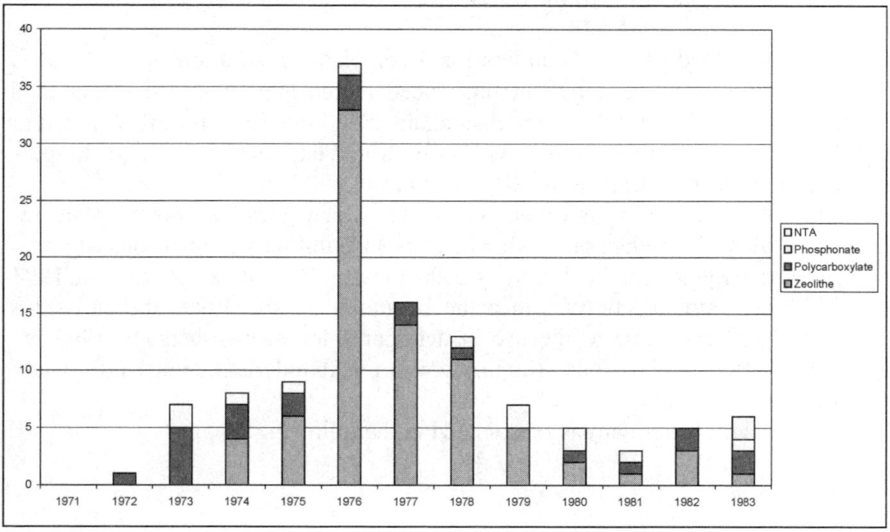

Source: Hartje, 1985: 25.

From 1976 the environmental performance of Zeolit was assessed in a large scale application that was supported by public funding (Nork, 1992: 229). It was concluded that environmental risks are not to be expected, but the health authorities were reluctant in giving a recommendation for the substitution. The federal health authorities cleaved to phosphates until 1988 when already 75% of all sold detergents were phosphate-free (Nork, 1992: 229 and 296).

Based on the assessment in 1980 an ordinance was enacted that came into force in 1981 and required the reduction of the content of phosphate by 22% and in a second step until 1984 by 50%. That regulation safeguarded the market for possible substitutes on a long term basis and gave the necessary incentives for furthering research and the build up of production capacities (Kemp, 2000). The regulative measures were furthered by the development of technical solutions but they never went beyond the technical possibilities.

Henkel which was one of the leading producers and the developer of Zeolite reduced the phosphate content by 50% already in 1981. The company had been able to build up considerable production capacities for Zeolites and was thereby able to reduce the price for this substitute from 10 DM/kg to 1 DM/kg (compared to phosphates: 1.30 DM/kg). Other producers followed this example with some time lag, because they experienced losses in turnover in other countries (Hartje, 1985: 40; Nork, 1992: 229 f.).

The adaptation of the competitors was eased because the economic ministry intervened in the enactment of the ordinance limiting the phosphate content and requested Henkel to offer licences to the other large detergent producers to produce Zeolites on their own. That intervention was meant to avoid a monopoly for the innovator Henkel. By this licensing it was possible to return at least parts of the R&D costs spent by Henkel that were estimated at 40 million DM (Nork, 1992: 274). The total costs of the development of a substitute are estimated at 250 million DM (Hartje, 1985: 40).

Zeolites do need other co-builders for a complete substitution of phosphates. The first phosphate free detergent introduced to the market in 1983 contained NTA as a co-builder. But the scepticism against the large scale use of NTA led to the development of combinations with polycarboxylates which enabled the producers to introduce phosphate free detergents from 1986 on.

Today, the substitution is almost complete, which goes beyond the legal requirement of a 50% reduction. Following this substitution the emissions of phosphates by detergents declined from 42,000 tons in 1975 to 2,000 tons in 1993 (former West Germany only). Since the beginning of the 1990s the emissions started to rise again, due to the use in detergents for dishwashers. In 1999 the emissions were 5,900 tons (http://www.umweltbundesamt.de/uba-info-daten/daten/wasch/trends.htm).

The diffusion in Germany is represented in the following graph:

Fig. 10. Market share of phosphate free detergents in Germany

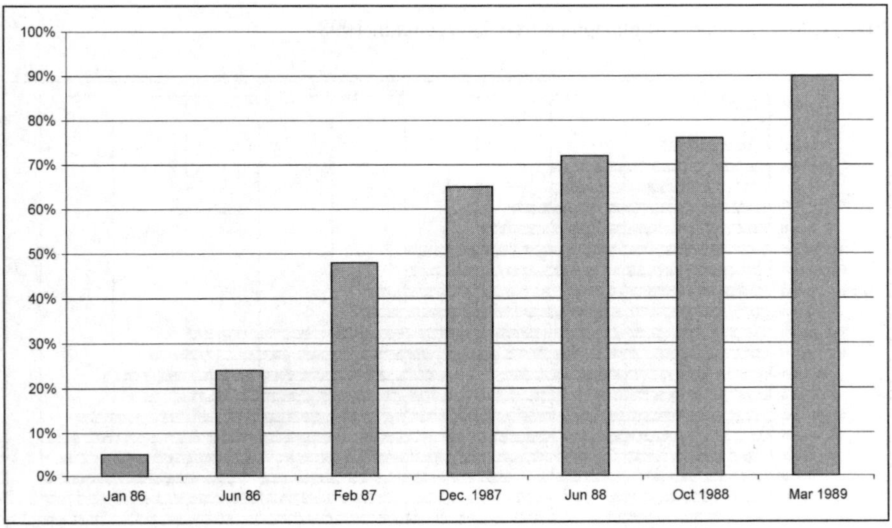

Source: Nork, 1992: 296.

Other countries adopted phosphate policies as well, the use was forbidden in Switzerland, in the Netherlands a voluntary agreement was stipulated that required a complete substitution by 1990. Austria, Norway and Italy adopted regulations limiting the maximum content. In Eastern Europe there are hardly any regulations regarding phosphates, in Poland and the Czech Republic the producers agreed voluntarily on a limitation. In Japan a voluntary agreement was adopted in 1979 to limit the content to 10%. As early as 1980 a phosphate free detergent was introduced to the market and from 1985 the market penetration was complete (http://www.jsda.org/e_history.html). In France a tax on phosphates in detergents was introduced in 1999 that led to a rise in selling prices of 10% (http://chemexpo.com/cmronline/stories/06_11_01/42_06_11_01.cfm; Barde, 2000). In the USA several states enacted regulations prohibiting the use of phosphates after acceptable substitutes had become available. Today, in about half of the States the use of phosphates is either forbidden or limited (ISSA, 1999).

Starting from the German market Zeolites are used today in detergents worldwide. A diffusion can be observed also in those countries where no regulations to limit the use of phosphates have been adopted. This is due to economic and technical advantages of Zeolites (Zeodet – Association of Detergent Zeolites Producers, 2000).

In 1993, the production capacities for Zeolites amounted to1.2 million t worldwide, of which 550 kt were situated in Europe, 390 kt in North America and 270 kt in the Far East. In 1995, the capacities rose to 1.5 million tons (Virta, 1995). For 1998 the worldwide consumption is estimated at 1.02 million tons (Virta, 2000). The higher consumption in Europe is explained by the higher market share of powder detergents, while in the US fluid detergents are in use for which citrates can be used as substitutes as well (Hartje, 1985: 39).

Fig. 11. Market shares of phosphate free detergents in 1998

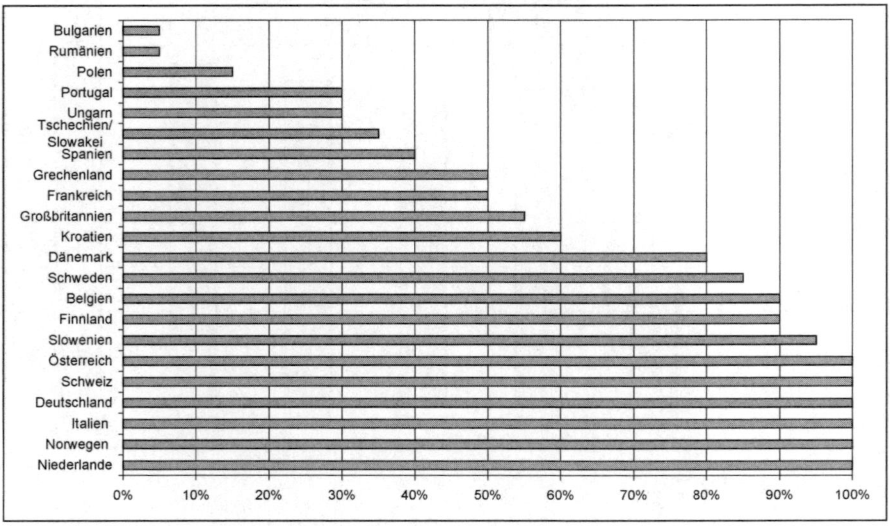

Source: Zeodet – Association of Detergent Zeolites Producers, 2000.

There were only few activities of international regimes or organisations in favour of the diffusion of the substitutes or of the supporting regulations. The Canadian-US joint commission for the protection of the Great Lakes put the issue of eutrophication and possible measures for a reduction of phosphates on the agenda. In the EU there is no regulation limiting the use of phosphate, but to the contrary, detergents with phosphate are still entitled to receive the European ecolabel. The emissions of phosphates have been an issue in the agreements for the protection of the North Sea and the Baltic Sea (OSPAR and HELCOM). Recommendations for a reduction were agreed on in the framework of HELCOM in 1988 (Lääne et al., 2002).

The European Union is supporting mainly the elimination of phosphates from waste water by a refitting of waste water treatments. The waste water directive that was enacted in 1991 and that should be fully implemented by the year 2005 requires an elimination of phosphates only in certain sensitive areas and for settlements with more than 10,000 inhabitants. For other regions limiting values for phosphates in waste waters are enacted. This directive led to an upgrading of waste water treatments with tertiary treatment of sewage. Against this background a lobbying for a rehabilitation of phosphate in detergents began in the 1990s by the European association of phosphate producers. The association made proposals for a recycling of phosphates from the waste waters (http://www.ceep-phosphates.org/Envidocs/performance.pdf). It remains open, however, if these actors will be successful.

4.7 Interim Conclusions

On the basis of the presented case studies, as well as several studies that have not been presented due to limited space, it is possible to draw some preliminary conclusions regarding innovation processes and the international diffusion of environmental technologies. Our studies reveal so far a considerable potential of lead markets for environmental innovations as summarised in the following overview:

Fig. 12. Lead markets for environmental technologies

An environmental lead market is the core of the world market for a product or process and is characterised by the following features:

- National policy or non-governmental influences successfully create a structure of incentives for users to adopt an innovation relating to a (manifest or latent) international environmental problem.
- The international dimension of the problem creates a potential demand in other geographic markets as well as the domestic market.
- Environmental lead markets are frequently initiated by national policy innovations (e.g. standards) which potentially diffuse to other countries. Policy innovation/diffusion and technical innovation/diffusion are closely interrelated.
- The diffusion of environmental policy innovations is supported both by horizontal imitation („benchmarking", „lesson-drawing") and by international organisations.
- The international diffusion of environmental innovations can be facilitated by a range of mechanisms other than policy diffusion, including cost reductions, export orientation and innovation superiority.

There are *demand*-driven lead markets (i.e. nations with higher environmental standards), which lead to a wide-spread adoption of environmentally friendly technologies. Examples of this phenomenon include the California exhaust gas standards for automobiles and the Swedish regulations on the use of cadmium. Other lead markets are driven by a *supply* of innovative technologies. Frequently, the producers of technologies seek to extend their markets and therefore lobby for international support for their technologies.

Regarding the pioneering countries that have successfully established their innovations in world markets, the following conclusions can be drawn: The pioneer country demonstrates the feasibility of its standards and regulations. Subsequently, the innovative regulation is adopted by other countries. A diffusion of the regulations is more likely if a country has a reputation as a pioneer. A very small number of countries today, mostly member states of the EU, serve as the benchmark for the environmental policy development. Our cases confirm once again the leading role of the Scandinavian countries in this respect. The frequent success of these countries in establishing lead markets underlines that great market size is not necessary. Even small countries like Sweden may push the international market to adopt their standards.

All of the countries identified as lead markets are highly integrated in world markets and demonstrate good overall economic performance. They are seen to have a high degree of technological competence, at least in the particular field of the innovation concerned.

The pioneer market, with its demanding environmental regulations can, however, also send out signals to the supply side beyond the domestic market. In such cases, competitive companies can advertise their ability to supply such demanding market areas as a sign of their technological competence. If there are scale effects, it can be cost-efficient to orient production to the highest standards.

Lead markets depend on policies and regulations, and therefore government agencies are frequently important actors in the process of innovation and diffusion. However, in two cases (chlorine-reduced pulp production and CFC/HFC-free refrigeration) NGOs, above all Greenpeace, took over the role of policymaker to a large extent. For the three-litre car and the promotion of wind energy, environmental NGOs were at least important players. The significance of multinational companies in the process of innovation is less clear, however. Several studies have stressed their importance for the diffusion of innovations. International organisations sometimes do play a role in diffusion, but are insignificant as to the innovation in the pioneer country. Learning and adoption also takes place in the form of country-to-country learning.

In most of the cases, subsidies were paid in the pioneering country, either directly – by reducing the costs of the innovation or its complementary goods – or indirectly – by increasing the benefit of an innovation. Energy taxes were important as a background variable in several cases. For the chemicals (phosphates, CFCs and cadmium), early prohibitions in the respective pioneering countries were important driving forces. Explicit political strategies to support the diffusion of policies as a means of extending markets are rare. The dependence of environmental innovations on political strategies should not imply that there is a causal relationship in which regulators force the adoption of a specific technology. Instead, policies usually take up existing technologies and support their diffusion. Regulations were tightened when substitutes were successful. In general, the policy style is characterised by flexibility and an orientation to innovation. Frequently, the lead countries have the image of a pioneer in environmental policy. Industry therefore might expect the diffusion of the policy innovations. Indeed, all cases confirm a demonstration effect of the policy measures on other countries. The adopted policies are transferable to other countries without many modifications. In general, regulations stimulate diversity rather than demanding a specific technical solution.

The economic risks for innovators and the risk reduction for adopters vary among the technologies, depending on the one hand on the necessary investments and on the other on possible subsidies that reduce the costs of adoption. Most of the case studies demonstrate that strict and early regulations hold the potential of advantages in exports, or at least that they bring no serious additional costs for pioneering.

Network externalities were important only in two cases (biomass CHP, where the availability of a district heating grid is an important factor for a high degree of market penetration, and catalytic converters, which require unleaded petrol). For other technologies (hydrogen- or electricity-powered cars), the lack of an appropriate infrastructure explains the failure of diffusion.

In a next step we apply the concept of lead markets to innovations in the stage of development or introduction to the market. By identifying emerging lead markets for environmental innovations, the stimulating and supporting policies could be optimised and R&D efforts could be adjusted more precisely.

5 The International Adoption of Photovoltaic Energy Conversion

5.1 Introduction

Photovoltaic solar energy (PV) is a fascinating alternative as a renewable energy. It is clean and silent and the main resource is obtained without any production and transportation cost; thus it is seemingly ideal for reducing CO2 emissions. However, the panels that convert solar radiation into electrical power are costly and energy intensive to manufacture, rendering electrical energy from PV cells one of the most expensive of all non-renewable and renewable resources. This is why its usage beyond certain niches remains marginal. It is still unclear whether the adoption of PV as a considerable energy source beyond niches will ever take off. This chapter addresses the prospect of solar energy from the perspective of the ability of single countries to render this technology internationally successful, that is, whether the success of photovoltaics in one country can entail its global success. The reason for this approach can be found in the effort of some countries, most notably Japan and Germany, to direct the widespread domestic adoption of solar cells to supply electricity for households. In order to assess the chances that single countries can propel a technology to global success, we discuss the factors that could drive a locally successful innovation abroad. At first glance, Japan and Germany do not look like the natural lead markets for photovoltaic energy conversion compared to the United States. Unlike the first two countries where sun irradiation is rather low, PV cells are more profitable in the US with its large, sparsely populated regions endowed with high sun irradiation but where remote households are often not connected to an electricity grid. Large developing countries such as China and India face a similar problem of electrification and are, therefore, future export markets.

Yet, solar energy would not have a chance on the world market without governmental intervention. Although governmental intervention to increase the export success of a domestic technology is tarnished as unfair trade policy, the character of solar energy as an environmental technology opens the door for politicians to use their tool box to organise a domestic success that is often necessary for the global competitiveness of an innovation. Negative externalities of non-renewable energies and an anticipated shortage of oil call for governmental support of renewable energy. Since the first oil crisis many countries, including the US, have introduced support programmes to kick off a mass market for PV cells. What Japan and Germany have managed so far is to create a vibrant domestic market with limited international effect. This paper discusses the question of whether a national government is able to create a lead market for photovoltaic energy conversion, that is, a domestic market that will be followed by other countries.

The chapter proceeds as follows: First, the international diffusion of PV systems from the PV cell's invention up to 2002 is discussed and the differences from country to country are explained with a simple regression model. In the following section the factors that might push a specific technology to commercial success abroad are discussed for the case of PV. The tentative answer to the main question given in this chapter is that the international success of PV is not considerably supported by its domestic success in Japan and Germany, because those countries have little lead market potential. The only potential leverage Japan has is cost reduction. With the energy production cost of solar cells unlikely to come close to that of conventionally generated electricity in the foreseeable future, this leverage effect seems to be slim, however.

A lead market is interpreted here as the regional market where the fate of an innovation is decided. If it sells there, the potential for global success is high; if it fails there, there is little chance for a global success. In that sense of a lead market, the United States is the lead market for PV, that is, the market where the question about the merit of PV as terrestrial energy source can be answered.

5.2 The Diffusion of Photovoltaic Energy Conversion

5.2.1 PV History

Photovoltaic energy conversion is the generation of electrical energy for households and industry by photovoltaic cells. This definition excludes all applications of PV cells in small devices such as calculators. PV power generation has seen a dynamic development in the 1970s and again in the 1990s, spurred by the subsidies of governments frightened by the leverage of the OPEC cartel or pushed by increasing public perception of risks caused by global warming or nuclear energy. The invention of PV cells, however, goes back to the 19th century. Photovoltaic energy conversion is based on the photoelectric effect discovered by Edmund Becquerel in 1839. Albert Einstein was awarded the Nobel Price for explaining the effect in an article published in 1904. The first solar cell that converted radiation of light into electric energy was developed in 1883 by an American inventor, Charles Fritts. The commercialisation phase of PV cells started in the 1950s after the transistor effect was discovered and explained. Pioneering work was done by AT&T and RCA of the US in the field of both crystalline and amorphous silicon (Johnstone, 1999). PV cells were commercialised mainly in the United States and by American companies because the first PV cells were very expensive and demand came virtually exclusively from the space industry to supply energy for satellites. However, other countries such as Japan, Germany and France entered the emerging PV industry already in the 1960s. For instance, Japan equipped a light house with a 242 W PV system in 1963 with PV cells manufactured by Sharp.

With the oil crisis in the 1970s governments in the industrialised world have initiated support programmes for research on and adoption of PV power conversion. Governments have supported the PV industry in various ways. All common instruments were used: research and development subsidies, political endorsements and target setting, demonstration projects and market stimulation incentives. R&D subsidies have the longest history. First, military and space related programmes were introduced in the US leading to the first PV cell powered satellite in 1958. R&D programmes around the world were introduced in the 1970s when the PV technology was still in its infancy and only expensive and low efficiency PV arrays were used. The public R&D budget was especially large in the United States, with federal support for terrestrial photovoltaic application in the 1970s and the massive funds generated by the Solar Photovoltaic Energy, Research, Development and Demonstration Act introduced in 1978. Germany and Japan took a similar path starting in the early 1980s. Japan, depending heavily on imported oil, initiated the Sunshine Program in 1973 but serious R&D support began after the second oil crisis at the end of the 1970s. Public R&D spending for PV climbed rapidly from around 1 billion yen ($4.5 Mio) in the late 1970s to 7 billion yen ($60 million) in the 1980s and 1990s (Watanabe et al., 2000), slightly more than the federal R&D budget in Germany. The heavy spending lasted officially until 2003, but the Ministry of Trade and Industry has found ways to continue the financial support beyond the planned cessation of public funds.

On the demand side, financing of demonstration systems and direct subsidies for private users were widely used by governments as policy instruments to support the adoption of PV energy conversion. Market incentives were introduced in the late 1970s. In the US, the Energy Tax Act of 1978 established a 10-% investment credit for photovoltaic applications. Broad terrestrial PV energy conversion started in the 1980s. Large PV panel facilities with more than 1 MW peak power were built in the United States; the biggest ever was Carrisa Plains with a capacity of 6.5 MW. Other countries as well put their hopes into large PV systems. Yet, when in the mid-1980s the OPEC threat waned and oil prices fell back to their pre-crises levels, interest in PV energy conversion faded as well. The large PV fields were not extended as planned but dismantled when they reached the end of their life cycle.

In the 1990s, however, the global warming issue boosted public support for PV and led some European countries and Japan to promote grid-connected photovoltaic systems as an alternative electricity source for households. Direct subsidies were given as tax credits or preferential loans and direct cash rebates for PV systems. The biggest programs are the roof programmes in Germany, Japan and – introduced only recently on the federal and state level – the USA. Japan's government initiated the New Sunshine Program in 1993 to promote PV technology and the residential dissemination programme to subsidise the adoption of small grid-connected PV systems for residential houses. Germany and Switzerland – with some European countries following the lead of the trio – introduced low interest loans and high feed-in tariffs for decentralised solar electricity generation on roof tops. Such subsidies attract house owners and other small investors who lack access to financial markets. Subsidies are commonly up to 50% of the total cost of a PV installation (Goldstein et al., 1999). Apart from direct subsidies, the most successful instrument in terms of adoption of renewable energy generators by private investors has been the renewable energy feed-in tariffs or buy-back rates. Feed-in tariffs are government-set purchase prices which utilities must pay for electricity produced from renewable energy facilities. Mostly, a preferential feed-in rate or "net metering" is offered, which means that electricity sold and purchased by the utility are equally priced. These subsidies, however, are not sufficient to make PV economically profitable for the user and some environmental commitment is required. Germany, however, introduced the most generous feed-in tariffs in 1999 with five times the retail price for electricity, rendering it profitable for private ventures to build PV systems (other countries have set an equal or lower tariff). The high feed-in tariffs in Germany have not only attracted house owners but also investors to once again construct large centralised PV fields with up to 4 MW peak power.

5.2.2 The Diffusion Pattern

The adoption of PV cells can be quantified by power of the cumulatively installed PV cells at their nominal maximum or peak power. Fig. 13 shows the build-up of PV power systems in several countries. Yet, this figure depends on the size of the country, underestimating the effort of small countries. The penetration rate as a measurement (e.g. application per population) controls for the size of the countries, making it easier to compare the countries based on their preference for a specific innovation. The penetration rate for photovoltaic energy conversion in the local market is characterised in this paper not as PV installed per household but as the ratio of installed power at peak and the electrical power equivalent of the solar irradiation in the respective country during one year. The latter is the power of solar irradiation that reaches the surface of a country in a year's interval. What is quantified with this ratio is the degree of usage of the available solar power within a country.

Taking the sun irradiation as the denominator, therefore, controls not only for size but also for availability of solar power. Although not all sun irradiation can be converted into electrical energy by PV cells (there is a theoretical maximum efficiency of around 32%), the efficiency depends mainly on the cell technology and to a much lesser degree on the geographical characteristics of a country.

Two measures for the maximum electrical power of the sun usable in a country are possible, one that multiplies the average solar irradiation with the whole surface of a country and one that takes only the surface of roofs of buildings into account. The first indicator relates solar energy usage to all parts of a country as usable in principle; the other considers only roof tops as relevant as locations of PV cell arrays. Because there are considerable differences from country to country depending on which measure is used, both have been used in the analysis. In Fig.

14 the penetration rates of PV cells of the top 5 countries is depicted using the total surface as reference.

Fig. 13. Installed PV power 1992-2001 by country

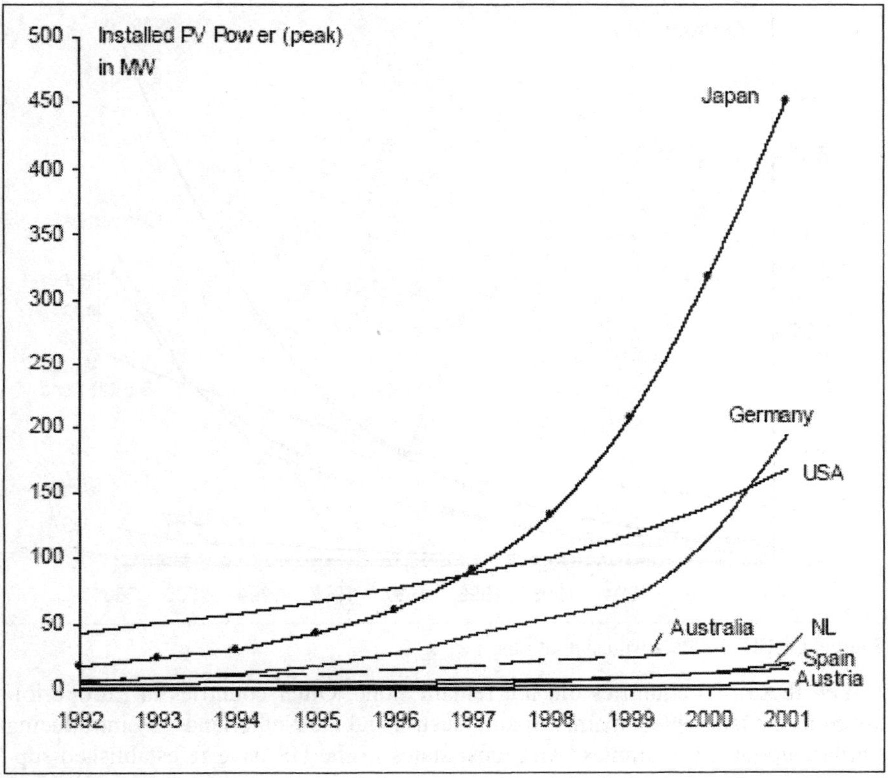

Source: OECD, 2002a.

Although data is only available for the 1990s, the graphics indicate that the United States used to be the market with the highest volume of installed PV power until the mid-1990s. Switzerland was the country with the highest ratio of usage and sun irradiation. This long time lead of one country resembled the general pattern of the diffusion of an innovation and it is not surprising that the US was the country that started the PV diffusion. However, in the second half of the 1990s an unusual pattern emerged. The United States was overtaken by two countries (Japan and Germany) in terms of installed PV systems and Switzerland in terms of penetration rate. This dynamic shift by these countries to the forefront of PV energy conversation reflects successful governmental intervention in the form of direct subsidies, low-interest loans, and high purchase prices for PV based electricity. A side effect of the subsidies was a shift in the structure of PV applications. While until then stand alone systems were the main application of PV, grid-connected roof top systems of private houses and commercial buildings became the main application of PV panels (see below).

Fig. 14. The diffusion of photovoltaic power installation 1992-2001 in several countries

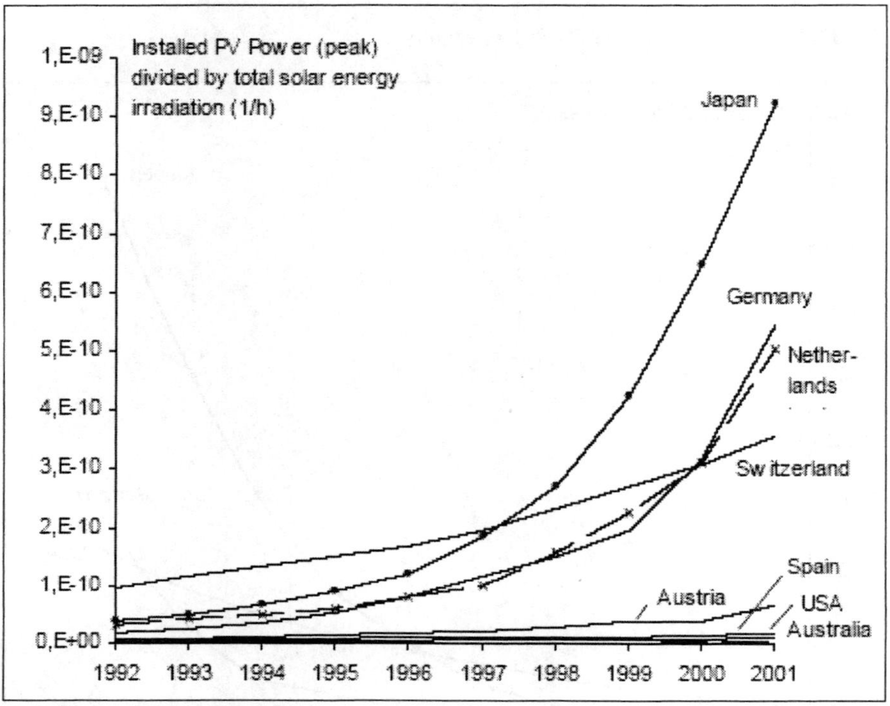

Source: OECD, 2002a, own calculations.

Yet, these two countries did not remain alone. Other countries in Europe followed in the late 1990s, mainly Spain, Austria and the Netherlands, by introducing similar support programmes. And most states in the US have re-established support "roof programmes" for PV systems as a reaction to local energy crises and worries about the dependence on oil from the Middle East. Germany and Japan have succeeded in creating a large domestic market for PV with high growth rates. Both use direct subsidies. While Germany uses high feed-in tariffs, Japan introduced a string of supporting measures. Governmental and public institutions were urged to install PV systems at facades and on roofs. In addition, PV systems were declared as building materials which opened tax-credit benefits and other preferences given to new housing to PV installations. These various incentives created a lively market for PV. However, in all countries the PV market is still dependent on the retention of subsidies (Holihan, 2000), which is apparent when support programmes are due to be phased out. At the time when the roof programmes in Germany and Japan were scheduled to be stopped in 2003, the domestic PV industry anticipated a strong decrease in demand and voiced new programmes to prevent the otherwise inevitable layoffs or even the destruction of the whole industry that was fostered by public funds.

Since only a few countries use PV panels to generate energy to a considerable amount, it is arguably not really a globally successful innovation. Two countries, however, have shown that in the presence of strong governmental commitment the PV industry can flourish and be considered locally successful. In the third section we will discuss the internationalisation mechanisms that those countries might initiate. Before, the effect of the various policy instruments on the nationally preferred design of PV energy conversion and the competitiveness of local industry is discussed.

5.2.3 Competing PV Designs and Policy Instruments

In almost all innovation ideas there are initially alternative designs that compete to become a globally dominant design. A design is a technical specification of an innovation idea (Utterback, 1994). The fax machine and the teletypewriter, for instance, are different designs for transmitting a text electronically. Designs compete on different levels. There are different designs of PV cells, but PV cells themselves compete against wind energy in the field of alternative energy. In general, different designs have different merits from country to country, so that countries would prefer different designs. For instance, countries in the sun belt would prefer solar energy among sources of alternative energy whereas countries with a windy coastal region prefer wind energy. Yet, standardisation advantages push for convergence and often globally dominant designs appear.

The country that has initially preferred the design that becomes the globally dominant design can be characterised as a lead market (Beise, 2001). Within governmental regulation specific designs are more or less supported. It is difficult to introduce an effective environmental policy that has no design bias at all. Often governments deliberately support one design over another to enhance the effectiveness of the intervention and the competitiveness of the local industry on the international market. This is called "picking the winner", because governments aim to promote at an early stage the innovation design that will become the globally dominant design enabling export opportunities for the domestic industry.

In Japan, environmental policy is derived from a combination of domestic environmental problems, the longing to reduce the dependency on oil and the government's sense of obligation to create new internationally competitive industries. This motivation led the government to invest considerable money in photovoltaic energy conversion. Photovoltaics are most appealing compared to other types of alternative energy because Japan has already a large semiconductor industry and PV cells are used for electronic devices such as calculators. Wind energy in contrast receives little public support. An official of the Japanese Ministry of Trade and Industry (METI) explicitly mentioned as one reason the fact that for wind energy the generator technology would have to be imported from Europe. Although there is not much wind in Japan, average solar irradiation in Japan is lower than in most other large countries as well. Another indication for the political choice of photovoltaic is that PV does not help reduce oil dependency or CO2 reduction. The preference for photovoltaic energy conversion seems more due to the strategy of world market domination as mass production is expected to be capable of driving down costs of production to a level that makes PV cells competitive for all kinds of applications.

The bias of governmental regulations towards specific innovation designs in alternative energy affects the technical choices to be made within PV technology as well. Within the photovoltaic technology, materials as well as system designs compete to become the dominant design. On the material side, traditionally, the United States market favoured the most expensive crystalline silicon because applications for extra-terrestrial and remote locations dominate, which require high-efficiency cells. In contrast, Japanese companies have always looked for a cheap substance for mass market applications, such as calculators and other appliances, and it was expected that amorphous silicon or thin film would do the trick. Europe somewhat settled in the middle between the two extremes using and producing mostly poly-crystalline silicon. Yet, the domination of crystalline silicon as the basic substance for PV cells appears to be much more stable than anticipated. In 2001 it still held a market share of 90% with a growing share of poly-crystalline silicon. The large scale production of amorphous silicon and thin-film PV cells faces many technical problems not expected after successful trials in the laboratory. Therefore, Japan was unable to start a bandwagon mass market based on cheap mass-produced PV cells. It appears that Japan's lead market potential relies solely on a technical breakthrough towards cheap PV cell production.

While governmental subsidies for the adoption of PV cells had lesser influence on materials for PV cells, it influenced the adoption of specific system designs. First of all, public subsidies in the front-runner countries for PV energy conversion are given explicitly for PV systems and feed-in tariffs in Germany are much higher for PV than for wind generators. In contrast, the EU policy aims to increase the usage of renewable energies in general, reflecting the diverse preferences within Europe. Second, most subsidies give preference to the adoption of proven older systems over new and unproven designs since the user receives an initial financial contribution and normally has to bear all the maintenance cost. And third, as already mentioned above, feed-in tariffs that have been applied so successfully in those front runner countries are only supporting the adoption of grid-connected PV systems. The result of this policy instrument is that grid-connected systems attracted all the capital for PV leaving non-grid connected technologies with little support to develop as well. Fig. 15 shows that the dynamic growth of PV energy conversion in Germany and Japan is solely due to grid-connected systems. Countries that offer only cash subsidies but no feed-in tariffs, such as Australia and the US, have lacked the dynamic of investments in grid-connected systems and remain focussed on off-grid applications. The mixture of incentives in Japan has led to a variety of off-grid and on-grid PV systems, whereas in Germany the extraordinarily high feed-in tariffs resulted in a dominance of grid-connected systems.

Fig. 15. On-grid and off-grid applications in Germany, Japan, the USA and Australia

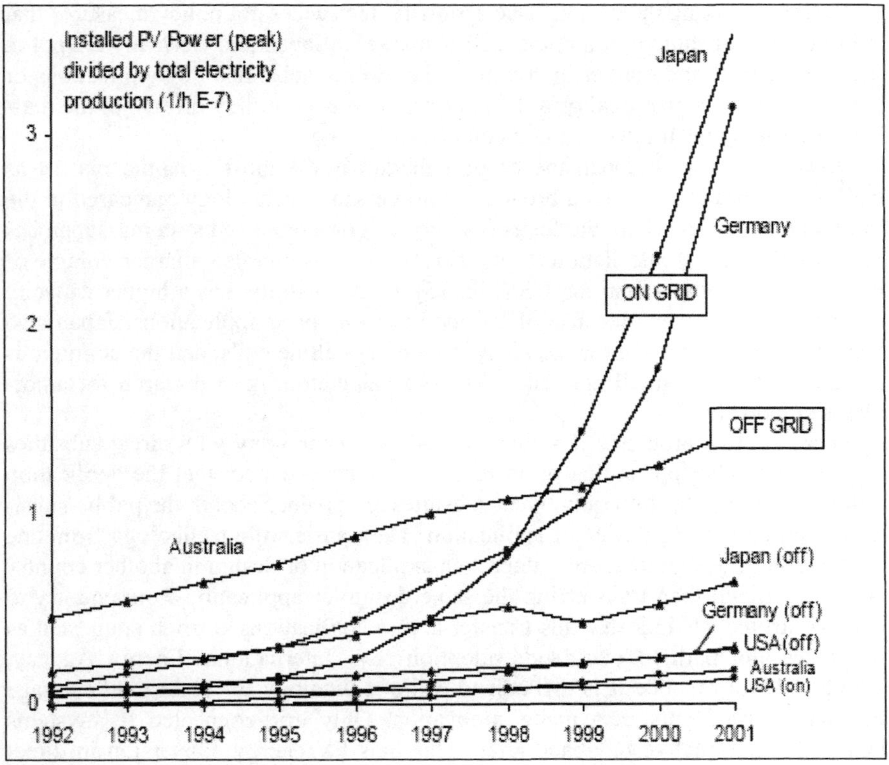

Source: OECD, 2002a.

In contrast to this market vigour in the two front runner countries, experts consider the non-grid connected market as the main global market (e.g. Fuhs, 2000) since in regions with no access to the electricity grid, where still 30% of world's population live, PV cells are or have the potential to become economically competitive against other generator types such as diesel engines (Holihan, 2000). Off grid is also the biggest market in the United States. The US government expects that the market share for grid-connected applications in the domestic market will remain low, around 17%, in the year 2020 (as cited by Holihan, 2000). In addition, the expected surge of PV applications due to region-wide electricity breakdowns, such as in the US, especially in California, and Italy in 2003, are again associated with battery-equipped non-grid connected systems. Although PV systems are modular in the way that different applications (grid-non-grid-connected) share the same components, companies that focus on grid-connected PV systems face design mismatch problems in the non-grid-connected market. First, grid-connected systems neglect the electricity storage technology that is important for non-grid but not for grid connected technologies. Second, connection to a public electricity grid requires a high quality AC-DC converter, since PV cells generate DC currency. For stand alone generators, either DC or a low quality converter is sufficient.

Therefore, taking the design issue seriously, the successful policy measures that led to the establishment of a domestic PV market in Japan and Germany are not in true accord with the market in countries that do not subsidise PV applications or that have no dense national grid. As long as there is no policy diffusion, the market for PV remains limited to these countries.

However, while in Japan the on-grid market is the most dynamic market as well, its PV policy supports a broader, more versatile technology compared to the European countries where the focus is solely on grid-connected systems. Japan has not only the largest installation of on-grid PV systems but also a larger volume of non-grid applications than the US (Fig. 15). Only Australia has a higher capacity of off-grid PV power. Because of PV modules for space applications, Japan also has a large production of the expensive mono-crystalline cells, and the continuous PV applications in small appliances such as calculators keep research for amorphous silicon alive.

There are two problems if a country pushes a technology with direct subsidies for the user. The first is that users in other countries expect that the application will be profitable for him only when subsidies are given. Second, the public subsidies often favour one design or application. The transfer of a technology from one application or design to another unproven application or design in another country is more difficult than transferring the same design or application from country to country. In the PV industry this transfer across applications is often suggested as the successful path to worldwide adoption (e.g. International Energy Agency, 2000b: 64). In practice it is difficult to sell a technology for mass market usage that has worked only in a niche application. Only grid-connected PV systems benefit from attractive pay-back rates. This puts PV energy conversion in direct competition with electricity production in central power stations and it is unlikely that this application will ever be profitable without subsidies. Although the transfer of grid-connected to non-grid connected applications is supported by the modular character of a PV system, a company that focuses on grid-connected solutions, as do the European manufacturers, will have problems with exporting their systems to countries that use mostly non-grid PV systems.

5.2.4 Domestic Markets and the Success of Manufacturers

It has often been suggested that differences in market penetration of PV cells affect corporate competitiveness. Porter (1990a) describes the local demand structure as one of the main nation-specific competitive advantages. User-producer-interaction theory, starting with Linder (1961) and further developed by Lundvall (1988), suggests that a dynamic local market rewards local companies more than foreign companies because of the efficiency of regional and cultural closeness for the perception of market preferences, communication with customers and feedback. The hypothesis has been supported by empirical studies on the micro level (e.g. Gemünden, 1981, Cooper and Kleinschmidt, 1987). If the local market has a lead role in the world, that is, if other markets follow its lead, then local firms are expected to profit more than firms in other countries. Their export performance should be better than that of other companies in the industry.

The PV industry, however, had to constantly adjust to changes of regional market dynamics, technological developments and varying intervention of national governments, accompanied by a continuous consolidation of the PV cell manufacturing industry. The shift in ownership of PV cell production reflects the swings in regional market dynamics. From the beginnings of the industry until today, a positive correlation between the local market dynamic and the commercial success of local firms becomes apparent. Initially, the PV applications in satellites created the first market for PV cells which gave US companies such as Arco Solar and Solarex a head start. They dominated the market for PV cells until the 1980s. With lots of sunny, flat and vacant regions on the one hand and an electricity hungry and high-income population on the other hand, the United States always looked (and still look) as the natural lead market for solar energy, that is, one untainted by governmental intervention in the adoption process. Yet, the lagging dynamic of the US market since the late 1980s has led US investors to leave the solar industry and to sell production facilities to foreign companies, notably to Siemens and ASE of Germany, and Sanyo and Kyocera of Japan. A boom in PV production in Europe initiated by national subsidies for the installation of solar cells opened large export markets for US and Japan manufacturers until sufficient production capacity could be built up in Europe. Yet, when the public programmes in Europe were temporarily phased out, PV cell production was reallocated to the US market again.

The late 1990s saw another consolidation process of the industry. By this time, the large European oil companies, BP and Shell, bought large chunks of PV production capacity. In Japan, Sharp aggressively invested in new production facilities and became worldwide the largest PV producer. In 2001 those three companies and Kyocera of Japan were in control of almost 60% of the world production capacity of PV panels with most of the other producers based in Europe and Japan as well. Concerning production location, Japan holds the lead with a 43% share of worldwide production. The United States' share decreased to about a quarter of the production of PV cells, down from 40% since the mid 1990s, while Europe increased its share to 23% (Butz, 2002). Europe is still a net PV cell importer; its biggest market, Germany, imported more than half of the total domestic installations in 2002 (International Energy Agency, 2003b).

The export success of PV cell and module exporters is still concentrated on grid-connected systems in the markets that subsidise PV applications (European countries and Japan). Japanese manufacturers have made little progress so far in the non-grid connected market, confirming the problem of design mismatch described above.

5.3 Factors of International Diffusion

5.3.1 Explaining the Adoption of Solar Energy

In this section some basic factors that can determine the adoption of photovoltaic energy conversion by a country are discussed and tested in a simple regression model. The aim is to explain the international differences in the penetration of PV energy conversion or why a country adopts PV cells more widely than other countries. To assess the question of whether other countries will adopt PV cells over time as much as the leading countries, it is essential to indicate the main adoption factors for PV. In the following section we discuss whether these factors are likely to spread worldwide. The front runner countries are the lead markets if the conditions in these countries that make local users adopt a specific technology imply increased incentives for users in other countries to adopt the same technology.

The historical overview already demonstrated that the regional adoption of PV cells had nothing to do with technological gaps between countries. Although PV technology may be science-driven or science-related (Pavitt and Soete, 1997), differences in adoption from country to country cannot be explained by differences in technological knowledge endowments among countries. The technological progress in photovoltaic technology was spurred by researchers and technicians in the US, Europe, Japan and Australia. The scientific and technical knowledge normally spreads worldwide quickly by articles published by the scientific community. In addition, the success of cell efficiency achieved in laboratories regularly means nothing for the efficiency of cells produced for the mass market. The productivity of production technology and, especially, the failure rate are the factors that determine the success of a manufacturer. And the incentives to invest in production facilities are normally determined by the local market size.

The main incentives for adopting a technology for a country in the first place are expected to be the sun irradiation (the benefit) in the country, the price of the innovation, the price of substitutes (electricity) and governmental incentives.

The relevance of these factors for the adoption of PV panels is tested using a simple linear regression model. The endogenous variable is either installations of PV panels in MW divided by the total electricity production in MWh or divided by total solar irradiation in MWh per year. The solar irradiation is measured in MWh per m^2. The average system price of PV panels per kW for systems with more than 10kw and the price of electricity for households is provided by the International Energy Agency (IEA). All prices are converted to purchasing power parities US-$. The IEA also made estimations on the financial contributions of governments to photovoltaics in the form of R&D funds, demonstration projects and market subsidies. All data is for the year 2002. However, data is only available for 13 countries, which renders the regression rather unreliable. Therefore, a panel regression for the years 1992 to 2002 was estimated. The panel includes 142 observations and allows for control of country-specific factors. The problem with a panel estimation is that the system price is only available for the year 2000 and the governmental funds for 2002. Therefore, the module prices are kept constant over the 10 year period and only the R&D funds are retained, because those are the only funds that do not vary considerably during the 1990s and they are an indicator of the overall effort of governments to support PV energy conversion. While prices for PV systems decline continuously over time it is assumed that the international price structure remains the same. The data of 2000 are thus used as a proxy for the price differences from country to country for the whole period. For the panel estimation a random effects GLS (generalised least squares) regression is applied. Only the results of the regressions with PV installations divided by electricity output as an endogenous variable are presented in the following table (results with the other variable are similar).

Table 2. Regression results for PV installation as a share of total electricity production

	OLS Reg. for 2002		GLS Reg. for 1992-2002	
	Coefficient	t-value	Coefficient	t-value
Exogenous Variables:				
Sun irradiation	0.027	0.27	0.074**	1.99
System price	-0.023	-1.67	-0.011***	-2.82
Electricity price	-0.158	-0.17	0.433	1.39
Public R&D budget	0.536	0.65	0.629**	2.18
Demonstration	5.727	1.66		
Market stimulation	1.581*	2.02		
Year			0.013***	7.87
Constant	0.204	1.01	27.53***	-7.90
/sigma_u			0.032	
/sigma_e			0.061	
Rho			0.218	
No. of obs.	13		142	
R^2 adj.	0.78			
R^2			within 0.365 between 0.726 overall 0.505	

All coefficients have the expected sign. However, due to data constraints, the estimations for the year 2002 are mostly insignificant. Only market stimulation funds have a significant effect on market penetration. In the panel estimation, most coefficients are significant. Only the electricity price has no effect. This seems to be caused by the high electricity prices in the Nordic countries where wind energy is used as the preferred alternative energy source. The results show that governmental instruments can create a home market for a technology even if there are natural disadvantages, in this case lack of solar irradiation. Among the governmental instruments, market stimulation has the biggest impact on adoption.

The estimation also shows that the adoption of PV panels are price sensitive. This explains the success of the roof-top initiatives where the prices of panels are subsidised. In contrast, high electricity prices in general have no effect on the adoption of all alternative energy sources, but only on those that are most profitable in the respective country.

The main result at this point is that Japan – and Germany – have become front runners in the adoption of PV panels because of preferential subsidies for PV systems by local governments. Taking the factors into account that have led to the adoption of PV energy conversion, two internationalisation mechanisms for PV technology are most promising. These mechanisms are the reduction of prices for PV systems and the adoption of policies to support the PV panels by many other governments. Those and other possible mechanisms are discussed in the next sections.

5.3.2 Price and Cost

Public subsidies for PV technologies aim to make PV cells an economical alternative as an energy resource. The biggest hope for the sustained adoption of photovoltaic energy conversion in the future without subsidies is the cost reduction effect of large production sizes and learning. If the cost can be reduced to the cost of the production of electricity from fossil resources, PV cells will be internationally adopted. Evidence for the price sensitivity of PV cells is depicted in Fig. 16.

Fig. 16. PV system prices and penetration rates (2001)

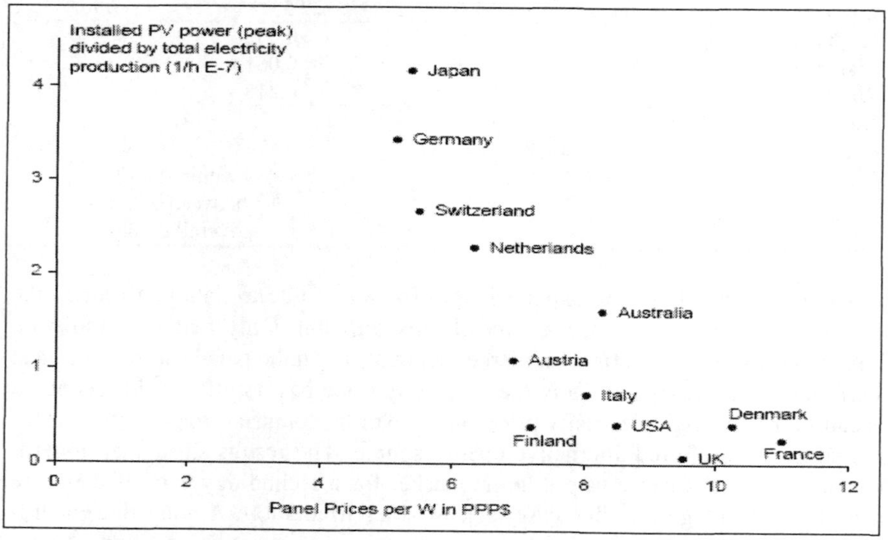

Source: OECD, 2002a.

While the prices for silicon cells are roughly the same worldwide, the prices for systems differ considerably due to pricing-to-market strategies, different competitive situations and market infrastructure. Lower prices for PV systems are associated with higher adoption rates. Lower prices are, therefore, an important success factor of photovoltaic energy conversion. The cost of PV cell production has indeed come down a long way from the beginnings to the present levels of production. Various studies have found that since modules have been industrially produced prices have fallen around 20% each doubling of the cumulative PV production (e.g. Watanabe et al., 2000, for a review see Harmon, 2000 and International Energy Agency, 2000a). These large cost reductions, however, have been mainly achieved by economies of scale, new automated production processes and increases in the efficiency of cells, and not so much through learning, which is defined as cost reductions in the same production unit. This would mean that the learning factor that is used for expectations about future cost reductions is overestimated. Indeed, the IEA finds that in the 1990s prices dropped by between 10 and 17% only (International Energy Agency, 2003b).

Fig. 17. Electricity pricing trends 1984-2002

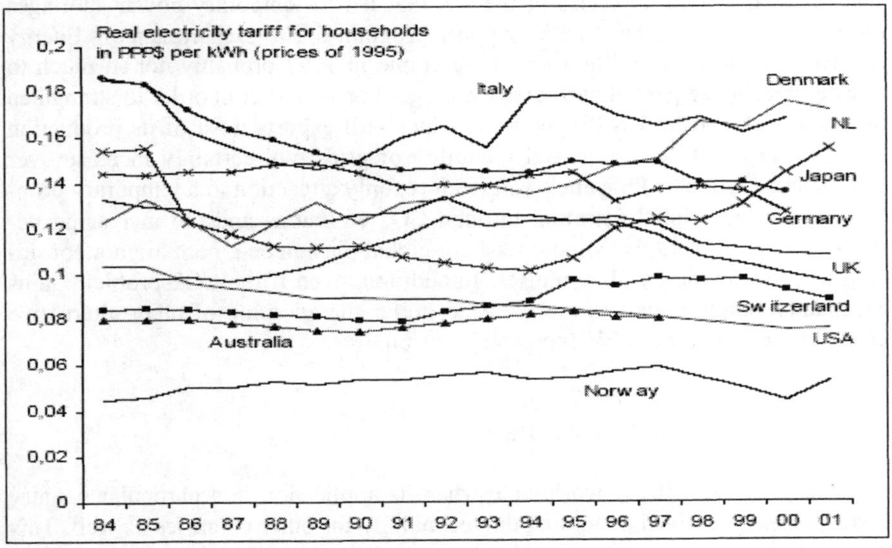

Source: OECD, 2002a.

Since PV cell cost is still a multiple of electricity by fossil fuels, it is expected that competitiveness in the general energy generation industry will not be reached in the near future. In addition to efficiency increases of fuel combustion generators and turbines the PV industry faces another trend that frustrates its economic sustainability. Although some countries, most prominently Denmark, have introduced energy taxes of electricity in order to increase the price competitiveness of renewable energies, there is no global trend of increasing electricity prices. In most countries electricity tariffs for households decreased during the last 15 years due to increased competition and production cost reductions (OECD 2002a, Fig. 17). The internationalisation of PV cells is, therefore, not supported by cost or price trends.

5.3.3 Demand Trends

In this section, we discuss whether there is a global trend that can spread the demand for PV cells worldwide. Yet, the answer is rather pessimistic. Up to now, the adoption of PV energy conversion is accompanied by motivations which vary over time and from country to country. In Japan, the front runner of the adoption of PV cells, a main concern is the dependence of oil imports from Arab nations and the international competitiveness of domestic industries. In contrast, the global warming issue and the reduction of CO2 became a major motivation for politicians in Europe to turn to solar energy. In the US, however, PV cells are mainly adopted to supply electricity at remote locations and as a backup for unreliable public electricity grids. The biggest market for PV cells is still the off-grid application in households and commercial units such as communication towers and satellites. The regional electricity crises in the US that led to temporary power shortages prompted states to prop up PV support programs. The Department of Energy (DOE) introduced the million roof programme in 1997 probably not so much to reduce greenhouse gases but to create a bigger home market in order to strengthen the home base of the US PV industry, which still exports most of its production (see Fig. 18). Yet, access to and reliability of grids will certainly increase over time. The adoption of PV panels is, therefore, only a reaction to a temporary problem. And while global warming through CO2 emissions and the increasing dependency on oil from the Middle East are global phenomena, both are not considered as problematic by all countries. In addition, even if the CO2 problem gains acceptance, many countries are likely to prefer the adoption of other alternative energy sources to that of PV energy conversion.

5.3.4 Transfer and Policy Diffusion

A technology can diffuse worldwide when its application in a particular country increases the perceived benefit of the technology for other countries as well. This means that either the perception changes, which is called a demonstration effect, or the benefit itself increases. The demonstration effect has been a major reason for the success of the light water nuclear reactor (Cowan, 1990). Energy production is normally associated with high investments which translate into high risks. The reliability of a new energy source is therefore an important adoption factor. Yet, the success of PV systems in Japan and Germany merely demonstrated that financial incentives can persuade house owners to invest in small PV units and can even persuade large-scale investors to erect commercial PV sites when high feed-in tariffs render electricity produced by PV cells profitable. However, neither Japan nor Germany demonstrate that PV energy conversion is economically reasonable or that it increases welfare. This means that only the diffusion of policy support programmes can transfer demand for PV cells abroad.

Policy diffusion is the adoption of the same public regulation or subsidies in many other countries worldwide. As we have shown previously (see chapter 2), we expect that the most important internationalisation mechanism for environmental innovations is policy diffusion. Developments in the PV industry seem to support this assertion bearing in mind that the mechanisms that internationalised certain electronic innovations – cost reductions and demand trends – are not sufficiently present in the case of PV energy conversion.

The most important success factor for the transfer of policies is the demonstration that a policy instrument is effective in solving an environmental problem while at the same time avoiding negative economic side effects. In addition, countries with large markets are often swiftly followed by export-oriented countries in the introduction of innovation-inducing environmental regulation if there is an opportunity to export the regulation-induced innovation. International organisations and international agreements can also spur the internationalisation of environmental regulation. Yet, the chances for the international diffusion of policies related to PV energy conversion are rather dim. The two biggest problems of PV right now are that all countries do not share the same motives and that PV currently does not solve an environmental problem. Instead, PV is often a more economical energy source in remote locations.

Within Europe, a major push for alternative energies is the recent directive on renewable energy of the European Union that promotes a doubling of the share of renewable energy by 2010. This directive, which has been adopted by several member states, puts pressure on the governments to promptly implement incentives that can quickly raise the adoption of renewable energies. This spurs the adoption of the instruments that have already been successfully introduced elsewhere, such as in Germany. As a result, German cash incentives for private investments in PV roof-top systems and governmental imposed feed-in tariffs have been adopted in France and Austria. Grid-connected PV technology has spread throughout most parts of Europe (International Energy Agency, 2002).

While the policies adopted in Germany and Japan have proven to be nationally successful, the likelihood of the diffusion of these policies worldwide is ambiguous. Grid-connection policies are inappropriate for countries where the biggest markets for PV cells are regions with less access to electricity grids. In those countries, policies that support the adoption of non-grid connected PV systems are more suitable. The mixture of policies in Japan has been successful in establishing a market for PV energy conversion. In particular the treatment of PV systems as building equipment matches the tax-incentives for housing popular worldwide. However, for an international adoption of a policy beyond Europe and Japan it must be shown that the policies that support the adoption of a new technology such as PV systems are fulfilling the targets of the national policy makers. Yet, those targets are diverse as has been discussed above and PV energy conversion is not a prime candidate for reaching all targets. Another possible scenario for policy diffusion is that the global warming problem becomes so severe that all countries are forced to participate in multilateral efforts to reduce CO2 emissions. Then, the successful policies on the national level are likely to be adopted internationally. Japan and Germany are the lead markets in this scenario because CO2 reduction is one of their main motivations. Another external shock that would increase diffusion of PV energy conversion would be a steep increase in the oil price.

While there are international organisations that promote the diffusion of PV cells as an energy source, such as the IEA and Greenpeace, their influence or commitment seems to be small compared to the activism that has led to the substitution of harmful substances, for instance CFCs in sprays or cadmium in paints. While policies are mainly discussed in multilateral conventions, multinational firms can become transfer agents as well. Multinational firms help standardise the roof-top panel design around the world. They transfer products that are successful in their home markets to markets worldwide. Since most of the PV manufacturers are based either in Japan or in Europe, Japanese and European panel designs penetrate the world market much better than US designs. In the US building-integrated and residential roof-integrated PV systems are said to be already mostly of European and Japanese design (Eckart, 1999). The biggest manufacturer, Sharp of Japan, has started to build up assembly facilities in the US and plans to do so in Europe to penetrate these overseas markets with its indigenous design. Most manufacturers are diversified large entities and are likely to promote their cell technology and panel designs in other applications within their operations. Anecdotal evidence for this leverage effect of multinational companies includes the fact that BP installs its gas stations worldwide with photovoltaic systems produced by BP Solar.

5.3.5 Competition

Domestic competition is a characteristic of lead markets. The higher the degree of local competition, the more likely it is to find a superior, economically reasonable application design. Competition would drive down prices, rendering the environmental innovation more price competitive and more intensive marketing activities would attract more users. It is evident that the competition in the Japanese PV market is the fiercest. The long-time governmental efforts to support a PV industry has led to a diverse group of PV manufacturers and panel assemblers that compete head to head. Evidence for a high degree of competition in Japan is the fluctuation of market shares. Kyocera, Sanyo and Sharp all obtained the largest market share once. No company ever dominates the market for long. Frequently, new large companies enter the market, bringing with them investment clout and the commitment to effectively compete in the market for a large market share.

Another indicator for competition are low or continuously decreasing prices. In other countries markets are moving fast as well and new companies enter the market. Continuously decreasing prices indicate the lack of cartels fixing prices. In contrast, in Germany, it is reported that the cost reductions of PV cells are not immediately passed on to buyers through lower prices, indicating a less competitive market structure (Butz, 2002). While Germany has attracted many small manufacturers of PV cells and systems, the comparatively small size of the firms can be expected to have a smaller effect on competition because their financial capability in marketing and price competition are very limited.

Porter and van der Linde (1995a) suggest that environmental regulation can have a similar effect to competition. It pushes companies to find new innovations in order to satisfy a new environmental obligation such as emission saving or fuel consumption innovations. These innovations might be economically reasonable even for companies that do not have to meet the environmental directive. In the PV case it would mean that the financial incentives to adopt PV systems together with the R&D subsidies could lead to the development of new technologies that would be profitable even without the subsidies. Although the public R&D subsidies for PV technologies aim exactly at this effect – to find materials and compounds that have a sufficiently high degree of efficiency accompanied by low costs – the subsidies for the adoption of PV are rather unlikely to accomplish that purpose. The Porter effect assumes that companies are complacent about specific innovation opportunities and are only actively seeking them when research is initiated by regulation. This, however, cannot be said about the photovoltaic industry, in which the innovation target is clear and numerous companies seek solutions to the problems.

5.3.6 Export

The export orientation of a country in a specific industry adds to its ability to commercialise innovations worldwide. A high export orientation of a country means that preferences of foreign markets are included in the design of innovations even if this lowers the attractiveness in the home market. Contrary to other industries, the export orientation of the US producers of PV system is stronger than that of the Japanese and European producers. The US export share of PV cells and modules grew continuously, reaching three quarters in the year 2000 (Fig. 18). A reverse trend is observable in Japan. The export share of Japan has been declining over time, dropping to around 10 to 30% (depending strongly on the yen-US-$ exchange rate). As a result of the buoyant market forecasts for Japan in contrast to stagnation in other countries, Japanese companies are focussing more and more on the domestic market.

The main export flows of PV cells and modules are from the US to Germany and Japan. About 50% of PV exports are shipped to Germany and 11% to Japan (trade data of 2000, Source: EIA). European and Japanese manufacturers develop and manufacture mainly for their domestic markets.

The reason for this is that although the United States was the initial lead market, US producers which built up large production capacity had to look abroad when the Federal tax credits expired in 1985 and their home market became sluggish. When Japan and Germany steeply increased the adoption of PV systems, the US production (already acquired by European companies) could deliver quickly. Holihan, (2000) describes the growing ability of US manufacturers to respond to foreign market preferences, as they "compensate for their distance from many end use markets with a willingness to place technically trained marketing representatives on site around the world." European and Japanese PV manufacturers on the contrary were busy serving the strong market growth in Europe and Japan and did not pursue export markets intensely. Only recently, after the market in Japan started to get saturated have the Japanese and European manufacturers turned to export markets with the building up of sales networks and assembly lines in the US and Europe.

Fig. 18. Exports of PV cells and modules from the USA

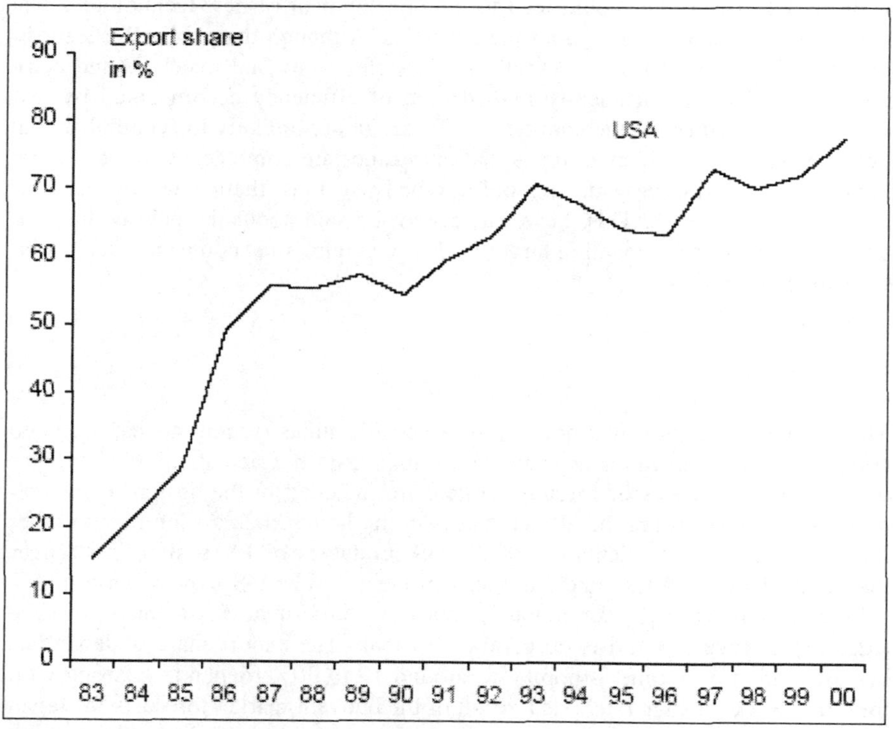

Source: OECD, 2002a.

The Japanese and the US government subsidise the adoption of domestic PV systems in developing countries. The German legislature has only recently (2001) introduced improved public export credit insurance for renewable technologies and an export promotion programme that mainly intends to provide German renewable energy technology manufacturers with information on export markets. The efforts of governments to spur exports of their domestic producers have not had a big volume effect on their exports yet. Again, the US seems to be more in tune with developing countries' markets, since non-grid-connected applications in rural areas are the main market. Over time US firms established a market strategy based on flexibility that puts much of the effort on the training of local sales people and customers in rural areas, enabling them to efficiently utilise and maintain a PV system.

5.4 Conclusions

In this chapter, we discussed the prospect of the international diffusion of photovoltaic energy conversion. The case of PV energy conversion is an illustration of the broader issue of how governments can create lead markets for eco-innovations in order to combine environmental aims with exports. The main political question of the exportability of eco-innovations is: While negative externalities call for governmental regulation, can a country become a lead market by governmental intervention in the market? The question of the international adoption of co-innovations that have been induced by governmental measures to protect the environment is an important one, because exports of eco-innovations can compensate for the cost disadvantages of the regulation for the local industry. Export chances encourage governments to introduce environmental regulation against the apprehensions of local businesses. While not all policy initiatives for solar energy were introduced to create an export industry, it is an argument often voiced by supporters of PV energy conversion. At least in Japan export chances are one criterion for governmental efforts to create a strong domestic market for PV.

There are several mechanisms that can make a technology internationally successful, despite many differences in preferences and market contexts from country to country. Eco-innovations have to overcome the additional obstacle that they are not economically efficient. Innovations in the electronic industry often overcome international differences because of the tremendous cost reductions of mass production. Eco-innovations normally do not achieve that level of cost reduction while they would need even bigger cost reduction to persuade users in other countries to adopt them. For eco-innovations the most import condition for international diffusion is therefore that they be environmentally efficient and that there be a global environmental problem they help solve. This is the basis for the global diffusion of eco-innovations. Environmental efficiency, the ability to solve environmental problems effectively and economically in a way that the costs are not higher than the negative effects of the environmental problem, is the starting point for global policy diffusion. The second condition is that the technological design favoured by the policies is compatible with foreign markets and, that the same design can be adapted in the follower markets. The aspect of design incompatibilities and design mismatch has not received much attention with policy makers yet, because of the too optimistic expectations that the experience and success of one design can be easily transferred by the domestically successful manufacturers to other designs that are appropriate for foreign markets.

Generous subsidies in Japan and Germany have succeeded in creating a local dynamic market for PV systems and promoting the global breakthrough of PV systems as well. A closer look, however, shows that the prospect of a world market for photovoltaic energy conversion is rather bleak. Judging by the internationalisation mechanisms that have made a technology internationally successful, the success of PV technology in Japan and Germany does not seem likely to lead to its global success soon.

The shortcomings of the domestic policies in Japan and Germany in starting an international bandwagon in the PV industry are that they focus on the cost reduction potential as the main internationalisation mechanism, while policy diffusion seems more important. PV energy conversion needs governmental subsidies to remain economical for a long time. The expected cost reduction that can be achieved by mass production in Japan is still not sufficient to render PV an economical alternative to traditional energy resources. In contrast, examples of globally successful eco-innovations have shown that global policy diffusion is a more effective internationalisation mechanism. If a policy instrument diffuses internationally, the innovation design responding to the policy instrument does so as well, thus raising the prospect of exports by the country that first introduced the policy. In the case of PV energy conversion, policy diffusion went only half way in few industrialised countries. Any further policy diffusion that would create a market similar to the one in Japan cannot be expected, because other countries would receive little economic benefit from adopting PV. In this case, the effectiveness of a policy instrument in combatting environmental problems is the most important success factor for the international diffusion of this policy instrument. Yet, the policies in the PV case are not successful in environmental terms. PV cells are efficient in supplying electricity for remote applications, where a grid-connection would be more costly.

However, PV systems are rather inappropriate for helping to solve the main environmental problems created by exhaustible energy conversion such as CO2 emissions in countries where PV energy conversion has been "successfully" applied. The production of PV cells itself is energy intensive. A mass production of PV cells, therefore, increases energy consumption for years until a large stock of PV applications can start lowering total consumption of depletable resources. In addition, policies that have worked well in Europe are not applicable in other countries. Feed-in tariffs are limited to grid connected markets. Non-grid-connected markets need other instruments. Yet, in the foreseeable future the only market for PV without subsidies is the non-grid market. PV energy conversion could help electrify developing countries. The problem with this scenario is that PV systems are more expensive than diesel generators and that the main target market is shrinking in the long run since more and more regions get access to a regional or national grid that is fed mostly by large central power generators.

When international policy diffusion is not achievable, then the United States remains the test bed for solar energy, where the fate of PV will be answered. With the energy production cost of solar cells unlikely to come close to that of conventionally generated electricity in the foreseeable future and the non-grid market the main economically feasible market, the US offers the conditions of a lead market and the leverage effects (size, competition, export orientation) to make it an international success. Thus, despite the efforts of Japan and Germany to create a local lead market, it seems that their measures will not be able to change the role of the United States as a test market. Only if PV experiences a breakthrough it can develop as a global innovation.

6 Fuel Cells in Stationary Applications

The analysis of factors that determine a leading position of a country with respect to a technology should not stop with an ex-post evaluation. The crucial question is, to what extent a lead market may be identified in the emerging stage of a technology. This section discusses the example of fuel cells for stationary applications as an emerging market. The different technologies are described and compared to each other as well as to conventional technologies for power production. The different fuel cell technologies can be understood as variations in the innovation design. Countries that are early in the development and adoption of innovation designs that later prove to be successful on the world market do have advantages as lead countries. Therefore, for each of the technologies that are under development today, it is analysed which countries and firms are the frontrunners.

Based on a literature survey, several factors are identified that are expected to be in favour of the development and market introduction. Among these are favourable conditions for combined heat and power generation (CHP), a favourable structure of energy prices, ambitious environmental policies that aim at internalising the environmental costs of energy production. In a next step, the policy programmes and framework conditions in the leading countries USA, Japan and Germany are compared and analysed on this background. We focus particularly on the patenting activities as well as the governmental funding for research and development of fuel cells in a comparative perspective in order to identify countries with advantages in R&D. The framework conditions for CHP technologies are analysed for each of the country. In respect to policies that support the introduction of fuel cells, special attention is given to the question in how far different sectors of policy making are co-ordinating their activities. In all of the countries, relevant policies are developed by the departments of the environment, industry, energy, and in the USA also by the department of defence. Finally, in this chapter we try to assess the different activities to stimulate the development and market introduction of fuel cells from a comparative perspective in order to assess respective lead market potential.

6.1 Innovation Designs

The principle of the fuel cell was already demonstrated by W.R. Grove in 1839. This technology started to be developed only around 1950, first in England, then also in Germany and the USA. This research was the basis for a NASA development programme that first applied fuel cells in the Gemini Program (1961) and in the Apollo Mission (Oertel and Fleischer, 2000). Fuel cells produce electricity without needing the detour using thermal energy. They are, like batteries, electrochemical devices. The preferred fuel is hydrogen; due to its high reactivity the need for (expensive) catalysts is minimised. At present however, hydrogen is reformed from natural gas (which is a process that diminishes the environmental advantages of fuel cells since CO2 and NOx is released). The common oxidation chemical is atmospheric oxygen, due to its ubiquitous availability.

Fuel cells can be applied very differently, e.g. for supplying individual electronic machines, or for powering automobiles, for heating and electricity supply in individual homes, and for stationary power stations of different sizes in the industrial and public energy supply. This case study concentrates on the partial market of fuel cells for stationary power generation combined with the utilisation of heat; as part of the same project, a further case study (see chapter 7) analyses the evolving market for mobile applications for cars. Due to capacity reasons, the partial market for fuel cells that supply heat and electricity to homes had to be left out.

In contrast to conventional power stations fuel cells have a high efficiency factor, even in the partial load area. The electrical efficiency factor is at around 40%, the overall efficiency factor when using thermal energy can be up to 80%. Another advantage is that there are virtually no NOx and SO2 emissions and that the machines are very quiet. The introduction of this technology is also closely connected to the hope that environmental advantages can be realised when compared to conventional power stations. Furthermore, they are seen as being a bridging or transitional technology for the introduction of hydrogen-based energy systems, synthesized with the help of solar energy.

In the last few years, the first efforts aiming at a commercialisation of fuel cells were undertaken mainly in Japan and in the USA. Here PAFC fuel cells were used (these models are described in more detail below). Research and development efforts as well as first demonstration installations will also lead to further advances with other models.

Fuel cells are classified by the type of electrolytes used, as well as by the processing temperature. Commercial chances are given to the 4 types that are introduced below (Phosphoric Acid Fuel Cells (PAFC), Proton Electrolyte Membrane Fuel Cells (PEFC), Molton Carbonate Fuel Cells (MCFC) and Solid Oxide Fuel Cells (SOFC)). The various cell types differ according to the operational temperature and the requirements for fuel pureness. Regarding the requirements for the fuel MCFC and SOFC cells have an advantages compared to the PAFC and PEM cells. Not portrayed are the Direct Methanol Fuel Cells (DMFC) that can be used for small consumers as well as in mobile applications up to about 50 kW and the Alkaline Fuel Cell (AFC) that had its first use in space projects but also has special requirements when it comes to fuel pureness. The further development of this cell type was stopped (Hirschenhofer et al., 1998).

A variety of different industrial sectors is taking part in the development and the manufacturing of fuel cells; these are chemistry (membranes, gaskets), ceramics (membrane, electrodes), catalysts, metal/carbon (bi-polar plates, corrosion protective films), process technology (heat exchangers, compressors, amongst others), electrical engineering, mechanical engineering, power installation construction (cell stacks, systems) and the electronics industry (portable applications).

Even though there were comprehensive research and development activities going on in these industrial sectors, it seems unrealistic that market forces alone will be able to force a large-scale introduction and use of fuel cells. Conventional technology for energy conversion has been tested and is available; the fuels for heat and power generation for these technologies are relatively cheap. Without further incentives or dramatic changes in the availability of fossil fuels, it cannot be expected that investments will be made into the barely tested fuel cell technology (Department of Energy, 2003). The main barriers are the high costs and risks that have to be taken to reduce the costs of this technology to a competitive level compared to conventional technologies.

For the industrial and public power supply that is being discussed here, it seems that high temperature fuel cells (MCFC and SOFC) are most suitable. These, though, are still in the early stages of development. Their performance spectrum ranges from capacities with few kW to several MW thereby covering micro gas turbines and motor CHPs all the way to combined cycle power stations.

Since the start of development in the 1960s there are now 650 stationary systems installed globally with an output level of over 10 kW each. As much as 65 of these were installed in 2003 (Cropper et al., 2003).

Fig. 19. Cumulative number of stationary fuel cells > 10 kW

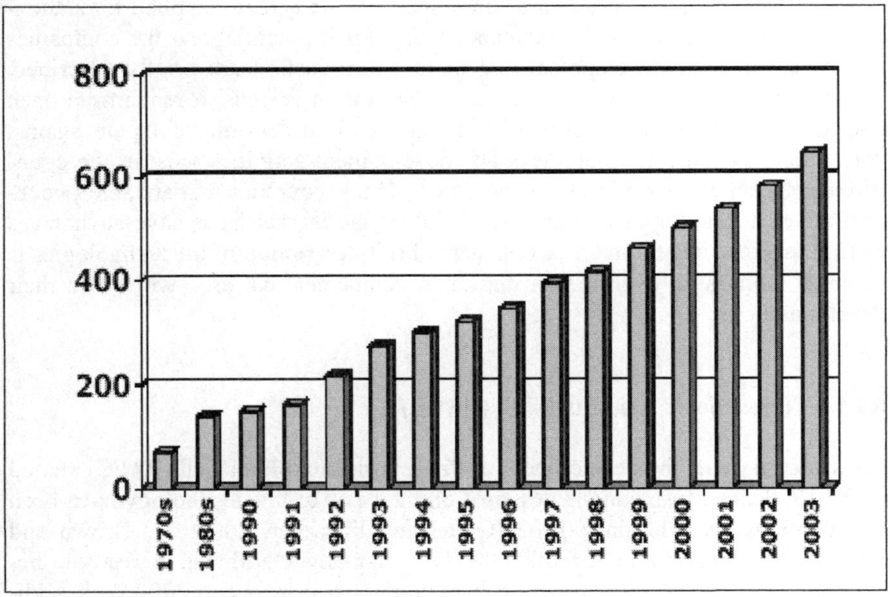

Source: Cropper, 2003.

Most facilities, according to this source, can be found in Japan (about 220), closely followed by North America (about 200). Europe is lagging behind with about 50 installations, while in the rest of the world a very small number is under operation (Cropper, 2002) In Japan research and testing has been strongly supported by government agencies since the early 1980s. The gas companies of Tokyo and Osaka have installed the world's largest demonstration units.

Most of the installed units are US made described in more detail below. They have been constructed and sold since the start of the 1990s as a limited series. In the USA the market launch was supported by a subsidy programme released by the Department of Defense (DoD).

Fuel cells compete with established technologies, e.g. gas and steam combined cycle turbines (CCGT) cogeneration plants that have an equal efficiency at least in the full load area and are meeting existing emission standards. In the low output sector motor-driven combined heat and power plants (CHPs based on internal combustion engine) are already on the market and micro-turbines are being developed. In order to be able to compete against these technologies, the price for fuel cells must be greatly reduced and long operation times must be proven. The German Federal Ministry of Economics (BMWi, 2001b: 47), responsible for energy policy, can be quoted with a requirement of EUR 1,250/kWel and 40,000 hours of operational use of fuel cells to become competitive compared to conventional energy technologies.

As with all CHP technology, assumptions regarding competitive prices for the installations strongly depend upon the expected electricity credit given. Due to deregulation, the decrease in electricity prices reduce the incentive to invest in CHP installations, and thus also in fuel cells.

In the following, the different technologies that are actually applied for stationary power production and in particular their market potential and the companies that focus on their development and market introduction are briefly described. These technologies represent the different innovation designs. It remains an open question, which of these innovation designs will successfully compete against conventional energy technologies. The development activities vary in the countries in respect to the different technologies. Hence, countries that are able to concentrate on technologies that are successful on the market later, have advantages as lead markets. Therefore, as a first step a brief description of the technologies is given as well as an overview on the main companies that are involved in their development.

6.1.1 Phosphoric Acid Fuel Cell (PAFC)

For stationary use, the development of Phosphoric Acid Fuel Cell (PAFC) started in the 1970s, and installations designed on the basis of this technology have been commercially on sale since 1992 (Oertel and Fleischer, 2000: 31; Brown and Jones, 1999: iv). Up to recently, the US company ONSI had a ready-to-be-connected module PC25C on sale with an output performance of 200 kWel. Additional companies that will have similar technologies on offer in the future are Fuji, Mitsubishi and Toshiba. At the moment the latter are concentrating on the Japanese market. According to other sources, Japan is even leading the use of such technology (BMWi, 2001b: 44, BINE, 2000). However, most of the installed units are of the US made type. All in all, 200 units of this type were set up globally; of which about half are still in operation. The installations were taken off the grid after a mean lifetime of 30,000 operational hours. During their lifetime, the electrical efficiency factor sank from 40% to 30-35% (Simader and Heissenberger, 1999: 26). In Germany alone, 15 units were installed, of which 10 are still in operation. 30 units were installed and put into operation in the US military sector. The disadvantages that are stressed are that investment costs are higher than with conventional motor CHP and that starting the utilities is a complex and time consuming task and therefore this technology is appropriate only for base load operation (Simader and Heissenberger, 1999: 24 f.). Investment costs are stated as being US$ 3000/kW (Department of Defense, 1998: 3). By manufacturing in mass production a reduction to about $1,300/kW is thought possible (Dienhart et al., 1998; Brown and Jones, 1999).

Another disadvantage is that the installations have to be kept at a temperature of between 40-50°C even when idle in order to avoid an over-crystallisation of the electrolyte (BINE, 2000). Furthermore, special requirements have to be adhered to vis-à-vis the nitrogen concentration of the gases used (BMWi, 2001b: 44).

In Japan, Fuji has PAFC units commercially on offer since the end of the 1990s and they were realised as CHP installations repeatedly in the past decade. In the recent past, additional installations have been constructed that use biogas as a fuel (Homma, 2000). In India the development of a stack by Bharat Heavy Electric has been underway since the end of the 1980s (Cropper, 2002).

6.1.2 Proton-Electrolyte-Membrane Fuel Cells (PEFC, PEM)

Proton-electrolyte-membrane fuel cells (PEFC, PEM) fuel cells were first developed in the 1960s; the reliability however was much lower than that of alkaline cells[6]. Only in the 1990s new impulses were provided with the introduction of new membrane types (Oertel and Fleischer, 2000: 31). In contrast to the high temperature cells described below, the low processing temperatures of about 80°C allow for, a swift operational start of the cell and quick load changes. The cell type is especially suitable for mobile applications as well as for small home units. Additionally, there are developments in the capacity range of more than 100 kW. With the considerable cost pressure on fuel cells in mobile applications there is also the hope that, for this type, larger cost cutting potential can be achieved for stationary applications (Theenhaus and Bonhoff, 1999).

The low operational temperature has the disadvantage that no processing steam can be won. A cost cutting potential is seen to be the reduction of the used platinum (BINE, 2000). The CO content in the used fuel has to be limited to 10-20 ppm, a higher concentration would destroy the cells (BINE, 2000). In order to stay

---

6 Alkaline fuel cells have been the first cell type; they were developed for application in spaceships by the NASA and were used in the Gemini program in the early 1960s for the first time.

within this limit, the hydrogen won from the reformation process has to be cleaned of CO.

PEFC and PEM with a size of 250 kWel are currently being tested in Canada/Vancouver by the company Ballard as well as in Berlin by the BEWAG, in the latter case supported by European research funds from the programme THERMIE (Oertel and Fleischer, 2000: 22). The costs for this installation are quoted as being US$ 8,000/kW (Lievonen et al., 2000: 65). The installation was delivered by the Canadian firm Alstom-Ballard. Of the total costs of about US$ 3.5 million 40% are financed by EU funds, 10% by Alstom and the remaining 50% by the participating electricity supply companies (Bewag, EdF, HEW, PreussenElektra and VEAG). Three further units of this type were planned in the years 2000 and 2001 for the Netherlands, Switzerland and Belgium (Pokojski, 2000: 399).

Ballard has been testing units with a capacity of 250 kW since 1997 and is planning the development of cells with a performance output of between 100 W and up to 1 MW. Other companies that are active in this technology sector are Analytic Power, Avista Labs, H Power, Plug Power, and Northwest Power Systems. The market launch of fuel cells that supply homes was expected in the near future (Brown and Jones, 1999: 12), the commercial sale of the 250 kW power stations was announced in 1998 for the year 2002 (Hirschenhofer et al., 1998: 1-15). In 1998 the companies Alstom and Ballard announced the construction of a PEFC fuel cell plant in Dresden for the year 2000. There the 250 kW unit that was tested in Berlin was supposed to be produced in series. This decision has been deferred to the year 2004.

Apart from the use in the mobile sector and in the already mentioned stationary applications, these fuel cells, developed by Siemens, are also in operation in submarines (Department of Defense, 1998: 3). In Japan PEFCs with very low capacities are being tested in the supply of homes (Homma, 2000).

6.1.3 Molton Carbonate Fuel Cells (MCFC)

For this cell type a commercial market launch is expected first, right after the PAFCs. That is why they are also described as fuel cells of the second generation. The operational temperature of MCFCs is around 600-650°C. Therefore, the heat generated can be used for the reformation of the fuel. Furthermore, expensive catalysts are omitted and the requirements for the pureness of the fuel being burned are lower.

In the USA the Energy Research Corporation (ECR) and MC-Power are working on the commercialisation; in Europe and Japan several companies are pursuing the development of this technology: Brandstofel Nederland, Deutsche Aerospace and Ansaldo (Italy); MTU Friedrichshafen, Hitachi, Ishikawajima-Harima Heavy Industries, Mitsubishi Electric Corporation and Toshiba Corporation. In 2003 a joint venture of MTU with the German utility RWE was founded that aims at starting a MCFC series production in 2006.

In the USA the companies Energy Research Cooperation (ERC) and MC-Power have realised demonstration projects with a capacity of 250 kWel to 1MWel. In Germany there is a unit with a capacity of 280 kWel capacity that the MTU tested in the years 1997-98 in Dorsten as contract work for Ruhrgas. The Stadtwerke Bielefeld started with the operation of a demonstration unit in the year 1999 (BINE, 2000). Another unit in a hospital was started in 2001 and seven further installations have been announced for 2003/04 (Cropper, 2002). The unit, developed by MTU, is supposed to radically reduce the costs by integrating the system elements in a single casing. The costs are expected to be EUR 1,200/kW. (http://www.h2guide.de/projekte/pfs12.html from 2.8.02). MTU is connected to the US company Energy Research Corp. (nowadays Fuel Cell Energy) by a licensing agreement. This company operated a 2 MW unit in Santa Clara, CA, during the years 1996 – 1997 (BINE, 2000, Brown and Jones, 1999: 18; Hirschenhofer et al., 1998: 1-16). In spite of a variety of problems arising from operating the unit, the company is planning a 2.8 MW installation with the same technology. The company is also participating, in cooperation with MTU, in a 300 kW MCFC unit in Friedrichshafen.

Fuel Cell Energy is developing a commercial unit with a performance of 250 kW and already has a production capacity of 50 MW/a in the USA at its disposal. By 2004, 1.5-3 MW units are also supposed to be available (Cropper, 2002).

In Japan several demonstration installations were set up, including a 1 MW unit in the year 1995 that was in operation until 2000. MITI and Nedo are planning further demonstration units in order to support the commercialisation process (Homma, 2000). The development was pursued by the company IHI that has announced two 300 kW installations for the year 2002 (Cropper, 2002) that is, however, still under development (Masaaki et al., 2003). Further units with a performance range of 75 kW to 1 MW are planned in Japan and the USA (Hirschenhofer et al., 1998: 1-17).

The Italian firm Ansaldo is developing MCFC units with sizes ranging from 100 kW to 30 MW. The market launch of a 500 kW unit as well as a several MW unit is scheduled for the year 2005 (Cropper, 2002).

In comparison to PAFC and PEFC cells, MCFC have advantages regarding the CO content of the fuel (CO is even used for the process in the MCFC procedure) and the higher process temperatures that facilitate the use of heat energy, e.g. as process steam. The disadvantage, though, is that the heating-up procedure takes several days and that special safety measures are necessary because of the highly corrosive carbonate smelt (BINE, 2000). In comparison to SOFC cells, described below, cheap material can be used for MCFC.

6.1.4 Solid Oxide Fuel Cells (SOFC)

The technological development of this cell type is being undertaken in the USA by Siemens-Westinghouse, AlliedSignals, SOFCo, Technology Management and Ztek. In Europe there are 8 companies, in Japan 7 and one is in Australia (Hirschenhofer et al., 1998: 5-1). Siemens-Westinghouse is seen to be the farthest.

The working temperature of SOFC can be up to 1,000°C and allows for an installation concept with integrated reformation and a flow-operated gas turbine. In comparison to MCFC there are no problems with corrosive materials. SOFC units are planned in the sizes 60-70 MWel by Siemens-Westinghouse. The worldwide first prototype was set up 1998 in Arnhem (NL) with a performance level of 100 kWel (BINE, 2000; Simader and Heissenberger, 1999: 30) and was moved to Essen (D) after a three year period of operation (Siemens, 2002). A 220 kW Siemens unit was put into operation in California. A 320 kW unit for RWE and a 1 MW unit for EnBW and EdF were planned for 2001 and 2002 (BINE, 2000). These planned installations, just as the one in California, are equipped with a flow-operated gas turbine. A commercial 250 kW unit was planned by Siemens-Westinghouse for 2003.

The British company Rolls-Royce has been active in the development of SOFCs since 1992 and is working on a unit that combines an 800 kW SOFC with a 200 kW gas turbine. A prototype is planned for 2004, the commercial launch for 2005/06 (Cropper, 2002).

In Japan a trial unit with a capacity of 15 kW that has been developed by Mitsubishi and Chubu Electric Power is currently in operation. Both companies are planning a commercial launch in the year 2004 (Homma, 2000; Cropper, 2002). Another Japanese company, Electric Power Development, is working on a 100 kW installation.

Concerning the electrical efficiency factor of about 50% (resp. 60% when combined with a turbine), SOFC power stations are comparable to conventional CCGT plants with a performance of 100 MW (electrical efficiency about 53%). An advantage, though, is that this efficiency factor can already be reached in the smaller units (from 100 kW onwards) and in the partial load operation, whereas smaller conventional installations of about 1 MW only show an electrical efficiency factor of 40%. In addition, separating the CO2 in the SOFC units is relatively simple as no mixing with the oxygen and nitrogen in the air takes place. Therefore carbon sequestration can be carried out much easier (Stimmig et al., 2000: 13). Furthermore, the emission of classic air pollutants by SOFCs is much lower so that one can speak about "near zero emission" in this case (Stimmig et al., 2000: 15).

Also for these installations a longer heating-up time is necessary. The high temperatures impose high requirements on the used material (BINE, 2000). Regarding the projected costs and the efficiency, SOFC cells are comparable with MCFC cells. An advantage of SOFC cells is above all that they can be combined with a CCGT power station as is foreseen because of their higher electricity efficiency (Brown and Jones, 1999: 25). However, such a combination is also being developed by Fuel Cell Energy for MCFC cells. Furthermore, SOFC cells, just like PEFC installations, though not MCFC or PAFC, are being tested in very small units.

A 1 MW unit that is planned by Siemens/Westinghouse combines a SOFC fuel cell with a gas turbine. Thereby the fuel cell replaces the furnace of a CCGT plant. With this unit, an electrical efficiency factor of 60% is expected (Hirschenhofer et al., 1998: 1-18). In the long-term perspective (until 2015), installations with a performance range of 50-60 MW are planned (Simader and Heissenberger, 1999: 30).

A test unit of a hybrid installation with a performance level of 220 kW was put into operation in the year 2000 in the USA. The electrical efficiency was stated as being 57% (Cirkel, 2000: 90). A further development direction by Siemens-Westinghouse is a "zero emission unit" for which the CO2 created is sequestered and stored in exploited oil fields. This technology is being developed together with Shell (Cirkel, 2000: 91). The Siemens-Westinghouse unit is supposed to cost US$ 1,500/kW (Lievonen et al., 2000: 65). The stack alone is quoted with US$ 700/kW, the material costs, however, are only US$ 7-15/kW. The major share is constituted by the assembly costs. This hints to a large cost-cutting potential (Hirschenhofer et al., 1998: 5-11).

In the framework of the US government's industry initiative SECA, the development of a commercial 5 kW SOFC is being strived for, one that can be applied in a variety of sectors. By combining several stacks, power stations that have a size of several hundred kWs can be planned. Through such a standardised cell for a variety of applications, competitive prices for the cells are expected to be reached a lot sooner.

6.1.5 Comparison of the Fuel Cell Types

Brown and Jones (1999: iv) compare the characteristics of the different cell types that can be considered for use in stationary units. At the same time assumptions on the prices and availability differ considerably from other sources.

High temperature cells have several advantages: Firstly, requirements regarding the fuel purity are low (with the exception of pollution by sulphur), secondly, a reform process for the separation of hydrogen out of the respective fuel can be dispensed with as the operational temperatures allow for an internal reform process, and thirdly, requirements of the catalysts being used are lower. Whereas with PEFC and PAFC platinum is used, for MCFC nickel is used and with SOFC perovskite, a substance family that describe ceramic crystals. These catalysts are much cheaper than platinum. A disadvantage, however, is the complex cell design and the higher maintenance requirements (Hirschenhofer et al., 1998: 1-5). It has not been possible up to now to demonstrate the reliability of high temperature cells during continuous operation d. The development status is restricted to pilot units.

Up to now, about 80% of the installed fuel cell facilities are based on PAFC technology. However, in 2003 most of the installed systems were based on MCFC technology (about 40%), followed by PAFC with about 35% and PEMFC with 20% (Cropper et al., 2003).

Table 3. Comparison of fuel cell technologies

Characteristics	Fuel Cell Types			
	PAFC	*PEFC*	*MCFC*	*SOFC*
Current development stage	Series	R&D	R&D	R&D
Begin of commercialisation	1992	2001	2002	2003
Market maturity	2005+	2005+	2005+	2005+
Expected installation costs (US$/kW)	1,500	1,300	1,300	1,300
Costs for the replacement of the stacks (US$/kW)	360	220	430	400
Lifetime of the stacks (hours)	60,000	40,000	50,000	40,000
Fixed operational costs per year (US$/kW)	30	30	8	20
Variable operational costs (US$/MWh)	1.4	1.4	2.0	2.5
Electrical efficiency factor (%)	37	36	52	63
Total efficiency factor	73	70	82	77
Usable temperature °F	250	160	1,050	400
Annual availability %	97	96	95	86

Source: Brown and Jones, 1999: iv.

It remains, however, unclear which of the technologies will be actually successful in competition with conventional energy technologies. The PAFC technology seems to be outdated and the recent overtaking of MCFC installations seems to prove this assumption. Regarding stationary applications the high temperature technologies MCFC and SOFC have advantages regarding the usable heat. However, PEM fuel cells might achieve more comprehensive learning and scale effects because of their utilisation in mobile applications.

6.1.6 Cost Comparison with Conventional Energy Technologies

Fuel cells are under high cost pressure as they, when compared to existing technology (combustion engine, conventional power stations, etc.), promise little or no additional value – the generated electricity has the same quality as from conventional generation. Only if there are major changes in the framework conditions for conventional technologies in terms of stricter emission standards, fuel cells may gain considerable advantages. Therefore, fuel cells are a substitute product. Other advantages include the marginally higher fuel efficiency, the slightly higher share of output of electricity, and an efficiency level that is largely independent from the work load and the power station size, as well as the possibility to use a variety of fuels. A disadvantage is the substantial investment costs.

Padró and Putsche (1999) compare investment costs and power production costs for different fuel cell technologies based on a literature analysis. The research is based on a variety of installation sizes ranging from a few kW to up to 100 MW. Accordingly, for SOFC and MCFC fuel cell system costs of US$ 600-1,000 are expected. For stationary PEMFC or PAFC units, however, higher costs (US$ 1,000-2,500) are generally expected. Power production costs are calculated to be US$ 0.06 to US$ 0.13 per kWh (pp. 17-22).

There are, however, some niche markets for which the higher installation costs seem to be acceptable already today. These are mainly applications for which a high reliability of electricity service is required. Due to the few moving parts fuel cells are expected to be a highly reliable technology, however, apart from PAFC the long term reliability has not been proven yet (Pehnt and Ramesohl, 2003).

Furthermore, a considerable rise in the share of decentralised power generation is expected. Pehnt and Ramesohl (2003) quote a study of Allied Business Intelligence which expect a rise from now 20 GW to 280 GW-350 GW worldwide in 2011. Another market survey of the German based utility RWE predicts a share of 30% of electricity produced by distributed power in Germany in 2015 of which a considerable share is likely to be provided by fuel cells.

6.1.7 Comparison of Environmental Impacts

Dienhart et al. (1998) compare a PEFC fuel cell with a motor-powered CHP and arrive at the result that the fuel saving value, depending on the system compared, is between 5 and 15%. In comparison to motor CHPs as well as production that is uncoupled to the power net, fuel cells show the lowest value in nearly all air pollutant categories. According to the calculated example given by the authors, in order to reach the comparative electricity price of a motor-driven CHP plant, the investment costs should not be above about EUR 850/kW. All in all, the authors claim that the ecological advantages of fuel cells in relation to motor-driven CHPs are not clear enough in order for a replacement to take place. The cost reduction potential, though, for motor-driven CHPs is seen as being pretty much exhausted (Bünger, 2000).

In contrast, a study by the US Department of Energy (Department of Energy, 2003: 5) highlights the environmental advantages. Here, however, fuel cell power stations are compared to the currently run coal, gas and oil power stations. In comparison to an average US power station, a natural gas run PAFC fuel cell emits only 0.2% of classic air pollutants. The CO2 emissions are quoted as being about 40% of the emissions of conventional power stations.

In a more extensive comparison of conventional technologies with high temperature fuel cells, Dienhart et al. (2000) conclude that fuel cells have advantages when it comes to the electrical efficiency factor, the combined heat and power (CHP) coefficient, the partial load behavior, the environmental effects, availability and – at least potentially – with regard to the maintenance expenditures and load change speed. The disadvantages of fuel cells are that dual fuel operation (gas and heating oil) is not possible and the operational starting time is considerably longer and much more costly after longer periods of shut-down. However, the overall efficiency factor during combined heat and power (CHP) operation and the temperature level of the processing heat are comparable. The competitive investment costs for the module (without the connection) are quoted as being EUR 700-1,050/kW. The fuel saving has a positive effect, the negative side is the fact that the stacks have to be replaced after about 5 years. The market in Germany for decentralised CHP installations within a performance range of 0.1-10 MW is around 500 MW/a. Export markets may eventually be established with the EU's objective of doubling of the CHP level from currently 9 to 18%. In the medium term the integration within coal power stations could represent a further new market segment. With the upcoming age-related replacement investments for power stations with a volume of 30,000 MWel up to 2010 in Germany, fuel cell systems could also profit from the promotion of CHPs (e.g. by obligatory quotas for CHP). However, a decentralisation of power production does not necessarily have to rely on fuel cells; this can also be achieved with conventional power stations.

Fritsche (1999) compares different fuel cell types with conventional CHPs of different sizes and a fuel cell power station with regard to emitted pollutants per 2 kWh thermal output and 1 kWh electrical output. The comparative standard therefore takes account of the higher heat level of conventional power stations. The author comes to the conclusion that fuel cells have the lowest level for all emitted "classic" pollutants. Concerning CO2, fuel cells are a bit behind (5-10%) the emissions of CHPs. All in all, this study sees no clear advantage for fuel cells; the much lower air pollutants though could be an advantage in areas heavily affected by this problem. The economic advantage of fuel cell power stations would only be given if the emission standards set for conventional power stations were tightened and therefore the operating costs made more expensive (Dienhart et al., 2000). Furthermore, fuel cells that are powered by pure hydrogen that in turn is produced by renewable energies have virtually no emissions.

6.1.8 Market for CHP Installations

The share of electricity generated in CHP utilities varies considerably in European countries. It ranges from more than 30% in the Netherlands to about 2% in France (Nitsch and Dienhart, 1998). CHP generated electricity constitutes the market potential for the fuel cells discussed here. The most promising markets for decentralised CHP installations are expected in Germany. These are accounted for with 2,700 units with a capacity ranging from 5 kWel to 4 MWel, totalling to a capacity of 1,450 MWel (that is 1.2% of the overall capacity for electricity generation) and a growth of 250 MW/a (Nitsch and Dienhart, 1998). Pehnt and Ramesohl (2003) quote scenarios of up to 50 GWel for domestic CHP utilities until 2020 in the EU-15 countries and a total of 190 GWel. However, the situation has changed dramatically after the liberalisation of electricity markets that lead to a decline in investments. The future of investments in CHP technologies remains unclear.

Whether fuel cells succeed in taking over a larger market share depends on the investment costs. The competitive costs of EUR 700-1,050/kW quoted in several studies are still relatively far away from the current prices. The only PAFC unit worth mentioning (in terms of output figures) costs US$ 3,000/kW, the Berlin PEFC is listed with US$/EUR 8,000, the Siemens-Westinghouse SOFC unit was announced with US$ 1,500/kW. However, considerable learning effects during the early diffusion phase can be expected. Based on experiences with other energy technologies a learning factor of between 0.75 and 0.9 can be assumed (Birnbaum et al., 1999).

Based on these target values and parameters Pehnt and Nitsch (2000) judge that in order to reach EUR 1,000/kWel, a starting point with a series production of EUR 5,000/kWel must be assumed, as well as an installed capacity of 5 MWel at the start of series manufacturing. Furthermore, a cumulative performance level of 700 MW is necessary in order to reach the given target value (Birnbaum et al., 1999: 86). Given the current growth rate of installations this can be expected until the year 2010 and it will lead to additional costs (compared to existing technologies) of about 360 million EUR.

6.2 Political Instruments

A variety of framework conditions influence the adoption of the fuel cell (Stolten and Höhlein, 2000; Department of Energy, 2003, Bünger, 2000; Birnbaum et al., 1999, Pehnt and Ramesohl, 2003). These can be differentiated in terms of, first, the factors that can be influenced by political measures and second the relatively static economic and regulatory frameworks:

Political Measures in Favour of Fuel Cell Introduction

- At the current stage of fuel cell development, that is largely still in the R&D phase, incentives for potential users are called for, as for example subsidising demonstration projects. Furthermore, it is called for further promotion of basic research, especially the reduction of cost risks for privately funded research. In order to achieve a signal effect that motivates private actors to invest in the development of fuel cells, long-term political measures are said to be necessary as well as the coherence of the measures of different policy sectors. Energy, environmental and industrial policy makers should not send out confusing and contradictory signals. The difficult phase of the market launch can be overcome through public procurement, thereby involving a range of different state actors. R&D activities should be supported by the inclusion of fuel cell technology in training courses at a university level.
- When it comes to market introduction, it is called for strategies that provide a stabilisation of the market prospects for fuel cell generated power. Important factors in this respect are the political framework for CHP in general, e.g. emission standards for CHP installations, measures for the support and promotion of CHPs and tax breaks for fuels and the infrastructure for heat usage. The conditions for CHP production are however still marred by uncertainty in most countries. Important in this respect are non discriminatory rules for third party ac-

cess to the power grid, i.e. clear, legally secured rules for the feed-in of surplus electricity and for the purchase of reserve and balancing power. The market introduction can be furthered by subsidising the prices for fuel cell generated electricity very much like prices for power from renewable sources. A frequent topic in the literature is the need to simplify existing regulations (e.g. training and allowing craftsmen to connect the gas as well as electric systems), just as it is necessary to harmonise this on a European level in order to allow for the export of the technology. This is also valid for fuel and safety standards. Furthermore, setting standards and norms for the operation of fuel cells is necessary in order to minimise possible liability risks.
- Finally, the chances of fuel cells depend on the framework conditions for conventional energy technologies. If environmental policies lead to an internalisation of environmental costs caused by energy production, the allowable investment costs for fuel cells are higher. However, since the costs of fuel cells are today 2 to 10 times higher than conventional technologies, it seems unrealistic that such strict measures are applied which bring the costs of conventional technologies on a comparable level. The instruments for such a strategy are GHG taxes, emission trading, stricter emission standards for classical air pollutants, etc.

Static Frameworks and Trends

- There is uncertainty about the market conditions for CHP, especially considering the liberalisation of the energy markets. Even though liberalisation at first led to a decline in energy prices and therefore was an unfavourable development for alternative technology, in the future liberalisation may be favourable for decentralised electricity generation because transmission and distribution costs could be saved.
- Among the various CHP technologies, advantages for fuel cells are ascribed due to the lower heating requirements in buildings as insulation has been improved and the increasing share of demand for electricity compared to the demand for heat. By this it is expected that the demand for heat is growing more slowly than the demand for electricity.
- The relationship between electricity and gas price is important: The smaller the ratio is, the less favourable it is for fuel cells. If the difference of prices for each kWh of gas is high, there are stronger incentives for a production of electricity.

6.3 Comparison of Fuel Cell Policies

6.3.1 USA

In the USA the research dealing with fuel cells is mainly financed by NASA, EPA, DoE and DoD on a federal level. With the funding, energy, environmental, industrial and military issues and objectives are pursued. Accordingly, a number of different state agencies are involved in the support of the development and application of fuel cells.

The NASA first developed fuel cells for the application in space travel in the 1960s. At present it is mainly involved in the development of smaller PEFCs that are also being used in space travel.

The programme of the Department of Energy (DoE) is co-financed by the research and development activities of industry. The share of industry in the R&D expenditures is 40%. The support for PAFC was finalised, the funding was shifted in 2002 in favour of MCFC and SOFC technologies. Targets of the support are cost reduction regarding the materials used as well as enlarging the production capacities in order to utilise scale effects (Department of Defense, 1998: 7). A programme for R&D support for stationary installations with high temperature cells was budgeted at about US$ 50 mn/a in the mid-1990s. The aim of the programme is to support the market launch of such units, not least owing to industrial-political reasons. A competitive industry is supposed to be created with these grants, using export chances as well. For the market launch support, the DoE has also, amongst other things, worked out national and international market analyses. The focus of the programme was on participating in financing the construction of the demonstration installations.

The Environmental Protection Agency (EPA) is supporting a SOFC demonstration installation together with the DoE. This unit has a performance capability of 1.3 MW and it is being constructed at an EPA laboratory. The construction of the installation was planned for 1998-99 (Department of Defense, 1998: 8).

The Department of Defense (DoD) has started a total of three programs for the promotion of fuel cells: (1) the DoD demonstration programme which financed the supply of PAFC units for military installations, (2) the DoD Climate Change Fuel Cell Programme out of which other installations receive their subsidies and (3) the Navy Environmental Quality Programme out of which a 250 kW PEFC unit for a naval base amounting to US$ 1.75 million was financed.

Research in the US was initially concentrated primarily on the development of PAFC units until their market introduction. Currently, the focus is shifted on MCFC and SOFC units (Brown and Jones, 1999: 8). In the year 1999 a public-private partnership for the further development of SOFC fuel cells was set up by the Department of Energy. The aim was to reduce the costs for this type from currently US$ 4,000/kW to US$ 400 within 10 years. This is supposed to be realised with the help of a 3-10 kW block that can be flexibly combined with different units and produced in larger numbers whereby further potential cost-cutting measures can be reached. This programme is designed to help the industry out of a Catch-22 situation: The price for fuel cells is currently too high to allow to sell larger numbers and, at the same time, the number of sold units is too small to allow viable cost reductions. Another objective of the programme is the realisation of an efficiency factor of 40-60%; when combined with steam turbines it should go far beyond this mark. The alliance, named Solid State Energy Conservation Alliance (SECA), includes industry, research and government agencies. The programme has been set up to run 10 years and the turnover is expected to be US$ 500 million, of which US$ 271 million are contributed from the public sector.

Apart from the financial grants, there are special regulations for patents on innovations developed within the programme framework. These patents must be made available to the other industrial corporations taking part in the programme for at least one year at "reasonable" licensing conditions and have to be offered non-exclusively. Thereby, the cooperative development of a single cell type is supposed to be made possible (Department of Energy, 2002: 20).

In coordination with the Department of Energy and within the framework of the DoD Fuel Cell Demonstration Program, the Department of Defense has installed a total of 30 of the ONSI PC-25 as demonstration units. Furthermore, in the fiscal year (FY) 1993 US$ 18 million and in the FY 1994 US$ 18.75 million were made available. The aim of the programme was to stimulate growth in the fuel cell industry and to examine the role of technology for the long-term energy strategy of the DoD (Brown and Jones, 1999: 27).

Through an investment support programme (Climate Change Fuel Cell Program, FY 95-97), the price of the ONSI installations was subsidised from US$ 3,000/kW to US$ 2,000/kW. Preferential treatment was given to those units that were installed in the US military sector. About US$ 18 million were spent for this programme (Brown and Jones, 1999: 7; Department of Defense, 1998: 11).

6.3.2 Japan

The development of fuel cells in Japan mainly took place within the frame of publicly financed programs that were undertaken by NEDO (New Energy and Industrial Technology Development Organization). Since 1993 their activities dealing with fuel cells are merged in the "New Sunshine Program". The programme is continuing on the support measures initiated in 1974. NEDO started with the PAFC development support in 1981 and with the MCFC technology in 1984. Research programs on SOFC were initiated in 1989 and on PEFC from 1992 onwards (Homma, 2001).

The so-called "Moonlight Project" started in 1981, was supposed to run for 17 years and had a cash volume of US$ 520 million. This as well as other energy and environmental projects were amalgamated into the New Sunshine Project in 1993. In the year 2002 the R&D budget for fuel cells was nearly doubled from US$ 119 million to US$ 220 million; for 2003 US$ 288 million are foreseen (Department of Energy, 2003).

As for the framework conditions regarding energy prices, it is worth mentioning that the Japanese electricity prices are the highest of all OECD states.

The high costs result from the comparatively high capital expenditure for power stations (higher costs for land, safety standards, compensation for the affected communities and an oligopolistic structure of the power station providers), higher fuel costs that are caused by environmental requirements and transport costs, demanding safety standards for power stations, an unfavourable relationship of the base and peak load, and finally, due to the refinancing of the subsidies supporting the use of local coal (International Energy Agency, 1999). The step-by-step liberalisation of the energy markets, begun in 1995, in connection with the market appearance of independent power producers, will only have an effect on some of these factors. Therefore, in spite of the price decline that has been taking place since the mid-1990s, prices will not reach the same level as in other OECD countries.

Fig. 20. Industry electricity prices 1980-1997

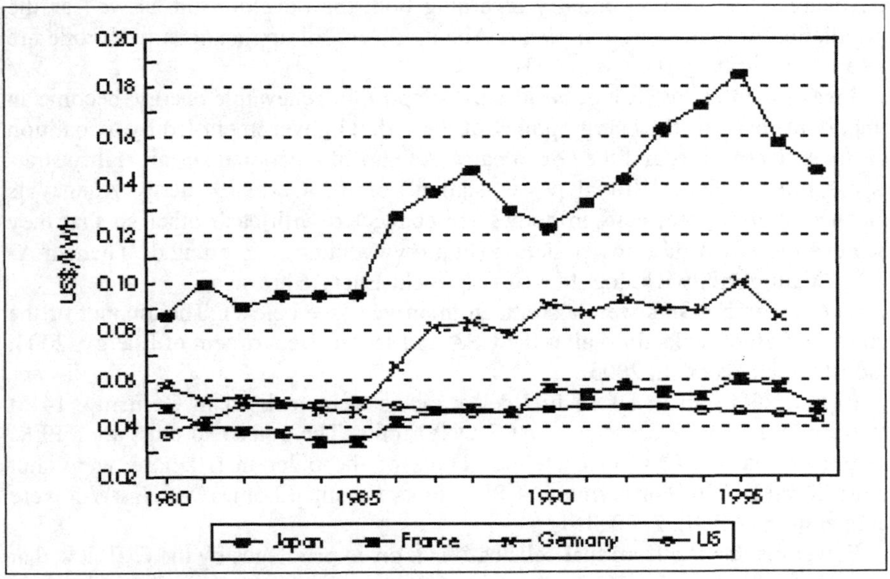

Source: International Energy Agency, 1999.

The market for combined heat and power production in Japan has had a favourable development since the mid-1990s; therefore the necessary regulatory framework and infrastructure for fuel cells are available. From the mid-1980s the number of sites grew from less than 50 to 550 in 2002 and the generating capacity from about 25 MW to about 450 MW (Japan Cogeneration Center http://www.cgc-japan.com/english/eng05.html). However, the number of sites and the generating capacity is far below that of Germany and the USA.

In Japan, the Tokyo Electric Power Company set up the world's largest PAFC unit, with a capacity of 11 MW (Brown and Jones, 1999: 7). A 1 MW MCFC unit was in operation from 1999 to 2000. Since 2000, the construction of a 300 kW installation is being supported and for 2004 the operation of a 750 kW installation is planned. The grant budget for R&D in this technology segment was US$ 17 million in 2002. About the same sum is envisaged for SOFC and PEFC development. PEFCs are supposed to be developed for both mobile as well as stationary applications. Altogether US$ 156 million have been made available for a 10 year programme; this amounts to four times the amount granted up to now (Department of Energy, 2003).

6.3.3 Germany

Industrial research activities in Germany date back to the 1950s, when companies such as Varta or Siemens searched for possible applications for alkaline fuel cells. In 1982 a 100kW installation was built for a military submarine. Daimler-Benz demonstrated the automobile application for the first time in 1985 (Geiger, 2003). Germany is the leading country regarding both the development as well as the installation of demonstration plants. About 75% of all applications in Europe are located in Germany (Geiger, 2003).

Investing in fuel cells has, besides the support for renewable energy, become an important focus of the energy policy of the federal government led by a coalition of Social Democrats and the Green party. As part of a national sustainability strategy a pilot project "Virtual power station" of the German Energy Agency is planned. Hereby fuel cells in homes are connected with each other so that they achieve the effect of a power station (http://www.bundesregierung.de/Themen-A-Z/Nachhaltige-Entwicklung-,9064/Pilotprojekt-Energie.htm).

The research grants were also much improved (see below). The amount of the grants therefore ranks third after the USA and Japan (Department of Energy, 2003, Industry Canada et al., 2003).

In mid-2000, all in all 16 fuel cell projects were realised in Germany, 14 of these with the above described PAFC ONSI units. The other two units are a PEM in Berlin and a MCFC in Bielefeld. Three of the older installations were shut down in mid-2000. Furthermore, 4 PEM units for small homes with 3 kWel were in operation (ASUE, 2000: 16).

Power production from fuel cells has been given privileges by the CHP law that came into effect on 1/4/2002. The aim of the law is, among other things, to support the market launch of fuel cells. For fuel cell units that are set up after the law came into force in 2002, the network operators have to pay a supplement above the agreed-to feed-in tariff for a time span of 10 years from the start of operation, amounting to 5.11 ct per kWh. This surcharge applies to new, small CHP installations. For older and bigger installations, lower surcharges are envisaged that are also degressive in character.

In addition, CHP installations are generally given preferential treatment by the law dealing with the introduction of the ecological tax reform. Since the stage 5 has come into force on the 1/1/2003, the law excludes energy self-production by units up to a capacity of 2 MW from the energy tax. Furthermore, CHP operators of installations with a yearly usage level of at least 60% are exempt from the ecological mineral-oil tax (0.366 ct/kWh for natural gas). At a yearly usage level of at least 70%, the exemption also covers the regular mineral-oil tax (0.184 ct/kWh for natural gas).

The Federal Ministry of Education and Research chose hydrogen technology and fuel cells as one of its main focus in its research activities. In this area, about EUR 110 million in research funds were spent between 1980 and 1996. In comparison, the public funding for the development of fuel cells in the USA was US$ 73 million a year and in Japan US$ 65 million (the figures are for 1995).

One interest of the federal government was the construction of a pilot and demonstration unit, realised by Solar Hydrogen Bavaria (Solar Wasserstoff Bayern, SWB), together with the state of Bavaria and partners in industry. Here a closed solar hydrogen system was supposed to be constructed, including the use of fuel cells. The focus of the grant activities, however, was in the area of fuel cells. Between 1990 and 1996 DM 79 million were spent, mainly for the development of SOFC, MCFC and PEFC fuel cells. In respect to the SOFC technology, the expectation has been expressed that domestic lignite can also be used for power generation (BMBF, 1996).

In the framework of non-nuclear energy research that was supported in the years 2001-2003 by the Federal Ministry of Economics and Labour with EUR 41 mn/year, fuel cells were one of the main research areas (BMWi, 2001a: 31). There is the hope that with this technology, a leading role can be taken in the world markets for climate protection technology and an advantage can be achieved in the sector of installation construction (BMWi, 2001a: 56f.). The aim of the research grants is to create a competitive industrial sector (BMWi, 2001b: 9).

Recently, the ministries of research and education, economy and the environment set up a new joint research programme ("Zukunfts Investitions Programm, ZIP") that aims to give support for the utilisation of renewable energy technologies. Between 2001 and 2003 EUR 65 million were granted for projects related to hydrogen and fuel cells (Geiger, 2003).

In Germany, high temperature cells are favoured for stationary applications. The development of these has been supported by the Federal Ministry of Economics and Labour since the start of the 1990s. The support was concentrated on the development of CHPs with an output of 0.2-1 MW (BMWi, 2001b: 46).

Wengel et al. (2000) discuss as to how far Germany can be seen as playing a leading role in the international development and introduction of fuel cells. As supportive aspects for the stationary employment of fuel cells, they list:

- Experience with support measures with broad effect (feeding-in/supply remuneration),
- willingness of consumers to invest in favour of the environment and to invest in private owned real estate,
- a good manufacturing infrastructure and well-educated craftsmen,
- a trend towards a favourable power-heat mix,
- redevelopment needs in decentralised heating units.

Impediments are:

- liberalised market with power station overcapacity and big suppliers (restrictive in the short term, maybe positive for FCs in the long term),
- dense, stable and relatively cheap electricity network.

Advantageous for the setting up of a lead market could be the high level of demand for off grid supply of electricity as here a higher willingness to pay exists. Fuel cells could be first used in off-grid areas or those that need a high level of reliability vis-à-vis the operation (hospitals, computer centers). From these niche areas, cost-cutting measures can be realised using the experience gained as well as the scaling effects. Further markets can then be exploited. Supportive policies that use these niches cannot be recognised at this stage in Germany in contrast to the USA.

6.3.4 European Union

Since the mid-1970s, fuel cell R&D is being supported (Department of Energy, 2003). The European Union participated in 135 research projects between 1989 and 1999; these had a project volume of ECU 381 million, of which EUR 92 million were financed by the European Union (Bahbout, 2000). Between 1995 and 1998, about EUR 80 million were spent (Lievonen et al., 2000: 68). In the year 2001, the budget was EUR 60 million (Department of Energy, 2003). With the sixth research framework programme, a further extension of the research activities is to be expected. In contrast to earlier research programs, targets for fuel cells as well as for the use of hydrogen as an energy carrier are explicitly named in the main objectives. For the period from 2003 to 2006, EUR 50 million a year are earmarked for the support of hydrogen and fuel cells (in comparison to $256 million in Japan and about $300 million in the USA for fuel cells alone) (http://www.forum-brennstoffzelle.de/index.php ?main=info&news=akt&akt=252).

The foci of the grants given up to now were support for a 250 kW PEFC unit in Germany, a 500 kW MCFC unit in the Netherlands and the development of SOFC stacks. In conjunction with the USA, a SOFC/micro-turbine installation with a capacity of 1 MW is expected to be supported (Department of Energy, 2003).

6.3.5 Canada

The research grants in Canada in the last 10 years have been mainly focusing on the development of PEFCs. CDN $ 179 million were spent between 1982 and 2002 for R&D grants (Industry Canada et al., 2003). The company Ballard Power Systems, located in Canada, is the leader in this sector and in 1997, joined an alliance with DaimlerChrysler and Ford Motors that has invested US$ 500-600 million in the development of fuel cells. In 2002, DaimlerChrysler announced further investments totalling US$ 1 billion over the next 4 years (Department of Energy, 2003).

A recent joint publication by several government agencies and companies wherein strategies for the commercialisation of fuel cells are developed, recommends focusing on supporting demonstration projects as well as the early stages of market launches. This could be supported by public acquisition programs, supporting research networks that include scientists and developers, and encouraging training and the technical infrastructure. Canada should, furthermore, take on a leading role when it comes to the international standardisation of fuel cells (Industry Canada et al., 2003).

6.3.6 Other Countries and International Activities

Fuel cells have been supported in South Korea since 1985. In the period from 1992 to 2000, US$ 20.9 million were spent for this. In Australia, the development of SOFCs has been promoted since 1992, including a US$ 15 million grant for the development of a 100 kW unit (Department of Energy, 2003).

In Italy, the development of fuel cells is being pursued by the company Ansaldo. It has concentrated on MCFC cells and has developed a 500 kW unit. Among the European countries Italy is second regarding the installed capacity, although far behind Germany (Cropper, 2003).

The International Energy Agency (IEA) has, in the framework of the "Implementation Agreements" in which 15 countries are taking part, set itself the target of encouraging the international cooperation in the development and introduction of fuel cells. As part of this programme, standards to test fuel cells were developed, networks of experts and international research cooperation were stimulated and market analyses were undertaken. This cooperation is supposed to be continued until the year 2003 (International Energy Agency, 1998; International Energy Agency, 2000c).

In 2002 a proposal for a World Bank support for installation in developing countries was issued. According to this programme up to 2,000 US$ per kW would be paid. In a first stage three demonstration projects should be selected, up to 2005 a total of 5-7 MW of fuel cells were expected to be funded (Cropper, 2003).

6.3.7 Comparison of the Research Activities

Japan, the USA and Germany are the most important countries worldwide with respect to research activities. As an indicator of the relative position of these countries, patent activities can be utilised. For an analysis, the patent databank INPADOC (International Patent Documentation) was searched for the key-word fuel cell (and the corresponding German, French, Italian and Spanish terms), the year of registration and the country of origin (priority country). Most of the patent activities take place in the three countries already mentioned. This corresponds with the data from the Delphi 98 study that is briefly described below, where the questioned experts saw the highest R&D levels as being in those three countries (FhG-ISI, 1998).

What is noticeable is that Japan started off quite early (at the beginning of the 1980s) with a large number of patent registrations that have remained at a high level since that time. In the USA, there has been a large rise in the number of patents since the mid-1990s; with a short time lag Germany has also reached this very high level. The drop for the year 2001 might be explained with a time lag in updating the databank.

Fig. 21. Patent registration for Japan (JPN), the USA (USA) and Germany (D)

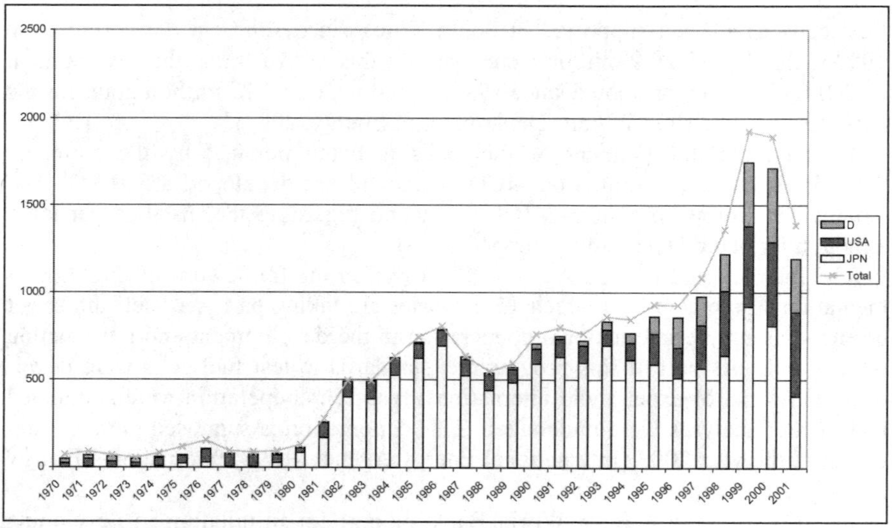

Datasource: International Patent Documentation (INPADOC).

Fig. 22. Public expenditure for R&D energy technology per capita

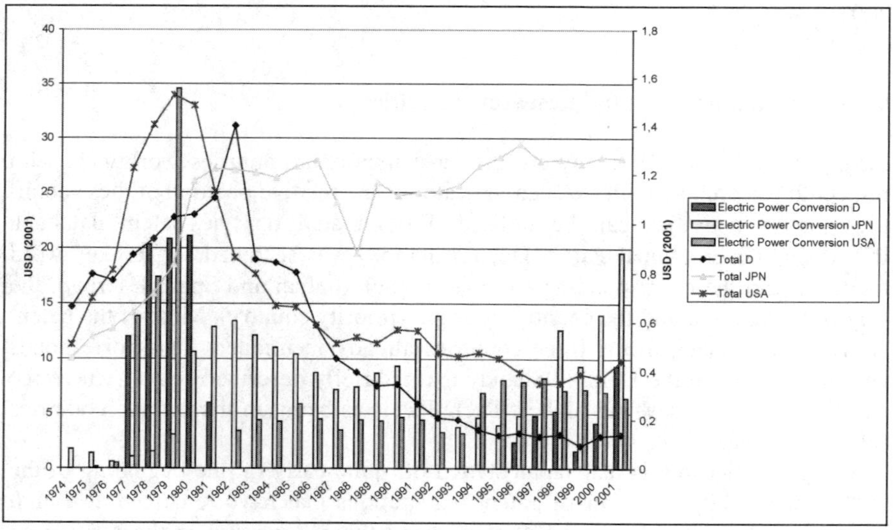

Datasource: IEA Energy Technology R&D Statistics; Government Energy Technology R&D Budgets http://data.iea.org/wds53/wds/eng/main.html.

The patent registrations in these three countries show a strong correlation with the public expenditure for energy research. In the following illustration, the per capita public R&D expenditures for general energy research in Japan, the USA and Germany are listed, as well as the per capita funding for "Electric Power Conversion" which includes inter alia the support for fuel cells.

In Germany and the USA, relatively big sums were provided for in the area of electric power conversion up to about 1980. These were considerably reduced afterwards. In Germany, the research funding was even completely stopped in 1995. In comparison, in Japan substantial funds have been put to use since about 1980. The USA and Germany have reached a comparable level only since the mid-1990s.

Barett (2002), in his patent analysis for the years 1999-2001, finds that 47% of the patents given out went to US organisations, 21% to German organisations and a further 16% to Japanese organisations. As another leading country, Canada is identified with 6% of the handed out patents. These results confirm that the USA, Japan and Germany are the leading countries in the research on fuel cell technologies; the US however has the highest share of patents. This may be explained with the choice of evaluated patent databanks. Barett, in his analysis, relates only to US patents and those of the World Intellectual Property Organisation (WIPO). The databank INPADOC being used here, however, contains data of 71 organisations that give out patents.

Despite the considerable efforts in the R&D of fuel cells, that can be read off the patent statistics, the introduction to a large scale market is according to a Delphi study of 1998 not close at hand. For the item *Solid electrolyte fuel cells with a performance level of several 10 MW can be applied for regional CHPs as well as for decentralised electricity stations,* the experts for chemistry and materials expect it in a mean by the year 2017, the experts for energy & natural resources, on the other hand, only by 2020. The expectations for CHP installations in homes are even further apart. Whereas the experts for energy & natural resources expect a broad distribution in the year 2020, the experts for construction & living expect the practical use of fuel cells for the decentralised energy supply of homes already in 2007. *Combined high temperature fuel cell gas and steam turbine power stations with efficiency factors of around 70% are on the market* is expected in a median for the year 2015 (FhG-ISI, 1998).

Stolten and Höhlein (2000) expect the market launch of fuel cells in 3-8 years, whereby first units for home energy supply, then busses, cars and, in the end, CHP installations are expected. The authors expect a very slow market penetration that could take 10-20 years and will not totally replace conventional technology.

6.3.8 Comparison of Energy Prices

The conditions for the use of fuel cells are better where electricity prices are high and gas prices are comparatively low. In the following graphics, the ratio of electricity to gas prices in Japan, the USA and Germany are illustrated.

Fig. 23. Relationship industrial electricity price/industrial gas price

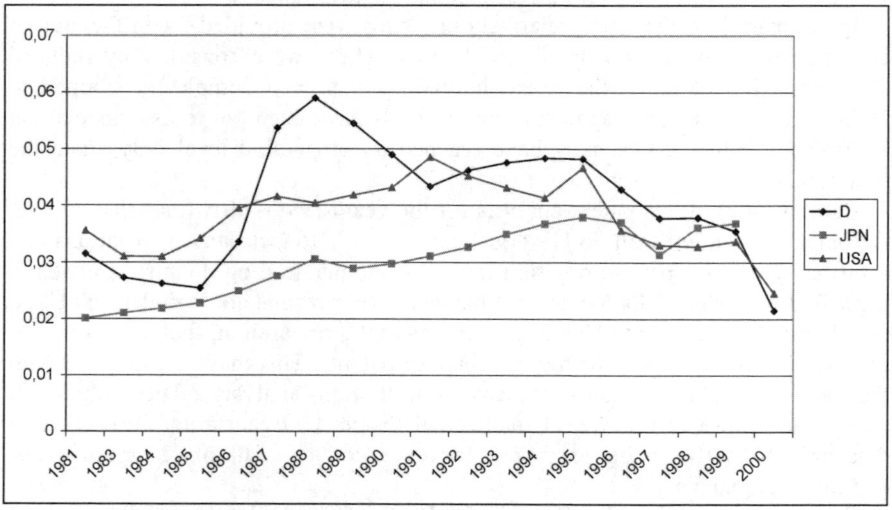

Datasource: IEA, Energy Prices and Taxes, several editions.

In both figures, electricity prices are those for industrial use. Electricity prices for households are less relevant for CHP plants that are studied here.

Fig. 24. Prices for industrial electricity/gas for energy generation

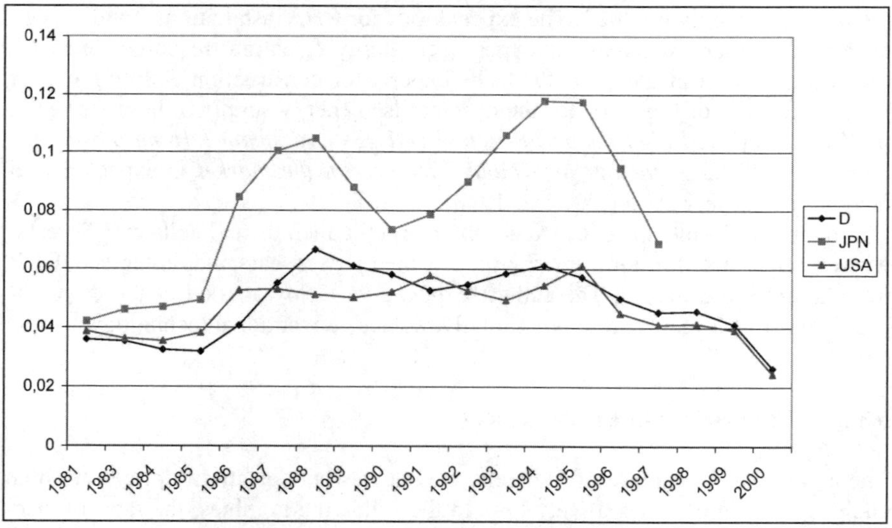

Datasource: IEA, Energy Prices and Taxes, several editions.

The falling electricity prices in all three countries lead to a worsening ratio of electricity to gas prices. However, the picture changes when gas prices are operationalised in a different way. In the above graphic, the price for natural gas in industry is used, whereas in the graphic below the price is based on gas used to produce electricity.

Depending on which gas price is used, country ranking changes substantially. Even though Japan shows higher prices in this market segment than Germany and the USA, the much higher electricity prices there lead to a much more favourable ratio for the purchase by industry.

Even if one can assume the cheaper gas prices for energy generation with the industrial CHP using fuel cells, the ratio between electricity and gas prices is the most favourable in Japan for the use of fuel cells. Germany and the USA are at about the same level.

6.4 Summarised Assessment

Against the background of the pressing climate change and the efforts undertaken in many different countries as well as on the international level to reduce the emissions of CO2, fuel cells might appear as a technology that provides a substantial contribution in this respect. Therefore, a worldwide market can be expected for this technology. It has, however to compete not only with conventional energy technologies, but also with CHP technologies as well as those for the utilisation of renewable energy. Up to now, the costs for fuel cells are not competitive. The analysis of the development and support activities in the most advanced countries reveals that there are still considerable efforts required until a large scale market introduction is possible. Up to now the applications are limited to niches or demonstration projects that require large subsidies.

It is not yet decided which of the innovation designs will be successful among the fuel cells and in competition with other technologies. There are advantages for high temperature fuel cells regarding the requirements on the fuel purity, the usable heat and the cost cutting potentials. However, PEM fuel cells are expected to be utilised for mobile applications, therefore learning and scale effects may be achieved earlier. It is hardly possible to locate regional differences in the stage of development of the different types among the countries. The USA are clearly ahead regarding PAFC fuel cells. Other development activities are carried out by companies that are active in several countries. For instance, Siemens-Westinghouse has roots in the US as well as in Europe, DaimlerChrysler is active in North America as well as in Europe through its subsidiary MTU. In general, however, Europe and particularly Germany is less behind of the USA and Japan in respect of high temperature fuel cells.

There are considerable differences regarding the support for fuel cells in the countries under consideration. A comparison of the political measures undertaken and the framework that were identified to be important for the introduction of fuel cells is listed in the following table. The code 1 corresponds to the most favourable situation compared to the other countries, and 3 to the least favourable. If two countries have almost the same value, a 2 was given that otherwise indicates a medium position

Table 4. Political measures in support of fuel cells

	CHP support	R&D support	Long-term perspective	Coherence/ Integration	Safeguard-ing of market entry	Internalisa-tion of external costs
USA	2	1	2	1	2	3
Germany	1	3	3	3	1	2
Japan	3	1	1	1	3	1

The USA, Japan and Germany could be identified as the lead countries with respect to research activities and the installation of the first demonstration units. The research activities depend heavily upon public funding. Market forces alone are still not sufficient in order to mobilise private capital for the development of fuel cells. Because of the considerable increase in R&D funding in the USA, in Japan, Germany and the EU in the last few years it can be expected that the advantage of the three countries will continue to grow in the future. Within this group of countries, though, Germany has the lowest R&D budget at its disposal even if one takes the EU funds into consideration. Therefore the advantage of the USA, where currently the most important production locations of fuel cell stacks can be found, can be further increased. The more favourable framework conditions and the higher R&D funding may explain that with regard to the number and performance level of the installed demonstration units, the USA and Japan, are ahead of Germany as well.

It is worth mentioning the high level of cooperation taking place between the different government agencies in the USA. The programs to date are advertised, tendered and administered by several departments. In Japan, the sponsorship is concentrated within the Ministry for Industry. In comparison, the supporting activities in Germany and the EU seem to be largely uncoordinated.

When it comes to the safeguarding of the market introduction of fuel cells, Germany can be ranked on the first place, due to its feed-in tariffs in favour of fuel cells. Since fuel cells are still in the stage of development, this instrument has no effects, yet. At best, it gives a long term signal for potential investors in the fuel cell development. The USA have had programs to subsidise the market introduction of fuel cells. By these grants it was possible to take over the leading role in the PAFC technology. Furthermore, its recent initiative on the promotion of SOFC primarily aims at preparing the market introduction of this type. Japan seems to concentrate on R&D programs rather than on market introduction.

The competitiveness of fuel cells is better compared to conventional technologies if the external costs of energy production are internalised. The degree of internalisation can be indicated by the energy cost and – related to this – the strictness of environmental policy. In this respect Japan has to be placed first, Germany second, while the USA is lagging the international trend in environmental and particularly in climate protection policies.

Table 5. Framework conditions for fuel cells

	Development Gas Price	Development Electricity Price	Relationship Gas/Electricity Price	Significance of Decentralised Energy Supply	Relationship Electricity/Heat Use[7]
USA	1	3	3	1	2
Germany	2	2	3	3	1
Japan	3	1	1	3	3

The effects of the liberalisation of energy markets vary among the studied countries. Generally, there is a decline in prices both for gas as well as for electricity. While low prices for fuel are favourable for the introduction of fuel cells, declining electricity prices are an impediment. The ranking regarding the respective prices is shown in table 5 above. Beyond the differences in prices, the ratio between the prices for gas and electricity is of importance. The higher the difference is, the higher is the added value of the introduction of fuel cells.

As for all CHP technologies fuel cells depend on the demand for decentralised energy supply as well as on the relationship between the demand for electricity and for heat. A higher demand for heat is advantageous for CHP technologies.

The conditions for the introduction of fuel cells depend directly on the general framework for CHP energy production. The ambitious European and German objective of doubling the share of CHP-generated electricity could lead to the market conditions for fuel cells being improved. However, this objective is not a binding commitment and up to now there is no directive issued. Furthermore, fuel cell technology is in competition with conventional CHP installations in this respect.

The costs of the existing units, already marketed in small numbers, cannot yet compete with conventional technology. In order to achieve learning and scaling effects, considerable public (co-)financing of the market introduction is necessary. The USA and Japan go to comparatively great lengths in subsidising the costs for demonstration installations. In Germany, besides the investment subsidies, feed-in tariffs for energy produced using fuel cells have been introduced recently. These are, however, not high enough to compensate for the higher investment costs of the fuel cell power generation. Mainly in the USA, demonstration installations in off-grid areas are being promoted. For these applications, higher costs are seen as being acceptable. With regard to public procurement in the USA, it is mainly the military sector that has come up with substantial funds. A corresponding use and implementation of niche applications in order to achieve learning and scaling effects isn't being undertaken in Germany with the exception of fuel cells that are used for submarines.

---

7 The relationship was calculated as the proportion of heat and electricity in final energy demand based on the 1999 figures in European Commission (2002a). According to this data, the demand for heat compared to electricity is 21% in Germany, 2.3% in the USA and 0.9% in Japan.

Expert questioned state that a market launch and gaining a substantial market share by the stationary fuel cells will only take place in 10-20 years. The securing of market success and the gaining of an advantage in international competition will depend on the experience and scaling effects gained by a step-by-step enlargement of niche applications during this time. The reduction of the current cost advantages by tightening environmental regulations for conventional power stations as well as lifting fuel prices would also be advantageous. In this respect, the strict Japanese standards are advantageous for the introduction of fuel cells. The strict environmental standards partly contribute to the high electricity price, therefore a more favourable electricity credit can be expected for fuel cells.

7 Fuel Cells for Mobile Applications

7.1 Introduction

Since Mercedes-Benz' ambitious development programme of the 1980s, fuel cells have been considered a technical alternative to the combustion engine. Currently, almost all major car manufacturers are developing fuel cell powered vehicles. A small number of prototypes of standard saloons and buses equipped with a fuel cell power train have already been tested in Japan, Europe, and California. Fuel cells are being pushed particularly by the California Clean Air Act that envisages the total eradication of pollutant emissions from cars. From a technical perspective, fuel cells are a realistic alternative to combustion engines, whereas the potential of electric cars, which were originally favoured by zero emission campaigns, is hampered by many practical limitations.

The fuel cell, therefore, is often considered the most plausible alternative to the combustion engine in future cars. Yet, persistently, the immense cost of fuel cell systems has caused their economic prospect to appear bleak. At the same time, other innovative engine designs, such as hybrid concepts and hydrogen fuelled cars, have received market approval and the endorsement of governments. The combustion engine, although a technology of the late nineteenth century, still offers potential for enhancements. Hence, it is far from clear whether the fuel cell will become a future dominant engine design.

In this chapter, the prospects of alternative car engine designs are assessed within a market-oriented framework for lead markets. We argue that the global success of a technology is not solely based on its technical merit, but primarily on the lead market role of a country, which refers to its ability to transfer an innovation design that is successful locally to other countries. Our major hypothesis is that whether or not a certain design will dominate and prevail worldwide depends – at least partly – on the lead market function of the country concerned. The design with the highest lead market advantage has the best chance of being successful on a global scale. Important factors for environmental lead markets are advantages with regard to prices, demand, transferability, export infrastructure and environmental regulation (see for details section 2.1)

Our analysis is based on the assumption that different innovation designs are preferred in specific countries. That is, there is no design that optimally fits all market contexts. Specific innovations only become globally and inter-temporally dominant if the first-mover country is characterised by nation-specific advantages: Our case studies reveal that the global success of internationally attractive environmental innovations is indeed triggered by certain pioneer countries that exhibit particular attributes which other countries lack. Country-specific environmental regulation, in particular, may be an incentive to adopt specific innovation designs in one country, but not in others.

Section 7.2 looks at the history of the combustion engine, which is still the globally dominant engine design. In section 7.3, we describe several alternative engine designs. Section 7.4 details the various environmental regulations applicable in the US, Japan and Europe. In section 7.5, we discuss various country-specific factors that increase the chances of a specific innovation design for its international diffusion. Section 7.6 summarises our findings.

7.2 Lead Markets in the Automobile Industry

In retrospect, it becomes clear that the United States was the leading market for auto mobilisation. The US has had the highest number of cars per capita since the early 1900s (Fig. 25).

Fig. 25. Penetration of passenger cars in several countries 1900-2001

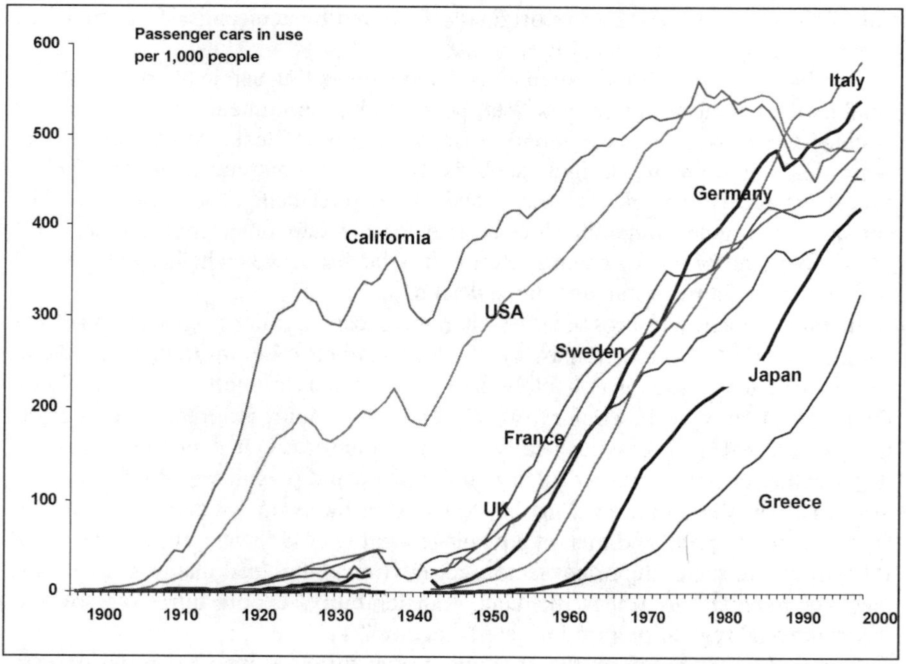

Sources: United Nations, several years, Mitchell, 1980 Federal Highway Administration, 2000.

What is more, the US was always the lead market for every type of energy that has been used over the last two centuries. The US led the way in energy substitution from wood via coal to oil and nuclear energy (Nakicenovic, 1986). The US was the first nation to switch from coal to oil which in turn established standards for nuclear reactors (Keck, 1980). Europe and Japan followed much later (Fig. 26).

Fig. 26. Share of oil as a primary energy supply in the US, UK, Japan & Germany 1900-2000

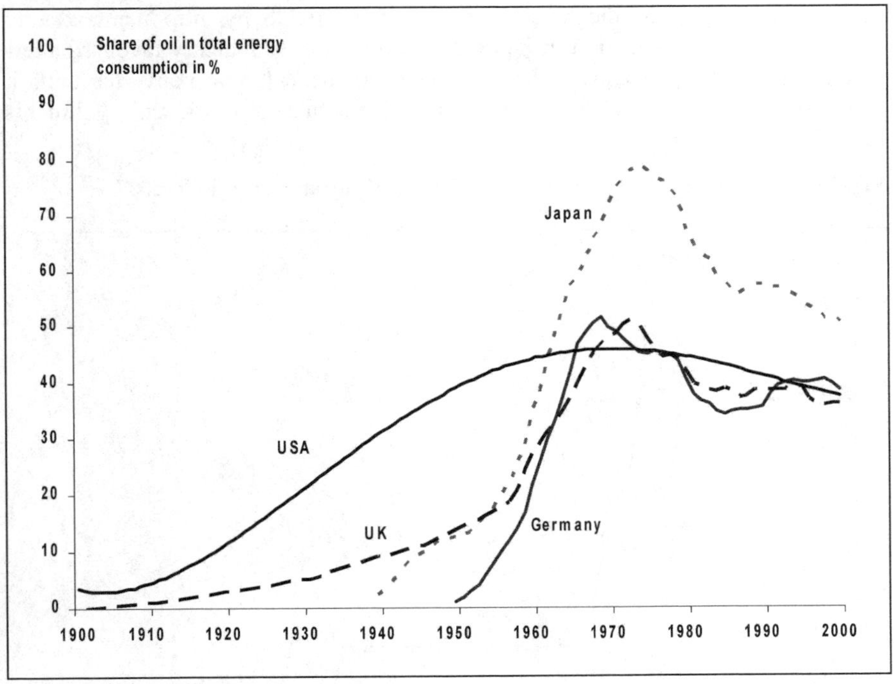

Sources: IEA/OECD (2002), Fisher (1973), own estimations.

Within the automobile industry, the choice of the dominant engine design over the past hundred years has also been made in the US. In the launch phase of the automobile, steam and electric engines competed with the combustion engine. In 1900, 40% of the 8,000 motor vehicles in the US were steam-powered, 38% were electric, and just 22% used an internal combustion engine fuelled by gasoline. Yet, the access of the US to oil helped establish gasoline cars as the dominant force in the market. The combustion engine was advantageous in the US because long distances could easily be accomplished by setting up filling stations that would solve the refuelling problem. Since recharging was time-consuming, electric cars were only advantageous within a small range, sufficient in small countries and cities but not in the US, where cars were used to drive longer distances than in any other country.

The US was also a pioneer in setting emission standards for cars (Fig. 27). California had to deal with the problems of increasing numbers of cars in cities such as Los Angeles and the corresponding air pollution long before other countries experienced the same problem. Thus the need to limit emissions of cars became apparent as early as the 1950s. UV rays transformed nitrogen oxide emissions from cars into a poisonous gas called smog. At the end of the 1970s, strict emission limits were introduced that effectively made a catalytic converter necessary. The catalytic converter became a global standard. This time, however, other reasons played a role (see section 4.5). For Japan the US market became the key market for automobiles in the 1970s. In order to support exports, the Japanese government anticipated the regulatory context in the US by introducing exactly the same clean air legislation in Japan. In Europe, the car industry favoured alternative engine designs and successfully resisted the catalytic converter until it eventually had to succumb because of its apparent success in reducing pollutants in the US and Japan.

Fig. 27. Emissions standards for NOx in the US, Germany and Japan 1970-2007

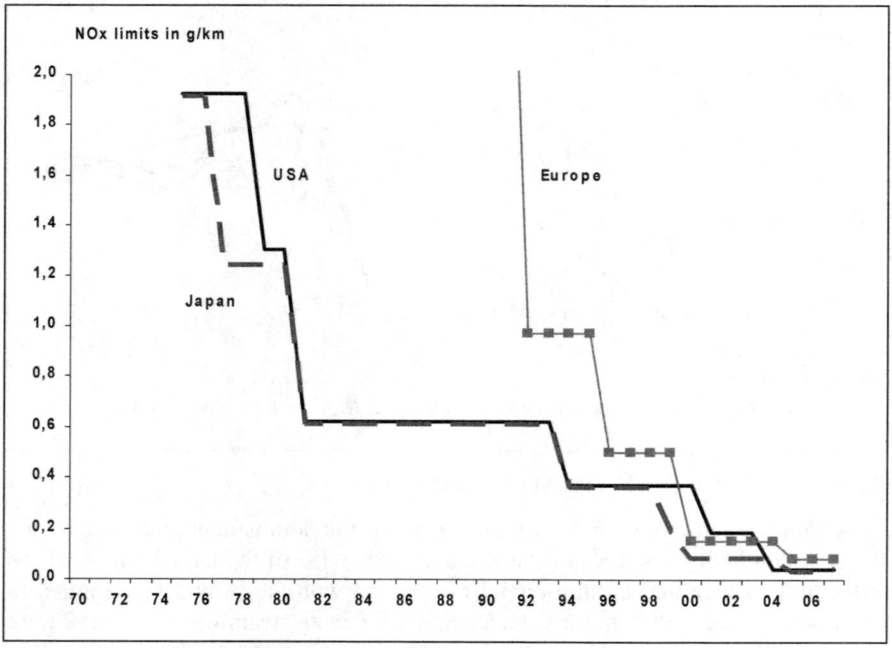

Sources: National regulatory offices.

However, the US is not the lead market for every innovation in the automobile industry. As the US society became more affluent after the Second World War, cars became bigger as well as more fuel consuming and innovation focussed on increased convenience. With the exception of the year immediately after the oil crisis, fuel prices remained low in real terms. In contrast, fuel prices in Europe followed an increasing trend, so that European car manufacturers developed more fuel-efficient cars. Demand gradually shifted to the diesel engine which is more fuel efficient than the gasoline engine. Innovations that increase fuel efficiency were first adopted in Europe and often only found their way into US and Japanese cars when they became much cheaper or when they not only reduced fuel consumption but also increased the performance of a car which is – according to car manufacturers – an important innovation success factor in Europe.

The regional technological lead market pattern is consistent with the socio-political context of the countries. In the US, pollutant emission reductions receive the most attention. Europe is most eager to reduce CO2, which is not a pollutant but a gas that causes the greenhouse effect, and therefore the focus is on increasing fuel efficiency. In Japan, restrictive speed limits, high vehicle density and toll roads reduce the demand for high-performance engine characteristics.

The varying national environmental preferences and regulations have resulted in different engine designs being favoured in each of the regions. There is no design that is the best design in all environmental contexts. However, countries may have an incentive to follow other countries and abandon their own preferences. For instance, the export orientation of industry and politics in Japan is somehow eclipsing environmental concerns and industrial policies masquerading as environmental regulation. Japan is therefore inclined to follow the US market context trying to influence the US towards the design that is favoured in Japan. In the following sections, we discuss the different designs and the ability of countries and regions to influence the adoption of their preferred design in other countries.

7.3 Fuel Cells and Alternative Innovation Designs

7.3.1 Fuel Cells

A fuel cell vehicle (FCV) is driven by an electric motor that is powered by a fuel cell. Fuel cells convert energy in the form of hydrogen into electricity. FCVs can be directly fuelled with hydrogen or, alternatively, fuels, such as gasoline or methanol, can be used and converted into hydrogen with an on-board reformer (Hekkert and van den Hoed, 2003). From an environmental perspective, the main advantage of the fuel cell is that it does not emit any pollutants during operation. However, hydrogen and oxygen have to be produced — either in a central production facility or on board the vehicle through conversion of conventional fuels. Moreover, taking into account the whole energy conversion process, FCVs consume slightly more energy than the best combustion engine cars.

The first fuel cells used for transport purposes were alkaline fuel cells (AFC), which were used in spacecrafts and submarines. AFCs are characterised by high energy density and a good cold start-up, but they require CO2-free oxygen to operate. High costs and the need for pure hydrogen and oxygen limit the economical use of AFCs in terrestrial applications (ATLAS, 2003). Today, the proton exchange membrane fuel cell (PEMFC) is generally considered the best option for mobile applications, especially for motor vehicles. The PEMFCs are operated at a relatively low temperature (80° C) and start up quickly. The main drawbacks are the costs of the catalyst and membranes (platinum) along with the necessity for the water produced to be removed.

7.3.2 Battery Electric Vehicles

Battery electric vehicles (BEVs) are equipped with an electric motor that is supplied with electrical energy from a battery. BEVs have been on the market since the dawn of the automobile industry. Today, General Motors, Chrysler, Nissan, Ford, Toyota and Solectria still offer electric vehicles. The market offers BEV models that range from two-seaters to minivans, sport utility vehicles (SUVs), and pickup trucks. A BEV is solely powered by an electric motor. It relies on a battery pack that must be recharged by an external electric power source. BEVs have the advantage that they do not produce any tailpipe emissions. Including the emissions of the power plants that produce the electricity for recharging, it is estimated that BEVs can cut CO2 emissions of cars by as much as 70% (Hekkert and van den Hoed, 2003).

The costs of BEVs are significantly higher than those of gasoline vehicles, mostly because of expensive small-volume batteries. Higher vehicle prices are only partially offset by the fact that fuel costs for electric batteries are about one-third of those of a gasoline-powered vehicle. The competitiveness of BEVs was expected to improve considerably. However, the expected progress in battery technology has not been realised. The main disadvantage of BEVs remains the low activity radius. Without recharging, the first-generation BEVs had a driving range of 50 to 80 miles. Technology advances now allow for travel distances of over 100 miles on the basis of a single battery charge (Union of Concerned Scientists, 2002). Since recharging is slow and requires a new infrastructure, BEVs so far are mainly used for special applications in small market niches.

7.3.3 Hybrid Electric Vehicles (HEVs)

Hybrid systems combine two different types of drive mechanisms, a gasoline or diesel combustion engine and an electric motor. One of the two types of engine is used according to the driving situation. For instance, the electric motor has advantages within city traffic, while the combustion engine is more efficient on highways. An electronic control device on board continuously evaluates which engine is better in which situation. The combination of the two engine types renders a hybrid car more fuel efficient than a car solely powered by a combustion engine, although the electric motor and battery increase the weight of HEVs.

A further advantage of HEVs is that emissions are low in situations when they are most undesirable. Since the battery is recharged by the combustion engine, the car does not need to be recharged externally as purely electric cars do. In stop-and-go situations in inner cities, for instance, the electric motor tends to be used. Several HEVs models have been available since 1997. To date, Toyota has sold 100,000 of its Prius Hybrid, mainly in Japan and the US (Hekkert and van den Hoed, 2003). The luxury saloon Crown Mild Hybrid and the first hybrid minivan, the Estima Hybrid, have both been available in Japan since 2002.

All current HEV models are powered by a gasoline engine. Although they offer a higher fuel-efficiency than comparable gasoline automobiles, HEVs are still less efficient than models with diesel engines. In addition, hybrid cars are more expensive than diesel cars. Besides higher prices, a further disadvantage of HEVs is the lower driving dynamic in comparison to traditional combustion engine cars. But the popularity of hybrid cars may increase if the electricity produced on board is used for additional functions that combustion engine cars cannot provide.

The hybrid concept is frequently considered as a transitional design that may facilitate the evolutionary transition to radically new engine technologies. But the European automobile industry is reluctant to develop hybrid cars, mainly due to the competing diesel engine and its advantages and popularity. On the other hand, combustion engine cars may slowly evolve in the direction of hybrid cars, because traditional combustion engines are already equipped with an electric motor that is required to start the engine. This electric motor could be upgraded in order to propel the car in specific situations, for instance at slow speed. Obviously, European manufacturers are not completely inactive with particular respect to HEVs: DaimlerChrysler, for instance, has developed a diesel hybrid concept.

7.3.4 Conventional Fuel Efficient Vehicles

Fuel efficient vehicles (FEVs) are conventional cars with combustion engines whose fuel consumption is low. With fuel prices being higher than in other regions, FEVs are most common in Europe. In Germany, the most fuel-efficient cars consume less than 4 litres per 100 km. There is a mix of technologies to reduce fuel consumption: Among the most frequently used approaches are the use of diesel engines and low-weight materials and the improvement of aerodynamics and combustion processes. These approaches are dominant partly because it is the most convenient development and partly because of market preferences (Beise and Rennings, 2003). Despite the use of low-weight materials, though, cars have become even heavier on average over time due to, above all, safety aspects, which, in addition to ecological aspects and aesthetic criteria, have turned out to be important.

Among various engine technologies, the common-rail or high-pressure direct fuel injection was most successful in the 1990s. It simultaneously improves combustion, lowers emissions, and increases car performance, notably acceleration. Today, most diesel engines are equipped with high-pressure injection. Modern injection systems have been developed by several car companies in Europe and Japan. Among these countries, Germany was the lead market: Most technologies to reduce consumption were adopted earlier in Germany than in other countries (see section 4.1). The US and Japanese markets lagged behind in this technical change, partly because fuel prices are much lower there. In addition, diesel cars are less popular in America because their pollutant emissions are higher than those of gasoline cars.

7.4 Regulations

7.4.1 USA

Because the USA experienced serious air pollution problems, it was the world's first country to regulate pollutant emissions of motor vehicles. Within the US, California, specifically, was authorised to implement its individual vehicle emissions control programs, because it suffered most from air pollution. Other states are allowed to choose between either the Californian or Federal programs. New York and Massachusetts, for example, have decided to implement the Californian standards. With particular respect to controls for nitrogen oxide and hydrocarbon emissions originating from passenger cars, the Californian regulations had a pioneering role in the US. California's Low Emissions Vehicle (LEV) Programme and the subsequent LEV2 Programme include stringent emissions standards as well as specific requirements for sales of advanced technology vehicles and zero emission vehicles, such as fuel-cell-powered cars (European Conference of Ministers of Transport, 2000).

In 1990, California initiated the gradual introduction of ZEVs through the implementation of the ZEV Programme, which originally implied a share of 10% of zero emission vehicles among all new vehicles sold in 2003 (California EPA Air Resources Board, 2003). However, as a result of pressure from the automobile industry, the programme was modified and allows for so-called "Partial Zero Emission Vehicles" (PZEVs) and ATPZEVs, i.e., "Advanced Technology Partial Zero Emission Vehicles", whereas vehicles based on traditional combustion engines do not qualify, even if these vehicles are fuel-efficient and thus low-polluting (Hekkert and van den Hoed, 2003). ATPZEVs are low-emission vehicles that are expected to support the development of ultimately competitive zero emission technologies. The ATPZEV option includes HEVs, which are subsidised in the US with a tax reduction of up to $2,000 (California EPA Air Resources Board, 2003). Due to the serious competition with HEVs, the chances of a large-scale market introduction of BEVs are drastically reduced.

In addition to pollutant emission controls, the Corporate Average Fuel Economy (CAFE) standard was introduced in 1975. The CAFE standards for new cars aim at limiting the fuel consumption of the whole US automobile fleet. The impact of the CAFE standards proved to be small, though: First of all, although overall fuel efficiency increased, the improvements were main ly reached in those years in which the oil prices increased substantially. Furthermore, manufacturers are allowed to violate target levels by paying fines. Second, a loophole in the regulation allowed for a market shift towards fuel-consuming light trucks that has offset almost all fuel efficiency improvements of saloons.

7.4.2 Japan

Traditionally, Japan's emission control regulation has followed US regulation. For example, Japan adopted the US Clean Air Act. The Japanese regulation behaviour has been commercially rather than environmentally motivated, since the US has been and still is the key market for the Japanese automobile industry. In line with US initiatives for zero emission vehicles, the Japanese government supported the development of battery-dependent electric vehicles. While the progress on electric vehicles fell short of expectations, manufacturers shifted their attention to hybrid engine designs (Åhman, 2003). The government reluctantly followed Japanese industry's reorientation, but started to support the development and adoption of hybrid cars. Furthermore, observing the pioneering activities of Mercedes-Benz on the fuel cell, Toyota urged the government to subsidise fuel cell development.

In contrast to electric cars, hybrid cars were received well by Japanese consumers, at least partly because hybrid cars are especially advantageous for stop-and-go traffic in cities. With direct subsidies from manufacturers and the government, which offers a cash incentive of around 2,000 $, the number of HEVs increased from nearly zero to around 50,000 between 1997 and 2000 (Hekkert and van den Hoed, 2003). Outside Japan, hybrid cars were not as successful: While low gasoline prices kept hybrid cars in the niche market of environmentally conscious buyers in the US, most Europeans seem to favour cars with powerful engines, which is not the best feature of hybrid cars. Interestingly, diesel cars were only accepted in Europe once they became as powerful as gasoline driven cars, although this was not the case in Japan. Finally, the second generation of the Toyota Prius, which was released in 2003 and exhibits features such as improved driving dynamics and higher fuel efficiency, demonstrates that the disadvantages of the hybrid design might be overcome.

7.4.3 Europe

While Europe has imitated the US regulation for pollutant emissions, such as nitrogen, Europe has a pioneering role in greenhouse gas regulation, specifically of carbon dioxide (CO2). Since CO2 reduction is possible through higher fuel-efficiency, European regulations aim at higher fuel efficiency of cars. Yet, the introduction of fuel consumption standards, such as the US CAFE standards, has been prevented by the European Automobile Manufacturers Association. Instead, this association offered a voluntary agreement to reduce average fleet consumption. Another reason why the CAFE standards have not diffused internationally might be the loophole in the regulation as described above. Moreover, low fuel price levels do not provide sufficient incentives for car producers to lower average fuel consumption (Bommer, 1996).

Nevertheless, in the 1990s, fuel efficiency ratios as low as 3-litres per 100 km became economically realistic. Fuel efficient cars in the range of 3 to 5 litres per 100 km have become more and more popular. Especially in Germany, the development of fuel-efficient cars was accelerated by regulations such as favourable tax treatment of fuel efficient cars and additional taxes on gasoline prices.

In 1998, the German Environmental Protection Agency (UBA) presented the results of a cost-benefit analysis suggesting that it will be much cheaper to realise greenhouse gas reductions and conserve resources with conventional vehicles powered by an optimised internal combustion engine than with fuel cell vehicles (Kolke, 1998). The UBA position characterises the priority of German and European environmental policy, which relies on the promotion of fuel efficient technologies.

Although French car manufacturers have boosted practical solutions in BEV development and several car manufacturers develop HEV concepts, BEVs and HEVs are still regarded as niche markets in Europe. However, the US and Japanese markets have become so important for several European automobile manufacturers that they are increasingly developing suitable models for export purposes.

7.5 The International Diffusion of Engine Designs

In this section, we discuss the determinants influencing the global success of one of the alternative engine designs. These are assessed by analysing whether a country is likely to be followed by other countries, i.e. whether a country has lead market characteristics. The design that is preferred by the market with the highest lead market potential has an international advantage and therefore the best chance of becoming the next globally accepted standard.

Since there is no zero emission regulation outside California and since FCVs and BEVs have major disadvantages compared to traditional engine design, all zero emission cars currently developed by the major manufacturers are aimed at the Californian market, one of the largest and most affluent markets in the world. Another reason is the "threat" that the Californian legislation is going to be adopted in other countries as well. The future of FCVs depends on the ability of the Californian market to influence other markets to follow the path of engine design towards zero emission designs. So far the Californian legislation has been changed so often that it is uncertain whether it will actually lead to the widespread adoption of a new engine design, and if it does, it is uncertain which specific technologies will ultimately be credited and supported by the ZEV Programme.

But the diffusion of the zero emission legislation is only one way of spreading FCVs. Beyond regulation, the cost reduction potential of mass production, demand trends and factor price trends such as the trend price of oil are the main factors in the internationalisation of engine designs. Cost is a crucial barrier for FCVs since the production cost of the current prototype is around \$ 1 million. Manufacturing cost reductions can be partly realised by economies of scale and learning curve gains. But the extent of cost reductions required for the fuel cell to become competitive against alternatives seems unrealistically high. Ongoing manufacturing cost analyses supported by the US Department of Energy indicate that an implementation of the current technology in automotive quantities (500,000 units/year) would result in costs of between \$195-325/kW. In addition, this cost represents today's current fuel cell performance scaled to high-volume manufacturing. But the cost of achieving parity with the performance, size and weight of a conventional vehicle is higher because current technology does not meet those requirements. Other studies even estimate numbers around $8,100 per kW for current FCV systems and cost reductions until 2010 that do not go beyond $1,000/kW (Morisot et al. 2002, cited by Hekkert and van den Hoed, 2003). The current cost of internal combustion engine vehicles is around $25-35/kW (Department of Energy, 2003: 39).

Another factor for the internationalisation of alternative car designs is fuel prices. The higher the oil price the more competitive the fuel efficient engine designs. Yet, there is no global oil or fuel price trend. As Fig. 28 shows, it was only in Europe that the fuel price tended to increase due to tax hikes in the past thus providing an incentive for fuel efficiency. In other major countries the fuel price follows the oil price. Although oil crises and conflicts in the Middle East temporarily pushed the oil price to record heights, no long-term increasing oil price trend could be detected in the past. Unless this pattern changes, fuel efficiency is not going to be an increasingly important feature of the next engine generation worldwide.

Fig. 28. Development of the price of gasoline in the US, Japan and Europe

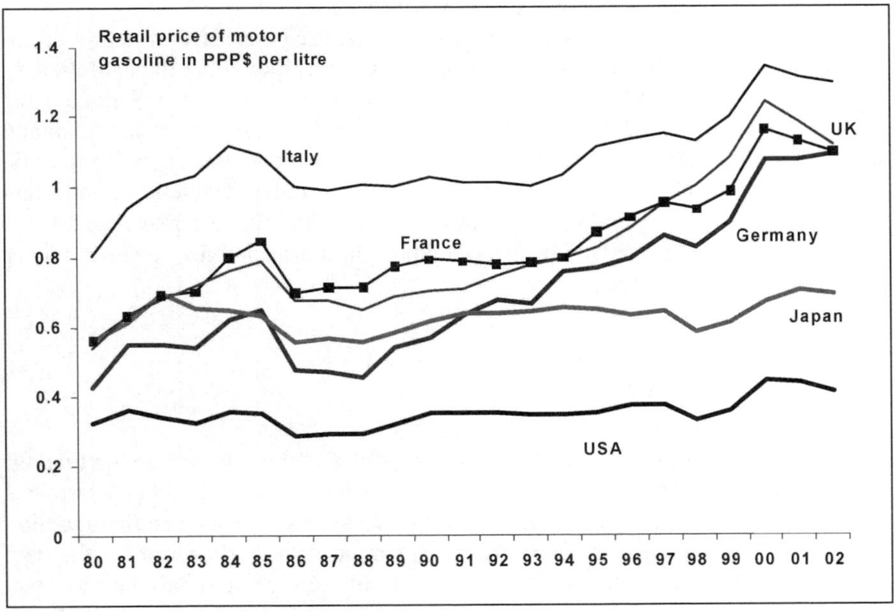

Source: OECD, 2002a.

Demand for zero emission cars can be induced by the globally increasing density of motor vehicles that worsen the pollution problem. But vehicle density already seems to be saturated in California and the US (Fig. 25). And as a result of previous emission regulations, total pollutant emissions are decreasing. Over time a similar trend can be expected in Europe and Japan, although vehicle density still has increased in these countries over the past years.

The most important internationalisation mechanism for alternative engine designs is the international policy diffusion. At this time, however, the adoption of zero emission regulation in Europe seems to be unlikely as zero emission cars offer no better fuel efficiency. Japan in contrast will follow the US legislation given the past experience on Japans environmental policy. However, this will not automatically favour the fuel cell, since the US regulation has been opened up for HEVs. It is possible that the Japanese market offers sufficient market size to lower the cost of HEVs to a level that makes them price-competitive when compared to traditional combustion engines. The Japanese manufacturers would certainly be able to transfer this cost advantage to diesel hybrids for the European market that offer a better fuel efficiency than pure diesel engines.

The international diffusion of European fuel-efficient engines, on the other hand, depends on a change in the fuel station infrastructure in the US and Japan as diesel fuel is not widely available for passenger cars at the present time. Overall hybrid technologies therefore have the best chance of diffusing internationally. They do not require diffusion of policies, since they can be optimised for different regulatory regimes and aims. They do not require changes to the national fuel station infrastructure, unlike fuel cell and diesel engines which would require infrastructure changes to become globally dominant.

However, it is also entirely possible that the three regions select different dominant designs in engine technology. In Europe, it seems likely that the evolutionary path towards more and more fuel efficient combustion engines will remain the dominant technical trajectory, while in Japan, which imports fewer cars than any other country, hybrid cars could well reach a significant market share. In the US, technological development will focus on improved catalyst technologies and fuel cells or electric cars gaining market share through high governmental and company subsidies, if the reduction of pollutant emissions continues to be a higher priority than fuel efficiency.

7.6 Conclusions

Right now several alternative engine designs for automobiles are competing for the next dominant design. We argue that not only technical merit alone determines which engine will win but also the ability of countries to influence the adoption decision of other countries. It is already apparent at an early phase of the new technology cycle that different countries prefer different designs based on national driving conditions and the regulatory context. The US prefers fuel cells, Japan hybrid cars and Europe sticks to the traditional engine design. In Table 6, we assess qualitatively which vehicle concept has the potential to become a globally dominant innovation design.

Commercialisation of BEVs was the original target of the Californian ZEV regulation, but it failed due to the unsatisfying performance characteristics of battery technology. There is no indication today that BEVs have the potential to become a dominant innovation design even at a national level.

Table 6. Lead market potentials of different alternative vehicle designs

Innovation Design	Most important regulation	Pilot market	Lead market potential	Major problem
Battery Electric Vehicles (BEVs)	Subsidies, strong ZEV regulation	US	Small, seen as niche market in addition to conventional cars	Problem that commercialisation of BEVs was objective of Californian ZEV initiative but failed, now all countries focus on other technologies
Fuel Cell Vehicles (FCVs)	Modified ZEV regulation with credits for ZEVs	Competition between US, Japan, Europe	Small for the next 20 years, due to high costs for vehicle and infrastructure	Problem that cost-benefit ratio is not competitive compared to HEVs and FEVs, even under conditions of mass production
Hybrid Electric Vehicles (HEVs)	Subsidies, fuel prices, tax incentives, modified ZEV regulation with credits for ZEVs	Japan	High, due to good technical performance and competitive costs	Risk if environmental regulations of the Californian ZEV type are enforced and diffused internationally
Fuel Efficient Vehicles (FEVs)	Subsidies, fuel prices, tax incentives, modified ZEV regulation with credits for ZEVs	Europe, esp. Germany	High, due to good technical performance and competitive costs	Risk if fuel prices and tax incentives of the European type are enforced and diffused worldwide; problem of lacking diesel acceptance in Japan and US (seen as "dirty technology" due to particulates)

Fuel cells were also supported by early developments of the ZEV initiative in California. Thus the US could be identified as a lead market for FCVs due to the regulatory push in California. FCVs are still in the phase of demonstration projects, while the ambitious time schedules for their launch has been postponed. FCVs are not expected to reach cost competitiveness within the next two decades. The only chance FCVs have of being adopted internationally in the medium term is the diffusion of ZEV regulations worldwide. A regulation is often adopted internationally when it is effective. ZEV regulations have however been watered down and now allow for a broad range of technologies, including HEV and potentially also FEVs. This and other reasons mean it is unlikely that strict ZEV regulations will be introduced in other countries.

The two remaining technologies with the potential of becoming a globally dominant design in the next decades are the HEVs and the FEVs. Both are economically competitive under given market and regulation trends which are: subsidies, moderately increasing fuel prices, tax incentives and modified ZEV regulations with credits for a broad range of technologies. Japan will further develop the

HEV to be valuable in other countries as well given the strong commitment of Japanese car manufacturers and the government to support exports.

European regulation and research concentrates on FEVs, respective policy instruments are fuel taxes and reductions of other taxes for car users. The global success of those technologies is supported by the preference of the European market for high performance. Innovations therefore have to match the driving dynamics Europeans are used to. Especially direct injection technologies for diesel cars have become a market success because of the combination of fuel efficiency and high performance. The success of the FEV innovation design favoured by European carmakers will depend crucially on the acceptance of diesel technology abroad, i.e. to overcome the image of diesel as a "dirty technology" due to diesel particulates. An improvement of the environmental performance is also needed to meet the strict US standards. It can be expected that both designs, FEV and HEV, will evolve with different regional importance (focus in US and Japan on HEV, focus in Europe on FEVs) in the years to come.

8 Technologies to Reduce Harmful Emissions in Diesel Vehicles

8.1 Introduction

The automobile sector is a central industry in all industrialised countries, contributing between 4% and 8% of GDP in OECD countries and providing between two and 4% of all jobs. The UN estimates that, for every skilled job in the automobile industry, 7 to 10 jobs are created in related sectors.

By the same token, however, both the production process and the operation of automobiles are associated with serious environmental risk and environmental damage. Road traffic is one of the biggest sources of atmospheric pollution and has a particularly strong impact on air quality in towns and cities. Vehicle exhausts contain the pollutants carbon monoxide, nitrogen oxides, hydrocarbons and particle mass. In spite of the reduction in exhaust contaminants achieved in industrialised countries for individual vehicles (using technology such as the 3-way catalytic converter), chances are that the continued increase in the number of kilometres driven as well as in the absolute number of automobiles on our roads will produce further increases in the overall burden through such contaminants (Ifeu, 2001), in addition to which vehicle emissions of carbon dioxides are a major contributor to the greenhouse effect.

The regulation of vehicle emissions is a political field which is strongly influenced by vested economic interests as well as ecological objectives. The highly technical regulating process for exhaust ceilings by the EU is a strongly politicised one, since it is pegged to the economic and political interests of member states. The automobile industry, however, is also actively involved in the regulating process. Indeed, it is important to analyse the industry's contribution to this process in order to understand its results (Arp, 2002). When the EU first began regulating exhaust ceilings, the desire to establish a uniform market through the standardisation of technical criteria in automobiles played a more substantial role in the development of ceilings than did environment-policy considerations. The fact that emissions standards within the EU have been consistently raised is not, however, owing to any greater value placed on ecological goals, but is attributable case by case to the respective special interests and strategies of the players involved as well as the political control concept inherent in the regulating process as economic integration is pursued (Arp, 2002). But economic and environmental goals are not necessarily contradictory. In principle, a reduction of pollution by automobiles is achieved by way of politically prescribed ceilings and the adherence thereto based on advanced vehicle engineering. The spread of such technology, however, is not simply a matter of the interplay of political regulation and response by carmakers. It is a complex process contingent on and shaped by a variety of factors.

Even beyond the borders of the European Union, economic integration through international automobile trading between Europe, the USA and Japan would appear to be instrumental in promoting the introduction of more stringent emissions standards. Indeed, even where individual national policy makers are implementing isolated environment strategies, growing trade intercourse among the different nations is helping to raise ecological standards in the countries involved in such trade. This application of more rigorous environment regulations as a result of greater economic integration is called the California Effect. For more than 30 years now, California – because of its high population level one of the key automobile markets in the US – has been setting the benchmark in the USA in terms of its strict emissions ceilings, with federal policy makers and individual states eventually following its lead whenever it moves the goalposts. This effect is easily explained. Carmakers who wish to remain in business on the Californian market are obliged to respond to the standards prescribed in that state by continually improving the emissions performance of their vehicles. Once automobile manufacturers have developed their products to comply with the stricter standards which this market compared to others imposes on them, they will have a vested interest in seeing the standards raised in other markets, thus enabling them to leverage their new-found competitive advantage and to manufacture their new products at a lower cost. This, in turn, leads to national governments promoting stricter standards in support of their domestic industries. At the end of the day, the automobile industry itself, normally opposed to more restrictive standards, actually works towards their introduction (Vogel, 1995; 1999). As a consequence, the afore-described markets which spearhead this development become lead markets, since they are responsible for the spread of political standards and green technologies.

The exhausts produced by diesel vehicles are also accountable for a substantial share of air pollution. Diesel technology remains under discussion for the following two reason: Firstly, the health hazard posed by particulate emissions (they damage the respiratory tracts and the cardiovascular system and are also carcinogenic) and the impact on the environment of nitrogen oxides (acidification and ozone formation) are still controversial issues. The biggest health hazard is probably posed by nanoparticles, the absolute number of which need not be reduced if, for example, the overall particle mass can be reduced by means of the better combustion of larger particles. The size of particles is contingent, among other factors, on the type of engine used, and there are concerns that, while modern engines featuring fuel-injection technology may produce less particle mass, they could nonetheless be producing larger amounts of ultra-fine particles and nanoparticles (Abdul-Khalek I. et al., 1998, Diabaté, 2003). A recent study by the German Federal Environmental Agency (UBA) estimates that particulate emissions from diesel engines cause 10,000 to 18,000 premature deaths in Germany through respiratory and cardiovascular diseases as well as lung cancer each year (Wichmann, 2003). Secondly, recent studies have indicated that particulate emissions contribute far more potently to the greenhouse effect than previously assumed (Jacobson, 2002). This finding is of particular significance given that German carmakers have entered self-imposed commitments which include a stronger marketing of diesel vehicles as a way of reducing emissions of carbon dioxide (VDA, 2000: 134).

The aim of this case study is to examine a) how emissions standards are devised and how they evolve, b) the markets which develop by regulating standards and c) the technological strategies carmakers use to conform with such standards. The subject of our study is the technology used to reduce particle mass (nitrogen oxides) in the exhaust emissions of diesel vehicle. We will discuss the extent to which and under which conditions lead markets develop for the applicable green technologies and which role policy makers play in steering such development.

8.2 Emissions Regulation in the Automobile Industry

The first exhaust standards to be introduced for passenger cars and heavy vehicles by the EU were included in its Directive 70/220/EEC. The ceilings it prescribed were far less stringent than those in Japan and the USA, with compliance requiring little to no technical modification. The primary objective of this directive was to create technically uniform standards to facilitate trade amongst EU member states. It was only in the early 1980s that the discourse on stricter emissions standards took on a sharper tone in Europe. Germany's federal government, followed by the Netherlands, Denmark and Greece, began to question its course of prioritising economic harmonisation over the reduction of hazardous emissions given clear evidence of environmental damage as well as mounting public pressure.

The regulating process set into motion at that time was strongly marked by the conflicts of interest among individual member states whose diverging positions were based on the technological competence of their national automobile industries and on their differing perceptions of the ecological problems involved. Germany, supported by Greece, Denmark and the Netherlands, insisted on emissions standards which would require the introduction of 3-way catalytic converters for petrol-engine cars – a technology with which sections of the German industry had already gained some experience. France, the UK, Spain and Italy opposed more stringent standards, since their national automobile industries favoured the lean combustion engine (a less efficient solution for reducing vehicle emissions) and thus exhibited engineering competence in this field. A broad-based and lengthy process of negotiation resulted in the passing of Directive 88/76, a compromise solution which graduated standards according to cubic capacity and which prescribed the 3-way catalytic converter for larger classes of vehicle. It was only four years later that Directive 89/458 laid down emissions ceilings which now prescribed the catalytic converter even for vehicles with less cubic capacity.

The 1991 Directive 91/441/EC and the 1994 Directive 94/12/EC stipulated the ceilings for the Euro 1 and Euro 2 standards, respectively, the latter making catalytic converters mandatory for all vehicle classes.[8] The standards for particles and nitrogen oxides in diesel exhaust outlined in Euro 2 remained far less stringent than those dictated by US and Japanese policy makers. The German government, in particular, had advocated stricter ceilings, failing, however, before the European Parliament in the face of a vigorous lobby campaign by the automobile industry. The industry had successfully pressed a case around its claim that the technology needed would generate disproportionately high costs given the level of reduction it would enable (Wurzel, 2002: 156).

The currently valid and future emissions ceilings for diesel cars (the Euro 3 standard and the Euro 4 standard as of 2005, respectively) were laid down in Directive 98/69 of 1998. This directive followed a four-year process of research, negotiation and discussion, which can roughly be grouped into two periods. The first consisted of the formulation of an initial proposal on future emissions ceilings by the EU Commission based on the Auto Oil I Programme from 1994 to 1996. The second period lasted from 1996 to 1998 and involved a public debate over the proposal and its ultimate resolution in the form of the said directive.

8.2.1 Auto Oil I

The Auto Oil I research programme involved participation by officials from the Commission, the Association of the European Oil Refining and Marketing Industry (Europia) and the Association of European Carmakers (ACEA). The aim of the programme was to provide policy makers with objective information about the most cost-efficient measures with which to reduce traffic pollution to a level which would satisfy the stipulations of the European Union's air purity standards (Com (96) 248 Final).

The Commission hoped the Auto Oil I Programme would enable it to push through tougher exhaust standards, to keep the costs for the industry moderate and to weaken the influence of individual member states – an influence which, in the 1980s, was such that it could practically block proposals by the Commission over quite a length of time. Prior to Auto Oil I, prospective emissions ceilings would be discussed and negotiated by the Motor Vehicle Emissions Group (MVEG) before the issue entered the EU's legislative process. MVEG members included representatives from EU governments, industry representatives and EU administrators. To avoid drawn-out discussions which would result in numerous compromises being made (as had been the case for the predecessor body, the Emissions Ceilings Group), the Commission collaborated with the industry only where Auto Oil I was concerned [9]. The Commission also hoped this would enable them to better incorporate and control both industries (Taminiau, 2001: 274).

A three-step procedure was adopted for the programme. First, the Commission stipulated future air quality goals for the EU, which were inspired by the WHO air

8 See section 4.5 for a detailed description of the negotiation process

9 MVEG, the EU Parliament and environmental organisations were merely given information about the ongoing status of the programme.

pollution ceilings. In a second step, a model was drawn up to ascertain how air quality would develop to the year 2010 if exhaust emissions were not reduced. The third part of the process involved outlining the contribution which each industry would have to make to improve air quality. The contributions of industry were to be made contingent on the costs and effectiveness of the measures decided on. Costs were to remain at a minimum, but effectiveness maximised. Three packages of measures to reduce exhaust emissions were given primary consideration: engine-modification measures, fuel optimisation and improvements in vehicle inspection (Goodwin, 1999).

The possible effects of reduction and the cost of individual measures were examined within the framework of the EPEFE technical research programme, i.e. the European Programme on Emissions, Fuels, and Engine Technologies. EPEFE was jointly run by the Association of European Carmakers (ACEA) and the Europia, the oil industry association, as part of the Auto Oil I Programme. The aim of EPEFE was to gain a better understanding of how engine technology and fuels interacted and what influence they had on pollutants in exhaust fumes. The programme ascertained the reduction potential inherent in individual technical measures and the costs involved. This information was then used to optimise standards.

8.2.2 Strategies Pursued by the Automobile Industry as Part of Auto Oil I

From the perspective of the industries involved, car makers and the oil industry, the Auto Oil I Programme presented a welcome method for determining future emissions ceilings. "The programme," explained one industry representative, "helped to determine and illustrate the actual costs of any further development." (ACEA, 2002).

Critics of the programme emphasised that both industry associations used their position in the programme to formulate unnecessarily high cost estimates and thus ensure that ceilings were only marginally reduced, so as to keep development costs from being incurred. They also, it was claimed, attempted to offload future costs to the respectively other industry (personal communications with Taschner, Rodt, and Taminiau, 2001). Since improvements in vehicle emissions levels can be achieved by either means of advances in vehicle engineering or by changes in the composition of fuels, each industry has a vested interest in seeing the regulations which govern the respectively other industry tightened, resulting in the achievement of environmental goals, while the bill for related costs is footed by others (Taminiau, 2001: 278). The strategy of industry associations to often put a high price tag on environmental protection technology, has been adequately substantiated in the past. Industry brandishes the threat of high costs, referring to the impediment such costs represent in terms of competitive strength and ultimately to the loss of jobs this would entail (Stockholm Environment Institute, 1999). According to critics, the success of industry is reflected in the fact that, given the pressure the industry exerted, the Commission's proposal for the Euro 3 and Euro 4 standards was twice as high as originally planned (personal communication Resch and Taminiau, 2001). The degree of influence wielded by the industry is said to be a consequence of its intimate incorporation into the Auto Oil I Programme and its leadership in terms of technological know-how coupled with the fact that the Commission was understaffed (Taminiau, 2001, personal communication Taschner, Wurzel, 2002).

8.2.3 Outcome of Auto Oil I

And yet the Commission's first proposal on future emissions standards was nonetheless to the disliking of the automobile industry, since the Commission's estimate burdened it with 765 million ECU p.a. against the only 3.1 million or so ECU p.a. it charged to the oil industry (Friedrich et al., 2000). The governments of the different EU member states took differing views on this proposal. Austria, Denmark, Finland, Germany and the Netherlands criticised it as being too slack. Greece, Portugal and Spain expressed their concern about the costs for the oil industry. Italy demanded more stringent restrictions on benzene. France and England alone welcomed the proposal (Wurzel, 2002: 166). The European Parliament deemed all the standards applied to be inadequate, putting forward their suggestion for lower ceilings at both readings of the directive concerned.

Table 7. Emissions ceilings

Pollutant (ceilings in g/km)	Commission Proposal	First reading, European Parliament	Joint position of the Council	Second reading, European Parliament	Mediation committee
2000	*Euro 3 (2000) binding values...*				
Nitrogen oxides (NO_x)	0.50	0.40	0.50	0.40	0.50
Particles (PM)	0.05	0.04	0.05	0.04	0.05
2005	*Euro 4 (2005)...*				
Nitrogen oxides (NO_x)	0.25 indicative value	0.19 mandatory value	0.25 indicative value	0.19 mandatory value	0.25 mandatory value
Particles (PM)	0.025 guide value	0.02 binding value	0.025 guide value	0.02 binding value	0.025 binding value

Sources: Friedrich et al., 2000, Taminiau 2003.

Bernhard Lange, the responsible reporting officer, had previously raised doubt about the cost estimates formulated for individual measures, criticising that they were too high. In light of the technology available and the development potential of such technology, it was possible, he said, to achieve the ceilings for petrol and diesel engines outlined in the proposal for the year 2000 at an earlier date than scheduled. Lange went on to explain that the costs associated with a reduction in nitrogen oxides had been overestimated. While he felt that the targets for 2005 were acceptable, he was convinced that they should be prescribed as mandatory rather than being guideline values. (Lange, 1997). Environmental organisations such as the European Environmental Bureau (EEB) likewise criticised the Commission's proposal, explaining that the ceilings it contained were too lax since the stipulated costs in no way reflected the actual costs incurred by technological development (personal communication Taschner).

A compromise between the EU Parliament, the Commission and the Council on these ceilings was ultimately tailored by the mediation committee. In the case of the upper limit for particle mass and nitrogen oxides, the Parliament only managed to some degree to assert its stance, though it was successful in calling for the standards scheduled for 2005 to be made mandatory and not, as originally planned, to be seen as indicative values. The standards for the year 2000 were not toughened (see Table 7). All further debate on the tightening of emissions ceilings is being conducted with a view to the Euro 4 standard due to become effective in 2005.

8.2.4 Outlook on Future Emissions Standards for Diesel Vehicles in the EU

We can expect to see more stringent emissions ceilings being put into place beyond the year 2005 (Euro 5). The Commission is planning to use the findings of the Clean Air for Europe (CAFE) programme as a basis for Euro 5. Commenced in 2001, the objective of the CAFE programme is to develop integrated, long-term political strategies for air quality conservation. Initial results are expected in mid-2005. Some of the items of focus in this programme include an examination of existing national and EU air conservation schemes, the preparation of a catalogue of measures to improve air quality, and the formulation of proposals for new EU directives. There are plans to put further restrictions on particle and nitrogen oxide emissions, with a change in the regulation meaning that particle emissions will no longer be gauged according to mass alone, but also according to size. The plans provide for an open, participative process versus a revised version of the Auto Oil I Programme. Initial activities within the EU Commission have been scheduled for this summer (personal communication Greening). It is too early at this stage to comment on the level of future values and on when they might be introduced. What is foreseeable is that future negotiations will see existing lines of conflict reaffirmed. Industry representatives, for instance, are already making their position clear that the transportation sector has contributed its share to air quality conservation and that the onus must now be on other industries to do their part. What's more, California's super ultra low vehicle emissions standard – the toughest of its kind in the world right now – is being rejected as too expensive for the industry (personal communication Greening).

There are also ongoing discussions at EU level about the Enhanced Environmentally Friendly Vehicle (EEV) scheme aimed, for one thing, at achieving an extensive degree of equality for all engine concepts and at further reducing emissions. According to the parties involved, this standard will only impact on passenger-vehicle emissions in the long term (personal communication Mönch).

8.2.5 Tax Incentives

In Germany, the D4 standard offers tax exemption for vehicles which meet the Euro 4 norm before it becomes effective in 2005. This policy is unparalleled in the EU. Tax incentives for specific technologies such as the particulate filter are not on the books at this point in time. In principle, however, individualised incentives are possible and something which environment associations have repeatedly called for (personal communication Rodt).

8.2.6 Assessing the Process from the Perspective of Technological Potential: Technology Forcing?

The Auto Oil I Programme sets out a profound revision of the EU regulation on emissions. For the first time ever, standards have been devised on the basis of cost/benefit considerations, where previous ceilings were lowered in response to the best-available technology (Friedrich et al., 2000). It is worth noting that, with its Auto Oil I Programme, the EU Commission is not pursuing policy goals aimed at promoting innovation, even though it could well assume that technological innovation would inevitably be forced upon the industry once a particular level of emissions ceilings was prescribed. As early as 1992, representatives of the EU Parliament taking part in a symposium on the future of emissions regulation warned that orienting future standards on the cost/benefit ratio and by-stepping the BAT principle could cost the automobile industry some of its competitive standing in the field of environment-relevant engineering (Wurzel, 2002: 157).

To assess current corporate strategies, it is essential to establish to what extent the standards decided in 1998 were technologically feasible at the time. Had the necessary technology been developed, or had it at least been foreseeable, these standards would have constituted nothing more than a response to the technological status quo. If the contrary is true and the technology needed had either not been developed or only in rudimentary form, these standards would have represented a case of technology forcing. As a rule, the prerequisite for introducing of certain standards in Europe is their technical practicability within the stipulated timeframe (personal communications with Mönch, Rodt), whereby the definition of "technically practicable" and the questions, what sort of time scope such practicability entails and what sort of costs will be involved are issues of debate.

In the view of the automobile industry the ceilings proposed by the European Parliament for Euro 3 and Euro 4 would have required a policy of technology forcing. Given the wave of criticism by environmental associations faced during the policy-making process as well as the briefing submitted by the reporting officer, the automobile industry ran a targeted lobby campaign spanning from the time the Commission put forward its proposal to the ultimate resolution of the directive, the aim of the campaign having been to prevent the Parliament from making any changes to the proposal that would entail further restrictions. At hearings, information forums and discussion sessions, the industry presented its cost estimates for any emissions-reduction measures and its view on necessary future exhaust standards, and moreover attributed only a minimal development potential to technologies which would enable reduced emissions (personal communications with Taschner, Rodt, Lange).

In the opinion of experts and those involved in the regulating process, the standards adopted for particulate and nitrogen oxide emissions for the Euro 3 norm, due to take effect in 2000, required no special development efforts on the part of carmakers. In this particular case, the industry had successfully flexed its muscles and would now need to make relatively minimal efforts to gear existing technologies to the new standards. It was only the values contained in Euro 4 (valid as of 2005) that would put more pressure on manufacturers in terms of technology development, requiring special development efforts and new engineering solutions altogether. This pressure was brought to bear on the industry by the Parliament, who turned the non-compulsory guideline values for 2005 as proposed by the Commission into binding ones (personal communication with Taschner, Lange, Mönch).

It is important to stress at this point that „development pressure" must always be seen as relative to the timeframe component. The Federal Environmental Agency, for example, came to the conclusion back in 1995 that particulate filters and NO_x traps designed to reduce nitrogen oxide and particulate emissions, i.e. vehicle features such as were necessary to conform with the standards as of 2005, could have been developed to market maturity by around 1998 if an adequate degree of effort had been exercised (Umweltbundesamt, 1995). In summary, we can say of Euro 4 that it was a time-delayed „soft" case of technology forcing. While the necessary technology was not yet available at the time, it was deemed feasible in principle. The only issue of contention was the timeframe required. The UBA and EEB both contended that the standards could have been introduced at a much earlier point in time if carmakers had been prepared to make the effort. Euro 3 was not a case of technology forcing, since compliance was possible subsequent to only minimal development efforts by the industry.

The relative nature of the term „technology forcing" becomes evident given the differing references made to the US regulating process. Environmental regulators there set stringent ceilings in conjunction with short timeframes, since air conservation policy is strongly focussed on reducing vehicle emissions. The industry, for its part, often cannot meet the stipulated values on time, thereby forcing deadlines to be postponed until the necessary technological status has been achieved. One example of this was illustrated by the efforts to introduce the 3-way catalytic converter, which was postponed several times in the 70s, even though the low emissions values this technology enabled made its introduction imperative. The industry had successfully asserted that it could not build it (see section 4.5). In its argumentation, the ACEA now points out that the proposals put forward by European environmentalists would lead to the same game of ceiling setting and non-compliance (personal communication ACEA). The environmentalists likewise refer to the regulatory style used in the US, though their line of argumentation is different. They say they do not want similarly strict standards as those in the USA, that in Europe the principle of technical feasibility applies, so that the standards introduced could be binding ones. In other words, although the proposals made by environmentalists may go beyond that which the automobile industry desires, they do take actual development potential into account. Environmentalists, too, wish to avoid the kind of situation which is apparent in the USA.

8.3 The Spread of Diesel Vehicles and Their Markets

The markets for technology which reduces harmful emissions in diesel cars are situated in regions with strict emissions regulations. Hence, diesel cars are subjected to the sharpest regulation in the USA, Japan and the EU, in all of which regions prevails the political will to introduce even tougher standards. The USA currently have the most stringent exhaust norms of all – norms which, at least on a political level, the EU considers to denote the way to the future and which are likely to influence the formulation of prospective EU standards (Walsh, 2000, personal communication Lange).

Within the United States, California has assumed the pioneer role, leading the way into the future on a platform of maximised emissions standards for automobiles. The regulations governing exhaust values, however, are far more complicated than in the EU. For one thing, California has issued a number of different standards, to which carmakers are required to conform using a dedicated table outlining the specifications for each section of their fleet. And varying values and predefined engine operating cycles apply for each emissions class. Stricter values are allocated for the first either 50,000 miles or five years of operation, for example, than for operations after 100,000 miles or 10 years. The currently strictest standard for diesel cars in California is the ULEV (Ultra Low Emission Vehicle) standard. As for 2004, the SULEV (Super Ultra Low Emission Vehicle) standard was announced. Both these standards apply for diesel and petrol vehicles alike.

Table 8. Emissions ceilings in California

Californian emissions standards for diesel and petrol cars, g/m (g/km)					
Norm	Year	Particles	Nitrogen oxides	Particles	Nitrogen oxides
		50,000 miles/5 years		*100,000 miles/10 years*	
ULEV		-	0.2 (0.124)	0.04 (0.025)	0.3 (0.186)
		50,000 miles/5 years		*120,000 miles/11 years*	
SULEV	2004	-	-	0.01 (0.006)	0.02 (0.012)

Source: www.dieselnet.com/standards.html.

The ceilings valid in Japan since 2002 slightly exceed those of the Euro 3 standard, with substantial restrictions governing diesel vehicles and their emissions in metropolitan centres. By the same token, however, diesel vehicles do not play much of a role in Japan. It is the EU market which provides the stimulus to develop technology that will reduce diesel emissions.

Table 9. Emissions ceilings in Japan

Japanese emissions standards for diesel cars, g/km			
Vehicle category	Year	Particles	Nitrogen oxides
Small sized cars	1997	0.08	0.4
(~1.25t)	2002	0.052	0.28
Medium sized cars	1998	0.08	0.4
(~1.25t)	2002	0.056	0.3
Light duty trucks	1997	0.08	0.4
(~1.7t)	2002	0.052	0.28

Source: ECMT, 2002.

Where use of the particulate filter is concerned, the picture we get when we look at the regulations which apply in the USA and Japan is this: In Japan, the ceilings for particulate matter could currently be met even without the use of filters, since the regulations there are less restrictive than the Euro 3 standard. Future measures are in preparation to further reduce hazardous emissions, though a timetable is not yet foreseeable. Whether or not a particulate filter is required to meet the ULEV standard which currently applies in California or whether the ceiling which lies somewhere between Euro 3 and Euro 4 can be satisfied through engine modification alone is not ascertainable from where we stand. The SULEV standard, to become applicable as of 2004 and which will restrict particulate emissions to less than half of the value defined by the Euro 4 norm to be put into effect in 2005, will make the use of a particulate filter necessary.

8.4 Market Development for Diesel Passenger Cars

In Europe, sales figures for diesel vehicles have risen considerably over recent years, the main purchasing incentives being the low price of diesel fuel (except in the UK) and the good mileage such vehicles normally offer. Rough calculations show that the higher purchasing price for diesel vehicles is balanced out within one to three years by the low fuel costs, good mileage and low maintenance costs (Brueckner, 2002).[10] In Austria, Belgium, France and Spain, more than 50% of all newly registered vehicles in 2002 were diesels. In Germany, the share of diesel vehicles was up from around 5% in 1975 to 38% in 2002. The biggest markets in Europe are presently Germany and France. In the first half of 2002, 20.5 and 23.5% of overall European turnover in the sector for diesel vehicles was generated by these two countries, respectively. Because the self-imposed commitments by the automobile industry to reduce CO2 emissions include a pledge to vigorously support the introduction of diesels, we can expect to see increasing marketing efforts in this area and a continued increase in the number of new registrations for diesel vehicles. A current forecast by Volkswagen puts the figure for the year 2005 at 50% of overall turnover from sales within the EU (Schindler, 2002).

10 It is important to note, however, that in Scandinavian countries, for instance, diesel passenger cars are subjected to a higher tax.

Fig. 29. Percentage of diesel vehicles based on the total number of new registrations of passenger cars in the years 1990, 1996, 2001 and 2002 in the European Union

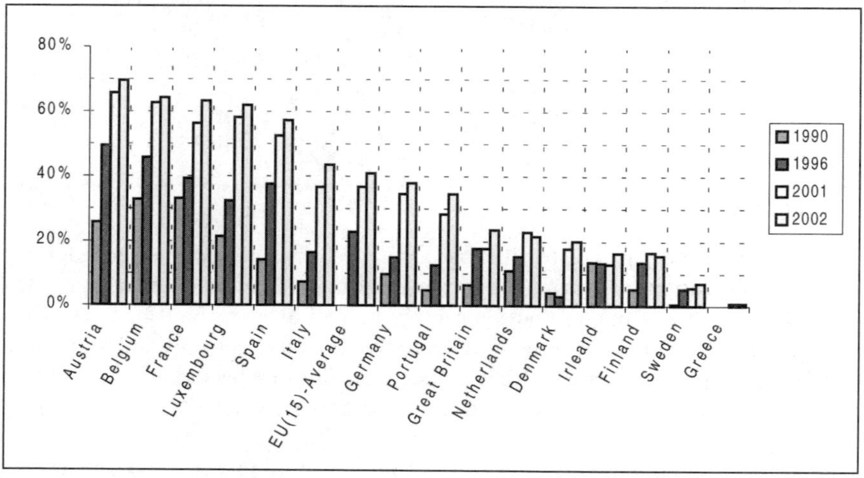

Source: Schindler, 2002.

Fig. 30. Share of diesel passenger cars against total new registrations in Germany

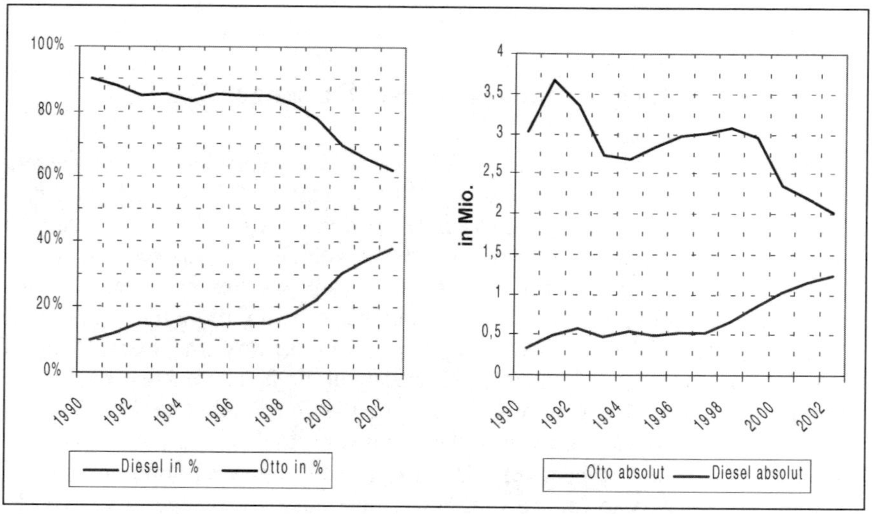

Source: Schindler, 2002.

With a market share of around 1%, the USA is not a factor in the equation as far as sales markets for diesel passenger cars are concerned. German manufacturers in the USA do, however, see a potential market there[11]. Even vehicles which conform to the Euro 4 norm, do not meet US emissions standards. Thus, to sell European diesels there will require further technological development. Given the growing market for diesel vehicles and the likelihood that exhaust standards will become even more restrictive, the market for technology which meets such standards is also experiencing growth. With respect to carmakers' competitive advantage and lead-market effects, two assumptions can be made. Firstly, long-term, global marketing strategies for diesel vehicles only make sense if such vehicles comply with the standards prescribed in all economic regions (i.e. in Europe, the USA and Japan). Secondly, lead markets governed by strict emissions standards, such as California or Germany, are likely to boost an ecologically aware buyer market open to the acceptance of vehicle offerings which enable premature compliance with emissions ceilings – with or possibly even without tax advantages playing a role.

Since compliance with emissions ceilings requires the use of technologies which car manufacturers purchase from their components suppliers, we can also expect strict standards to produce lead-market effects in corresponding supplier industries – a theory exemplified by the fact that the first suppliers of 3-way catalytic converters still maintain the biggest market shares to this day (see section 4.5).

8.5 Technologies Designed to Reduce Hazardous Emissions

A whole range of suitable technologies is at different stages of development, each being pursued by the automobile industry with different levels of enthusiasm. We can categorise the technology applicable to diesel engines into two groups: exhaust treatment and engine modifications. Based on the present-day status of development, certain methods of exhaust treatment require fuel to contain less than 10 ppm of sulphur. Current ceilings for nitrogen oxides and particulate emissions can be met using existing technologies. Compliance with the Euro 4 or SULEV standards, however, requires making considerable engine modifications and then combining them with exhaust treatment technology.

8.5.1 Engine Modification

The two pollutants which exhaust treatment using standardised oxidising converters has not been able to sufficiently reduce are nitrogen oxides (NO_x) and particles. To understand how engine modifications can effectively reduce them, it is

11 A high-ranking symposium was held in California in 2002 with the backing of the environmental agencies in that state. There have also been repeated statements of intent by German carmakers to step up marketing efforts there in support of diesel passenger cars (Handelsblatt, 2003a).

important to understand how these substances are created during the combustion process.

The problem with diesel-based technology, in particular, is that direct injection is likely to cause a local surplus of fuel in the cylinder's combustion chamber. A lack of oxygen leads to insufficient combustion, as a result of which particles are produced (Wachter, 2002). NO_x is generally created when the combustion temperature is high, when the combustion temperature remains at its maximum for a long period and when a particular fuel-air mix is produced. While the simplest solution would be to reduce the combustion temperature, this would automatically increase particle emissions. The share of NO_x produced is always contingent on the share of particles produced and vice versa (Carstens et al., 2001). The aim of any engine modification must therefore be to achieve an effective trade-off between the different emission reduction measures.

8.5.1.1 Exhaust Gas Recirculation

One effective method of reducing NO_x is exhaust gas recirculation (EGR). EGR redistributes some of the exhaust into the charge air. Adding exhaust gas to the fresh air diminishes the concentration of oxygen in the fuel-air mixture contained in the combustion chamber, which in turn causes combustion to be "slowed down", enabling the maximum combustion temperature to be reduced and thus less NO_x to be produced. In diesel engines, the EGR system can presently only operate in partial load. Developers are now working on adapting EGR for full load operation, so as to achieve further reductions of NO_x – the prerequisite, however, is the development of new materials and compound materials as well as cooling for the recirculated exhaust (Flaig and Zimmermann, 2000). EGR can effect substantial reductions in NO_x emissions, but it also increases fuel consumption and particulate emissions. An optimal trade-off can, however, be found (Wachter, 2002).

8.5.1.2 Direct Injection Systems

Increasingly, modern diesel engines are being designed to feature electronically controlled high-pressure injection systems only. The benefits of such systems are improved running smoothness and better mileage. The high pressure these systems use distributes fuel evenly and finely in the combustion chamber. Hence, combustion is improved and less particles are produced (Pucher, 2002).

Leading carmakers currently subscribe to two main variations on the injection system, one of which is the unit-injector technology by Bosch, used mainly by the VW Group, and the other being the common-rail concept used by all other major manufacturers. The rule is: The higher the injection pressure, the better is the distribution of fuel in the combustion chamber, resulting in less particulate emissions in exhaust. While a high degree of injection pressure may not prevent NO_x emissions, again, an optimal trade-off between NO_x and particles can be found. Future developments will see the concept of direct injection being further enhanced through pilot- or pre-injection, improvements to the injection process and multiple injection (Dorenkamp and Stehr, 2001).

8.5.1.3 Homogeneous Combustion

Given its reliance on heterogeneous combustion which causes fuel surpluses in individual parts of the combustion chamber and thus prevents full combustion, diesel-engine technology is clearly inferior to petrol-engine systems in terms of particulate emissions. Carmakers intend to switch to homogeneous combustion in order to neutralise this drawback. The virtue of a diesel engine (i.e. its better mileage) could, however, remain unaffected. Compression firing of a homogeneous mix illustrates that consistent temperature distribution within a homogeneous combustion process can drastically reduce NO_x generation without producing any significant amount of particulate emissions (Kahrstedt and Buchwald, 2001). To date, however, it has only been possible to use homogeneous combustion in conjunction with low rotational speeds and in partial load. High demands are also made on the electronic control of the combustion process. Things are currently still at a very early stage of development.

8.5.2 Exhaust Treatment

8.5.2.1 Particulate Filters

Particulate filters help to radically reduce particulate emissions. The filter is integrated into the exhaust area, where it captures the particles contained in the exhaust. These particles eventually clog up the filter, causing exhaust counter-pressure to be increased and larger amounts of fuel to be consumed. It is therefore necessary to regenerate the filter at regular intervals by burning off the particles. Their combustion along with the oxygen contained in the exhaust requires a temperature of over 600°C, i.e. a temperature which diesel exhaust in passenger cars can hardly achieve, even at full throttle (Michelin et al., 2002). Regeneration measures therefore need to be undertaken, so as to ensure that the filter is either properly regenerated as of a certain particulate load (discontinuous regeneration) or that filter loading is restricted (continuous regeneration). Regeneration measures can be subdivided into active and passive systems, whereby active systems require heat, while passive ones generally utilise catalytic effects (Herrmann et al., 2001). Table 10 lists different regeneration measures which are normally combined.

Table 10. The categorisation of regeneration measures

	Active	Passive
Continuous	Generation of reactive components: Plasma technology (ozone, OH radicals, NO2)	Generation of reactive components: CRT system (NO2 effect)
Discontinuous	Burner Engine modifications (e.g. multiple injection)	Fuel additive Catalytically coated filter

Source: Herrmann et al., 2001.

8.5.2.2 Catalytic Converters for the Reduction of Nitrogen Oxides

Two concepts are currently considered to be particularly promising: The SCR (selective catalytic reduction) converter uses ammonia to oxidise nitrogen oxides into nitrogen and water. Since safety considerations prevent the use of ammonia, however, urea is generally used, disintegrating into ammonia in the hot exhaust gas. The SCR converter is regarded as a future technology in commercial vehicle engineering, even though this field of development still harbours problems which need solving (e.g. the absence of an infrastructure for urea). While the SCR converter has so far been deemed too big for use in passenger cars, the technology could in principle, be used for such vehicles (Elsener et al., 2001).

The NO_x adsorber converter (also referred to as the NO_x storage converter or NO_x trap) is amongst the technologies currently enjoying the most attention in terms of development efforts. Indeed, a model for passenger cars with direct-injection petrol engines has already been developed to series maturity and has for some time now been available on the market in Europe. (Krebs and Theobald, 2001). In contrast to conventional converters, which normally convert NO_x to N_2, adsorber converters store (or adsorb) nitrogen oxides (much like a sponge would) until their capacity is exhausted. Once this eventuates, the engine electronics temporarily switch from their standard lean operation to low-oxygen operation, allowing the converter to regenerate itself (Pischinger et al., 2003).

8.6 Carmakers' Technological Development Strategy

To meet the Euro 3 norm, it was necessary to advance the technological status quo, so as to achieve improvements in injection technology, in combustion chamber design and in the design of exhaust treatment systems (VDA, 1998). Euro 3 required no more than the enhancement of conventional technology.

The technology needed to satisfy the demands of Euro 4, on the other hand, was not yet clear when the standard was drawn up in 1998. All the parties involved agreed that the standard would be technically feasible only after a time of development, with different estimates made as to how long this would take. Technical surveys, however, concluded that it was possible to meet the stipulated ceilings either through engine modification or exhaust treatment measures (Neunzig and Wallentowitz, 1998, Faiz et al., 1996, Umweltbundesamt, 1995). In its yearbook 2000, however, the Association of the German Automobile Industry (VDA) set out the guidelines for future developments: The goal of engineers, it stated, was, where possible, to prevent emissions being produced at all, rather than filtering them out later (VDA, 2000). In the meantime, engine modifications are seen to be a sufficient means of achieving compliance with Euro 4 for small and medium-size engines, with particulate filter systems for the reduction of nitrogen oxides and, if necessary, catalytic converters being used in particularly heavy, high-performance vehicles only (Schindler, 2002).

According to the VDA guideline, automobile manufacturers focus on coming up with engine modifications – as indicated by Audi's and VW's finished development of a number of Euro-4-compatible models. As a consequence, a call by the federal environment minister[12] in 1999 to introduce a particulate filter system onto the market by way of self-initiative was rejected on the grounds that it constituted a construction regulation which was unacceptable in principle, given that such regulation served to distort competition. The association also denied the existence of production-series-type particulate filters (VDA, 2000: 151). It is moreover assumed that agreement has been reached within the automobile industry not to launch exhaust-treatment technology such as particulate filters or NO_x traps onto the market prematurely (personal communication Rodt).

8.6.1 Peugeot Introduces the Particulate Filter

In late 1999, the French automobile Group PSA Peugeot Citroen was the first manufacturer to introduce a particulate filter system for diesel passenger cars in France. In May 2000, the system was launched on the German market, too. First introduced as a standard series feature in a premium-class car, the FAP system (Filtre à particules) has since been used in other models, all the way down to lower middle-class vehicles[13]. This system now allowed particulate emissions to be reduced to 0.001g/km, i.e. well below the ceiling of 0.025g/km as stipulated for the EU as of 2005.

Peugeot introduced the FAP system, it says, to make use of the competitive advantage which such environment-friendly technology offers, the Group's concrete objective being to use particulate filters to increase market share for its vehicles.

12 The environment ministry addressed the issue with manufacturers after a survey by the Fraunhofer Institute for Toxicology and Aerosol Research had recommended introducing filters in light of the health hazard posed by particles.

13 The particulate filter was first introduced as a standard series feature in the model 807 (premium class) in May 2000. It was then successively included in the Peugeot 406 and 307, likewise as a standard series feature (though only for the 307 version with a 2-litre-cubic-capacity engine). The filter is not available for vehicle models below the Golf class (206 and 106) – not even as an extra.

This strategy differs from that of other manufacturers such as VW or Audi, whose aim is to secure competitive advantage through early compliance with the Euro 4 standard, the specifications of which are mirrored in Germany's own D4 norm (tax-incentive standards). This technology allowed Peugeot to reduce its emissions of particle mass to almost zero, though it does not contribute to reducing nitrogen oxides[14].

The German market has dual significance in Peugeot's strategy. First, it is the biggest market for environmental technology, so Peugeot counted on a good deal of demand for vehicles with particulate filters. Second, Germany is a key reference and test market; advancements in the automobile sector which are successful in Germany would generate demand stimulus in other markets.

Peugeot presumed that the filter would be a success in Germany and anticipated that the purchasing behaviour there would be emulated in other countries. Given its vision (as well as the lower costs resulting of uniformity in production), it offered this filter as a standard in all other markets as well (personal communication Schalberger). For Peugeot, the German market was a calculated lead market which would create demand stimulus in other countries if the particulate filter proved successful there. The response Peugeot's introduction of its filter solicited from other carmakers was predominantly subdued. Even though Peugeot proved that, using the filter, it was possible to achieve an emissions standard, at least for particulate emissions, which fell far below the Euro 4 norm and did so five years in advance of the date specified by regulators, manufacturers maintained their official course aimed at complying with emissions ceilings through engine modifications. Even the emerging public discourse of the day about the health hazard posed by particles and the need for the filter did not effect any change in this position.

German manufacturers had substantial reservations about the technical feasibility of the particulate filter, arguing that there could be no certainty as to their durability and that the filter would cause a higher degree of fuel consumption. One of the reasons the FAP system was publicly dismissed was Mercedes' unfavourable experience with the technology. After the company had fitted a number of its models for the US market with the particulate filter 20 years previously, it was forced to take it from the market again because regeneration of the filter did not work[15]. As a consequence of this fiasco, Mercedes did not continue development on the particulate filter (Wüst, 2000). According to the people at DaimlerChrysler and Volkswagen, exhaust treatment measures aimed at enabling compliance with the Euro 4 limit had not been in the pipeline at the time – except for heavy VW automobiles (Wüst, 2000).

---

14 Peugeot is currently further developing its FAP system in the hope of making it eligible for tax incentives on the basis that it will reduce nitrogen oxide emissions.

15 The material of which the filter is made could not take the strain of the high temperatures to which it was exposed during regeneration and it broke. There was also an absence of reliability about whether or not the temperature necessary for regeneration would always be reached; in the event that it was not, the filters clogged up and the vehicles simply broke down.

And yet Peugeot's lead was remarkable in one way: Normally, automobile manufacturers agree on a common course when it comes to certain themes. They do so via their national trade associations. It is unusual for a player to break away from this practice (personal communication Roth). Peugeot's introduction of the particulate filter was something akin to the introduction of the 3-way catalytic converter, only this time its was a French group that launched the technology on the market and the German manufacturers who were intent on preventing this technology from asserting itself.

8.6.2 Long-Term Testing by ADAC and the Federal Environmental Agency

In August 2001, Germany's premier automobile club, ADAC, and the Federal Environmental Agency (UBA) published the results of long-term testing which examined the durability of the FAP system. The test found not only that the filter drastically reduced particulate emissions (especially ultra-fine particles), but it also disproved the validity of the scepticism other manufacturers had vis-à-vis the particulate filter. Functionality remained intact even after a driving distance of 80,000 km, nor did the testers establish any significant increase in fuel consumption (Umweltbundesamt, 2001). ADAC and UBA therefore advised other manufacturers to switch their focus away from the graduated Euro 4 plan and instead follow PSA's lead to reduce particulate emissions to practically zero by using the filter (Fröhlich-Merz, 2001). Even before the particulate filter was introduced, its manufacturers had contacted UBA, requesting confirmation of the environmental tolerability of the additive it contained. The idea to test the filter was a joint decision by UBA and ADAC, whose aim it was to prove the functionality of the filter and to generate awareness for the technology among the greater public. This unlikely coalition between ADAC and UBA was established because of ADAC's vested interest in clean technology, given that it understands its role in connection with health matters to be one of a protector of consumer interests. As far as ADAC is concerned, the health of motorists needs to be protected if motoring is to remain an attractive proposition in the long term (personal communications with Rodt and Demmel).

This proof of the particulate filter's functionality hugely increased public pressure on carmakers, with environmental organisations and the media demanding of the other manufacturers that they close ranks with Peugeot. From Germany's government, in turn, they demanded that use of the particulate filter in new vehicles be given special tax consideration.

German carmakers found themselves in the uncomfortable position of having to defend their own strategy centred on engine modification. There was no longer any room for doubt about the functionality of the filter. Peugeot offered other manufacturers licensing agreements on production of its FAP system. The stance of the other carmakers saw no significant change, however. They continued to reject the filter, though they did make changes to their official communication strategy. Public doubt about the functionality of the technology was expressed in press releases and statements in the year 2001, which referred to the fact that the Euro 4 standard made no specifications regarding the technology to be used, that the particulate filter did not solve the problem of nitrogen oxides and that it was important to take a holistic approach to the reduction of hazardous emissions. In this regard, it was proclaimed, Peugeot's particulate filter is nothing more than a marketing stunt (VDI, 2001, personal communications with Giesen, Skibbe, Metz). Filters, the opponents said, should only be used where no other technological solutions were conceivable as a means of conforming with Euro 4.

8.6.3 Automobile Manufacturers' Current Technological Strategies

While it is difficult to define a timeframe within which a change of strategy took place, 2002 did see an increase in the number of individual companies testifying that they would at least consider early introduction of diesel filters (FTD, 2003). This development may have something to do with an initiative launched in November 2002 entitled "No diesels without a filter", the aim of which was to push through tax breaks for particulate filters (with a deadline set for 1 July 2003) using pressure instruments such as the media, PR measures, lobbying, public campaigns and advertising measures.[16] This was a demand to which Germany's federal environment minister, Jürgen Trittin, gave his verbal backing, though he did not initiate any concrete measures.

Still under pressure from the public domain, German carmakers defended their strategies. VW's CEO Pischetsrieder, for one, publicly announced that a filter would cost between 200 and 600 euros, depending on engine size, a cost which VW wished to spare its customers. Pischetsrieder went on to say that his company's development efforts had been oriented on the formal political criteria which demanded that emissions of both particles and nitrogen oxides be reduced to the level prescribed by Euro 4. It was left to the automobile industry, he explained, to decide which technology it would use. At the same time, Pischetsrieder left all options open by claiming that a particulate filter had never been ruled out. (FTD 19/2/2003, Zeit 27/3/2003, Welt 6/4/2003). Similar arguments were forthcoming from spokespeople at Mercedes and from the president of the carmakers'

---

16 A joint initiative entered into by the Federal Environmental Agency, the German arm of the World Health Organization, Greenpeace, BUND (an environmental conservation organisation), Germany's Child Protection Association and ADAC (the automobile club) and coordinated by the Environment Support Society of Germany (DUH), this project calls for (and the call is echoed in the media) special tax considerations for particulate filters, for Euro-3-conform diesels with particulate filters to be eligible to the same tax incentives as Euro-4-conform diesels which do not feature such filters, and special tax considerations for the retrofitting of older vehicles. Diesel filters, the group argues, are available in principle to all carmakers. There is no proof, it says, that they cause increased fuel consumption. And a German initiative is necessary, since EU-wide regulation would be too lengthy a process. The reason for the group's public commitment is the health risk posed by particulate emissions. (Resch, 2002).

association (VDA), Bernd Gottschalk, who described the targeted endorsement of particulate filters as discontinuous government policy which manufacturers could not focus on (Spiegel 11/2003, Rheinische Post 2/4/2003).

In addition to the rhetoric confusion created by official rejection and acceptance, the indications in the spring of 2003 were that other automobile manufacturers were now working on particulate filters. Press reports, unconfirmed by the carmakers themselves, claimed that the international motor show in Frankfurt in the autumn of 2003 (the IAA) would see Audi, BMW, DaimlerChrysler, Toyota and even Volkswagen showcasing a particulate filter (FAZ 12/04/2003). In February 2003, Ford was the first to break with the consensus among automobile manufacturers that particulate filters would only be used where no other alternative was possible (Reinking, 2003). The current strategies can be summarised as follows:[17]

Ford was the first manufacturer in Germany to announce (in early 2002) that its development cooperation with the PSA Group would produce not only a new generation of engine, but that the partners would be looking to find ways of enhancing particulate filters. A filter which produces less particle ash, it explained, would be on the market well before 2005 (Von der Weiden, 2002). Ford fixed its sights on a second-generation additive system with longer regeneration and maintenance intervals. The development of more advanced diesel engines in a joint effort with the PSA Group is aimed at achieving compliance with the Euro 4 norm (personal communication Hennen). The FAP system is now also featured in a number of Fiat and Lancia models.

At the same time, Toyota announced its system for exhaust treatment – a system which would drastically reduce both particulate matter and nitrogen oxides in exhaust and thus by far outperform the standards stipulated in Euro 4. Its so-called DPNR system (Diesel Particulate NO_x Reduction) is to be put to market by the end of 2003 (Menzel, 2002). Renault plans to be the first carmaker (in the second quarter of 2003) to introduce a series-standard particulate filter which features a catalytically coated filter element rather than requiring an additive, while undertaking engine modifications to reduce nitrogen oxides (Renault, 2003). Both these manufacturers intend to meet the Euro 4 standard at an earlier-than-prescribed date, enabling buyers to take advantage of the vehicle-tax benefits associated with the D4 norm.

We are meanwhile seeing a change in strategy at PSA. Whereas, at the time when it introduced the particulate filter, the company focused on gaining competi-

---

17 We determined current engineering strategies based on the written and telephone interviews we conducted. Given the political sensitivity of this topic and the commitment to confidentiality on the part of the engineers interviewed, these strategies ought to be viewed as trends or proclaimed intentions rather than fixed developments. If, on the other hand, we look at the course of development based on past announcements by the companies involved, we can establish that, if nothing else, introduction of the particulate filter at least effected a change in the companies' PR campaigns. We were not able to determine how long the individual companies had been working on their respective technologies or when exactly they were due to be launched on the market.

tive advantage by offering clean technology at no extra cost, its development of an integrated system (in conjunction with Ford) to reduce nitrogen oxide emissions by way of engine modifications is now aimed at benefiting from the tax advantages of compliance with the D4 norm.

Volkswagen, on the other hand, continues to favour another strategy. This carmaker only intends to introduce a filter system as series standard in vehicles which would otherwise not be able to meet the Euro 4 norm, while particulate filters will only be available for its smaller models at an extra charge – since Volkswagen has doubts about the demand for particulate filters among buyers (Reinking, 2003). Audi, a VW subsidiary, nonetheless plans to introduce a particulate filter as of autumn 2003, though likewise only as an extra.

We can currently identify four different exhaust treatment systems developed by different companies. Three of them (FAP, CRT, Renault) are strictly particulate filter systems, each based on a different regeneration strategy. The FAP system is the only one to date used as a series feature. Toyota's DPNR system is the only one which claims to reduce both particle and nitrogen oxide emissions.

Peugeot's FAP System

Regeneration of the filter element is initiated in the event that the exhaust backpressure measured by a pressure sensor exceeds a certain limit. This is the case every 400 to 600 km (depending on the style of driving), for which the following two measures are responsible:

- Multiple injections, regulated by common-rail injection, cause the exhaust temperature to be raised to over 450°C.
- An additive which envelopes the particles is mixed into the fuel, causing the particles to be combusted at a temperature of only around 400°C.

The additive is stored in a separate tank, from which it is successively dispensed into the fuel. To ensure the system runs smoothly, the filter requires cleaning every 80,000 km (as part of the inspection job) to cleanse it from all the residue produced by the additive. The tank is then refilled with fresh additive. This filter removes more than 99.9% of all particulate matter (Michelin et al., 2002).

The CRT System

Another system for the reduction of particles is the CRT system (Continuously Regenerating Trap), which features an oxidising catalyst positioned before the particulate filter to oxidise the NO and NO_2 contained in the exhaust gas. The particulate matter stored in the filter is systematically combusted, using NO_2, at temperatures starting at 250°C, i.e. at temperatures which are substantially lower than that required for oxidisation using oxygen. This system, which requires fuel with a sulphuric content of less than 10 ppm, is already being successfully tested in commercial vehicles such as city buses and selected fleets. It has not, however, been developed to series maturity for passenger cars. The CRT system is being worked on by Johnson Matthey, a chemicals company with a vast amount of experience in catalytic technology (Herrmann et al., 2001).

The "Renault System"

Renault has co-operated with Ibiden, Engelhard and Eberspächer to develop a particulate filter system which requires no additives. Like the filter element used in the FAP system, this element is made of silicon carbide and features one-end-open/one-end-closed functionality. Again, like the FAP system, regeneration is initiated periodically – every 300 to 500 km, depending on the style of driving. Here too multiple injections temporarily raise the exhaust temperature to reach as much as 570°C. A catalytic coating on the filter ensures that particulate matter is combusted even at this temperature. Renault additionally intends to fit its models with an improved oxidising catalyst and a system of exhaust gas recirculation (Renault, 2003).

Toyota's DPNR System

Japan's Toyota has developed a new exhaust gas treatment system (DPNR or Diesel Particulate and NO_x Reduction System) for the reduction of both particles and nitrogen oxides. The DPNR catalyst has a porous ceramic structure with a special coating which can store and dissolve NO_x. The system also features high exhaust gas recirculation rates as well as a low combustion temperature, enabling nitrogen oxide emissions to be further reduced. The discharging of NO_x in the catalyst causes the monovalent generation of reactive oxygen, which oxidises the particulate matter. Excess oxygen ensures that the particles combust very rapidly. The combustion process and decomposition of the NO contained in the NO_x storage catalyst is initiated by the system control, which temporarily switches to a richer-combustion mode. This releases NO and reactive oxygen, which respond to carbon monoxide and hydrocarbon to produce N_2, water and CO2. The particulate matter is combusted together with the reactive oxygen (Paquet, 2001).

8.7 Strategies by Components Suppliers

Individual manufacturers do not build particulate filter systems as complete systems (just as they do not build whole catalytic converters for exhaust gas). Different manufacturers produce individual modules. The first thing needed to filtrate particles is the filter material itself. Additional components are then needed, depending on the regeneration strategy used. Additive-based regeneration requires a measuring-out system for the additive, while regeneration using a catalytically coated filter requires an effective coating. In a final step, a components manufacturer then „cans" the particulate filter system in a metal casing and integrates it into the exhaust system (personal communication Stöpler).

Product development by suppliers is strongly contingent on the engineering strategies of the carmakers. Despite the fact that individual production steps are separated, the companies involved, from those who produce filter systems to the carmakers, co-operate closely. Collaboration with carmakers is the normal procedure. In their work, manufacturers of filter material are least of all dependent on the specifications made by carmakers. Their products are quasi independent of the type of regeneration the filter uses and of the type of automobile in question (personal communication Rippe, personal communication Teubner). And yet filter manufacturers do join forces with car manufacturers and satisfy their wishes, even though their most important partners are other components suppliers (personal communication Vogt). Manufacturers of catalytic coating and additives enter a medium level of cooperation with carmakers, since these products need to be specifically adapted to the demands of individual carmakers (personal communication Teubner). The closest cooperation with the automobile industry is maintained by "canners" – the manufacturers of exhaust systems. Their job is to develop complete particulate filter systems – in conjunction with automobile companies – and to gear such systems to engine management apparatus (personal communications with Stöpler, Stüttem, Teubner).

8.7.1 The Companies

The only filter material so far used as series standard is produced by the Japanese firm Ibiden (Michelin et al., 2002). A ceramic structure made of silicon carbide, it is currently being used by Peugeot, with Renault and Toyota also planning to do so. This material is present-day standard, even though other companies produce filters for diesel cars. Corning, a leading manufacturer of catalyst substrates, offers a filter made of Cordierite. The people at NGK, likewise a manufacturer of substrate material for catalytic converters, have developed a filter made of silicon carbide. Emitec, originally a producer of metal catalysts, is also in the process of developing a particulate filter. HJS Fahrzeugtechnik, a small vehicle-technology firm, which to date has been building particulate filters made of sintered metal, recently sold the rights for the manufacturing, further development and sale of its filter to Bosch (Westfalenpost, 2003), with Bosch anticipating rapid growth in the demand for particulate filters for diesel cars (Handelsblatt, 2003b).

Where the production of additives is concerned, two firms, Rhodia and Octel, lead the market. Rhodia manufactures Eolys, an additive already used as a series feature in Peugeot's FAP system. The leading manufacturers of catalytic coatings, Engelhard, Johnson Matthey and OMG, also dominate the market for coatings for 3-way catalytic converters. Engelhard will be the first to take catalytic coating for Renault's particulate filter system to market (personal communication Scherm).

The manufacturers of exhaust systems act as system integrators. Their job is to develop systems which meet the demands of carmakers and which can be integrated into their respective makes of automobile. Faurecia, one of the world's major components suppliers, once belonged to the PSA Group, and even today Peugeot still holds the majority of shares in the company (personal communication Teubner). The FAP system was developed in cooperation with Faurecia and Tenneco Automotive Gillet (personal communication Stöpler, Michelin et al., 2002). Other suppliers include Eberspächer, which manufactures particulate filters for Renault, Zeuna Stärker and Friedrich Boysen. The customer structure of these companies is generally broad-based, though there are exceptions. Friedrich Boysen, for instance, manufactures exhaust systems for BMW (personal communication Teubner). Almost all these companies confirm that they develop their particulate filter systems upon commission by major German carmakers.

8.7.2 Research & Development

Particulate filter technology is by no means a new issue for components suppliers, with initial development activity for commercial and off-road vehicles dating back to the late 1980s (Treiber 2003, Glück 2003, Rippe 2003, Vogt 2003, Scherm 2003, Teubner 2003). The expertise for such development was generally provided by experience gained in the development of catalytic converters (personal communications with Treiber, Rippe, Vogt, Scherm). Given the increasing spread of diesel cars, the discourse surrounding the hazard of particulate emissions and the advances made in diesel technology, manufacturers all stepped up their research efforts on particulate filters in the 1990s. Added impetus was provided by market introduction of the FAP system, which prompted more demand for particulate filters by other carmakers (personal communications with Glück, Rippe, Vogt, Scherm). Even at this stage, other automobile manufacturers already feared losing competitive edge and therefore called for development efforts to be undertaken in the area of particulate filters (personal communication Glück). The "No diesel without a filter" initiative is currently putting tremendous pressure on carmakers (and they are doing so on suppliers) to introduce particulate filters (personal communication Treiber, Rippe). NO_x storage catalysts and enhanced oxidising catalysts are also being developed for passenger cars.

8.7.3 Assessment from a Supplier Perspective

The technological strategies subscribed to by carmakers (with the exception of Ford) are aimed at developing diesel filter systems independently of any cooperation with the PSA Group. Suppliers emphasise their close cooperation with manufacturers. By the same token, however, they are keeping a lid on any information concerning the current status of developments. Engelhard, for instance, offers a catalytic coating which is compatible with all filter types available. While this technology has been on the market since 2001 (personal communication Scherm), it still needs to be adapted to satisfy the demands of vehicle manufacturers in terms of their regeneration strategies and engine management systems. Before the system can be used, therefore, a certain amount of time is first required for preparation. We were not able to find out just how much time is needed and what sort of difficulties might arise. Renault intends to use this system as series standard in its vehicles. Developments are also ongoing in collaboration with a German carmaker. Upon inquiry, we were given to understand that all the manufacturer products involved (filter material, additives, coatings) had been developed to maturity. The problems that present themselves are system integration into vehicles and the regeneration strategy (personal communications with Stüttem, Stöpler, Teubner).

The best practicable means in the area of particulate filter technology are presently considered to be additive-based systems and systems with catalytically coated filters. In the long term, the use of additives is to be avoided. For one thing because they are not completely combusted, leaving ash residue in the filter. For another the additive-based solution is considered to be too expensive (personal communication Treiber). According to the experts, most carmakers currently favour a solution which does not involve the use of additives (personal communications with Stüttem, Treiber, Teubner). To achieve the Euro 4 norm, however, additive-based systems will probably still be widely used. The CRT system is regarded as being too large, and hence too complicated, to integrate into the exhaust system. Another dilemma is sulphur sensitivity (personal communications with Rippe, Teubner).

Based on this information, we can conclude that other vehicle manufacturers, too, would be in a position to introduce particulate filters in a relatively short span of time. The only explanation for the fact that they have not previously been used is that carmakers have adhered strictly to the political stipulations governing emissions ceilings, despite the technological advances made.

8.8 Outlook and Discussion

It is clear that introduction of the filter by Peugeot and the support of ADAC and UBA have accelerated development activities by other manufacturers. The VDA policy to only make use of filters where necessary and by no means any earlier than such time, would appear to have been rendered no longer applicable. According to Peugeot, it has sold 450,000 cars fitted with diesel filters around the world since 1999, 35,000 of them in Germany. Peugeot also supplies its FAP system to Ford, Lancia and Fiat. The changed technological strategies will affect the components supplying industry, even though such implications are not yet foreseeable. If the filter technology should become more wide-spread and buyer demand continue to increase, Germany could be said to play the role of a lead market. Right now, this technology is gaining acceptance among manufacturers – a fact which substantiates the possibility of a lead market being established.

The evolution of a lead market has been boosted by UBA and ADAC support, by its endorsement on the part of a number of other private players as well as by the media impact such support has generated. Had it not been for the public discourse initiated by these players concerning the health hazard posed by particulate mass, other manufacturers would have been able to continue to pursue their individual technological courses of development and would have introduced or even begun to develop particulate filters either at a much later date or not at all. The effectiveness of public pressure on automobile manufacturers is a fact verified by components suppliers for particulate filters.

In the case of the diesel filter, one manufacturer has made use of a pilot market with particular environmental preferences and no political regulation in an effort to create competitive advantage for itself vis-à-vis its market rivals. The course opted for by the EU Commission to determine ceilings in accordance with the cost principle versus their effectiveness, resulting in too lax and, more importantly, too future-oriented emissions ceilings, has retarded the spread of particulate filters. By introducing this technology, Peugeot proved that it was possible to comply with the Euro 4 standard on particles five years earlier than the industry had claimed in the Auto Oil I Programme. Although it is not yet foreseeable whether or not and, if so, when, diesel-filter technology will be more widely used, it is obvious that diesel engine technology in cars will only continue to have market viability around the world in combination with diesel filters. The export of diesel cars to California, for example, is only possible if diesel filters or similar technology is used. If we look at the long-term tendency with respect to emissions regulation and the discussion surrounding zero-emission vehicles, it becomes clear that diesel cars can only maintain a competitive standing vis-à-vis engine concepts such as fuel cells if they fall in the category of "almost-zero-emission vehicles". The same applies to less-developed technologies for reducing nitrogen oxides. It will only be possible to export diesel cars to the USA and Japan (provided that the ceilings which apply in that country become more restrictive) if considerable advances are made in emissions-reduction technology.

An analysis of the components suppliers for particulate filters reveals that a dynamic industry exists, broad sections of which are dependent on the development plans of car manufacturers and which are experiencing growth. Bosch, one such supplier, intends to embark on the production of diesel filters with a view to the USA as one of its target markets (Handelsblatt, 2003b). Stricter emissions ceilings for particulate mass would be likely to have a positive effect on the industry. There are also first indications that suppliers for Peugeot have gained competitive advantage in the area of particulate filter systems. As the German Newspaper Handelsblatt reports, the PSA suppliers Tenneco, Faurecia and Ibiden are currently facing strong demand for their products since a growing number of car manufacturers intend to introduce particulate filters earlier then 2005. Other firms like Bosch will not be able to put their filter systems on the market until 2005 (Handelsblatt, 2003c)

Cooperation by PSA with Ford, Fiat and Lancia and the experience gained ahead of other firms implies an extra competitive edge. Other suppliers are developing different types of filter systems in cooperation with other carmakers, but a lead-market for PSA and their suppliers' products is gaining shape.

Representatives of the supplier industry have confirmed that, subsequent to the introduction of the filter by Peugeot, other carmakers stepped up development efforts. We can therefore presume that the wakeup call issued through Peugeot's activities has led automobile manufacturers to run the dual strategy of publicly discrediting the filter, but striving, internally, to occupy part of the market on which Peugeot has set its foot.

Rather than negotiating emissions ceilings, as in the past, with some sections of the automobile industry in favour of tighter standards (given the technological competence at their disposal) and other sections opposed to such restrictions, the Auto Oil I Programme saw the industry united in its backing for the introduction of the highest possible ceilings. This may have something to do with the fact that the automobile industry had hoped to achieve reductions in hazardous emissions by minimising the level of pollutants in fuel and thus offloading the costs involved on the oil industry. It may, however, also have to do with the fact that the industry did not recognise the possible competitive advantage and the export opportunities for low-emission vehicles. The lead-market effects we observed in connection with our case study can be summarised as follows:

- There is an ecologically sensitised market for technologies to reduce harmful emissions in diesel exhaust beyond the stipulated ceilings.
- In view of the tougher ceilings which we can expect to see in future, the automobile industry itself will deem it wise in the long term to forge ahead with the development of environment-friendly technology.
- Introduction of the particulate filter by Peugeot illustrated that a buyer market existed even before its "forced" introduction as prescribed by emissions regulations.
- Introduction by Peugeot of the particulate filter also demonstrated that technological development times can be substantially shorter than predicted by the industry.
- It is possible to converge political strategies in the area of environmental policy. One thing that would make sense, for instance, would be to combine the reduction of CO2 emissions through the greater spread of diesel vehicles with a reduction in particulate emissions.
- Concerning the public commitment of private players towards promoting more environmentally friendly technologies, there is a need on the part of policy makers to initiate further improvements.
- For the automobile industry, stricter emissions ceilings do not necessarily produce competition-distorting costs, but are likely to create competitive advantage.

Epilogue: German car manufacturers, the particulate filter and the 60th international motor show in Frankfurt/Germany

From the 11th to the 21st of September 2003, the 60th international motor show (IAA) was held in Frankfurt/Main, Germany. It is one of biggest and most important motor shows in the world and certainly the most important one for German car manufacturers. Most of the German car producers have announced the presentation of particulate filter systems for a number of their passenger car models during the IAA. These announcements are laudable, but one must not forget that they come four years too late. It was in 1999, when Peugeot first introduced their particulate filter system and German car manufactures had nothing better to do then impertinently discredit Peugeot's new technology in public. Their dismissive attitude has not only decreased their chances in gaining competitive advantage in a growing technology field but also shown the manufacturers' ignorance towards environmental and consumer protection. For more than 20 years, scientists, environmental organisations as well as federal agencies have been warning about the hazards related to particulate emissions in diesel exhausts but German car manufacturers reaction were ignorant and inflexible and protracted the development of new environmental technologies. Their behaviour demonstrated not only lack of responsibility beyond bureaucratic regulation but also the neglect of stakeholder inclusion into corporate management.

9 Lead Markets for VOC-Reduced Paints

Emissions of Volatile Organic Compounds (VOC)[18] contribute to the creation of ozone in the troposphere and subsequently to 'summer smog'. The most important sources of VOC emissions are the combustion of fossil fuels and the usage of solvents in lacquers, paints and glues.

Fig. 31. VOC emissions Germany 1990-2000

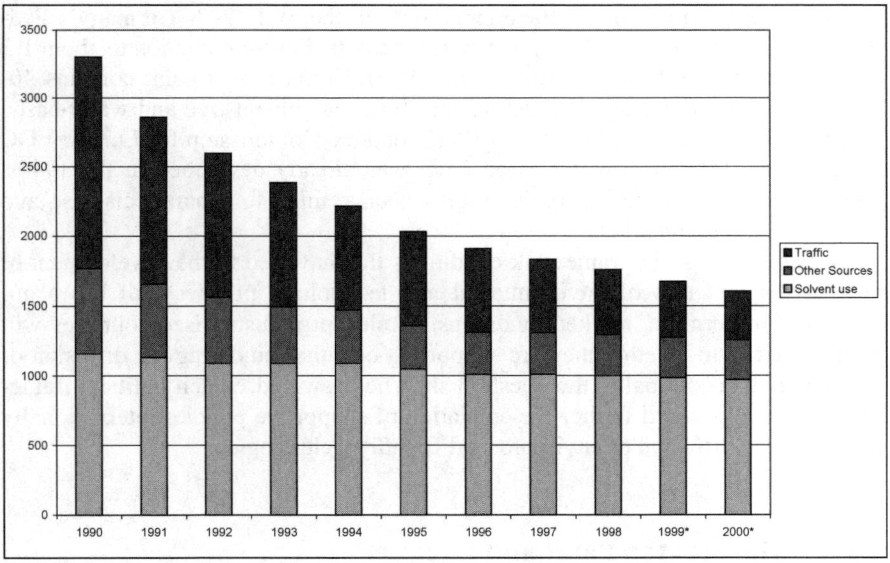

Source: Federal Environmental Agency "Daten zur Umwelt" several editions.

As emissions resulting from incineration and combustion VOCs have been subject to air pollution policies in all industrialised countries in recent years. Significant reductions in emissions have been achieved, for instance, by equipping internal combustion engines with catalysts. Also, from the early 1990s, authorisation procedures have been put into place to regulate emissions from industrial plants. Solvent-related emissions from plants requiring official authorisation amount to

[18] There is no definition available for Volatile Organic Compounds (VOC) that is commonly accepted. Some definitions rely on pressure (> 10 Pa at 20°C), others on the boiling-point (e.g. < 250°C) or the photochemical potential (Decopaint, 2000).

about 20% whereas 80% result from small-scale plants, painters and the do-it-yourself (DIY) sector (Bizer and Führ, 2000: 2). Accordingly, there has been rather little success in reducing VOC emissions from solvent use when compared to internal combustion engines or incineration plants. As a result, in Germany the share of this type of use of the total emissions has increased from about 30% in the early nineties to about 60% in 1999 while total emissions have decreased slightly to 1,015 kt/a in 1999 from about 1,160 kt in 1990 (Umweltbundesamt, 2002).

According to the European 'National Ceilings Directive' of 2001 a further reduction to less than 995 kt/a has to be achieved by 2010. Thus, further efforts to reduce emissions are required. However, potentials to reach further reductions by means of purifying exhaust gases appear to be almost exhausted. Consequently, efforts to achieve further reductions increasingly focus on products that are low in solvent.

A number of substitutes for solvent based paints have been developed to provide for alternatives to conventional lacquer, paint and glue. This relates to a significant potential to further reduce emissions. In the mid-1990s Germany's Federal Environment Agency (UBA) estimated the potential for reduction to about 1/3 (i.e. 300 kt) for 2005 (c.f. Berner et al., 1996). Conventional paint contains 40-70% of solvent whereas powdered lacquer function solvent-free and water-based and high solid paint contain only 5-15% (Economic Commission for Europe/VOC Task Force, 1990: 12). Water-based paint was already developed in the 1940s, however, only since the 1980s have they been refined for commercial use and distributed through markets.

In what follows, the framework conditions that have led to the development of alternatives in terms of environmental and technology policies will be reconstructed. Furthermore, market conditions in relevant industrialised countries will be analysed as to whether they are supporting or rather hindering the diffusion of new technologies. Finally, the question shall be answered, which political framework conditions could further the emulation of supportive policies internationally as well as the diffusion of environmental friendly technologies.

9.1 Markets for Paint and Lacquer

9.1.1 The Economic Salience of Paint and Solvent

In 1997 about 25 million tons of paint and related products worth about EUR 50 billion were sold worldwide. 80% of the world market is almost evenly distributed between the most important economic regions North America, Western Europe and East Asia. Germany, France, Italy and the UK constitute 75% of the Western European market. Decorative paints for buildings represent with 55-70% by far the most important market segment (CEN, 2000). This market share will thus be addressed in detail in the following paragraphs.

In Europe, the consumption of decorative paint (i.e. paint that is used to protect and decorate buildings) amounts to an annual emission of VOCs of about 580 kt.

Another 138-253 kt result from the utilisation of solvents and for cleaning purposes (Decopaint, 2000: 45).

The paint industries in the European Union plus the 10 first-round accession countries comprise 1,300 larger and 3,200 very small enterprises with a total of 122,000 employees. Roughly 50% of their production is covered by the ten largest companies (compared to about a third worldwide) (CEN, 2000). The annual production volume of these countries amounts to 3.8 million tons (Decopaint, 2000: i). Raw materials are provided by about 200 enterprises, the most important of which are multinational chemical corporations. On the demand side there are 165,000 painter businesses and a considerable DIY sector (from about 30% in Greece to about 70% in Scandinavian countries).

A number of diverse intermediate products are utilised in the processing of paint and lacquer. With regard to quantities solvents amount to 25% of these. With 12%, however, the value of this product segment is below average.

Table 11. Consumption and value of raw materials as of 1996

	Quantity (ktonnes)	% Tonnage	% Value
Solvents	1,420	24.2	12.0
Coloured Pigments	225	3.8	15.1
White pigments	880	15.0	34.0
Resins	1,775	30.2	34.3
Extenders	750	12.8	3.3
Water	735	12.5	-
Additives	90	1.5	1.3
TOTAL	5,875	100.0	100.0

Source: Decopaint, 2000: 15.

In Europe, about 200 companies are producers of intermediate products for lacquer and paint. Furthermore, there are more than 100 producers of resin, the most important of which are DSM Resin, BASF, Bayer, Hoechst and Rohm & Haas (Decopaint, 2000: 15). Only a small share of their total production – 1,775 kt out of 33,336 kt – flows into paint. The turnover from resin that flows into paint production is stated at EUR 1.5 billion (Decopaint, 2000: 16). Solvent is produced by more than 100 companies and is dominated by a few large petrochemical corporations (BP, Total-Fina, Shell, Exxon). Multinational chemical corporations (BASF, Hoechst) are also important producers of solvents. The share of solvents that is used in the production of coats and laminations is stated to be 25-30% of the total production, equalling a turnover of EUR 500-600 million. The market for pigments is also largely concentrated in a few hands. A total of five manufacturers produce 90% of the most important anorganic pigment, TiO2, while four producers (BASF, Ciba, Hoechst and successors and Zeneca) cover 2/3 of the demand for organic pigments. There is no comparable market domination with regard to additives as most producers are specialised on a few components.

Leading non-European manufacturers are Dexter, Dupont, Ferro, HB Fuller, Lilly, PPG Industries, Sherwin Williams and Valspar for the USA and Kansai Paint and Nippon Paint in Japan (Decopaint, 2000: 33).

Table 12. Leading European paint manufacturers as of 1996

Company (owner)	Nationality	Market share (%)
Akzo Nobel	NL	17.9
ICI	UK	9.2
Sigma-Kalon (Total-Fina)	B/F/UK	8.0
Herberts (Hoechst)	D	7.0
BASF[19]	D	4.8
PPG Industries	USA	2.6
Becker	Se	2.4
Tikkurila	Fi	2.0
Jotun	N	1.9
Top 9 together		44.2

Decopaint, 2000: 19.

With respect to countries, in 1990, Germany held a share of 24.6% in world trade, the Netherlands 10.7%, UK 10.1% and the USA 9.2% (Bonifant, 1994: 208). Through acquisitions within Europe shares should have shifted, although Europe, by a margin, remains the leading region with regard to the world market in total.

Fig. 32. Domestic sales volume of paints and lacquers

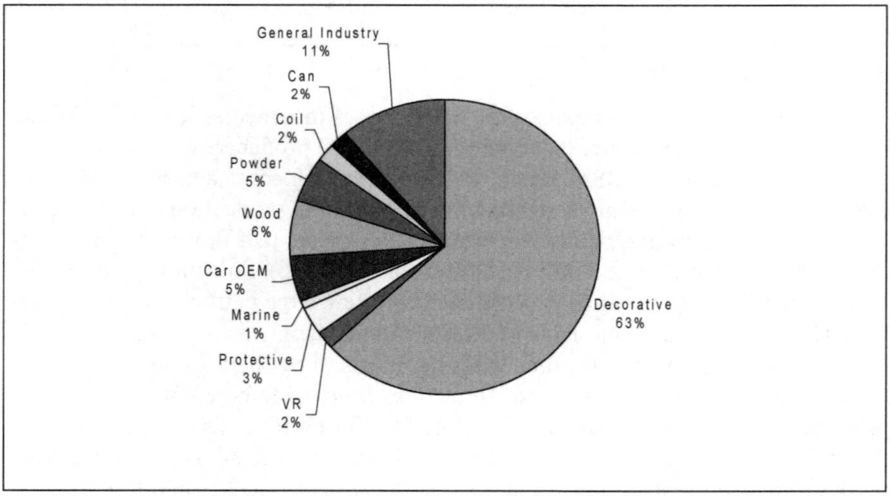

With regard to car repair lacquer the market is even more concentrated and dominated by six companies (Dupont, PPG, Akzo Nobel, BASF, Max Meyer, Herberts). Through the sale of Herberts to Dupont and ICI Autocolor to PPG,

19 Has been sold recently to Akzo Nobel.

these US companies succeeded in expanding their market share to over 50% (Entec/PRA, 2000: 27). The market for car repair lacquer has a worldwide volume of 6 billion Euros per year, about 660 kt are produced for this market segment alone (BASF, 2002). This market segment is particularly affected by the European directive on solvents since car repair lacquer is used at sites that are addressed by this legislation. It is expected that a transformation to water-based systems will have been implemented by 2007 as a result of that directive.

The trade employs some 100,000 workers in more than 3,000 enterprises. This market is less concentrated, however, the largest 90 of these companies provide 72% of the total demand (Decopaint, 2000: 18). Divided by segments of consumption, the 2001 sales of 5.5 million tons of paint and lacquer are distributed as shown in Fig. 32.

Given the paramount importance of decorative paint and the fact that a reduction in consumption of solvent within this segment can virtually exclusively be achieved by product innovations, these will be primarily addressed in the following analysis. The total production of decorative paint in 1997 was about 3,344 kt. Within Europe, this production is distributed as presented in Table 13.

Table 13. Regional markets for decorative paints

	National production decorative paints (kt)	Sales volume[20] in million EUR	Imports all paints (kt)	Exports all paints (kt)
Austria	65	n.a.	48.5	29.7
Belgium	79	109	94.3	94.2
Denmark	52	177	24.9	59.4
Finland	32	81	24.0	29.3
France	432	1,049	112.2	123.5
Germany	860	1,300	121.2	297
Greece	90	16	23.2	9.7
Ireland	25	89	22.6	4.0
Italy	408	570	60.8	156
Luxemburg	3	n.a.		
Netherlands	179 ('98)	381	76.7	95.6
Portugal	87	222	28.4	11.1
Spain	489	673	55.9	47.6
Sweden	95	71	38.4	71.7
UK	448[21]	401	82.0	199.0
Total	3,344	5,209		

Source: Decopaint, 2000: 21 f.

20 According to the national associations.

21 Calculated on the basis of an estimated 1,3 kg per litre.

The market is characterised by the following trends:

- Concentration/rationalisation: The number of important paint manufacturers has decreased from more than 2,000 to about 1,300 through mergers and acquisitions. In 1999 the market share of the top ten producers increased from 30% to 50%.
- Specialisation on core businesses: In recent years, large paint manufacturers have aimed to dominate few sectors rather than covering the whole market range.
- Expansion of markets/internationalisation: Accessing new markets, predominantly by means of acquisition of businesses.
- Increased intensity of competition amongst producers.
- Accelerated technical change and modernisation of production plants.
- The most important driving forces for technical change are environmental requirements and consumer demands.

Increased competition and modernisation leads to an increase in research efforts, the closure of old factories and the set up of new ones. Research expenditure for paint has been stated at around EUR 250-300 million p.a. This amount has been preceded by a considerable growth since the mid-eighties, whereas in the fifties and early 1980s efforts for research and development had been restricted as production relied on hitherto developed methods (Decopaint, 2000: 32-36). According to a large Dutch producer its number of employees working in research and development has risen by 60% between 1985 and 1990. Another large paint manufacturer states that 80% of its R&D budget is earmarked for environmental concerns (Mol 1995 cited in Decopaint, 2000: 36). From the USA it is reported that more than 50% of the R&D expenditure is spent on water-based substances in response to regulative measures (Pollano et al., 2000). Producers of raw materials conduct the bigger part of research efforts. By far the largest contributor is the group of resin manufacturers. A large part of research endeavours is invested in improving the performance of paints that are low in VOC.

9.1.2 Consumption

The diffusion of water-based paints varies significantly with regard to their utilisation. Furthermore, internationally comparable time series on the diffusion of water based paints in the different countries over meaningful time periods are not available. The following table provides a survey with regard to market share of water-based paint in the decorative paint segment. This segment comprises the paint used in construction businesses which traditionally feature a high share of water-based paint.

The comparatively high shares for Austria and Denmark are explained with regulations in both countries, in the case of Germany it is explained with a high degree of environmental awareness (Decopaint, 2000: 24). The share of paint sold to DIY sector varies between 24% (Spain) and 48% (UK). Generally, the share is higher in northern countries. Crucial determinants are labour costs, the share of privately owned houses and fashion (Decopaint, 2000: 27). For the USA an increase in the share of water-based indoor paint is reported from 16% in 1979 to 84% in 1996, and in the share of outdoor wall paint from 60% to 71%. Considering other areas of consumption a further increase in low-in-solvent paint is expected (Pollano et al., 2000).

Table 14. Market shares for water-based decorative paint

Country/State	Share (%)
Germany	82
Austria	81
Portugal	80
Denmark	79
Spain	74
Netherlands	69
Sweden	68
UK/Ireland	67 (Ireland)
Belgium	66
Finland	61
Greece	61
Italy	58
France	57
*California***	*82*

Source: Decopaint, 2000: 24; **Data for California only for architectural paints from Californian Environmental Protection Agency, 1999: 95.

Fig. 33. Market share for water-based automotive paints in Germany, Europe, NAFTA and Asia (in million cars)

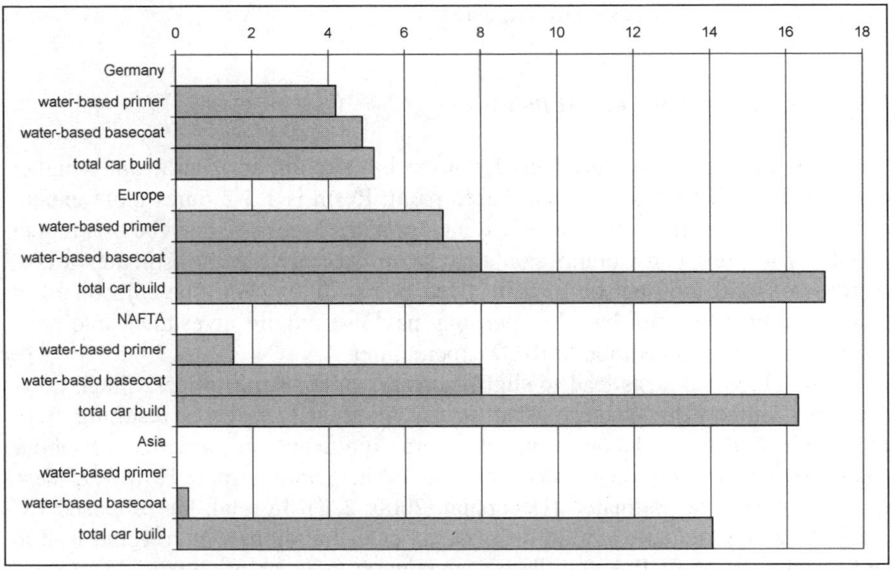

Source: European Coatings Journal 7-8/2002, http://www.coatings.de/articles/dupont.pdf (19/06/2003), own representation.

Fig. 34. Share of water based coatings against other segments

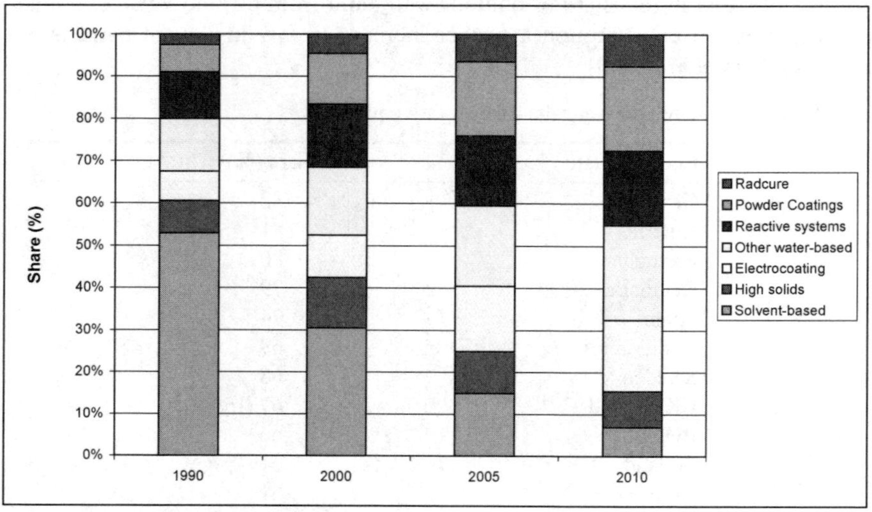

Datasource: http://www.coatings.de/rcn/rchoward.cfm (19/6/2003).

More notable differences can be observed regarding the spraying of cars. In Germany, water-based lacquers prevail in terms of basic lacquering as well as with coating. Opposed to this, solvent-based paint remains dominant in the rest of Europe, North America and Asia.

A further expansion of the usage of water-based lacquer is expected within this segment. With regard to other segments of lacquer and paint consumption a shift towards low-solvent paint is also expected.

9.1.3 Costs of Low Solvent Paints

The costs of intermediate products for water-based paint are significantly higher than for those that go into solvent-based paint. Resin is 1.3-2 times more expensive and solvent which – to a lesser extent – remains necessary must be of a higher quality. The European Commission's study on decorative paint estimates a cost increase of EUR 0.60 per kg of paint (Decopaint, 2000: 217). The adjustment of paint in respect to water-based dispensing may also require investment into new, stainless facilities in addition to R&D expenditures.

These additional costs lead to slight increases in consumer prices which, however, are unlikely to aversely affect sales. Additional expenses resulting from increased intensity of labour could be more significant, in particular as labour costs provide for a significant share of costs in the painting trade. However, these expenses cannot be estimated (Decopaint, 2000: 222). In total, the proposed EU guideline could facilitate a 56 kt decrease in VOC emissions which would lead to additional costs of EUR 300 million at maximum (Decopaint, 2000: 223). Countries with a high proportion in DIY can expect to be least affected by the increasing costs. Furthermore, the promotion of more expensive paint that is low in solvent or solvent-free could have a negative impact on the business of professional painters as it may lead to an expansion of the DIY sector. Painter businesses in Europe are stated at 165,000 with 1.6 million employees. Professional consumption at the same time allows for further regulation as compared to the DIY sector, for instance by means of health and safety regulations.

9.2 VOC Regulations

A number of diverse policy instruments are being applied to reduce consumption of solvent-based paints. Yet, there are regulations addressing the VOC content of paints in four EU countries. Labelling programmes, voluntary agreements with industry or awareness campaigns regarding reduction in emissions are conducted in many other EU countries and accession states.

The measures taken by various states and the European Union can be shown in a diffusion curve that represents individual instruments. It only evaluates product standards that go beyond health and safety regulations, voluntary obligations, eco-taxes on solvent and eco-labels. Other instruments, such as subsidies, production standards and health and safety standards are not included. Health and safety standards with regard to VOC solvents vary significantly across Europe. For instance, limits for the use of the chlorine-hydrocarbon-trichlorethylene vary between 50 mg/m^3 (TLV) in Norway and 550 mg/m^3 (TWA) in UK. Similar variances can be found regarding chlorine-free solvents, e.g. Toluol, for which the maximum allowable concentration [MAK] is 380 mg/m^3 in Austria as opposed to 94 mg/m^3 (TWA) in Denmark (Altnau, 2001).

In what follows, the most important regulative measures of European countries, the USA and the European Union as well as the most important activities conducted under the UNECE protocol to limit trans-boundary emissions will be illustrated.

9.2.1 Comparison of Most Important Regulative Measures

Austria

Austria has enacted far-reaching regulations to limit the content of solvent in paint since an early point of time. The basis of these regulations is the ozone act of 1992. Taking 1988 as year of reference, the law aims for reductions in emissions of at least 40% by the end of 1996, 60% by the end of 2001 and 70% or more by the end of 2006 (BGBl 210/1992 as cited in Vitovec et al., 1998: 53). The 40% reduction in the paint, lacquer and glue sector has been achieved (Vitovec et al., 1998: 53). However, this is partially a result of an autonomous development of the market and cannot solely be attributed to the regulation (Decopaint, 2000: 53).

The first solvent regulation that was decided on in 1991 aimed to incrementally reduce to a maximum of 10% the content of organic solvent in certain preparations (amongst others paint, lacquer, glue). As of 1/1/1996 only products that comply with these conditions should be authorised. The assumptions regarding technical feasibility proved overly optimistic and failed to meet critical requirements such as durability and quality of the products. Thus, the 1995 amendment sought a modification that differentiates limits with respect to areas of consumption and solvent and furthermore entails a number of exemptions (Vitovec et al., 1998: 56). Subsequently, the use of organic solvent in paint, lacquer and glue decreased from 53,772 tons in 1990 to 25,986 tons in 1995 while a further reduction to 22,472 tons was expected for 2000. The mean content of solvents in paint and lacquer has decreased from 39% to 22%, for glue from 4.7% to 3.5% (Vitovec et al., 1998: 57).

For wood lacquer and varnish there is a national eco-label which preconditions the product to be water-based. Furthermore, a number of paint producers voluntarily indicate the content of VOC on the packaging (Decopaint, 2000: 54).

Germany

In Germany, far-reaching targets regarding VOC reduction were developed early. The select committee of the German Bundestag on 'precaution to protect the atmosphere' demanded a 75-80% reduction by 2005 as early as 1990 (Enquete Kommission 1990). This target was adopted by a high-profile ozone symposium in 1991 (BMU/Bayrisches Staatsministerium 1991).

In the mid-1990s the Federal Environment Agency (UBA) developed a regulation on solvent that followed Austrian and Anglo-American examples. This regulation should have led to a limitation of VOC rates (g/l, minus respective water contents). The rate of VOC was adopted from Californian and British legislation (Berner et al., 1996: 16). In the long run it was aimed for VOC rates of 250 g/l which could already be achieved by low-in-solvent systems. In contrast, conventional solvent lacquer features VOC rates of 400-700 g/l. With respect to authorisation procedures for lacquering installations it was required to consider the VOC rate alongside the quantity of solvents that were being consumed per year and per hour to decide upon the necessity for an authorisation (Berner et al., 1996: 16f.). However, this regulation was not enacted.

Germany also was a pioneer regarding the limitation of VOC emissions from industrial plants. VOC limits for new installations as well as for old installations, with a given time schedule, were defined in the TA Luft (Technical Instruction Air) in accordance with the BImSchV 4 (Federal Emissions Regulation) of 24/7/1985. The technical instructions regulating the authorisation of installations were further intensified in 1991.

The 1999 European guideline on solvent was implemented by the BImSchV 31 of 21/8/2001 (solvent regulation). This regulation addresses installations in certain branches of the industry when they go beyond limits in solvent consumption as defined in the regulation. Solvent with certain dangerous characteristics according to the GefStoffV (hazardous substances regulation) are to be replaced by less dangerous substitutes as far as possible. Firms with solvent-consuming installations are required to produce an annual solvent balance sheet. They can also present reduction plans which entitle them to alleviations regarding the implementation of measures to comply with emission norms.

Since 1980 there is a comparatively successful national eco-label (Blauer Engel, i.e. 'blue angel') that determines, among other things, limits to VOC contents (Bizer and Führ, 2000: 9). The market share of paint carrying the eco-label is stated at 70% (Decopaint, 2000: 57). Nonetheless, with regard to professional consumption one finds market penetration to be weak at about 15% despite health and safety obligations that require the use of low-in-solvent paint and lacquer.

In 1984 authorities and industry entered into a voluntary agreement to reduce by 25% VOC emission from all paints by 1991 (Decopaint, 2000: 58). However, no more than a 10% reduction was achieved as innovative products were not accepted by the market (Bizer and Führ, 2000: 9). In the meantime, the industrial association VCI acknowledges a need for further reduction. Jointly with the Federal Ministry for the Environment (BMU) it worked out an environmental action target that expects a 70-80% reduction compared to 1988 as a year of reference (BMU and VCI, 1997). This target has been included in the EU's National Ceilings Directive as it can achieve a limitation of ozone concentration to a rate of 120 mg/m^3 as recommended by the WHO.

The Federal Environment Agency (UBA) has been collecting and disseminating information regarding products that are low in solvents for years. The establishment of a web site www.umweltbundesamt.de/voc on low-in-solvent products is a recent example for this information activity. A survey on the UBA's research activities can be found in UBA 2002.

Netherlands

As of 2000 professional painters in the Netherlands are prohibited the indoor use of paint with a high content of VOC. The regulation provides for a limit which should have been further reduced in 2002. However, 90% of wall paint used indoor is water-based already today. Thus, the regulation is not expected to have a meaningful effect. Rather, a potential for reduction is seen with paints based on artificial resins (Decopaint, 2000: 59f.).

A taxation of paint with high levels of VOC has been tested in one Dutch city. As a result, sales of solvent based paints increased as higher prices were considered to indicate higher quality, too (Decopaint, 2000: 60).

There is an agreement between the paint industry, DIY traders, environmental associations and the construction union to label paint with respect to their VOC content (Decopaint, 2000: 60).

In the Netherlands the industry has co-operated with the government since 1986 in developing a strategy for VOC reduction (KWS 2000). The target was to reduce emission of VOC (without consideration of emission from traffic) by 50% by 2000. Reasons for cooperation were possibilities to influence policy measures, to negotiate a generous time frame regarding implementation and to prevent surprising policies up to the year 2000. The influence the industry managed to exert was rooted primarily in its almost complete monopoly regarding information on recent technological developments. Industry did not attempt to protect the continuance of small enterprises that were seen to lack the capacity to comply with regulations (Mol, 1995).

Another voluntary agreement was concluded between paint industry, unions and health authorities in 1990 to improve health and work safety. Paint was classified according to four risk categories and it was agreed to support the use of paint from lower categories. However, the agreement was hardly complied with (Decopaint, 2000: 61).

Spain

Spain introduced a national eco-label for low-in-solvent paint in 1994. Furthermore, the content of VOC is voluntarily indicated on the packaging (Decopaint, 2000: 61).

Sweden

In Sweden only water-based paint is permitted for professional painters in indoor decoration since 1987. This rule is considered to have been the model for the Dutch regulation of 2000 (Decopaint, 2000: 62). Furthermore, there is a labelling pointing to the emission of VOC in the indoor air (Decopaint, 2000: 62).

Switzerland

Switzerland is a pioneer regarding the introduction of economic instruments to reduce solvent consumption. As concluded in 1997, a levy of SFr 2 (about EUR 1.35) per kg VOC is charged since 2000. An increase to SFr 3 (about EUR 2.05) has been announced for 2003. The regulation also includes products that contain solvents.

Furthermore, there is a voluntary agreement between authorities and the paint industry to reduce VOC contents by 25% in the period from 1985 to 1990 (Decopaint, 2000: 63).

United Kingdom

In the United Kingdom it was determined in the Environmental Protection Act in 1990 that standards will be developed regarding the authorisation of production plants that process paint (Bonifant, 1994: 207). This regulation gave incentives to use low solvent paints.

Furthermore, there is a classification – developed by the industrial association and a trade firm – which informs about the content of VOC (ranging from minimum to very high) and is applied on packaging alongside warning labels (Decopaint, 2000: 63).

Denmark

Paint with a high content of VOC is subject to particularly strict health and safety regulations in Denmark. As early as 1972, so-called MAL codes were introduced to indicate VOC contents and health hazard. There is a general obligation requiring substitution with less harmful substances wherever this is technically feasible. With regard to paint used by consumers a regulation is currently being prepared.

Ultimately, water-based paint is affected, too, by the prohibition of APEO which came into force in 1999 (Decopaint, 2000: 55).

Since 1989 there is a voluntary agreement between authorities and the paint industry according to which paint containing VOC should not be used for indoor wall paint. Also, consumers should be given instructions on the usage of water-based paint and water-based paint should also be used outdoor where possible (Decopaint, 2000: 56).

Finland

In Finland there is an agreement between the paint industry, painters' firms and the association of painters regarding the limitation of VOC contents in indoor paint (Decopaint, 2000: 56).

France

Since 1992 there is a national eco-label which defines limits for the maximum content of VOC. Furthermore, a voluntary agreement between authorities and the paint industry was concluded in 1986 in order to reduce by 25% paint-related emissions of VOC by 1991. VOC contents were reduced by 16.5%, however, consumption increased by 20% in the same period (Decopaint, 2000: 57).

Czech Republic

In the Czech Republic there is a reduced VAT – 5% as opposed to 22% -for paint that is low in VOC. A national eco-label requires paint to be water-based (Decopaint, 2000: 54f.).

USA

Emissions of VOC have been subject to regulations both on state and federal level since the 1970s. Technical guidelines regarding the authorisation of plants that process paint containing solvent were elaborated within the Clean Air Act. Compliance with its emission limits could be achieved by the application of filter installations or by usage of paint with reduced solvent content. In California, a first regulation to limit contents of VOC in paint was enacted as early as 1966.

In 1990 the Clean Air Act was amended in order to include eleven more industrial sectors into authorisation procedures. Furthermore, it was determined to develop a national regulation to limit VOC contents in decorative paint (Bonifant, 1994: 207).

In 1996, the EPA produced a proposal to limit VOC contents in decorative paint. A fee of US$ 0.0028/g VOC to be charged when exceeding the limit was part of this proposal (Decopaint, 2000: 64). Limits to the content of VOC in building paint came into force in September 1999. The passing of a unified national regulation was supported by the industrial association (NPCA, http://www.paint.org/ind_issue/ib_march00.pdf). A group of entrepreneurs attempted to bring down the regulation at court, although without success (Maty, 2000).

There are more far-reaching regulations at state level. Limits have been demanded for Southern California that, by 2006, will be well below the EPA proposal. For California altogether, higher limits than in South California are still valid and it has been decided to tighten them further in between 2001 and 2008 (Decopaint, 2000: 65). Californian product standards are differentiated along product groups containing 300 individual limits for the content of solvents (http://www.uni-duisburg.de/FB7/FG15/documents/VOC-kurzfassung.html, 16/9/2002). Limits were defined in the late 1980s, partially with very long transition periods up to 2000 (http://www.uni-duisburg.de/FB7/FG15/documents/VOC-kurzfassung.html, 16/9/2002; Bower 1991). Other states that have enacted product regulations are Kentucky, Massachusetts, Washington, Oregon, New Jersey and New York. These regulations are partially stricter than federal regulation (NPCA, http: //www.paint.org/ind_issue/ib_march00.pdf). EPA requirements will at best lead to changes in products as paint producers hitherto orientated themselves with respect to stricter obligations of individual states (Vratsanos, 2001).

European Union

The European directive on solvents – discussed since 1990 and in force since 1999 – defines sectors for which member states are obliged to develop implementation plans as well as to monitor and reduce emissions. The directive affects only those sectors which use solvents and products containing solvent in *stationary* installations. These sectors include the printing industry, the distribution of fuels, the chemical industry and a number of paint-processing sectors (Council Directive 1999/13/EC). Within these sectors, a reduction of solvent-consumption by means of substituting conventional paint can be expected as this facilitates implementation regarding the monitoring of emission limits.

According to the European Decopaint study the 1999 European directive on solvents will not contribute to a significant reduction of emissions from paint. This justifies a genuine regulation on decorative paint products as planned by the European Commission (Decopaint, 2000: ii). The directive on solvents exclusively regulates industrial use of solvent. The translation into national law has to follow in several steps by 2007.

Further relevant is the 'National Ceiling Directive' as passed in 2001. This directive defines limits for a number of air pollutants, including VOC, which have to be achieved by 2010 and 2020 respectively. Member states are required to produce reduction programmes elaborating how they will comply with these targets by October 2002. Reports on implementation and compliance are to be submitted to the Commission regularly.

Within the framework of the European eco-label, established in 1992, criteria for decorative paints were developed in 1996, one of which is the content of VOC. Currently (9/2002), 28 companies are participating in the eco-label scheme (http://europa.eu.int/comm/environment/ecolabel/consumers/db_indoorpaint.htm, 10.9. 2002). Compared to the number of 1,300 significant paint producers, this level of participation is hardly meaningful.

Although incentives to develop paint with a low content of VOC have possibly been provided, the European eco-label has failed – according to this study – to bring about a shift in the market. The planned guideline to determine national limits to VOC emissions provides for a framework as well as the necessity for a guideline on products. With the exception of solvent producers, industrial representatives and representatives of national authorities interviewed for this study would appreciate such a guideline. Representatives of dependent sectors lobby for long transition periods (Decopaint, 2000: ii). The edict of a regulation is preferred to other instruments (financial, voluntary, information related) (Decopaint, 2000: iii).

The regulations proposed in the Decopaint study go beyond environmental standards of other countries. However, it is assumed that similar regulations will diffuse internationally and that European companies would then be in a position to exploit their experience with low-VOC paint on non-European markets (Decopaint, 2000: viii).

Members of the European industrial association CEPE have declared a voluntary obligation to reduce VOC contents in paint. 12 groups of products were formed in this respect. Contents of VOC are to be indicated on packaging and to be reduced in two phases of three and six years. The declaration anticipates in particular future EU regulations (Decopaint, 2000: 53).

UN/ECE

Since 1991 national targets for reductions of VOC emissions have been agreed within the framework of the UN/ECE Convention on Long-Range Trans-Boundary Air Pollution. The protocol was signed on 21/11/1991. Most states, including Germany, have pledged to reduce their VOC emissions by 30% by 1999 as compared to 1988 (Rentz et al., 1993). A Task Force led by France and Germany has worked out a concept for reduction of VOC emissions in ECE states (Economic Commission for Europe/VOC Task Force, 1990). Further reductions were agreed on at the 1999 Gothenburg conference. The reduction target was expanded to 40% with 1990 as a new year of reference. Germany has pledged a reduction of 69% by 2010 in the protocol (Umweltbundesamt, 2002). 25 European states, including 13 members of the EU, as well as the USA and Canada, have signed the protocol.

According to the European Commission considerable efforts are necessary to achieve these targets. The Commission has identified two sectors within which reductions would be most cost-effective. These are the coating of motor vehicles and paint consumption both by professional painters and DIY consumers.

9.2.2 Summarised Evaluation of Policy Measures

The analysis of individual measures from various European states, the EU and the USA can be represented as a diffusion curve of individual instruments. It only evaluates product standards that go beyond health and safety regulations, voluntary obligations, eco-taxes on solvent and eco-labels. Subsidies, production standards and health and safety standards need to be excluded from this evaluation. Only roughly half of the countries examined have introduced any of these measures. Given the passing of the EU guideline on solvents and the necessity to translate it into national law as well as the new and far-reaching reduction targets of the UN/ECE protocol, a further diffusion of regulations is to be expected.

As yet, the diffusion process shows a slow increase in countries that have introduced any regulation at all since the mid-1980s. Individual instruments of this regulation feature striking differences: Voluntary obligations have primarily been introduced in the 1980s, since then only one more country has been added. Product labels have seen a strong increase since the early nineties. Taxes, to the contrary, have only been introduced in the recent past. Finally, product regulations are characterised by the lowest increase in the adoption curve. On average, surveyed countries have adopted two of the measures examined.

Fig. 35. Diffusion of product related VOC regulation

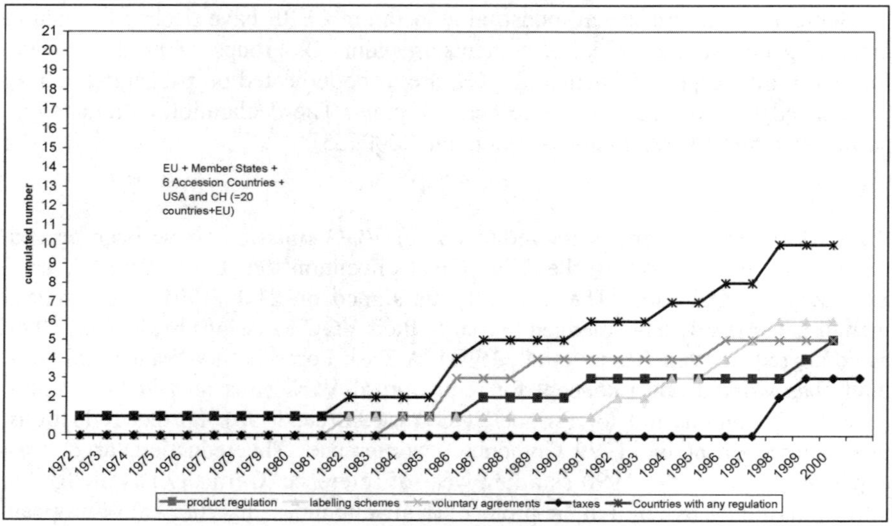

9.3 Effects of Regulations

Referring to the recently passed European guideline on solvents, large paint producers and the European Industrial Association emphasise the availability of paint that is low in VOC. Manufacturers maintain their traditional VOC-based products claiming a lack of consumer demand for environmentally friendly alternatives and the absence of regulations in most countries. Thus, producers fear a loss of market share if they would deliberately give up on present product lines. Henceforth, the European Association of Paint Manufacturers (CEPE) and a number of national paint producers have demanded regulations to limit contents of VOC in decorative paint. The association put forth a proposal in 1996 that defined limits for VOC contents of paint that differ according to areas of consumption. These limits could be tightened yet again in a second phase (CEPE News 1/2001). A regulation could prevent an unlevelled playing field amongst members. Besides, a unified European regulation could facilitate a minimisation of the product range which would increase efficiency and reduce costs (Decopaint, 2000: 37). At the same time, producers of highly specialised niche products with VOC-rich contents point to the indispensability of these products with regard to certain uses (Decopaint, 2000: 37).

In contrast, the European Association of Solvent Producers (ESIG) opposes further regulation of paints. As a result of the proposed guideline on solvents for decorative paint, the association estimates a loss in sales of up to EUR 100 million which would be linked to the loss of 2,000-4,000 jobs out of about 10,000 altogether. However, the Decopaint study concludes that large companies in this sector are able to bear these losses as the solvent business is of minor importance. This notwithstanding, small enterprises would be burdened with a disproportionate share of the costs.

Manufacturers of resin expect that with an additional product regulation it will be necessary to develop new intermediate products which would imply considerable R&D efforts. Given a commonly binding regulation, these costs could be burdened upon paint producers. High research intensity would, however, be advantageous to large companies with the appropriate potential (Decopaint, 2000: 216).

When comparing the countries there is a significant variety in the consumption of substitutes that are solvent-free or low in solvent. However, the data available is not satisfactory in terms of time series. Data regarding production is available for a few years only. Longer time series exist regarding emissions from solvent consumption. This data is provided by the European Environment Agency within its UNECE Task Force Inventories and Projections.

Fig. 36 relates emission data to population to make the data comparable. This shows the biggest reductions in Austria and Germany, albeit from a very high level.

Eurostat provides statistics for the years 1995 to 2000 regarding production quantities, external trade and values grouped according to the following NACE categories:

- 24.30.11.50 and 24.30.11.70 – paint and lacquer dispersed or solved in an aqueous medium
- 24.30.12.25, 24.30.12.30 and 24.30.12.70 – solvent with a content of volatile organic compounds of more than 50%
- 24.30.12.29, 24.30.12.50 and 24.30.12.90 – paint and lacquer dispersed in a non-aqueous medium

The respective NACE categories differ according to the basic substance used. For the evaluation and missing values the various categories have been added up using an interpolated method. The sum of water-based paint and lacquer that was sold in the domestic market was related to products with non-aqueous solvent as well as those with very high contents of solvent. At this, the market shares vary between some 70% and just above 30%. Hence, a lead market cannot be clearly identified.

In the same period external trade with paint based on aqueous media has expanded significantly. The biggest share of the expansion fell on Germany, which at the same time tripled its active trade balance from about EUR 30 million to EUR 90 million. Sweden also recorded a significant expansion in exports.

Fig. 36. VOC emissions from solvent use

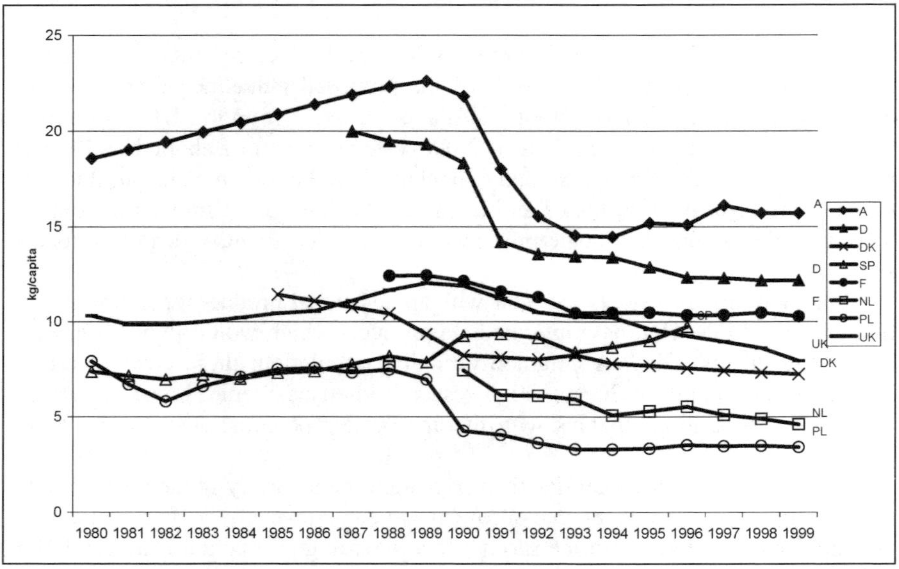

Fig. 37. Market shares of low solvent products

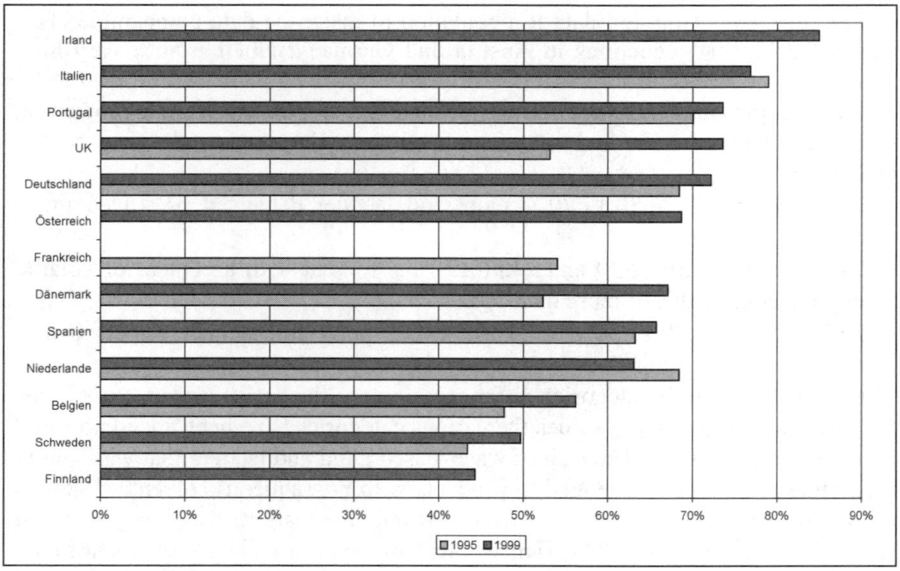

Fig. 38. EU trade balances for paints

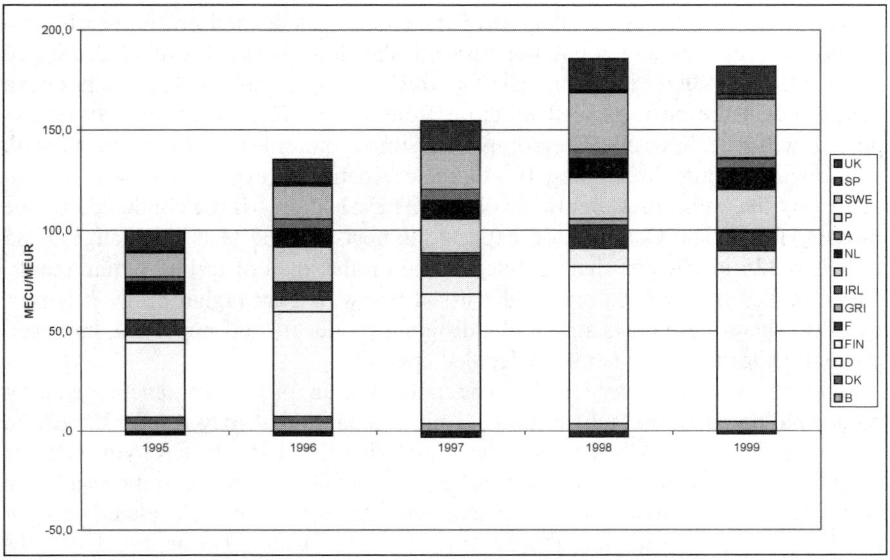

To what extent these expansions in export sales depend on the development of new products or whether the exports are rather traditional paint low in or free of solvents cannot be gathered from these aggregated figures.

9.4 Solvent-Based Paints and the Reformulation of the European Chemical Policy

The current debate on a re-regulation of the European chemical policy is expected to have additional impacts on innovation and the diffusion of environmental technologies and hence also for the production of paints. It is a question open to investigation if the new regulations are likely to increase the costs and therefore lead to disadvantages compared to other regions or vice versa, if the new regulations are likely to stimulate environmental innovations that are marketable also in regions outside the European Union.

The outline of the future European chemical regulation was published in 2001 in the White Book "Strategy for a future chemicals policy" (COM(2001)88 final). In its core the former distinction between new chemicals and existing chemicals is abandoned. Under the current regulation, existing chemicals are those substances that have been marketed already before the enactment of the current regulations in 1982. For these chemicals the requirements to provide data on possible environmental and health effects are far lower compared to the requirements for new chemicals that have to be carefully examined before the marketing is permitted. Regarding both the number and the amount of production the existing chemicals represent by far the larger share of substances yet with insufficient data about possible risks.

The requirements for an analysis of the substances depend on the yearly production figures. The new regulation distinguishes four different levels (>1 t/a; >10 t/a; > 100 t/a; >1,000 t/a). Chemicals for which an encompassing analysis has been conducted in the past, as well as those from which little exposure may be expected, will receive a relief regarding the testing requirements. For chemicals with a production volume exceeding 100 t/a the evaluation of the test data will be conducted by the authorities, below this level the evaluation will be conducted by the industry itself. The Commission expects the costs for the tests in a range of 85 kEUR to 325 kEUR per chemical depending on the level of testing requirements. Other studies that will be briefly discussed below, expect higher costs. It is proposed to share these costs among the different producers and importers, however, procedures for this have not been decided upon.

Substances with a very high toxic potential, in particular cancerogenic or mutagenic potential are subject to a permit procedure that may restrict the use to certain applications. All of theses steps are symbolised in the acronym REACH (registration, evaluation and authorisation of chemicals). The current regulation provides little incentives for the collection and assessment of risk related data for existing chemicals. Although this became obligatory from 1993 on, the data gathering and evaluation was very slow and only for very few chemicals the assessment procedures were actually concluded. This is likely to be different under the planned regulation because if at a certain deadline the assessment is not concluded, a producer will lose the authorisation of production. Compared to the current regulation, the burden of supplying information about possible risks is shifted from the authorities that currently have to prove that a chemical is harmful to justify specific regulatory measures towards the firms that now have to prove that a chemical is harmless in order to keep the permission to produce the substance.

The risk management is based mainly on a preliminary evaluation by the producers which is part of the data that have to be submitted to the authorities and which shall contain recommendations for risk reducing measures. A control of the data and the evaluation will be performed mainly on a random basis.

As opposed to the current regulation the risk evaluation covers only specified applications of the substances. If new applications are developed, data has to be collected and evaluated as well. Unlike previously, this duty is also extended to the professional users of chemicals. They have to provide data on applications to the producers and if they open up new applications they are responsible for the collecting of data and its evaluation as well.

For the existing chemicals that are already on the market, certain deadlines are proposed for the data to be collected. The deadlines depend also on the volume of production and range from 2005 (>1,000t/a) to end of 2012 (>1t/a). This long period should ensure that the necessary time is given to test the chemicals and to avoid a high cost burden at a certain point of time.

Currently, 100,000 registered chemicals exist of which about 90% are actually produced for the market and 30,000 substances exceed the amount of 1 t/y. Out of these, 10,000 chemicals exceed 10 t/y and 2,500 > 1,000 t/y. The authorisation procedure is to be expected for about 1,400 chemicals.

Several studies have been conducted to assess the costs of the new regulatory scheme, which vary considerably in their results and which triggered a fierce public debate on the future chemical policy. Business associations are in opposition to the proposed regulations because they perceive them as implying unbearable costs for the producers and users, in particular for SME. According to business actors, the regulation weakens the competitiveness and the innovativeness of the affected enterprises. The existence of many enterprises is expected to be at risk and likewise the loss of jobs is expected. These economic risks on the one hand are not balanced with the only marginal improvements in the safety of the use of chemicals on the other hand. Several studies have been presented that should provide evidence for the economic drawbacks (CEFIC, 2002, Institute for Health and Environment, 2001, Arthur D. Little, 2002b).

The studies can be distinguished regarding the estimation of the direct costs, that are mainly the costs for the testing of the chemicals and indirect costs that may arise because the production of low volume chemicals may be abandoned and by this, products in later stages of the production chain may be affected as well. It is widely feared that there may occur a large scale substitution by imported products. However, it is not yet decided how the import of substances that are part of a product will be treated.

Estimations of the direct costs differ according to the assumptions about the costs for single testing procedure. They range from 1.4 billion EUR to 20 billion EUR. The European Commission expects 2.1 billion EUR (European Commission, 2001), a study commissioned by DG enterprises and conducted by Risk & Policy Analysts and Statistics Sweden estimates the testing costs with 1.4 – 7 billion EUR with 3.7 billion EUR being the most likely value (Risk and Policy Analysis and Statistics Sweden, 2002). The European business association CEFIC estimates the costs depending on the number of chemicals that fall under the new regulation. In case of 30,000 substances the costs may range between 7-10 billion EUR while in case of 70,000 substances that have to be tested this may 15-20 billion EUR (CEFIC, 2002). A study commissioned by the British Environmental Ministry estimates the testing costs at 8.68 billion EUR. In this study it is questioned if the necessary testing capacities are available until the time limit of 2012 (Institute for Health and Environment, 2001).

It is argued by business associations that a large share of the costs has to be borne by the producers of low volume fine- and speciality chemicals. However, the German Advisory Council on the Environment points out that even for this segment of the sector the share of testing costs on the total turnover ranges between 0.2 and 0.39%, while for the overall sector the share ranges from 0.06% to 0.12% (German Advisory Council on the Environment, 2003). Furthermore, the Council argues that over time learning effects may occur and the costs of testing per chemical is likely to decrease with the accumulation of experience.

The indirect effects arise from the cease of production for chemicals with a high share of testing costs compared to turnover and profit. The study of Arthur D. Little that was commissioned by the German business association BDI develops three different scenarios that vary regarding the testing costs. Even for the modest scenario a decline of gross product by 1.4% is expected for the industry and by 0.4% for the total economy, accompanied by a loss of 150,000 jobs. The most extreme scenario predicts a loss in gross product by 20.2% for the industry and 6.4% for the total economy, and a loss of 2.35 million jobs (Arthur D. Little, 2002b). These effects are calculated for Germany only. The German business associations VCI expects that 20 to 40% of the chemicals with a production <100 t/a may be discontinued, other sources expect that a share of two third of the products of small and medium enterprises may be taken from the market (VCI, 2003; Ahrens, 2002). However, the German Council on the Environment pointed out that these studies do not provide a business as usual scenario and that a considerable number of substances maybe would have been discontinued in any case (German Advisory Council on the Environment, 2003). Furthermore, the Council questions in its evaluation of the ADL study the appropriateness of the methods that are used. The study tends to overestimate negative effects and underestimates, partially even ignores positive effects.

Potentially positive effects may arise in the area of health and safety. A study commissioned by the European Commission estimates the potential savings in the area of health at 18 to 54 billion EUR for a period of 30 years (Risk and Policy Analysis, 2003). A study by Pearce and Koundri (2003) concludes that the savings in the area of health and extended life expectancy exceed the costs of the regulations. It has to be noted, however, that the effects on natural systems, e.g. the preservation of biodiversity can hardly be depicted in economic models. Therefore, additional positive effects may be taken into account.

The effects of the future policy on innovations are difficult to predict. It has been argued that already today the innovativeness of European chemical companies is lower compared to the level of innovation in the USA and Japan due to the higher requirements of chemical testing (Fleischer et al., 2000). The new requirements even imply an additional burden by extending the testing requirements on existing chemicals, therefore additional disadvantages may be expected (Ahrens, 2002). The study of Fleischer et al. has been criticised regarding their choice of indicators and because recent trends in the registering of new chemicals have not been considered sufficiently (German Advisory Council on the Environment, 2003 with additional references; Nordbeck and Faust, 2002). Apart from the negative effects that arise from additional testing costs there are positive effects that may occur. The current regulatory framework treats new chemicals much stricter than existing chemicals. It is only for new chemicals that extensive testing procedures are required. Therefore incentives were given that existing chemicals were used and recombined for new applications. The proposed new scheme lowers the costs for testing new chemicals, provides an equal burden to existing chemicals and thereby relocates the testing burden in favour of new chemicals. Compared to USA and Japan where existing chemicals are privileged in the same way as in the current European regulation, additional incentives for innovation are likely to arise.

Several studies stress that the need of a long-term and strict regulation of chemicals directs the innovation activities towards environmentally friendly substitutes (Jacob, 1999, Stevens, 2000, German Advisory Council on the Environment, 2003 with additional references). The proposed regulation has a transition period of more than ten years that is likely to give room for the adaptation to the new requirements and to develop environmentally friendly alternatives. Furthermore, environmental regulation may safeguard the marketing of environmental innovations; therefore they provide additional incentives for innovators. However, the new regulation provides only little substantial direction for potential innovators. It is only the high volume and high risk chemicals that fall under the requirements of authorisation which provides substantial objectives, while apart from this only procedural matters are regulated and the actual results of the testing and evaluation cannot be anticipated. It has not yet been decided if there will be a general obligation for substitution if alternatives are available or if the authorisation procedure just leads to certain requirements regarding the processing of these substances. Furthermore, the list of chemicals with high concern has not been decided upon, yet.

Under the current regulatory regime the development and the marketing of new chemicals in general only took place in large companies that disposed over the necessary resources for development, testing and registration. The proposed new regulation may provide opportunities for the development of new chemicals also for small and medium-sized companies because of the elimination of testing requirements for low volume chemicals and the lesser requirements for small and medium volume chemicals. This may level out at least partially the perceived disadvantages of producers of low volume chemicals. However, the innovativeness of SME depends on other influencing factors as well.

The influence of regulation on competitiveness depends on comparable market conditions in foreign countries. As mentioned above, the European Union is a front-runner in reformulating the chemical policy. Unlike the current regulation in the industrialised countries the distinction between existing and new chemicals is planned to be abandoned. This has also implications for the international trade with chemicals. Imported chemicals have to be tested in the same way as chemicals produced in Europe. Up to now it is not clear how to treat chemicals that are part of a product that is imported. Since the European Union constitutes the worldwide largest single market for chemicals it is unlikely that this border adjustment may lead to a withdrawal of imports to the European market unless the testing costs exceed the profit which may be gained from substances that are produced in the European Union as well.

If the European legislation will prove that an encompassing testing and evaluation is practicable and does not lead to major economic drawbacks it is likely that foreign countries follow this example and adjust their chemical regulations accordingly. Regarding the export of chemicals European producers may even gain advantages through the regulation: They may offer products that are permitted on the market with the strictest environmental requirements. If foreign countries follow the European example the European producers may have a first mover advantage in offering well tested chemicals.

But even if the regulation does not diffuse to countries outside Europe it is likely that the European regime will have a considerable impact in other countries because of *complementary* regulations. The European regulation gives strong incentives for an encompassing collection of information about possible risks of chemicals. If an assessment is not provided to the authorities the substance concerned must not be produced after a fixed deadline anymore. In other countries, with the US as the most prominent example, liability rules are of greater importance than the European regulation. Generally, liability rules provide incentives that no additional information about the risks of a chemical are collected, because if it is proven in a law suit that a firm may have had knowledge about harmful effects it may be condemned to pay compensation. In case the European risk assessments on chemicals are publicly available an American firm may not ignore this information without running the risk of high compensation payments. This may explain the high level opposition of the American chemicals industry association and even the State Department against the planned European regulation which is, however, substantiated with the feared testing costs for the importers of chemicals. Such a complementary effect may give a strong incentive to harmonise the chemical regulation because at best there may develop a competition in uncovering possible harmful effects.

Table 15 provides a summarised evaluation of the possible effects on innovation and competitiveness of European firms.

Table 15. Effects of REACH on innovation and competitiveness

Issues	Negative effects	Positive effects
Testing costs	Additional testing costs absorbs R&D capacities	Lowering of costs for testing of new chemicals Dismissal of testing requirements for low production chemicals
Long term objectives	Lack of substantial targets for new chemicals except for those falling under the authorisation procedure	Potentially safeguarding of markets for environmental friendly substitutes; long term regulation allows for early adaptation
Treatment of existing versus new chemicals	-	Equal treatment of existing and new chemicals
Testing costs	Testing costs cannot be imposed to foreign firms (unless they import their chemicals to the EU)	-
Market effects	Chemicals used as intermediates or as part of final product may be privileged (depending on the border adjustment)	Label "Chemicals tested under REACH" may be advantageous in foreign markets
Diffusion of regulation	-	Likely if European regulation proves its feasibility
Complementary regulation	-	Negative testing results will have immediate impacts in countries with liability rules

The influence of the new regulatory regime on paints with low solvents remains difficult to assess. As for solvents these are typically chemicals with a large production volume of more than 1,000 tons/year. Therefore, a detailed risk assessment has to be produced at an early point of time. The direct costs for testing will remain low compared to the total turnover that is achieved with these substances. For the same reason it is not very likely that the European production is substituted by imports on a large scale. Furthermore, imported solvents are required to produce the same testing data. It is unlikely that solvents will be in the group of chemicals with high concern since these are mainly CMR chemicals, and the use as solvent open to the environment would be prohibited already today. The same holds true for chemicals used for the production of low solvent paints as far as they are produced in large quantities. However, paints do contain also a great variety of additives that are produced in small quantities only. It is argued that the direct testing costs may exceed the profit that can be achieved by the production of small quantities of chemicals and therefore the producers may cease the production. In this case there might be a substitution by imports of ready made paints and hence a loss in market shares for the European producers. This depends, however, on the design of the border adjustment: If chemicals that are part of a final product have to be tested in the same way, the importers of paints will have to bear the same costs.

The current R&D efforts in the development of low solvent products are likely to profit from the lowering of testing requirements for new chemicals and for those substances that are produced in very low volume. By this, it can be expected that new chemicals are more often used in the production of paints. This is likely to open up market opportunities also in non-European countries.

Finally, chemicals that are used in the production of paints for which the testing reveals some adverse properties are likely to come under pressure also in non-European countries. This may be due to a loss in export opportunities or due to liability rules in the respective countries. On the other hand, chemicals that have proven their harmlessness and that received the label of being tested under REACH are likely to have an advantage also in foreign countries.

To what extent these effects on innovation and competitiveness apply for paints with low solvent depends on (1) the results of the testing procedures and (2) on the final design of the new regulation, in particular in respect of the border adjustment and in respect of the measures that have to be taken for chemicals with adverse properties. The shift of testing requirements in favour of new chemicals and to the disadvantage of existing chemicals is likely to stimulate innovations that are able to find markets also in non-EU countries.

10 Potentials for Substituting Paper by Electronic Media

10.1 Introduction

Paper consumption and production cause a variety of environmental pressures. They range from soil erosion and species loss to air and water pollution – among others through various highly toxic compounds – and a variety of problems associated with dumping or incinerating waste paper. The production and consumption of paper also involves many transportation activities.

The average annual growth rate of global paper consumption is of an order of magnitude of 3% (Source of data unless stated otherwise: FAO Forestry Statistics http://apps.fao.org). In Western Europe – where per capita consumption is about three times as high as the worldwide average of 55 kg per year but still only slightly more than half as high as in the US (van den Reek, 1999) – the corresponding rate of growth is slightly lower (about 2,8%). For the foreseeable future further increases at similar rates are expected.

Total paper consumption can be divided into graphical papers (42% of total paper consumption), packaging papers and paperboard, household and sanitary papers (tissues) and others such as filter papers. Graphical papers comprise newsprint (about 30% of graphical papers) and writing and printing papers. In Western Europe the share of graphical papers is approximately half of total paper consumption.

The consumption of newsprint increases at annual rates of some 2% globally, the corresponding rate for writing and printing paper is 3.5%. In Western Europe the rate of increase is 2.5% for newsprint and 3.1% for writing and printing papers.

National peculiarities play a role for paper consumption as is revealed by differences in specific paper consumption (paper consumption per unit of gross domestic product (GDP)) in different countries (van den Reek, 1999). The highest specific consumption of newsprint in Western Europe is found in UK (1.7 kg per 1,000 EUR of GDP), compared to values of around 0.5 kg per 1,000 EUR of GDP in France and Italy. For writing and printing papers the United Kingdom has the highest specific consumption as well (5.1 kg per 1,000 EUR of GDP) compared to 3 kg in Italy and 3.7 kg in Germany.

The increase in paper consumption could be reduced in some areas of application through the use of emerging electronic media. The present chapter investigates the markets for some of these technologies in order to identify the mechanisms of their international diffusion. In particular, we apply the lead market concept to see which conditions determine an early adoption and a subsequent international diffusion of technologies with potentials for substituting paper (henceforth: paper saving technologies).

In the past, increases in paper consumption have at least partly cancelled out reductions of specific environmental pressures, therefore technologies which have a potential for substituting paper are clearly relevant from the point of view of sustainability. In particular, it could be hoped that developing countries, when their incomes rise, avoid some of the increase in paper consumption that industrial countries experienced in the past. Innovations in this field are not driven by environmental concerns, however. Thus the present case study constitutes an example of sustainability innovations the adoption of which is almost exclusively motivated by private economic incentives.

In the remainder of this chapter we proceed as follows: In section 10.2 we demonstrate the potentials for substituting paper applications through electronic media. In section 10.3 we describe the cluster of relevant technologies and characterise the markets for these technologies. Section 10.4 describes policies which promote the development and diffusion of these technologies. In section 10.5 we summarise the motives and conditions for the early adoption and international diffusion, focusing on the factors emphasised by the lead market concept. Section 10.6 concludes and points out consequences for policy.

10.2 Potentials for Substituting Graphical Papers Through Electronic Media

Applications of graphical papers can be substituted for by the use of electronic media. Even today, most information does not have to be printed on paper for documentation purposes any more. Electronic media also allow to select a subset of information to be printed on paper for easy reading. In future, new technologies will evolve which allow reading from screens almost equivalent to paper sheets. The application of paper for some legal purposes which still prevails may become obsolete as electronic signatures become more wide-spread.

Even with the emergence of new technologies, worldwide consumption of graphical papers will increase at rates of some 2% annually in the foreseeable future. A study (BCG 1999) estimates that in 2003 some 5.2 million tons of paper are substituted for by electronic media. Compared to a status-quo scenario – i.e. one in which electronic media with a potential to substitute for paper do not diffuse further – the consumption of graphical papers would thus be reduced by some 5%.

The rate at which paper is substituted for by electronic media is determined firstly by their rate of diffusion to the demographic groups which traditionally use paper products. It is secondly determined by the likelihood that users switch from paper applications to electronic media. This likelihood depends on whether electronic media offer lower costs or higher user value on the one hand and on the importance of traditional reading habits on the other. Therefore different applications of graphical papers are subject to substitution to different degrees.

Table 16 shows expected short term substitution effects for different paper applications. Paper directories – because of the significantly lower cost and the higher user value of electronic media, resulting from their timeliness and their capacity to search, select and link information – are most likely to be substituted for. However, this results in a small reduction of paper consumption only, as directories account for a small share of the consumption of graphical papers. The same is true for catalogues and books. Electronic catalogues offer the same cost and user advantages as electronic directories, however, internet access has not yet as widely diffused to the traditional users of catalogues. In the case of many books, traditional reading habits prevent readers from shifting to electronic media, although this is not the case for information oriented books such as encyclopaedias.

Table 16. Substitution of paper applications (million tons)

	Demand 1996	Forecasted demand 2003		Substitution effects	
		Without substitution	With substitution		
Newspapers	28.5	27.7	25.7	-2.0	-7
Magazines	13.8	15.6	14.6	-1.0	-6
Catalogues	5.7	7.3	6.6	-0.7	-10
Books	4.2	4.9	4.5	-0.4	-8
Directories	2.2	2.5	2.0	-0.5	-20
Total	54.4	58.0	53.4	-4.6	-8

Newspapers including indirect effects (through reduced revenues from advertising) of -0.4 million tons.
Source: The Boston Consulting Group, 1999- Exhibit 8, 10-14.

Although in the short run the percentage at which paper versions are substituted for is rather low for newspapers and magazines, the amount of paper saved is significant because of the high share of newspapers and magazines in the demand for graphical papers. The substitution will concern traditional newspapers, in particular nationals, and free-sheets more than locals and tabloids. Professional magazines are more strongly affected than consumer magazines. An indirect dampening effect could arise if classified advertisements are shifted to the internet, thus undermining the economic foundations of newspapers. Since the mid-eighties the circulation of newspapers is decreasing in Europe as well as in the US. The main reason seems to be a decreasing interest of young people in printed news and their increasing interest in new media instead. Competition from electronic media is also made responsible for decreased sales of magazines while the number of magazines and their volume increases.

Independently of the substitution of paper applications through electronic media, a strong increase in the consumption of office papers is to be expected. Their largest sub-segment – cut-size paper – grows at rates of 6% annually (van den Reek, 1999;The Boston Consulting Group, 1999). This trend is accelerated by the substitution of some paper applications. An ever increasing amount of information which is received via electronic media is printed on personal printers. The ease of electronic storage even supports the inclination to print documents several times instead of storing them in paper versions. On the other hand, however, electronic media also allow a very easy pre-selection of a relevant subset of information which is then to be printed.

The BCG-study reckons that in the near future only 30% of the information previously acquired on paper will be received via electronic media. If half of this information is printed, some of it even multiple times, the increase in cut-size paper will be just 17% of the amount saved of other graphical papers.

However, the rate of substitution of cut-size papers for other graphical papers crucially depends on the amount of information contained in different paper applications. One study (Göttsching 1999, quoted by van den Reek, 1999) makes the extreme assumption that one kilogram of cut-size paper holds 1 MB of Information while the same amount of newsprint contains 10 MB.

The view that electronic media offer significant potentials for a reduction of the growth rate of paper consumption is confirmed by several other studies. A study (European Commission DG XIII/E, 1996) estimated that within a six year period a share of 5 to 15% of the printing market would be covered by electronic media. Just one application of electronic media, printing on demand (POD), could reduce the consumption of graphical papers by 6% within a 20 year period, by reducing overprint which for books amounts to 35 to 50% (van den Reek, 1999). Another application, email, if it substitutes half of all the information now contained on business papers within the next 20 years and if 10% of it is printed, will result in a reduction of the consumption of graphical papers by 4% (van den Reek, 1999).

10.3 Technologies and Applications and Their Diffusion

Potentials to substitute for paper arise because electronic media permit to select a subset of electronically coded information before it is printed on paper for documentation or reading. Some of the remaining functions of paper may soon be taken over by new electronic media thus expanding the substitution potentials. As electronic media diffuse, they will communicate among each other more frequently, thus promoting paper substitution.

A great variety of electronic media jointly determine the potentials to substitute for paper. This cluster of technologies comprises hard- and software components as well as rules and standards. It is not always evident if they compete with or complement each other; frequently "old" technologies which are well developed and have broadly diffused are combined in new applications with technologies which are just being introduced. Thus the technologies considered in this section will generally not be regarded from the perspective of competing innovation designs.

10.3.1 Cross-Section Technologies and Applications

Paper saving technologies will substitute paper applications in enterprises and in households. Besides technologies related rather to businesses or consumers, there are cross-section technologies supporting both, paper substitution in offices and at home.

10.3.1.1 Information and Communication Technologies

Information and communication technologies (ICT) constitute the basis for the potentials to substitute for paper. They comprise telecommunication services, other ICT services, hard- and software. ICT markets make up for a share of gross domestic product (GDP) of 10% in Japan and of 8% each in Germany and the US (OECD, 2002b). Software accounts for less than 10% of ICT markets on average, this segment is the fastest growing, though (16% annually). The software market has a higher share of all ICT markets in the US than in Germany, in Japan its share is smaller than in the two other countries. Among all firms in the ICT sector, software companies have the highest R&D intensity; patents for software account for 4 to 10% of all patents, depending on the method of measurement.

Among the world's top 50 ICT firms 26 are based in the US, accounting for 47% of revenues (OECD, 2002b: 62 f.). 12 of the top 50 ICT firms are based in Japan with a share of revenues of 31%. Germany has two firms among the top 50 (Siemens, ranking 4th, and Deutsche Telekom, ranking 17th). Of the 26 US firms, five are electronics and component manufacturers, another five produce ICT equipment and systems; 13 of the US based firms provide telecommunication and ICT services or software. Of the 12 top Japanese firms 7 provide electronics and components, 3 make ICT equipment and systems and the remaining two provide services. The top 10 ICT services firms are based in the US except for one which is partly based in France (Cap Gemini Ernst and Young, ranking 10th among ICT services firms). Of the top 10 software firms two are based outside the US: SAP in Germany (3rd among software companies) and Softbank in Japan (5th).

The demand for ICT is partly reflected in figures about internet use (see below). Additional hints are contained in statistics on ICT investment. In 2000 the share of ICT investment in total non-residential investment was roughly 15% in Germany and in Japan (data for Japan for 1999), while it was 30% in the US (OECD, 2002b: 22). Compared to Japan, a much higher share of German ICT investment was in software, while Japan invested more heavily in communications equipment; the US allocated an even higher share of its ICT investment to software.

10.3.1.2 The Internet

A prerequisite for a pre-selection of information is the ready availability of this information in digital form and the easy access to this information. The internet provides easy access to a vast amount of digital information for a very large number of people. From the perspective of expected reductions of paper consumption the online availability of newspapers and magazines is of particular importance. On the access side not only the share of the population connected to the web is relevant but also its demographic composition.

Online Offers

The supply of information on the internet increases rapidly. From 1997 to 2000 the number of internet hosts has at least doubled in all countries for which data are available (OECD, 2002b). In the US which have the largest number of internet hosts in relation to their population the number increased by 300%. In Germany the increase was 270%, but in relation to the population the number of internet hosts is small compared to the US or to the Scandinavian countries.

Nearly all publishing houses offer electronic versions of their newspapers and magazines besides their printed versions. The Spiegel Online magazine reports 34 million contacts per month. Although no large revenues are collected from electronic papers, two thirds of the German publishing houses reported a balanced cost-revenue situation for their electronic products in a survey (Shaker Verlag, 2002).

More recently the tendency has increased to request payment for content on the internet. Examples are financial information or test reports. Some newspapers charge for their online versions. Several publishers offer access to their archives for fees. As the trend to paid content gains momentum so that customers would have to pay twice – one can expect that electronic information may be actually substituted for printed information instead of being used as a supplement only.

Internet Access and Use

Time series of the shares of population which have access to or actually use the internet have to be collected from different sources the comparability of which is restricted.[22] Internet use is closely correlated to the availability of personal computers (PC) (Köllinger, 2003). The diffusion of PC differs considerably in different countries. The diffusion ratio (the number of PC in relation to the population) was 39% in the US compared to 16% in the European Union in the mid-1990s. Within Europe the Netherlands had a ratio of 24% while Spain had one of 9% only. Countries where PC had widely spread also had a high share of PC connected to the internet. In Europe this share was some 30% compared to over 40% in the US in 1996.

Among the countries compared in Table 17, Sweden has the highest share of population with internet access, even ahead of the US, while Germany has the lowest access ratio. In Japan internet access is ahead of that in Germany but behind that in the US. Japan is, however, the leading nation with respect to the use of mobile internet access, more people are using mobile access than fixed line connections. The number of i-mode customers increased to 20 million persons by February 2001 (more than 15% of the population).

---

22 An overview of the sources of information can be found in Table A-1 in Blazejczak and Edler, (2003).

Table 17. Share of population with internet access in %

							Change in percentage points	
	1997	1998	1999	2000	2001	2002	2001/1997	2002/1997
Finland	20.4	27.9	38.1	43.9	na	51.9		31.5
Germany	4.7	8.7	15.0	29.0	34.5	38.9		34.2
Japan	8.0	11.1	15.5	37.2	40.4	na	32.4	
Sweden	21.3	33.0	44.3	56.4	63.6	67.8		46.5
USA	21.0	27.8	39.4	59.9	59.8	59.1		38.1

Last available month in each year.
Sources: Table A-1 in Blazejczak and Edler, 2003.

The German Institute for Economic Research (Köllinger, 2003) reckons that in early 2003 nearly 39 million people in Germany were using the internet, corresponding to some 47% of the population.[23] Based on a diffusion model explicitly accounting for network effects (Bass, 1969) the trend describing the number of new users is estimated to have peaked in 2000 and to level off by 2008, resulting in the typical S-shaped penetration curve. Thus, the number of internet users in Germany is forecasted to increase much slower in future and to reach a limit of some 48 million persons, equivalent to 59% of the population or almost 90% of the 15 to 64-year old (Fig. 39).

The estimate is based on the assumption that internet use is closely related to the use of PC. The complexity of this technology is assumed to limit the potential number of users to younger, formally well educated persons. If, however, alternative easy to handle access technologies become available, this limit needs not to be binding.

A comprehensive assessment of the "networked readiness" of different countries is presented by the World Economic Forum (World Economic Forum, 2003). It is based on a wide range of variables covering market and political environments, regulatory frameworks, infrastructure and usage of ICT as well as indicators of personal, business and government readiness. By the Networked Readiness Index (NRI) the United States hold the second position while Germany ranks 10th. The most "networked ready" country is Finland; other Nordic countries also rank on top positions. The UK is ahead of Germany (7th position), while France follows behind (19th). Japan occupies the 20th rank. Japan has a poor performance of the political/regulatory environment contrasted to a high ranking with respect to infrastructure due to its competitive and cheap broadband services. With respect to individual usage Japan ranks 6th ahead of the US (7th) and Germany (17th) while it lags behind in business usage (Germany 1st, US 3rd, Japan 23rd) and government usage (US 6th, Germany 20th, Japan 41st).

23 Differences to the figures in table 17 are due to different definitions and delimitations. See Köllinger, 2003: 481 and Blazejczak and Edler, 2003, table A-1.

Fig. 39. Number of internet users in Germany

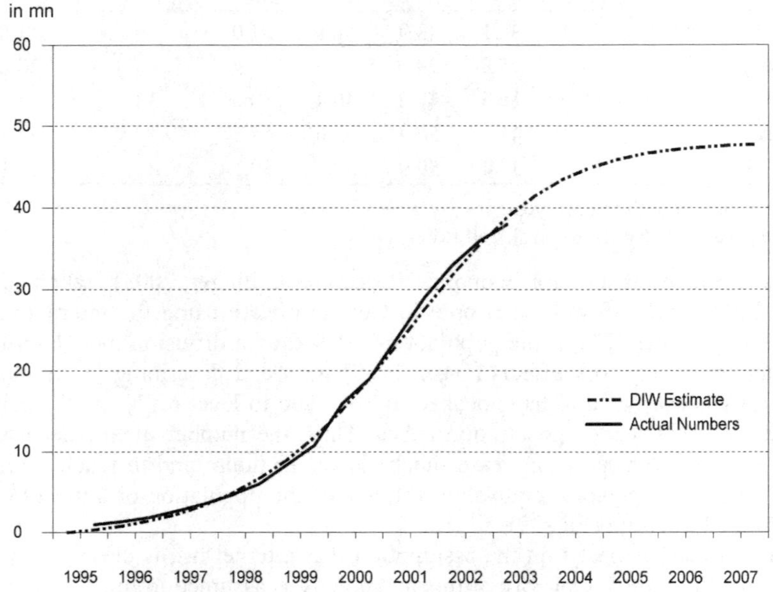

Sources: Ferderal Statistical Office; Nielsen NetRatings; GfK-Online-Monitor; Calculations by DIW Berlin.

DIW Berlin

The population using the internet significantly differs from overall population by age, education, income and sex (for details see Blazejczak and Edler, 2003).

- The internet is used primarily by young people.
- Persons with higher formal education are more likely to be online.
- The probability that a person uses the internet increases with household income.
- With the notable exception of the US more men than women use the internet.

In part, the number of new users increases more rapidly for those groups in which internet users are still underrepresented.[24] This results in the structure of internet users corresponding more closely to the overall population. However, there may remain a group of less educated persons without internet access at least as long as simply to operate, inexpensive alternative access technologies are not available.

For the US a detailed account of online activities is available (OECD, 2002b: 197). The three activities in which the highest shares of internet users are involved, are potentially paper saving: e-mail (84% of internet users), production/service information search (67%), and news, weather, sports (62%). Other, traditionally paper intensive activities, in which internet users are involved to a

24 GfK (quoted according to www.absatzwirtschaft.de).

lesser share, are e.g. product/service purchases (39%), government services search (31%), and online banking (18%).

The BCG-study (1999) has evaluated the correspondence between the demographic structure of internet users and of users of various paper applications. The correspondence is regarded as high for professional journals and non-fiction books. For tabloids, children's books, supplements and direct mail it is judged to be low; for other paper applications it is in between these extremes.

10.3.2 Business-Related Technologies and Applications

10.3.2.1 Electronic Document and Form Management

Electronic document and form management can be viewed as part of the broader movement to business process automation, relating not only to enterprises but to government agencies and non-profit organisations as well. It is estimated that companies currently process 80% of their forms and documents manually (Cardiff, 2002). For the US, the annual costs for processing paper documents are estimated to be above 350 billion US$; processing a single paper document costs 30 to 165 US$ (Gates, 1999: 51). For printed forms over 22 billion US$ are spent annually.

Electronic document and form management technologies have a potential to save paper as electronically generated documents and forms are stored, retrieved, processed and distributed electronically without copying the information on paper.

Technologies essential to this process include – in addition to internet technologies – document management systems and electronic signatures. The diffusion of these technologies is primarily driven by the objectives of higher productivity and improved service quality while lowering expenditures for materials like paper plays a lesser role.

10.3.2.2 Document Management Systems

Document Management Systems (DMS) are programs which permit an integrated administration – i.e. storage, retrieval and processing – of heterogeneous documents including graphics, active documents (e.g. spreadsheets) and multimedia applications. For this purpose DMS integrate a variety of technologies including text management, imaging, navigation, multimedia, forms processing and workflow management.

DMS have been applied since about 1980. Since around 1990 a hybrid data management concept has been generally applied supplementing the original object orientation by relational and associative capabilities. Advanced DMS also allow to administer the programs by which the documents have been generated and contain workflow components. Currently DMS are developing towards Knowledge Management Systems (KMS) which process digital information for the support of decision processes.

DMS store documents either as non-coded information (NCI), i.e. as an image, or as coded information (CI). CI documents have a much higher potential to save paper, as they can be searched and retrieved electronically according to their content and be electronically modified and processed. As more documents are generated on computers and mailed electronically their share increases. The content of NCI-documents can be made electronically accessible by optical character recognition (OCR-) software.

The adoption of DMS is motivated by cost savings mainly trough reduced time for retrieval, handling, copying and distribution of documents as well as reduced need for storage space. Also, the same degree of data security can be achieved at lower costs than for paper archives. Paper savings are significant only for some businesses with mass distribution of documents such as banks or insurance companies. The introduction of DMS is frequently associated with an overall optimisation of business processes resulting in productivity increases which often exceed direct cost savings.

The potentials of DMS to provide opportunities to substitute for paper depend on the development of several other technologies. Concerning hardware, increased speed of processors and storage capacities as well as advanced displays are crucial. On the software side the capabilities of OCR software and the integration of application software and communication systems are essential. For embedding DMS into computer networks differentiated access and encryption technologies need to be further developed. The – exclusively – electronic generation and management of documents and forms can be promoted by the adoption of open standards such as XML and PDF. Finally, legal and regulatory changes which treat electronic documents equivalent to hand signed paper ones will further extend substitution potentials.

DMS markets comprise soft- and hardware as well as services segments; system suppliers integrate these segments. The markets for DMS are dominated by US suppliers. Large international companies are increasingly entering this market; among them US-based firms such as IBM and Microsoft as well as non-US firms like SAP and Canon (Concord Equity Research, 2002). In Germany some 200 suppliers can be identified; German suppliers have a rather strong position in the international market for electronic archiving systems (Kampffmeyer, 2002: 7). In the emerging KMS market newly founded US firms are leading besides Microsoft and Lotus (Kampffmeyer, 2002: 15).

Around electronic document and form management a great variety of services has originated. Their importance can be demonstrated by two examples. Cardiff Software, founded in 1991, with its main office in Vista, CA, and some 15 branches in the US and other countries, is a leading supplier of software and services for forms and document based business processes. The company offers programs which allow the design of forms, their electronic publishing or mailing and their evaluation, including programs to transfer information from printed forms into digital representations. In part, the innovations of the company are protected by patents. Cardiff co-operates in strategic alliances with a number of hardware and software suppliers. Among Cardiff's 20,000 customers are small as well as large enterprises, public administrations as well as academic and other non-profit institutions. In Tokyo, Japan, Zetta Technology Inc. develops programs primarily for public administrations to create forms and store and process information. The company focuses on links of their programs to workflow components and B2B applications. Primary objectives of their programs are reduced manpower and improved data quality; paper savings are not an explicit aim.

Data on the diffusion of electronic document and form management systems are not readily available. The motives that drive adoption as well as obstacles to diffusion can be demonstrated by the examples of the Tokyo Marine Group. This company with its headquarters in Tokyo, Japan, is a large insurance company employing some 14,000 persons. Its paper consumption amounted to 7,440 tons in 2000, representing costs of 1.7 billion yen which was only slightly less than costs for electricity (2.3 billion yen). Two third of paper consumption are forms, 23% are computer printouts and the remaining 12% are copies. Compared to 1997, paper consumption has been reduced by 225 tons due to a variety of measures. They included standardisation of forms, directing computer output to CD-ROM and the utilisation of the LAN for the distribution of internal manuals. In addition, double-sided copying and printing is promoted e.g. by registering the share of double-sided copies at each copier. In 2000 the company-wide target of 55% double sided printouts was achieved; for subsequent years targets individually adjusted for each department were formulated. By consent of the tax authorities certain documents can now be stored electronically, saving some 700,000 sheets of paper annually. Another 100,000 sheets of paper per year were saved by converting 40 internal forms to electronic format. In the long run it is intended to reduce the number of forms first to half, then to 20%. Legal requirements still demand to conduct large parts of the correspondence with customers in paper form.

Other large Japanese companies also make large efforts to reduce their paper consumption. Koyo Seiko, an international producer of automobile parts and mechatronic equipment planned to reduce its paper consumption of 1997 by 40%, most of it (35%) having already been achieved by 2001. To reduce the consumption of copying paper, the companies emphasises electronic data exchange and workflow systems. Computer printouts are to be saved by digital storage or even renunciation of certain reports. To implement the paper reduction objective the company has set up Paper Usage Environmental Subcommittees in each establishment.

10.3.2.3 Electronic Signatures

For written communication – in e-commerce, public administration, and personal interaction – it is frequently essential that the sender of a document can be identified and that the content of the document can be verified. In the "paper world" seals, letter-heads, and – primarily – manual signatures serve these purposes. To substitute paper in these applications, equivalent electronic alternatives need to be available which reach a similar degree of acceptance.

Electronic signatures – in a general sense, according to ISO-standards – are technologies which ensure the authenticity and integrity of electronic data. The

German law (Signaturgesetz 1997 und -verordnung) originally defined electronic signatures in a narrower sense as a particular technology: the combination of a private key to sign documents and of a certified public key to test the signature; the certification serves to relate the electronic key to natural persons. The new law (Signaturgesetz 2000) adopts the broader, technologically neutral definition of the European directive of 1999 of electronic signatures as all possible alternatives to manual signatures. The European directive also defines Advanced Electronic Signatures and Qualified Electronic Signatures. Advanced Electronic Signatures have to

- be attributable exclusively to the issuer;
- allow to identify the issuer;
- be generated by means under the sole control of the issuer;
- be linked to the data in a way that allows to identify later changes.

Procedures to guaranty these features are specified in appendices to the European directive. Qualified Electronic Signatures have to be constructed according to these procedures and be certified by independent agencies.

The European directive has been implemented by the member states in different way, resulting in some divergence concerning the legal status of electronic signatures and the regulation of certification (for details see Langenbach and Ulrich, 2002). The German law is rather detailed and restrictive with respect to the legal acceptance of electronic signatures, whereas countries such as the UK and France in principle treat manual and electronic signatures equivalently. A particularity in Finland is its experiment with digital identity cards which can be used to issue electronic signatures. Concerning certification services Germany and some other European countries introduced public supervision while other countries, e.g. the UK and France, rely on self regulation.

In Germany the electronic storage of data is regulated by a number of laws (Handelsgesetzbuch, Zivilprozessordnung, Abgabenordnung, Grundsätze ordnungsgemäßer Speicherbuchführung); for personal data specific rules (Bundesdatenschutzgesetz) apply. Except for a few documents (e.g. opening balance sheets, annual accounts, customs declaration), an exclusively electronic storage of documents is permitted if certain basic conditions (e.g. complete and unchanged storage for the legally required periods) are made sure. Certain documents, e.g. freight documents must be reproducible as an image. Differently from the UK and the US, the value as a proof of electronically stored documents is lower than for manually signed paper documents in Germany. It is expected that the development of electronic signatures will abandon this imbalance.

10.3.2.4 Electronic Services

The electronic execution of business-to-business processes offers a number of potentials for paper savings. This can be illustrated by the example of the services offered by the Japan Quality Assurance Association (JQA) which – with a staff of 800 – conducts quality controls. As an innovative product JQA offers a web based environmental auditing system for small and medium size companies; the system has been implemented for some 60 metal bashing firms and is planned to be realised for foundries.

The system has been developed in cooperation with a systems supplier (NEC), a consulting firm (Deloitte Tohmatsu) and the business association of Japanese metal bashing companies (JMBA). It consists of a number of check-lists based on standard office software which can be adjusted according to the specifics of individual companies. Participating firms can use these lists to set up a data bank which forms the core of an environmental management system. Part of the information is accessible by JQA for auditing.

The web-based auditing process – compared to traditional on-site procedures – saves considerable amounts of paper. This is not an explicit objective, but rather a side effect. The primary objective are cost savings through economies of scale; depending on the number of participating enterprises, cost savings amount to 50 to 90%, simultaneously the time required for the audit is reduced from one year to about four months.

10.3.3 Consumer-Oriented Technologies and Applications

10.3.3.1 E-Books

E-books are devices specifically designed to make digitally coded books, journals and newspapers accessible to readers on a screen. They are intended to offer an ease of reading at last as good as paper issues. At the same time they offer additional functions, e.g. search, links, tags and comments. E-books can combine texts with other media such as sound and pictures. Contents of e-books can also be easily updated. E-books also provide opportunities for new organisational arrangements; e.g. e-book content rented from libraries could loose its readability at a specified date thus eliminating the need for a return.

If e-books would become widely accepted, they would obviously have a large potential to save paper. In order to access the chances and obstacles for their further diffusion, it makes sense to distinguish between the hardware or platform technology (basically the reading devices) and the software, consisting of reading and library administration programs.

The platform technology of e-books can be either mono-functional devices (e-books in a narrower sense) or multi-functional mobile devices such as Personal Digital Assistants (PDA), Tablet PC or Notebooks. The market for mono-functional devices is dominated by a US firm (Gemstar) which basically provides content according to the dominating Open E-Book (OEB) standard. Recently, multi-functional readers, in particular PDA, have become more important. A number of large US and Japanese firms are offering PDA with capabilities to display e-books, including Compaq, HP, Palm, Casio and Sony. It is expected that in future Tablet PC will be of significance for the diffusion of e-books. Tablet PC resemble books or notepads. They have the size of a ordinary sheet of paper (DIN A4), are 2 cm thick and weigh some 1.5 kg. They are operated with a pencil. Tablet PC are offered by a number of large computer firms including Compaq, National Semiconductor, Toshiba, Sony, and Fujitsu Siemens. For 2003 already sales of 400,000 units are expected, corresponding to 1% of the worldwide notebook market. A large leap in the use of e-books is imaginable if e-paper products (see below) succeed commercially.

Originally the PDF-format – which constitutes a de-facto standard for electronic publishing on the internet – was used as the software to read e-books. However, as this software lacks the capacity administer texts, the Open E-Book (OEB) standard established itself as a dominant alternative; different companies (e.g. Microsoft, Palm, Adobe) offer e-book readers based on this standard. Cross-media-publishing software to generate e-book content, based e.g. on XML, as well as software to administer access play a crucial role for the diffusion of e-books.

The Open E-Book Forum (OeBF)[25] is an international initiative of some 75 firms with stakes in the e-book market; they comprise hardware and software companies, publishing houses and other organisations, e.g. associations of authors. The objective of OeBF is to promote the diffusion of e-books, particularly through standardisation.

Approximately 40,000 titles, most of them in English language, of some 400 publishing houses are available in an e-book format. From 2001 to 2002 a doubling of sales – from 0.5 to 1 million books – has been estimated, most of these sales in the US.

In addition to hardware and software requirements regulatory arrangements are a crucial determinant of the future diffusion of e-book. They relate to intellectual property rights and touch upon data security and electronic signatures. Not the least important diffusion factors are prices of reading devices and of content; in German speaking countries the legal requirement of binding prices for books may constitute an obstacle to a rapid diffusion.

10.3.3.2 Electronic Paper

The term electronic paper (e-paper) is used to describe displays which have certain functional properties comparable to paper. These properties are flexibility, readability from different angles and under different light conditions, and visual brightness. Contrary to printed paper, the information content is not fixed, however, but can be readily changed. In addition, e-paper has a much lower energy consumption than displays in use now (1/1,000 of a LCD display), it is also expected that e-paper will be much cheaper than existing displays.

The basic component of e-paper is "electronic ink" consisting of pigmented balls with very small diameter (100 micrometers) embedded into a plastic layer. Differently coloured balls can be brought to the surface and thus be made visible by applying an electric current; in total they produce the desired pattern. Contrary to existing displays no background illumination is needed. So far the technology has been developed for black and white representations, but colour displays are also conceptualised.

---

25 www.openebook.org.

Presently two alternative technological designs of e-paper are being pursued by two US companies, both co-operating closely with foreign firms (e.g. in Japan and Germany) some of which contribute own technologies or capital. One firm – Gyricon Media located at Ann Arbor, Michigan, USA, founded in 2000 as a spin-off of the Xerox Palo Alto Research Centre – develops a concept where black and white beads gyrate in a double foil filled with a lubricant as a current is applied; matrix addressed printed transistors generate the desired picture. The distinguishing feature of this technology is its bi-stability. A first commercial application has been electronic posters for department stores; the texts to be displayed are transmitted via a wireless local area network (WLAN).

Another company – E-Ink Corporation based at Cambridge, Mass., USA, founded in 1997 – uses the laws of electrophoresis, the movements of electrically charged particles in fluids. Black and white particles fixed in transparent micro-capsules are moved upwards – thus becoming visible. The micro-capsules can be fixed to any electrically conductive material similar to ink. E-Ink directs its activities towards displays for mobile applications such as PDA. An e-book based on E-Inks technology is to be marketed in Japan. According to its roadmap the company will gradually increase the resolution of its displays, develop colour displays and produce multi-page displays. E-Ink has strategically co-operated with technology firms such as Phillips (Netherlands) and TOPPAN (Japan). It has acquired capital from a number of investors, among them technology firms (e.g. Motorola, Lucent) and media companies (e.g. Hearst, Vivendi (France)).

Currently the e-paper technology is in the phase of the development of prototypes and in an early market introduction stage. A broad diffusion into fields of application – where it will unfold its potentials to substitute paper such as digital newspapers, books, and journals – is not be expected before several years from today. An indicator that the potentials of e-paper are nevertheless judged to be of strategic importance can be seen in the fact that the Sony company has established a task force reporting directly to the board of directors which is supposed to guarantee a favourable starting position for the company as soon as the technology takes off.

10.3.3.3 Printing on Demand

A large share (35 to 50%) of books and other printed paper products is regularly not sold. This overprint can be reduced significantly by printing documents on demand only. Printing-on-demand (POD) describes the services of specialised suppliers to produce electronically stored documents in paper form on the demand of customers or in a form adapted to the needs of specific users. Hardware suppliers like Xerox and Kodak have developed specialised printing equipment for this purpose. For editions below 800 copies POD is generally cheaper than offset printing. One of the first firms to enter this market was Lightning Printing in 1997. An annual growth rate of 20% of this market has been estimated. Since about 1998 it has also become common to print newspapers close to their point of sale.

10.4 Policy Framework

The technologies dealt with in this case study are examples of economically viable technologies with large potentials to reduce at least some kinds of environmental pressures. Their adoption does not depend on environmental regulation and in most instances is not even motivated by environmental concerns. Even policies that are directly aimed at eliminating paper are primarily motivated by expected increases in productivity or improvements of the quality of output. Besides government policies business and stakeholder activities play a role for the diffusion of paper saving technologies.

10.4.1 Public Policies

Public policies play an important role for the adoption and diffusion of technologies with potentials to reduce paper consumption as ICT regularly display network externalities and many ICT services are non-rival and non-exclusive. However, the appropriate role of government is primarily one of moderating, facilitating, and leading (World Economic Forum, 2003). Therefore strategies and action plans play an important role. To implement these plans, programs have been developed in many countries to support R&D, to improve access to electronic media, to promote the application of these technologies – particularly for public administration- and to support the development of standards.

10.4.1.1 IT Strategies and Action Plans

In practically all OECD countries IT strategies and action plans exist (OECD, 2002b). Policies outlined in these plans comprise R&D programmes as well as measures to promote technology diffusion. The promotion of access for under-privileged groups is addressed. A further crucial element of all plans are attempts to improve the security of electronic communication. Many countries (14 out of 21 responding to an OECD questionnaire) have implemented policies to promote broadband infrastructure and applications (OECD, 2002b: 246). The importance of wide-spread availability and use of broadband networks has also been recognised by the European Council and is reflected in the eEurope 2005 Action Plan (European Commission, 2002b: 16-18). Software development – as ICT R&D in general – has traditionally been supported via defence subsidisation or procurement programs, particularly in the US. Meanwhile software policies are viewed as a means to promote economy wide productivity and competitiveness. On the supply side, software policies relate to R&D, intellectual property rights, standards, and ICT professional skills. On the demand side they comprise government procurement, incentives for private sector use, and training and information; in addition international trade and foreign direct investment are promoted. Many countries also are aware of the importance of competition in the ICT industry. In Japan, for example, the Ministry of Economy, Trade and Industry commissions software development work and holds public contests for creative software.

For Germany, policies at the level of the *European Union* are highly relevant. European ICT strategies date back to the e-commerce communication in 1997 followed by the adoption of a series of directives, e.g. on electronic commerce (2000) and electronic signatures (2000). In 2002 the European Commission proposed a comprehensive action plan "eEurope 2005" succeeding an earlier plan (eEurope 2002) as part of the Lisbon strategy which aims at making the EU the most advanced knowledge based economy by 2010 (European Commission, 2002b). eEurope 2005 acknowledges the interdependencies of demand and supply on ICT markets and promotes actions on both sides.

On the demand side it aims at

- modern online public services including
  e-government,
  e-learning,
  e-health services, and
- a dynamic e-business environment.

At the supply side it targets

- a wide-spread availability of broadband access at competitive prices and
- a secure information infrastructure.

The action plan comprises as instruments

- the revision and adaptation of legislation at the national and European level,
- the exchange of experiences and of good practices,
- the benchmarking of progress, and
- the co-ordination of relevant existing policies by a steering group.

Although the prime objective of the action plan is to provide a favourable environment for private investment, it will require significant public resources which will be met by using and re-focusing existing community programs including structural funds.

Corresponding to the EU action plan eEurope 2005, in *Germany* the Federal Government is preparing a programme "Information Society Germany 2006". It will be based on two existing strategic programs, namely the Action Programme[26] of 1999, evaluated in a progress report in 2002[27], and a 10-point programme "Internet for All". Central fields of action in the Action Programme as well as in the equal access programmes Internet for All which are to be implemented jointly by public policy, business and society, include

- lowering the costs of access to the internet, mainly through deregulation,
- promoting the use of multimedia in education,
- adapting the legal framework and supporting self-regulation of business,
- consulting small and medium-size enterprises on e-commerce,
- promoting R&D, e.g. on semiconductors, search-engines and other software,

---

26 Action programme "Innovation und Arbeitsplätze in der Informationsgesellschaft des 21. Jahrhunderts" of September 1999.

27 Progress report "Informationsgesellschaft Deutschland" of March 2002.

- improving infrastructure, e.g. 3rd generation networks, digital broadcasting, high-speed research networks,
- facilitating e-government, e.g. by introducing electronic public procurement.

To implement the German strategy a number of operational programs exist. A cornerstone is the internet initiative of the German business community D21, the largest public-private partnership in Germany. Other activities include a monitoring of the information economy, a network of competence centres for e-commerce to assist SME, and the financial support of demonstration projects of e-commerce activities of SME. Several laws in Germany have already been or are in the process of adaptation to electronic business in correspondence with European directives.[28]

Japan has developed a strategy to promote ICT in order to make Japan the most advanced information society in the world by 2005. The "e-Japan Priority Policy Programme 2002" is administered in the prime ministers cabinet. It comprises 318 actions, organised in five policy fields

- promotion of the most advanced ICT-networks,
- development of human capital,
- promotion of e-commerce,
- digitalisation of administrations and application of ICT in other public domains,
- promotion of security in advanced ICT.

In total, these actions create considerable opportunities for paper savings (see below for more details on e-government initiatives). For their implementation a number of specific policies and programmes have been designed, e.g.

- a financing system for the development of fibre-optic and broadband networks,
- various R&D programmes, focusing on the networking of information-related home appliances and on the convergence of telecommunications and broadcasting,
- technology diffusion promotion, including the establishment of local public networks,
- legal provisions for electronic signatures (put into force in 2001), intellectual property rights, internet sales etc.,
- support of ICT skills development.

In the *USA* the National Telecommunications and Information Administration (NTIA) is principally responsible for advising the President on domestic and international telecommunications and information policy issues; it also acts as an advocate of US commercial interests overseas. NTIA is responsible for spectrum management and conducts cutting-edge research in its laboratory. It also administers grant programs. It is particularly concerned with bridging the digital divide nationally and internationally. From 2001 on, NTIA has requested a 200% increase in its funds to some 250 million US$ annually, mostly for grant programs. As its goals for 2000 to 2005 NTIA has stated to

- promote open markets and encourage competition,

---

28 Gesetz zum Elektronischen Geschäftsverkehr von 2001, Gesetz zur Anpassung der Formvorschriften im Privatrecht, Signaturgesetz.

– ensure that spectrum management provides the greatest benefit to all people,
– advance the public interest in telecommunications, mass media, and information,
– promote the availability and sources of advanced telecommunications and information services.

Among the programs of NTIA are the Technology Opportunity Programme (TOP) promoting the development of the National Information Infrastructure. Since 1994 TOP has awarded 378 projects with 118 million US$ which were matched by some 180 million US$ in non-Federal funds.

Governments have also engaged in *international activities*. An example is the Declaration on Authentication for Electronic Commerce adopted in Ottawa in 1998 (OECD, 2002b: 244). It outlines a number of actions to promote electronic authentication technologies and mechanisms. It recommends consideration of the Model Law on Electronic Commerce adopted by the United Nations Commission on International Trade Law of 1996 and emphasises cooperation with business and user representatives. Seventeen OECD member countries have meanwhile amended laws so as to give recognition to electronic signatures, in most other member countries legislation is under way. Other issues on the international agenda – discussed e.g. at the OECD, the WTO, the European Council, the Global Business Dialogue (GBDe) or ICANN – are e.g. administration of the internet, cyber-crimes, free trade on the internet, or consumer protection.

10.4.1.2 The US Government Paperwork Elimination Act

Although not motivated by environmental concerns, the Government Paperwork Elimination Act (GPEA) in the US is a case of legislation directly and explicitly aimed at the substitution of paperwork by electronic media. The GPEA was enacted in 1998. It establishes an equal ranking of paper documents with electronic documents in all administrative processes unless particular objections exist. Persons and institutions that have to provide information to the administration or have to store information are to be permitted to do this in electronic format from October 2003 on. Government agencies are obliged to develop plans for the implementation of suitable technologies and to report annually. The Office of Management and Budget is charged with supervising the implementation.

In the context of this regulation questions of technological standard setting play an important role. In particular it is debated whether the government should prescribe particular standards or even technological solutions for DMS, electronic signatures or other data security issues. A widely shared consensus has emerged from the discussions that government regulation should be neutral with respect to technology as in the present early stage of application advantages and disadvantages of alternative solutions cannot be accessed reliably.

Environmental benefits from a substitution for paper of ICT solutions are not being discussed in the context the GPEA. Generally one expects an improved efficiency of administrative procedures through their reorganisation; these effects will show for administrations themselves as well as for companies and citizens which are obliged to provide information.

10.4.1.3 E-Government Initiatives

Under the eEurope 2002 Action Plan all Member States of the European Union had agreed to provide all basic public services online by 2002. Within its eEurope 2005 plan (see above) the European Commission has proposed a series of actions to further promote e-government (European Commission, 2002b). They include providing broadband connections for all public administrations by 2005, ensuring interoperability and interactivity of public services, organising significant parts of public procurement electronically, and establishing public internet access points.

In December 2002 an e-government law was enacted in the US. It implemented the US government's strategy for promoting the application of IT in federal administrations under the supervision of a newly installed directorate for information technology and e-government in the Office for Management and Budget. From a comprehensive list of proposed actions, a number of 24 were given priority for public funding. They covered communication

- between government and citizens (G2C),
- between government and business (G2B),
- among government agencies (G2G), and
- effectiveness and efficiency within government initiatives.
- E-authentication was dealt with as a separate cross-section issue.

Some initiatives are to be expected to have a large potential for paper savings, e.g. electronic tax filing and foreign trade related declarations in electronic form. Similarly large paper savings could result from switching to electronic communication between administrations (e.g. e-Grant) and use of internet technologies for internal procedures (e.g. e-Payroll, e-Travel, e-Training).

In 2002 the US federal government spent 2.9 billion US$ on e-government programs, and an annual growth of 12% is planned. Its total annual expenditures for information technology are in an order of magnitude of 50 billion US$. For the initiatives of the e-government act 45 million US$ were available in 2002, to be increased to 150 million in 2006. The implementation of the initiatives is to be outsourced to private firms, cost savings are to shared between administrations and contractors.

Within the "e-Japan Priority Policy Program 2002" one focus is on the digitalisation of administrations and the application of ICT in other public domains which is quite similar to the e-government initiative in the US. The primary objective of this policy field is a reorganisation of administrations such that information in electronic form becomes equivalent to information on paper. Based on an evaluation of ICT use in administrations a catalogue of measures was designed, including

- the provision of information in electronic form,
- electronic communication with administrations, primarily electronic applications and filing, e.g. of tax and foreign trade data,
- electronic payment of taxes and fees,
- electronic public procurement,
- paperless internal communication, e.g. in legislation.

Each of these fields is further detailed. For internal communication between administrations 57 procedures were identified which can be made paperless in 2002/3. Each government department is requested to develop rules for paperless documentation. Simultaneously internal and external computer networks are improved and extended with particular emphasis on connecting lower level administrations (prefectures). These activities are supported by training programs.

The European Commission, DG Enterprise, established a market observatory, the "European e-Business Market Watch" (European Commission Enterprise Directorate General, 2002). It monitors developments in 15 industry sectors including publishing, printing, audio-visual services and telecommunications as well as computer related services, focusing on the usage of ICT and e-business activities.

10.4.2 Industry and Stakeholder Activities

In the early 1990s a Paper Task Force was established in the US, led by the Environmental Defence Fund, an environmental NGO, involving several large companies, including e.g. Time Inc., one of the world's leading publishing houses (Environmental Defence Fund, 1995). The Paper Task Force developed a number of recommendations. Among other suggestions, it proposed source reductions by systematically identifying opportunities and taking action to reduce the use of paper "... where consistent with functional considerations". As one follow up the Alliance for Environmental Innovation, an NGO working with business, set up projects with companies to implement some of the Paper Task Force's recommendations (Alliance for Environmental Innovation, 1999). The Alliance for Environmental Innovation is currently planning to develop projects focusing on the substitution of paper by electronic media.[29]

One project of the Alliance for Environmental Innovation was with the Bank of America, the largest Bank in the US created by the merger 1998 of BankAmercia and NationsBank (Alliance for Environmental Innovation, 1999: 5 ff.). In 1997, BankAmerica's central purchasing organisation bought 23,750 tons of paper. Among other measures the bank promoted electronic communication to reduce paper use. It expanded the use of e-mail and voice mail and turned to providing reports and manuals online or on CD-ROM. Information covering 15,000 hardcopy documents is now posted on the bank's intranet. In the mid-1990s the bank maintained an inventory of 20,000 stock form items and publications. By 1999, Bank of America has consolidated this inventory to some 4,000 forms, with the most frequently used 1,500 forms available via print on demand. Significant paper savings are also achieved by sending out much fewer but more targeted direct mails. Applying new "data-mining" technologies on its data warehouse of current and potential customers and focusing mailing on just 10% of the list increases direct mail response rates by 75% and cuts paper use by 90%.

---

[29] Personal communication with J. Cefola.

Some paper intensive businesses are beginning to realise that the environmental benefits of the application of paper saving electronic media can be used in marketing. German Telecom for example promotes electronic billing via the internet instead of mailing paper invoices by hinting to their beneficial environmental effects through paper savings.

A large number of industry initiatives exist which promote the exchange of information and try to develop standards for technologies with potentials for paper savings. Some examples are given below

- In Germany the industry association for optical information systems (Verband Optische Informationssysteme; VOI) play a major role for standardisation for electronic archiving systems
- About 10 years ago, a working group electronic publishing (Arbeitskreis elektronisches Publizieren; AKEP) of the publisher commission of the German booksellers association (Verleger-Ausschuss im Börsenverein des Deutschen Buchhandels) was established. It is concerned with working out rules for electronic publishing. Its main issues are content management, online publishing, training, e-learning, digital workflow, paid content, and legal issues.
- The European Commission has established a Document Lifecycle Management (DLM) Forum to discuss questions related to DMS at a European scale.
- The DMS industry has established an international association, the Association for Information and Image Management (AIIM) with a European Branch called AIIM International Europe.
- The Xforms Working Group, part of the World Wide Web Consortium, develops XML standards for online forms; members of this working group are Intel, Microsoft, Xerox, Netscape/AOL, HP, IBM, Cardiff Software and others.
- Many leading firms with stakes in the e-book market are co-operating in the international Open e-Book Forum (OeBF) on standards and other issues.

These associations often co-operate with public administrations which play an important role as a mediator and often provide sovereign protection of agreements. The European Commission in its eEurope 2005 Action Plan for example, states as an objective that by the end of 2003 the private sector, supported by the Commission and the Member States, should have developed interoperable e-business solutions for transactions, security, signatures, procurement and payments (European Commission, 2002b: 15).

10.5 Diffusion Factors

Countries are regarded as lead markets for particular technologies if these technologies

- are adopted first; and
- diffuse to other countries.

In previous sections we have presented evidence of various kinds on the adoption and diffusion of technologies with potentials to substitute for paper. This evidence suggested that the US are a lead market for a cluster of cross-section technologies and for a cluster of business related paper saving technologies while Japan may emerge as the lead market for consumer oriented paper saving technologies.

In the present section we discuss the motivations that have led to an early adoption and the forces that drive the internationalisation of paper saving technologies. According to the lead market concept and the framework for analysis adopted in this study we focus on demand side factors. It should be noted, however, that – contrary to other technologies analysed in this study – technological competence has played an important and maybe decisive role in establishing the lead market positions of the US and Japan for the ICT technologies described in the present case study; this has been shown in the previous sections.

Prices and costs played a minor role for the early adoption of the three technological clusters (cross-section technologies, business-related technologies, and consumer-oriented technologies). The costs of paper applications that are to be substituted for are not particularly high in any of the countries investigated, and the costs of electronic alternatives are not particularly low in any of them compared to the other countries. The functional advantages and productivity increases that are the main drivers for firms to introduce these technologies do seem to have approximately the same weight in any of the three countries under investigation. Some of the functional advantages of electronic substitutes for paper may be more important for the long distances in the US, though. More importantly, an established infrastructure for other – e.g. military – purposes in the US may have reduced the additional costs for the adoption of some paper saving technologies.

Differences in *demand trends* have some significance for an early adoption of consumer oriented paper saving technologies in Japan, where an openness for new electronic gadgets prevails. Policies with regard to electronic signatures also were different, the US have been leading in recognising them as equivalent to conventional signatures; this has had a significant influence on the adoption of business related paper saving technologies. The same applies to e-government initiatives which were more timely and pronounced in the US than in Germany or Japan. Environmental awareness is different in the countries under investigation but has had hardly any influence on the adoption of paper saving technologies. However, it may gain some importance for international diffusion in future; some firms and NGO begin to use environmental benefits as an argument to persuade agents to use electronic alternatives for paper.

If a country has adopted a technology early and has demonstrated its feasibility and its economic (or political) benefits, the likelihood of a *transfer* of this technology to other countries increases. Likewise, if the demand for a technology is partly or exclusively driven by regulation or subsidisation, *policy diffusion* to other countries paves the way to an internationalisation of the technology.

It is quite obvious from the experience of the lead market countries that electronic paper alternatives lead to considerable productivity gains and cost savings as well as improvements of products and services. This is probably the main reason for the quick international diffusion of these technologies from the early adopters to other highly industrialised countries. Diffusion to less advanced industrialised countries is somewhat retarded as they need to develop the necessary physical and human capital infrastructure and appropriate institutions. It can be observed, however, that ICT policies diffuse very quickly not only to highly advanced but also to less advanced industrialised OECD countries as the policy objectives – improved productivity and competitiveness – are generally highly valued. Business initiatives besides public policies play an important role in the diffusion process of rules and standards.

Much of the technology with potentials for paper savings – particularly in the business domain – is software. The international language standard for software is English. This may have created an *export advantage* for firms in the leading US market.

10.6 Summary and Conclusions

Considerable potentials exist to substitute for paper applications by the use of electronic media, mainly by selecting a subset of information before printing. The use of these potentials is determined by economic advantages, in most cases increases of labour productivity, rarely paper savings. While there is some awareness of social objectives – mitigating a digital divide – environmental motives hardly play any role at all. The potentials to substitute paper by electronic media is based on a complex cluster of technologies, combined into a large number of applications. Some technologies which are currently being developed such as e-paper may massively broaden substitution potentials.

Technologies and applications with potentials to substitute for paper applications (paper saving technologies for short) can be grouped into three broad clusters: cross-section technologies such as the internet, business-related technologies like Document Management Systems (DMS), and consumer-oriented technologies like e-books. A country is considered a lead market for one of these clusters if the respective technologies are adopted first in this country and the technologies subsequently diffuse internationally. Evidence of different kind suggests that the US are a lead market for cross-section and for business related paper saving technologies while Japan may emerge as the lead market for consumer oriented paper saving technologies.

While technological competence has played an important and maybe decisive role in establishing the lead market positions of the US and Japan in the respective paper saving technologies, demand factors have played an important role as well. In the US, military demand has led to the early creation of a well developed infrastructure which has reduced the additional cost of the adoption of some paper saving technologies. In Japan, positive attitudes towards new electronic gadgets facilitate the adoption of consumer-oriented paper saving technologies.

The demonstration in the lead market countries of considerable productivity gains and cost savings as well as improvements of products and services is the main reason for the quick international diffusion of paper saving technologies from the early adopters to other highly industrialised countries. A quick diffusion of ICT policies to highly advanced as well as less advanced industrialised OECD countries also boosted internationalisation; business initiatives and a multinational perspective of many firms besides public policies play an important role in the diffusion process of rules and standards. Diffusion of paper saving technologies to less advanced countries is retarded as they need to develop the necessary physical and human capital infrastructure and appropriate institutions.

Even though there are economic incentives to adopt paper saving technologies, policy plays a vital role for the development of these technologies. Public policies support R&D, create a favourable environment for the adoption and use of these technologies, and promote them by applying them in public administrations. Governments have also engaged in international activities. Besides public policies, business and stakeholder activities – led and facilitated by government – play a role for the diffusion of paper saving technologies.

In almost all OECD countries IT strategies and action plans exist. They do not refer to the potentials (and risks) of ICT for sustainable development, however. Usually there exist also funding schemes for implementing these action plans. The US is the most advanced country with respect to e-government activities; the US Government Paperwork Elimination Act is explicitly aimed at the substitution of paperwork by electronic media. In Europe the European Union plays a prominent role for promoting ICT use and e-government. Due to the global nature of ICT applications, governments have engaged in a variety of international cooperations mostly concerned with developing standards. To this end, governments work together nationally and internationally with a large number of industry initiatives. Some NGO and some paper intensive businesses are beginning to realise the potential environmental benefits of the application of paper saving electronic media.

On summary, it can be stated that applications of ICT, while they may show both positive and negative effects on sustainable development, have considerable potentials for reducing paper consumption. Most applications can be expected to eventually diffuse because of their economic advantages for businesses or consumers. Still, because of the public goods character of many ICT services and network externalities, there is a role of governments for the development and diffusion of ICT, mainly as moderator and leader. This role implies inter alia the establishment of rules and standards, education and training, the use of ICT in e-government, and addressing digital divides. Governments are aware of these challenges and have tackled them. Early public policies have contributed to the lead market position of the USA in some paper saving technologies. There is, however, a lack of consciousness as to the potentials of ICT to reduce environmental pressures not only relative to GDP but also in absolute terms. From the perspective of sustainable development it seems to be essential that governments lead in integrating this objective of reducing paper consumption substantively into ICT policies.

11 Technologies for Paper Recycling

11.1 The Development of the Utilisation of Recovered Waste Paper in Germany and in the International Context

The utilisation of used, post-consumption material for the production of paper looks back on a long tradition. In a historical perspective the production of paper was based on rags and other used textile materials before fibre generated from wood – first mechanically then by thermo-chemical processes – became the dominant source for paper production. Since then the re-use of paper and board as a source for secondary fibre is an old practice in the paper industry. To produce certain grades of paper and board from secondary fibre is economically attractive as it avoids first of all the high energy costs for the production of certain primary fibre types.

The big consumer countries play a pre-eminent role in the production of secondary fibre not least because of the high potential supply of used paper material. The re-use of fibre is especially advantageous in those consumer countries which either have high energy prices and/or have a small supply of primary fibre.

A long term comparison of the relation between the supply of waste paper and the production of new paper and board shows that Germany and Japan always had a higher ratio than the US and the average of all countries. This was already true in the 1960s and in the early 1970s[30] when no environmental regulation existed yet, so that the use of secondary fibre from waste paper at that time was predominantly ruled by its cost advantages.

At the beginning of the 1960s Japan had the highest ratio between the supply of domestic waste paper and the production of paper and board, followed by a period in which both Germany and Japan were the leading countries. Since the mid-1980s Germany alone is in the lead, showing a doubling in the ratio from 30% to 60% over a period of 40 years (1961-2001), while in Japan the increase amounts to 20 percentage points (from 40% to 60%) over the same period. A comparable increase – starting from a lower level – can be observed in the US (which did pick up considerably in the last years) and in the rest of the world.

---

30 An early environmental regulation for the collection of used paper was implemented in the year 1975 in Sweden.

Fig. 40. Relation between supply of waste and production of paper and cardboard in selected countries between 1961 and 2001

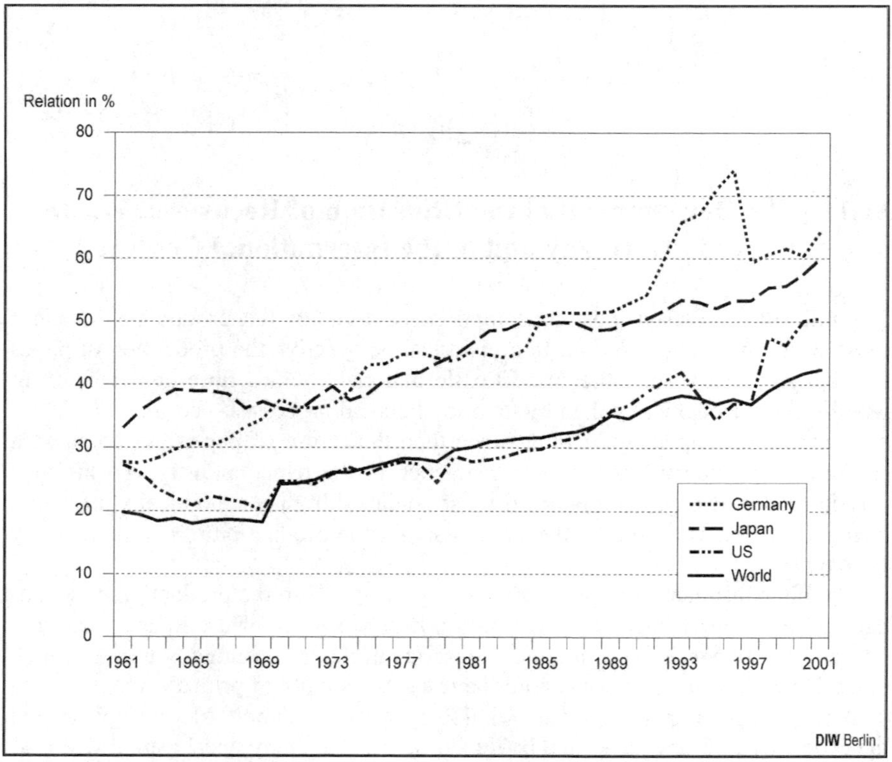

Sources: FAO, Japan Paper Association, calculations by DIW Berlin.

The increase in the relation between the supply of waste paper and the production of paper and board can therefore be characterised as a worldwide phenomenon. The countries Japan and foremost Germany could sustain their leading position in this development, while the US picked up in recent years without closing the gap completely.

Different indicators which measure the relation between the supply and usage of waste paper on the one hand and the production and consumption of new paper and board on the other hand are used depending on the special interest in question. For an evaluation of the effectiveness of (national) collection systems it makes sense to define the recovery rate, which measures the relation between the amount of recovered waste paper and the total consumption of paper. The utilisation rate is defined as the relation between utilisation of waste paper and the production of new paper and board. It indicates to what extent secondary fibre is used for the paper production in a country.

Fig. 41. Different definitions of waste paper quotas. Data for Germany 1991 to 2001.

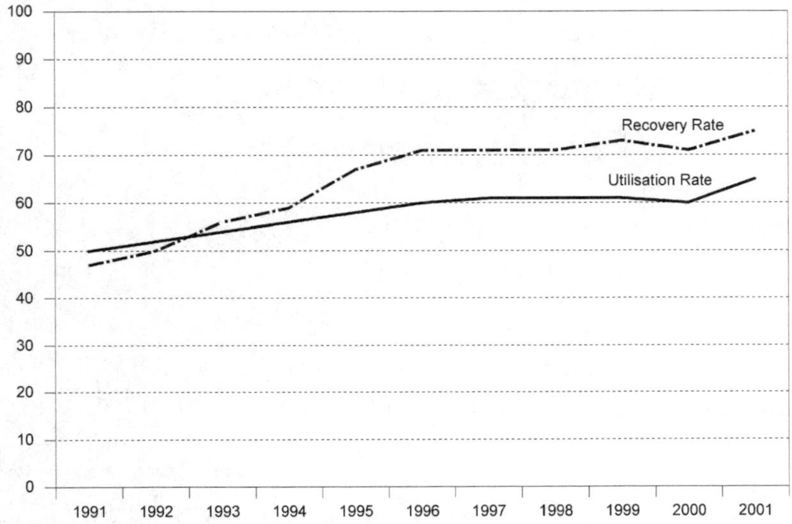

Source: VDP.

DIW Berlin

Looking at the recovery- and the utilisation rate in an European context clearly shows that Germany is in the lead concerning the (quantitative) effectiveness of its waste paper collection system. It is followed by the environmentally pro-active Scandinavian countries and the Netherlands. The United Kingdom is lagging for this indicator, but leading with respect to the utilisation rate, a mere consequence of its small domestic production of paper and board. Given their high production and their rich supply of primary fibre Finland and Sweden have very low utilisation rates.

The potential for the use of secondary fibre is quite different for different paper grades. The use of secondary fibre is traditionally high for the production of packaging paper and board. The utilisation rate is well above 90% without a further increase in the last years. In contrast to this development the utilisation rate for newsprint has significantly increased over the last ten years, starting from 70% to over 110%[31]. The utilisation rate for sanitary paper (80%) is also above average (65%) and has increased by 20 percentage points.

---

[31] The – apparent – utilisation rate is defined as the weight of the used paper in the relation to the weight of the produced paper. Due to the loss of fibre and additives, e.g. mineral fillers and coating pigments, while processing waste paper into secondary paper, the apparent utilisation rate can be above 100%. The weight of additives can amount to 40% of total weight, e.g. for coated paper.

Fig. 42. Utilisation and recovery rate of waste paper in European countries in 2000 in %

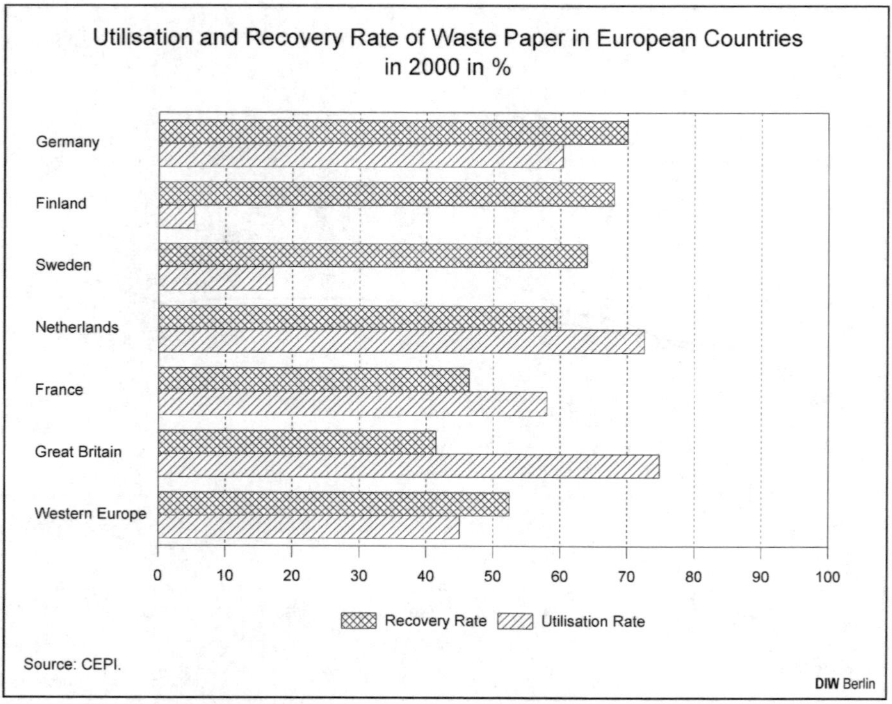

Well below average and without any noticeable increase is the rate for technical and special paper and board. For the quantitatively important grade of printing and office paper the utilisation rate has more than doubled over a ten year period. A further increase seems likely given the most recent development. Starting from a low level but showing strong increase in the last years is the utilisation rate for other graph paper, a paper grade with high demands regarding visual quality.

On the assumption that in the future innovative technologies in recovered paper treatment and in paper production will be implemented there seems to exist a large potential for a future increase in the utilisation of secondary fibre in paper production. The saturation rate for some paper grades has already been reached or seems very close, e.g. for newsprint and for packaging paper and board. Therefore the future development will depend mostly on a further increase in the utilisation of secondary fibre for the production of higher quality paper grades. New technologies in recycling and paper making play a crucial role in widening the technological options to potentials to paper recycling.

Fig. 43. Utilisation rate for different paper grades in Germany 1991 to 2001

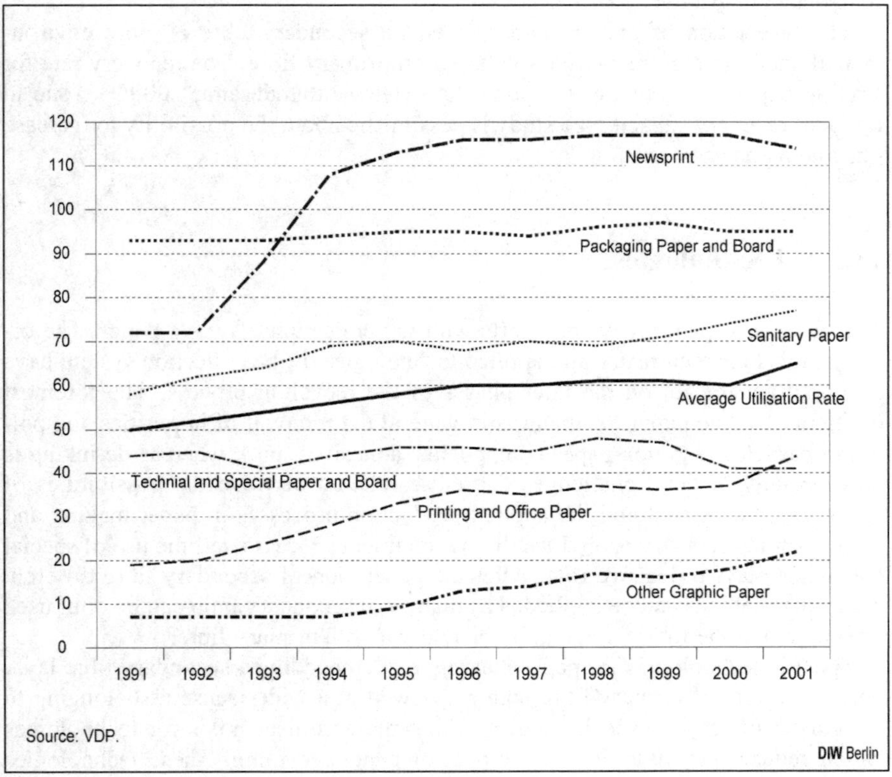

11.2 Environmental Impacts

A recent study commissioned by the German Environmental Agency (UBA) on the life cycle assessment for graphic papers produced many results helpful for the evaluation of the ecological effects of the utilisation of secondary fibre in the production of graphic papers (Umweltbundesamt, 2000). The study focused on newsprint, magazine and office paper produced on the basis of either primary or secondary fibre. As alternatives to recycling the report studied incineration or land-fill. In total the study analyzed more than 100 processes with respect to a variety of environmental impacts (atmospheric ozone, eutrophication of waters and soils, acidification, emissions of SO2 and NO_x, health damage, damages to eco-systems, resource consumption, usage/consumption of open space and green house effect). The environmental impact of the consumption of graphic paper in Germany relate foremost to the usage/consumption of open space, greenhouse gas emissions (11.8 mn ton CO2 equivalent) and acidification. The life cycle assessment demonstrates that the recycling of waste paper is more environmental friendly than incineration while land-fill is the most harmful option from an environmental perspective.

The production of graphic paper based on secondary fibre is more environmental friendly than the production based on primary fibre. The recovery rate for graphic paper in Germany is around 80% (Umweltbundesamt, 2000: 3), due to limits of recovery capacity the study is pessimistic about the possibility to increase this rate in the short term.

11.3 Technologies

The process of paper recycling starts with the collection of waste paper. The organisational characteristics and applied technologies of the collection system have an important impact on the later phases of the recycling process. The foremost problem of waste paper treatment is in general the removal of impurities and polluting particles (e.g. non-paper components, adhesives, ink), whereas de-inking is an especially difficult challenge. The close relation between the possibilities of waste paper treatment and the applied production processes in paper making and in the printing industry is obvious. In the treatment process itself the use of special chemicals plays a decisive role. After the generation of secondary fibre different bleaching methods can be applied. The quality of secondary pulp can be optimised with regard to the future use, e.g. by blending it with primary fibre.

Specific technologies for paper making, e.g. embedding a secondary fibre layer between layers of primary fibre, can be viewed in a wider sense as belonging to the cluster of recycling technologies. The same argument holds for technologies which reduce the environmental impact of paper recycling. These technologies focus on reducing water consumption and on lower waste water pollution.

11.3.1 Collection of Waste Paper[32]

To guarantee certain characteristics of paper products it is necessary to control the input of fibre for certain characteristics, e.g. strength. Mixed waste paper contains different types of fibre which cannot be separated after treatment, so that the resulting pulp can only be used for lower qualities of paper. It is therefore worthwhile to collect and sort waste paper according to fibre characteristics which are defined in certain classification schemes. These schemes normally include other parameters like type and extent of impurities in addition to fibre quality. The applied classification schemes differ substantially between countries. Attempts by the Confederation of European Paper Industries (CEPI) to standardise these schemes were not really successful. An example illustrates the consequences: the British classification gives more importance to fibre type than the German, so that waste paper sorting in Germany is less oriented to fibre type. As a consequence

[32] McKinney, 1995b

certain secondary fibre qualities like wood-free secondary pulp are available in Germany to a lesser extent.

The collection of waste paper can be organised either as a user delivery scheme or as a pick-up scheme or as combination of these two principal types. To characterise collection systems it is also useful to distinguish between systems with and without sorting and between systems with different sequences of sorting and collecting (before/after collecting). User delivery schemes have smalls costs (at least if the opportunity costs of households are neglected), yield a low recovery rate and produce higher quality of waste paper. In comparison pick-up schemes have higher costs, higher recovery rates but generate a lower quality of waste paper. In general the quality of waste paper can be improved by pre- and post-collection sorting, the option of pre-collection sorting depending on the willingness of households to participate.

Paper becomes waste paper in different stages of its life-cycle, for each of which specific collection systems may exist. Between 5 and 15% of the produced paper becomes pre consumer waste, especially before and in the printing process and in packaging. Pre-consumer waste is traditionally completely recycled, as there is a strong demand for this high quality waste paper, especially woodfree paper grades. Woodfree waste paper is used for tissue production. This demand and increasing disposal costs are the main factors for an extension of the collection of office papers which is a relatively unregulated segment of the waste paper market. The necessary quality grades require pre selection in this field.

Part of packages already becomes waste in shops, this type of clean waste paper is often collected by specialised traders or paper producers in specialised systems. The same is true for waste paper from printing for which the separation of woodfree and wood containing paper is of importance.

11.3.2 Treatment of Waste Paper[33]

Technologies for the treatment of waste paper are to a large extent based on technologies which are also used in the pulping process for primary fibre. The technologies are adapted to the special problems of waste paper treatment and are supplemented by additional process steps like cleaning, stickies handling and deinking. The innovation process for these technologies is of incremental nature, it is characterised by the following conditions:

- the necessity to treat waste paper which becomes more and more contaminated, the contamination becoming more diffuse and complicated over time
- preparing the generated secondary fibre for the usage in a widening spectrum of paper grades (starting from packaging, then sanitary paper to newsprint and finally graphic paper)
- the necessity to reduce the environmental impact of waste paper treatment, especially to reduce water consumption
- the growing importance of automated process control.

[33] McKinney, 1995a.

The removal of polluting particles is not only important for the quality of the produced secondary pulp (e.g. fibre strength and visual brightness) but also has impacts on the runability of the paper machine. What is viewed as a harmful polluting particle depends on the future use of the produced pulp. For example filling minerals are seen as unwanted if the secondary pulp is used to produce sanitary paper, but are not a problem if the final use is graphic paper. In particular the involved machinery is different for the treatment of recycled packages and for the treatment – especially de-inking – of paper. The following remarks will focus on the steps involved in paper recycling.

The first non-paper components already enter in the process of paper-production. Additives in paper production include clay, lime, color pigments, etc. These additives cause no problems at all as long as pre-consumer waste paper is recycled to produce the same paper grade a second time. Other additives enter in different processing steps, especially in printing. Examples are ink, adhesives, paper clips and chemical additives. The removal of some of these additives can be complex and expensive. More polluting additives enter during the use of paper, e.g. feed leftovers which may pose health risks.

Post-consumer waste paper is normally a mix of different paper grades and qualities, nevertheless the basic treatment processes are the same as for pre-consumer waste. A complex problem in waste paper treatment is the removal of adhesives in the form of stickies. The amount and variety of chemical components of stickies have grown over the years. The use of dispersable, water-soluble or at least easier resolvable adhesives would reduce the problems of stickies removal noticeably.[34]

A second complex problem is de-inking. Normally washing and flotation processes or a combination of both are used to remove printing inks while methods like sieving have been substituted. A variety of chemicals is added to the process to improve the results. Of course, the properties of the used printing inks have a strong impact on the results of the de-inking process. In principle it is possible to use inks[35] which are easier to remove but even slight cost differences often prevent the wide-spread use of new products.

The processes in waste paper treatment plants normally consist of four stages:

- pulping: dissolving paper into fibre and other components (impurities) avoiding degradation of fibre quality as far as possible
- separation of large and small non-paper components: removal of large (e.g. paper clips, plastic foils) and small impurities (e.g. adhesives, ink) loosing as little fibre quantity as possible
- additional process steps: e.g. dispersion units for the size reduction of impurities in order to improve the visual appearance of the secondary fibre and to improve the runability of the paper machine

---

34 Tests with 3M Post It Notes have demonstrated that the dispersible adhesives used in this product causes no problems in recycling although it is unclear which are the exact properties responsible for this result.

35 An example for the use of easier to remove ink is the ink used to print phone directories in Germany.

– compression and drying processes: not necessary if the pulp is used on the production site.

Conventional waste paper treatment plants have only one water circulation system. Modern plants may have two water circles (one acid and one alkaline) or one cold and one hot circle or a combination of both. Other variants include e.g. de-inking sections which are operated completely without chemical agents[36] (in Europe) and de-inking sections based completely on chemical de-inking (in the US). Different technological paths have also been chosen in Europe and Japan, e.g. in the process of digesting waste paper without size reduction for impurities. Plants in Europe bet on high consistency, while plants in Japan work with low consistency and additional digesting process steps.

The process water is cleaned between different process steps (e.g. by micro flotation) and is re-used as far as possible (principle of closed loops). The produced sludge is de-watered before it is either used as land-fill or incinerated.

Bleaching may be necessary to improve the visual quality of secondary fibre depending on the quality and characteristics of the waste paper and the intended future use of the fibre. Bleaching is done by using oxidizing chemical agents. The most common agent is hydrogen peroxide, in other cases oxygen or ozone (not for wood containing waste paper) are used while nowadays chlorine is only used in rare cases. In general the basic principles resemble the technology for bleaching primary pulp.

11.4 Policy Measures and Regulatory Approaches

In Germany the separated collection of paper in households started in 1985. Since 1991 the enacted packaging regulation sets binding goals for certain recovery rates of different paper grades. Japan has obtained high recovery rates without obligatory goals. Japanese households are even willing to pre select waste paper and a network of small dealers is organising the collection system.

The regulation of waste paper collection was pioneered by Sweden in 1975[37]. Germany was one of the first countries in Europe which enacted binding recovery rates. Today a Commission Directive exists.

The regulation for waste paper recovery and indirect subsidisation e.g. through the green dot label ("Grüner Punkt") had a large positive impact on the supply of waste paper. As demand firstly did not keep up the over-supply resulted in sinking prices (occasionally negative prices) for waste paper and forced some of the traditional waste paper traders out of the market or in other niches of the waste market. Some countries tried to stabilise the prices of waste paper, the Netherlands e.g.

---

[36] Chemical agents are used in waste water treatment, however.

[37] Binding recovery rates exist for newsprint and cardboard, while in the last years voluntary agreements have been implemented for office and printing paper. See Blazejczak and Edler, 1998.

applied managed stock piling and Sweden gave permission for regional monopoles in paper collection.

Some countries like Denmark or Sweden require the pre-selection of waste paper. These and other countries have regulations, which give paper recycling a priority over incineration.

Other policy measures aim for the enlargement of the market for waste paper and for products from secondary fibre. Examples for this type of measures are ecological labelling (e.g. Nordic White Swan, Blue Angel, European Flower), public procurement guidelines (e.g. US), and voluntary agreements (e.g. with newspaper publishers in the UK).

Ecological labeling of paper products with a high content of secondary fibre is one measure to enlarge the demand for this type of paper. According to the ongoing standardisation of ecolabelling (ISO 14020 series of standards) three types of labels are distinguished:

- ISO-Type I (ISO 14024): labels awarded by third parties (private or governmental) based on verified criteria
- ISO-Type II (ISO 14021): labels for self-declared environmental claims (not verified)
- ISO-Type III (ISO 14025): environmental product declarations EPD in quantitative terms (verified)

Examples for ISO-Type I ecological labels are the Nordic White Swan, the German Blue Angel and the European Flower. Each these labels exist for a broad spectrum of products, paper being one of the early labelled products.

The Nordic Swan for example is a common (multi-national) ecological label in Denmark, Iceland, Finland, Norway and Sweden, which has been introduced in 1989 on resolution of the Nordic Council. The objective of the label is to provide information to consumers to enable them to select products that are the least harmful to the environment. The Nordic Swan is given for different paper grades, e.g. office paper, printing paper and sanitary paper. The rules[38] are revised every 2 to 3 years and cover a broad set of environmental criteria, not only the use of secondary fibre. The European Flower is a (supra-national) ecological label awarded by the European Commission, the label for copying and graphic paper, which does not relate to the use of secondary paper, is not widely used throughout Europe.

The German Blue Angel is awarded for recycled paper (100% recycled fibre, at least from 65% low grade, medium grade or craft-containing waste paper) and for newsprint previously made of waste paper and bleached free from chlorine (more than 80% must be recycled paper).[39] In Japan an eco-label is awarded for printing paper which contains more than 70% waste paper in the pulp mixture. In the US an eco-label is awarded for printing and writing paper (containing at least between 20% and 50% post-consumer waste paper depending on the paper type), coated

---

38 The rules are defined in a council in which the respective national bodies (mostly standardisation organisations) collaborate.

39 The Blue Angel is awarded for a large variety of products, e.g. for copy machines and printers. For these two products the ability to use recycled paper is one of the applied criteria.

printing paper (minimum 10% post-consumer waste paper) and newsprint (at least 40% recovered waste paper and minimum 25% old newspaper). For most of the awarded products additional environmental oriented criteria (other than content of secondary fibre) are required. Criteria applied include forestry, chemicals used for production, emissions (e.g. toxic emissions and CO2 emissions from fossil fuels), energy use as well as properties in use and waste related issues.

Public procurement is another widely used measure to enlarge the market for paper produced from secondary fibre. In Germany specific laws and regulations allow public bodies to include environmental criteria in their procurement decisions. Several guidelines assist the public decision makers by giving advice, e.g. the Federal Environmental Agency (UBA) publishes a handbook for environmental friendly procurement (Umweltbundesamt, 1999) and some state governments also have developed corresponding information material. Buying paper with recycled content plays a role in most of these guidelines.

Green procurement is also a topic in the US (Takase, 2002). The Resource Conservation and Recovery Act (1976) and the Executive Order 13101 Greening the Government Through Waste Prevention, Recycling and Federal Acquisition from the year 1998 play an important role. Under the Resource Conservation and Recovery Act the Environmental protection Agency (EPA) developed comprehensive procurement guidelines, paper and paper products being one of the eight product categories under consideration. Based on Executive Order 13101 which encourages federal agencies to buy environmentally preferable and/or bio-based products EPA has developed a guidance on Environmentally Preferable Purchasing (EPP) based on several mostly environmentally based principles. A database of environmental information for products and services has been developed which contains information about criteria, product attributes and vendor lists. Paper products are one of several important product categories in the database with recycled content being one of the product attributes listed.

The green procurement policy in Japan[40] is defined by the Action Plan for Greening Government Operations for the years 1996 to 2000 and by the Law on Promotion of Green Purchasing[41] of 2001. The action plan lists as specific targets the content of secondary pulp (more than 20%) and the total production volume (no increase) as specific targets.[42] The law on the promotion of green purchasing aims to provide information about environmental-friendly products to public organisations.[43] Paper is one of the designated procurement items for which certain environmental criteria have to be considered. Content of recycled fibre is the dominant criterion[44] for paper products. The required content of recycled fibre is with one exception (50% for OCR paper) between 70% and 100%, the latter applying for hygienic paper.

40 See Takase, 2002.

41 See http://www.env.go.jp/en/lar/green/index.html.

42 A evaluation shows that the target for recycled content has been more than reached while the target of stabilisation of total production has been missed.

43 See for details http://www.env.go.jp/en/lar/green/2.pdf.

44 Other criteria are weight (for coated paper) and bleaching.

Japan has established in form of a public-private partnership a specialised Paper Recycling Promotion Center (PRPC) which, besides other activities, actively promotes new fields of application in which recycled fibre can be used outside the traditional markets. Examples of proposed new markets for secondary fibre are construction of houses with components based on used paper.

12 Regulations Promoting Socially Responsible Investment

12.1 Introduction

Socially responsible investment (SRI) has experienced a strong change from being a rather exotic idea of a few environmentally or socially motivated groups to new markets in the finance business. While in the beginning of modern socially responsible investment lower profitability was to be accepted by the socially or environmentally motivated investors, there is now a large variety of investment products available and a relevant part of them is designed to achieve the same or even higher yields than the competing conventional products. Typical investment products with an SRI component are investment funds, which consider social and/or environmental aspects within their investment strategy. Besides SRI funds there is a large variety of other types of investment products, such as pension funds, life insurances which can also be designed with an SRI component.

Even though the SRI issue has become very prominent within the scientific as well as the financial world, there is not yet a fixed definition for socially responsible investment available. Furthermore there are some language problems, especially in German speaking countries. Here in the nineties the expression "Grünes Geld" ("green money") was rather more popular than expressions such as "sozial verantwortliches Investieren" (= socially responsible investment) or "ökologisch-ethisches Investieren" (= ecologic-ethical investment). In the case study we adapted a definition for SRI from UK-SIF:

Socially responsible investment combines investors' financial objectives with their commitment to social concerns such as social justice, economic development, peace, religious values or a healthy environment.[45] *(UK Social Investment Forum, without year).*

Often quoted for the oldest roots of SRI are the American Quakers who in the sixteenth century refused to invest in slave labour and pay taxes which supported war because it went against their belief in the equality of humankind (see Vandenberg, 2002: 18). The first socially responsible investment fund, introduced in 1928, is the Pioneer Fund. It served church groups who wanted to avoid supporting "sins" such as alcohol, tobacco, gambling and weapons.

---

[45] See UK Social Investment Forum (eds.) online www.uksif.org. We included religious values, in order to include religious motivated investment strategies.

Due to the religious roots of SRI, investments which take religious motivations into account are also to be considered as socially responsible. Consequently, this also includes Muslim or other religious funds. By the way, nowadays Christian institutions in Europe are more and more considering to apply SRI strategies within the management of their assets and so form an important market to the SRI rating organisations.

Contemporary ethical investment can be traced back to the movements of the 1960s and 1970s, when the political climate was marked by campaigns and crusades for civil rights, the environment, peace, anti-consumerism, anti-militarism, anti-racism, anti-apartheid (etc.). In 1971, the Pax World Fund was founded, which as a result of the anti-Vietnam-war movement refused to invest in weapons, and became the first ethical investment fund in the United States. Since then, 175 mutual funds have followed suit in applying social screens to their portfolios (Social Investment Forum, 2001).

12.2 Design of SRI Products

Today there is a wide range of financial products, which can be designed with an SRI policy. In general this option is open to all financial products which are based on the build up of capital such as

- investment funds,
- pension funds, and
- insurances.

The application of an SRI policy is also possible for financial assets of private or public institutions. Here churches and charity organisations become more and more active.

In order to realise an SRI policy, different strategies are applied (UK Social Investment Forum, without year, Mistra, 2001: 8). These strategies once were developed independently but now they are increasingly combined. The different SRI strategies consist of:

- *Negative screening:* For the selection of shares, bonds, investment funds or other investment opportunities certain exclusion criteria (e.g. armament, nuclear power, tobacco) are applied which prevent investments in these businesses perceived as negative.
- *Positive screening:* When determining the investment universe outrider enterprises are selected. The outrider position can be interpreted in different ways. Some selection procedures identify the outriders of each industry sector, and hence also consider e.g. the sustainability leaders in car production and the utilities sector (best-of-class approach). Other selection procedures focus on industry sectors or selected businesses which are particularly well contributing to environmental protection or sustainable development. This results in investments e.g. in bicycle manufacturing, mobile phones or environmental protection technologies (best-of-class approach).

- *Active engagement:* Technically, active engagement means the use of voting and further shareholder rights. Besides the use of shareholder rights there is already a long-standing tradition of institutional investors to discuss financial risks and opportunities with the companies directly. As an SRI strategy this dialogue is extended on SRI issues in order to foster a stronger consideration of ecological and social issues in general or to address certain existing problems in these areas.

It has to be pointed out that the intensity of the SRI policy can vary a lot. For example SRI funds in German-speaking countries usually apply SRI selection procedures which combine both positive and negative screening. Their SRI selection procedure demands relevant research which in some cases leads to considerable additional expenditure compared to conventional investment funds.

On the other hand in the USA the simple use of a small set of exclusion criteria is wide-spread. When the size of the American SRI market is calculated pension funds are considered as socially responsible as soon as they use at least one exclusion criterion.

For the lead market project it is necessary to distinguish the sustainable design from the competing design. In the case of SRI the competing design is simply financial products without an SRI policy.

12.3 Regulations Promoting SRI

12.3.1 Existing Types

Regulations promoting SRI are quite new in the history of SRI. The first and by now famous declaration rule for UK pension funds was introduced in 1998 and came into force in 2000. It is obvious that SRI is not a result of regulations but regulations are a result of SRI: When policy makers realised the beneficial effects of SRI the discussed regulations were developed in order to promote the further development of the market.

In the case study we distinguish between regulations promoting SRI directly and those which promote SRI indirectly (see Fig. 44). Regulations promoting SRI directly are rare and easy to distinguish. They include the following types:

- Mandatory disclosure of the SRI policy: This is an obligation for financial institutions investing in equities to disclose to their customers, if and how ecological and ethical issues are taken into account in the investment policy. This obligation is known to be imposed on pension funds but might apply for common investment funds or insurances too.
- The obligation to consider ecological and ethical aspects in the investment policy: This obligation can be imposed by law or charter on to state-controlled capital stocks or on to foundations.
- Tax relief for ecological-ethical investments: For instance relief can be made available in the taxation of revenues arising from ecological-ethical investments. Tax incentives for certain companies or technologies are not to be in-

cluded in this category. These are considered as indirectly supportive regulations.

The indirect supportive regulations for SRI are numerous. Sometimes they can have a significant impact on the SRI market, as shown by the German Law for Renewable Energy. According to this law electricity generated by renewable resources receives a fixed price which is significantly higher than the market price. This law made direct investments in wind energy so attractive that it represents a major part of the German SRI market.

Less obvious is the SRI promoting effect of legal restraints requiring the use of environmental technologies. These regulations might lead to economic success for the companies providing the environmental technologies and influence the SRI funds which have invested there. However, it would be very difficult to determine the effects on SRI of the various legal restraints for industry. Some regulations for industry might also be met with progress-integrated measures (i.e. without new technologies) and thus would not promote SRI.

Since it is very difficult to distinguish indirect regulations promoting SRI and as they were not designed to promote SRI, they are not taken into account in our analysis.

Fig. 44. Delimitation of SRI-supporting regulations

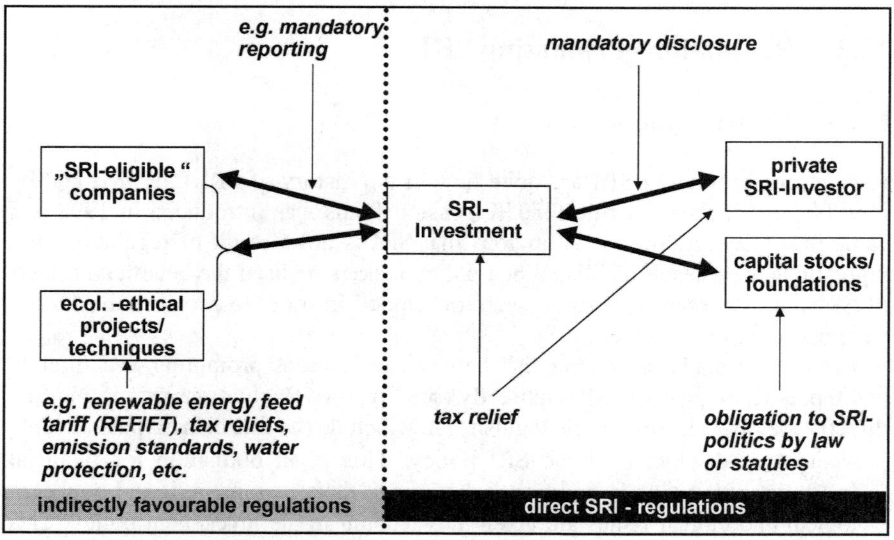

Source: Loew, 2002: 7.

12.3.2 International Diffusion of SRI Regulations

Geographically the analysis was focussed on Europe, Australia, New Zealand, Canada and the US. Thus the most important markets for SRI were considered and it can be assumed that all the countries which introduced SRI related regulations are included. The SRI disclosure regulation is the one which is most diffused. It came into force in four countries and is being discussed seriously in three other countries (see Table 18).

Table 18. International diffusion of SRI regulations

Country	Mandatory disclosure (year = effective date)	Other SRI Regulations (year = effective date)	Memorandum item: self-obligation
EU	Actually dismissed. [46]		
S	-	1998 [47]	
GB	2000		2002 [48]
DK	-	-	
NL	-	1996 [49]	
B	Discussion	Discussion [50]	
D	2002	-	
A	Discussion	-	
CH	-	-	
F	2001	2001 [51](5)	
I	-	Discussion [52]	
USA	-	-	
CA	Discussion		
AU	2002		
NZ	Dismissed		

Source: Loew, 2002: 8.

A legal commitment to consider ecological-ethical aspects in the investment-policy is only known to exist in Sweden. This affects the newly created state controlled funds for the assurance of the national pension system. A similar commitment was discussed in France, but was dismissed. The executive board of the French national retirement reserve funds has to report the ecological-ethical impact of the investments (to the supervisory board) instead.

46 EU: mandatory disclosure was suggested but dismissed.

47 Sweden: Reserve fund of the national pension has to consider SRI aspects in its investment policy.

48 GB/International: London Principles, a voluntary initiative of the British finance sector developed for the Johannesburg conference.

49 Netherlands: Tax relief according to "Regeling Groenprojekten". The new centre-right government discusses severe austerities.

50 Belgium: Proposal for tax relief similar to NL.

51 France: The board of directors of the reserve fund for the national pension has to discuss ecological and ethical consequences of the investment policy in its internal annual meetings.

52 Italy: bank-foundations are requested to consider SRI in their investment policy.

Tax-relief for SRI is not widespread as well. The only example is to be found in the Netherlands where the tax-allowances caused a major increase in the affected investments. However, the new conservative government started to retract the tax-incentives (in the middle of 2002).

12.3.3 Effectiveness of SRI Regulations

The effectiveness of the regulation is mainly estimated according to plausible consideration. The SRI disclosure has – at least in theory – a broad effect. Those providers who do not take SRI aspects into account are required to provide a negative report. Potential investors can thus distinguish funds according to their commitment to SRI and can invest in SRI funds. Moreover, providers are continually forced to consider SRI since they have to give a statement on their investment policy when the contract is signed and – depending on the national regulation – in their annual account. This led to a considerable number of UK pension fund providers stating that they would discuss ecological-ethical questions with the companies they invest in and thereby attempt to improve those ecological-ethical performances.

In estimating the effectiveness of the SRI disclosure regulation, the implementation and the scope of application have to be taken into account. The German regulation, for instance, only applies to certain subsidised pension schemes („Riesterrente", private and occupational) and thus covers only a very limited number.

In contrast, all pension funds in the UK are affected and therefore a bigger proportion of the market is included than in Germany. Moreover, UK pension funds have to make a statement every year without exception. In Australia, all investment funds have to make an annual disclosure.

A low efficiency should be generated from regulations requiring state-controlled capital stocks or foundations to consider ecological aspects since it can be assumed that those invest directly in equities rather than in investment funds. Therefore, they are more likely to seek external advice or SRI rankings than to increase demand for ecological-ethical investment funds.

Tax allowances have, as can be seen in the example of the Netherlands, a significant impact on the demand for SRI. To what extent there are spillover effects on the market as a whole has not been investigated but they can be expected.

12.3.4 Window of Opportunities to Introduce Regulations

Most SRI supportive regulations were discussed and implemented during reforms of the pension systems. SRI associations and green parties usually led the initiative. Disappointments, e.g. in New Zealand were a result of a lack of support from other groups. Whether this was caused by a lack of persuasion work or by an unfavourable political situation has not been examined.

The situation in the US highlights the importance of general reforms for the introduction of SRI regulations. Up to now there have been no regulations and the political attitudes of the Bush-administration give no cause for hope. However, the Enron-bankruptcy led way to demands for more transparency and more control in the financial sector. The US-based Social Investment Forum tries to benefit from this process.

Moreover, it is clear that in most cases centre-left governments introduced the observed regulations. The regulations are rescrutinised after a change in government. The new conservative government in the Netherlands is an example and also the German conservative opposition has already indicated that it would annul the SRI disclosure regulation if it came into force.

All direct SRI regulations were introduced in the last 6 years. The SRI disclosure regulation introduced in the UK served as an example for many other countries. Hopefully possible future conservative governments in Europe would not endanger this development.

12.4 Market Development

Even though a variety of studies on the market development of SRI is available, it is still difficult to give a comprehensive international overview. One major problem is that most of the studies focus on SRI funds and neglect other types of SRI financial products, such as SRI pension funds or insurances with SRI components.

For this reason international development of SRI funds is used as an indicator for the development of the whole market. The limitations of this indicator can be demonstrated by analysing the structure of the British SRI market. Here the volume of SRI funds form only a little part of the overall volume of the national SRI market.

12.4.1 International Development of SRI Investment Funds

The last Europe-wide investigation on SRI funds has been carried out by the SIRI Group (SIRI Group, 2002). The study covers social, ethical and ecological funds, which were distributed in Europe at the end of 2001. The results show, that the market for SRI funds grew dynamically in the past years (Fig. 45). From 1999 to 2001 the number of SRI funds rose by more than 70%. At the end of 2001 there were 280 SRI funds available. Despite this strong growth rate the absolute figures show that SRI funds still compete in a niche market. For example approximately 6000 investment funds are distributed only in Germany. Most of the European SRI funds (62 funds) come from the UK (Fig. 46). France ranks second with 38 funds, Sweden follows with 34 funds, and Belgium with 33 funds. According to the SIRI study Germany reaches the fifth place with 22 funds.[53]

---

[53] Funds from Luxembourg were assigned to countries were the parent company has its office. This explains in essence the differences as against the analysis of www.nachhaltiges-investment.org.

Fig. 45. Number of SRI funds 1980 to 2001

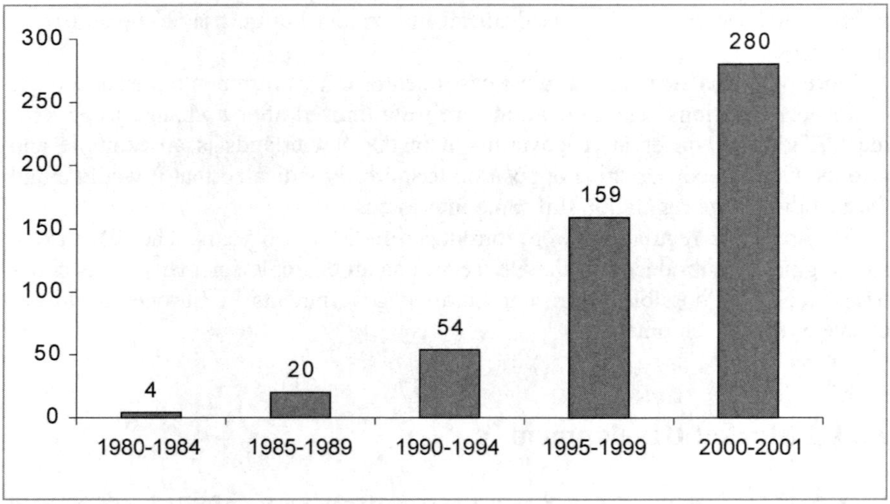

Source: SIRI Group, 2002: 6.

Fig. 46. Number of SRI funds per country by summer 2001

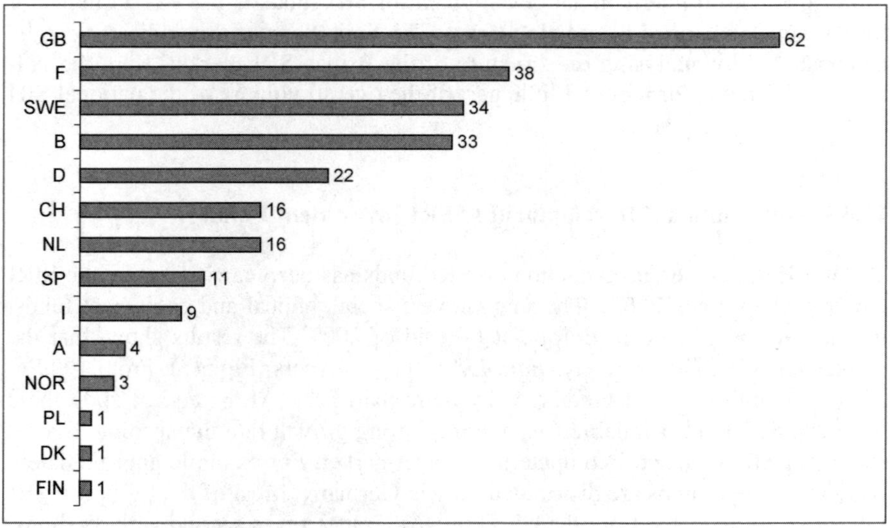

Source: SIRI Group, 2002: 8.

Fig. 47. SRI funds by volume in million EUR

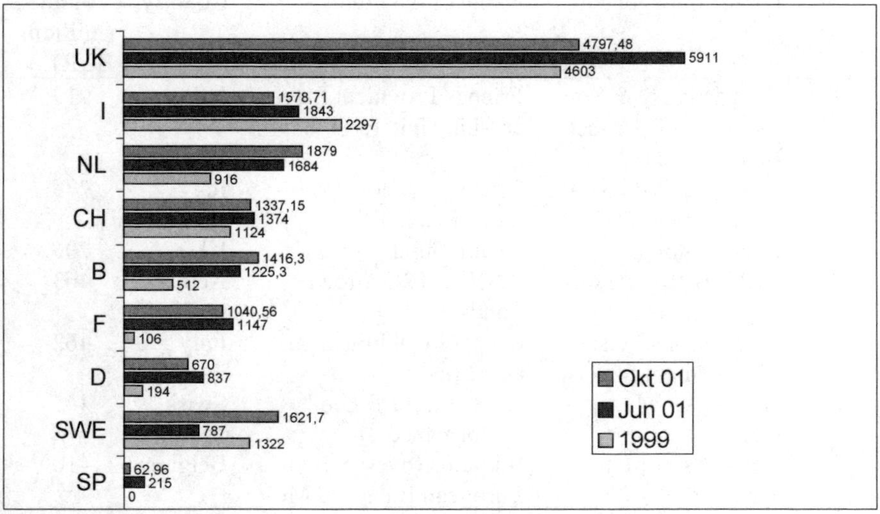

Source: SIRI Group, 2002: 7.

A different picture develops, when the amount of money invested is considered (Fig. 47). Even then the British market is obviously leading, but no clear second and third place can be identified. There is only little difference with regard to the volumes of the money invested by SRI funds in Sweden, Italy the Netherlands and others. In some countries, e.g. France the recent growth rates are visible. Within three years, from 1999 to 2001, the total volume of SRI funds in Europe has grown by 30% from EUR 11.1 billion to EUR 14.4 billion.

Up to now SRI funds are usually much smaller than conventional funds. While conventional investment funds manage an average volume of EUR 140 million the average SRI fund only reaches the size of EUR 51 million. These figures demonstrate that the SRI funds are still young.

The largest funds are originated in the UK and Italy (see Table 19). The top UK Funds have reached this considerable size as they are offered in one of the most developed SRI markets. The rather surprising result for Italy might be caused by the so-called bank-foundations which serve charity purposes and are asked to consider SRI criteria according to their statutory aims also within their investment policy (Loew, 2002:42).

Table 19. The top 10 SRI funds in Europe, 31/12/2001

Position	Funds Management	Name of the Fund	Country	Volume (million EUR)
1	Friends Ivory & Sime Plc (now ISIS Asset Management)	Friends Provident Stewardship Unit Trust	UK	919
2	Sanpaolo-IMI Asset Management SGR	Sanpaolo Azionario Internazionale Etico	Italy	775
3	Framlington	Health Fund	UK	700
4	ABN AMRO Asset Management	ABN AMRO Groen Fonds	Netherlands	463
5	Sanpaolo-IMI Asset Management SGR	Sanpaolo Obbligazionario Etico	Italy	462
6	UBS Asset Management	UBS (Lux) EF Eco-Performance	Swiss	445
7	Dexia Asset Management	Stimulus Invest Stimulus European Balanced Medium	Belgium	410
8	SNS Asset Management	ASN Aandelen fonds N.V.	Netherlands	292
9	Henderson Global Investors	NPI Global Care Growth	UK	274
10	ING Fund Management B.V. and ING Bank Fondsen Beheer B.V.	ING Bank Duurzaam Rendement Fonds	Netherlands	254

Source: SIRI Group, 2002.

12.4.2 Structure of the SRI Market in the UK

Socially responsible investment in the UK was for a long time dominated by the insurance company Friends Provident which offered a range of SRI funds. In the end of the nineties some pension funds made first steps towards SRI by investing part of their assets according to SRI criteria (Sparkes, 2003: 340). Then in 1998 the declaration rule for British pension funds was introduced which on one hand made sure that it is legal for SRI funds to apply SRI policies and on the other hand triggered an intense discussion on SRI in the management of SRI funds The SRI activities within the pension funds market were further promoted in 1999 by the announcement of three very large pension schemes that they would incorporate SRI principles in their investment policy.

In 2000 and 2001 a number of large insurance companies decided to apply SRI criteria across all their equity funds. Before these companies just offered a selection of SRI products, mainly SRI funds and SRI pension funds. Their decision to expand the SRI policy on all their equity assets nearly doubled the volume of the money invested under SRI policies.

Fig. 48. Development and structure of the SRI market in the UK

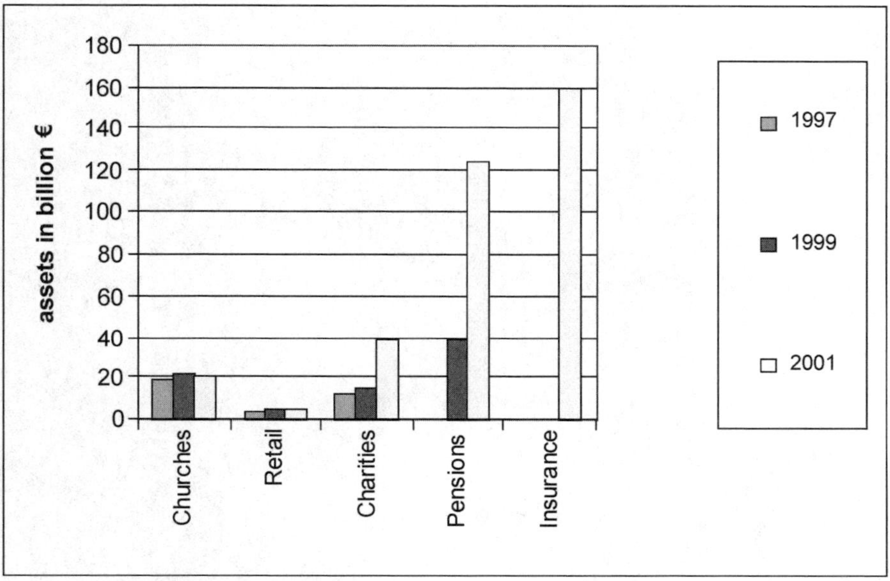

Source: Sparkes, 2003: 349.

12.4.3 Further Development

It is not yet clear whether the continental European insurance companies will follow the British example. Already there are first indications that this development might become real. The largest pension funds in Europe, PGGM and recently also the Stichting Shell Pensionfonds decided to at least partly administer their assets taking SRI aspects into account (Bergius, 2002, Sustainable asset management (SAM), 2003). Apparently the background is rather economical than ethical and social considerations. The CEO of PGGM, Roderick Munsters, said in an interview that he is convinced that a SRI policy is improving the yields in the long run, because companies which seriously consider human rights, environment and social politics, are usually characterised by a management that identifies new developments earlier. It is expected that this development will continue and SRI leaves its niche market position and becomes mainstream.

13 Comparison of In-Depth Case Studies

13.1 Introduction

The aim of the comparison of the in-depth case studies is to further determine which policy-driven measures and other factors facilitate the emergence of lead-markets. Starting point are the case studies and the respective analysis grids containing a number of factors which were considered to be important and selected on the basis of the relevant theoretical approaches and conclusions of the first part of the research project.

The comparison of the in-depth case studies is quantitative in nature. It is based on how often factors *considered* to be of importance for the creation of a lead market were *found* to be relevant in the respective case studies. The results of the in-depth case studies are then linked to the preliminary empirical findings and conclusions of the literature studies in the first part of the book. It is our aim to further refine the first conclusions and increase their plausibility.

13.2 Frequency Distribution

To undertake a quantitative analysis of the in depth-case studies, the entries of the analysis grids were converted into a binary relevant/non relevant code. 40 out of the grid's 44 factors were considered. The factors *Specification of the innovation design, Competing Designs, Promising Markets,* and *Stability of the Lead Market Position* were not considered since they were either too qualitative to be converted into a simple relevant/non-relevant statement or served to describe the respective innovation. Factors found to be relevant for the creation of a (prospective) lead market were assigned the value of 1, factors found to be of no or very little significance were assigned the value of 0. Table 20 shows how many factors were how often found to be relevant. For example nine factors were found to be relevant in eight (all) case studies. Only two factors were found to be relevant in zero (no) case studies.

A first interpretation of Table 20 is that most factors *considered* to be relevant for the creation of lead-markets during the initial phase of the research project, although differing in frequency, were *found* to be relevant. 75% of all factors were found to be relevant in at least four of the conducted case studies. This underlines the general appropriateness of the selected factors. Furthermore, nine factors are relevant in all case studies while only two were relevant in none of the cases. The vast majority was found to be relevant in some of the cases. This underlines that there are apparently only very few constant or universal factors related to the emergence of lead markets. Every lead market therefore emerges under different circumstances. This purely quantitative analysis, however, does not allow any conclusions regarding the importance of a single factor in relation to other relevant factors.

Table 20. Frequency distribution

Frequency of relevance in case studies	Number of Factors	Percentage of all factors	Subtotals
8	9	22.50	22.5
7	5	12.5	35.0
6	4	10.0	45.0
5	5	12.5	57.5
4	7	17.5	75.0
3	6	15.0	90.0
2	2	5.0	95.0
1	0	0.0	95.0
0	2	5.0	100
Total	40	100	100

A ranking of the factors according to their frequency of relevance shows the following result. Only two factors were found to be never relevant in any of the case studies *Monopolistic demand for the innovation* and *Additional incentives for exporting*. The absence of any special measures to promote the internationalisation of emerging technologies indicates potential room for further political measures. Considering the factors which where found to be relevant in all case studies, it is not surprising that all underlying environmental problems had international dimensions. It is difficult to imagine the international diffusion of an environmentally sound technology without the existence of an environmental problem of international dimensions. The same applies to *state agencies* and *multinational firms* as actors, whose central involvement could be expected. It is however interesting to note that international agendas were also relevant in all cases. This indicates that new and different types of international governance are effective in promoting green innovations.

Regarding the type of factors which are relevant in all case studies, it is striking that four out of the total of nine (*Allows a variety of innovation designs, flexible* and *innovation friendly policy style* and *instrumentation* as well as *flexible regulations)* refer in one way or the other to a flexible policy style. This result indicates a certain role for the state in setting environmental regulation with respect to the economically successful resolution of the problem.

Fig. 49. Ranking of the factors

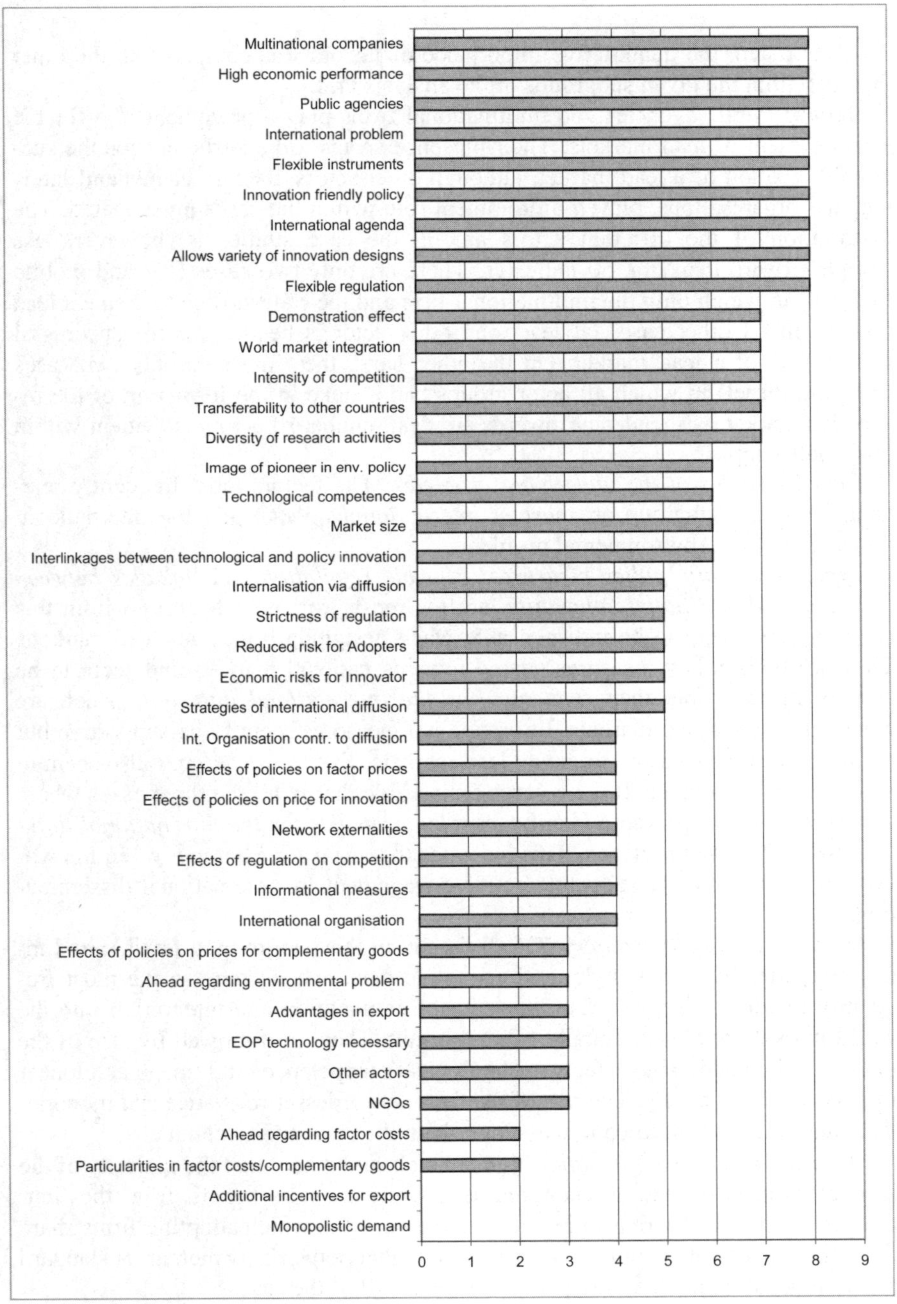

13.3 Analysis of Factor Subgroups

As a next step, the quantitative importance of factors was compared to the other factors within the given subgroups of the analysis grid.

Actors: Public agencies and multinational firms play a prominent role for the establishment of lead markets. Their presence seems to be sufficient for the successful creation of a lead market, although other actors, namely NGOs and international organisations, played a prominent role within the cases investigated. The distribution of the different actors among the case studies is, however, less straightforward than Fig. 50 indicates. There are only two cases (PV and mobile fuel cell) in which only the multinational firm and the state suffice to create a lead market. In all other cases, at least one other actor is needed for the successful constitution of a lead market. On the other hand, there are also only two cases (SRI and diesel) in which all actor groups had a stake in the formation of the respective market. No tendency towards an ideal number of actors is evident within this small sample.

Characteristics of the underlying problems: The factors most frequently relevant from this subgroup are *part of international agenda* and the international dimension of the environmental problem.

Types of specific policy measures: Flexible regulation and *linkages between technological and policy innovation* are the most prominent features within this subgroup and seem to be indispensable when designing policy for lead markets. They are both policy measures geared towards national markets and seem to be slightly more visible then *strategies for the international diffusion*, which are aimed at international markets. Informational measures seem to be supportive but not an obligatory measure to create lead markets. *Export advantages* also seem to be of lesser importance. It is however remarkable that in all the three cases where *export advantages* played a significant role, *strategies for the international diffusion* were also of importance. This indicates that *export advantages* of an innovation do not necessarily substitute active engagement for international dissemination.

Determinants of the country: Of all factors in this subgroup, a flexible and innovation friendly policy style, and economic performance rank as the most frequently important factors. Also, intensity of competition and integration into the world market are almost equally often relevant. They are followed by size of the market had considerable effects, technological competence, and image as pioneer in environmental policy. The rest of the factors is of lesser relevance and monopolistic demand never seemed to play any role in the case studies conducted.

Determinants of the innovation: It can be observed here that the majority of the innovators have to take an economic risk while adopters benefit from the first-movers' activities. There is only one case (solvents) in which adopting firms share the same risks as innovators. It is also notable that networks, which are a standard aim in innovation policy, only played a role in half of the cases.

Fig. 50. Frequency of relevancy according to subgroups

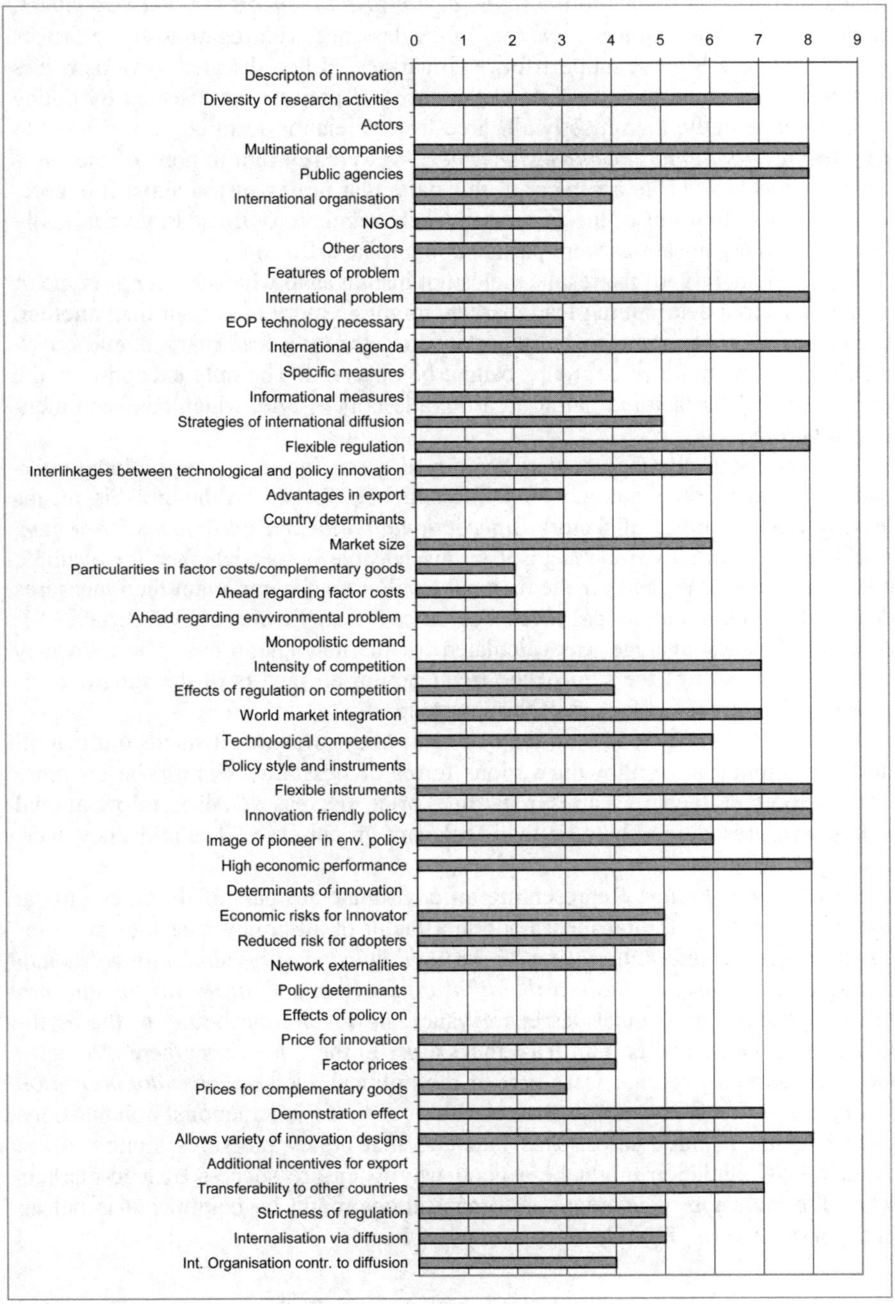

Determinants of the policies: The three most important policy determinants are *allows a variety of innovation designs*, *demonstration effects for other countries*, and *transferability to other countries*. Policy designed with regard to those factors should yield the biggest support for lead markets. Policy directed towards prices was only relevant in three or four of the cases. If prices were affected by policy within a case study, then mostly all three factors relating to prices were found to be relevant. *Additional incentives for exporting* were relevant in none of the cases which seems to indicate a neglect of this particular policy instruments. It is noteworthy that in four out of the five cases where regulation diffused internationally international organisations were participating in the diffusion.

This first analysis of the results yields not insight as to whether a certain type or group of factors determining lead markets might be more important than another. Factors of all types seem to be important in generating lead-markets and cross-relationships within the subgroups cannot be observed. The only exception is the importance of the factors relating to a flexible policy style, which has been mentioned before.

As a next step, the factors were regrouped according to policy (national/international) and market (national und international) factors. Although this means leaving out a number of factors (*international/national environmental problem*, *End of Pipe solutions necessary*), it seems feasible to ask whether for example policy measures designed for the national level are more important then measures designed for the international level. For an overview of the results see table 51. Also, a relevancy average was calculated for the new subgroups. The relevancy factor is the result of the sum of the frequency of all factors of the subgroup divided by the number of factors of the subgroup.

National Policy: Considering the national policy measures it stands out that all measures aiming at or allowing various forms of flexibility seem to be far more often important then measures regarding price decreases. Also, informational policy measures were only to be found relevant in four cases. The relevancy average is 5.4.

International Policy: Representing an environmental part of the international agenda seems to be the far most important factor of all policy measures at an international level. *Internationalisation through diffusion of regulation*, *involvement of international organisation in the diffusion process*, and *strategies for international diffusion* are of much lesser relevance, however contributing to the establishment of lead markets in at least four cases. In the five cases where *strategies for international diffusion* were part of the political agenda, *internationalisation through diffusion of regulation* was relevant four times. International organisations were relevant in three cases. This indicates that policy measures aiming at the diffusion of regulation might be a good way to ensure success of lead-markets while the inclusion of international organisations might be helpful but is not an indispensable asset. The relevancy average is 5.5.

Fig. 51. Frequency distribution according to new subgroups

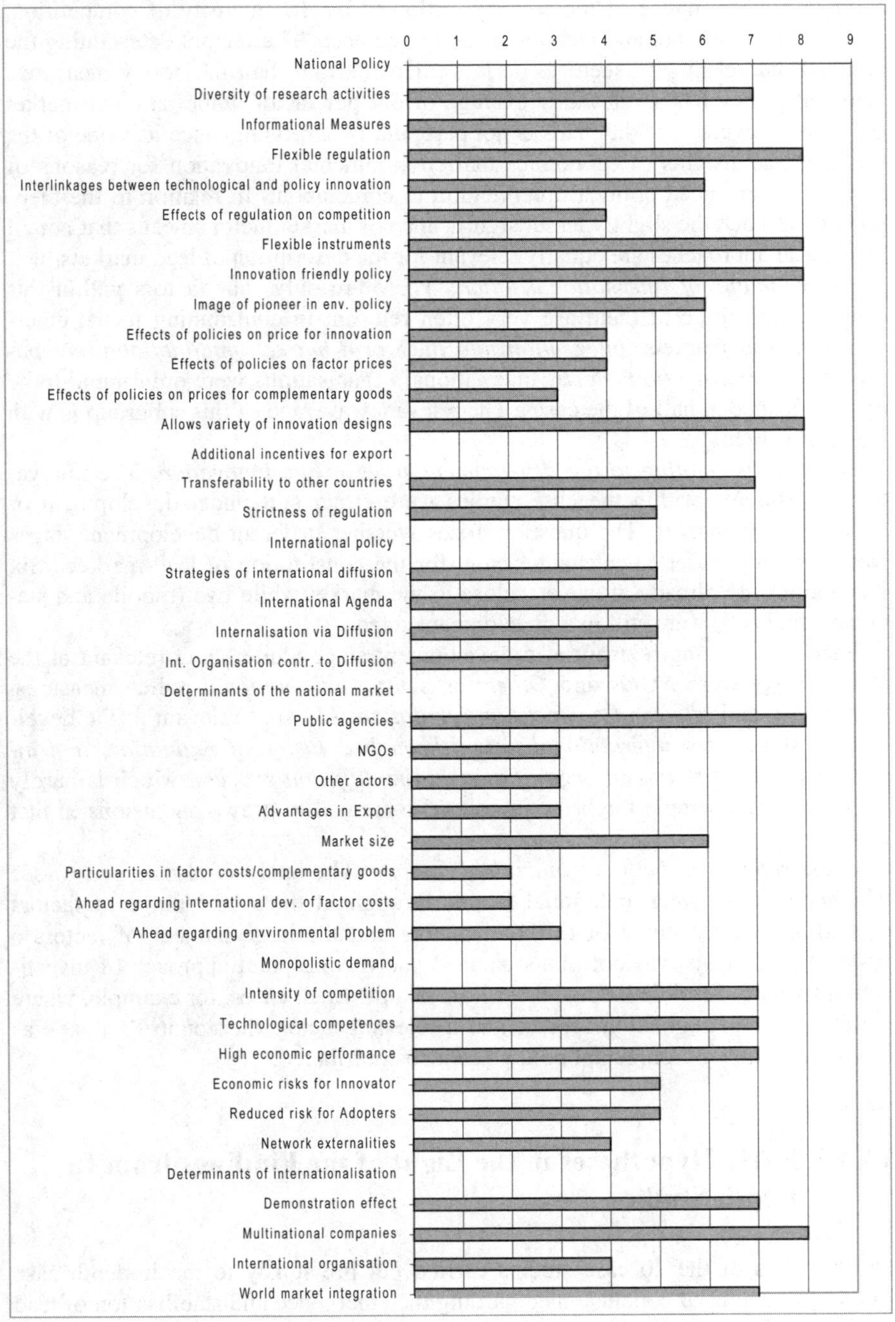

Determinants of the National Market: The most often relevant factor is the economic performance of the country, followed by the intensity of competition, the size of the market and technological competence. The factors determining the national market in sum seem to be less often relevant than the policy measures. National policy has a relevancy average of 5.4 per factor while national market only has an average of 4.3. This is not particularly surprising since it is one of the fundamental insights of economics that environmental innovation for reasons of market failures need political intervention to come about. In relation to the theoretical approach the slightly lesser significance of market factors means that not all theoretical approaches are equally relevant for the description of lead markets.

Determinants of Internationalisation: There are only four factors within this category, but three of them are very often relevant in contributing to the emergence of lead markets: *integration into the world market*, *multinational companies*, and *demonstration effects*. International organisations were only found to be of significance in half of the cases. The relevancy average of this subgroup is with 6.5 relatively high.

Differences relating to the development stage of the innovation: The innovations considered within the case studies were either still under development or already at the market. The question arises whether different development stages were entailing different relevant factors for the constitution of lead-markets. Six innovations are already at or very close to the market while two (mobile and stationary fuel cell) were still in a development stage.

Factors *not* being relevant at a development stage while being relevant at the market stage were *NGOs* and *Others* as actors, *informational* policy measures, *factor cost,* and *effects of competition regulation.* Also not relevant at the development stage were *internationalisation through diffusion of regulation, and involvement of international organisation in the diffusion process*, which is hardly surprising. The sample might be in general too small to draw conclusions in that respect.

Cross-references between individual factors: The analysis also aimed to see whether links between individual factors throughout the whole range of factors existed. Given the range of different factors and the huge number of factors a systematic analysis was not undertaken. A more conceptual approach of investigating likely or feasible links yielded little results. In all cases, for example, where the strictness of regulation represented a relevant factor, the country's image as lead country in environmental policy had also contributed.

13.4 Early Hypotheses in the Light of the Findings from In-Depth Studies

On the basis of the 20 case studies carried out previously to the in-depth case studies, a number of conclusions regarding the emergence and stabilisation of lead markets and the international diffusion of environmental technologies were laid out in the first part of the book. Those conclusions shall now be reconsidered on the light of the findings of the eight in depth case studies.

(1) It was assumed that lead markets are stimulated by higher preferences for environmental goods, specific support measures or policy intervention. Environmental innovations were predominantly ascribed to state and NGO activity. This assumption is supported by the in-depth case studies. Policy measures were found to be more often relevant then other factors. Also, the state was an important actor in all cases. NGO activity however was only relevant in three of the cases. But the picture of a wholly state driven lead market creation is misleading, since other actors and international organisations were relevant factors in cases when NGOs were not. Since the analysis of the factor scheme is purely quantitative, nothing can be said about causality relation and the importance of each actor in each case.

(2) It was assumed that there are demand and supply driven lead markets. As to the assumption of demand driven lead markets it can be said that in the majority of the cases high environmental standards were at least co-driving the respective lead market. This is for example the case in the US regulations on the use of solvents. In four cases the lead market was supply and demand driven at the same time. In the cases of solvents, recycling, photovoltaic and mobile fuel cell high environmental standards and technological competence were found to be relevant.

(3) It was assumed that the effective demonstration of the feasibility of certain environmental standards by a pioneer country will support the diffusion of regulation. This assumption is also supported, since in seven out of eight cases, demonstration effects were found to be relevant.

(4) It was assumed that countries identified as lead markets are highly integrated into world markets and show good economic performance as well as high technological competence in the field of the respective innovation. These assumptions can be largely supported. While economic performance was a relevant factor in all cases, integration into world markets was a relevant factor in seven and high technological competence in six cases.

(5) It was assumed that pioneer markets with high environmental regulation can send out signals to supply sources outside the domestic market and activate them to make their products fulfil higher standards. This assumption is also confirmed, since the corresponding factors were found to be relevant in many cases.

(6) It was assumed that peculiarities regarding factor prices or prices of complementary goods are of almost no significance. This assumption cannot fully be supported. Evidence for the relevance regarding factor prices or prices of complementary goods was only found in few cases, but this finding cannot be generalised since their role depends strongly on the phase of the innovation process and competition.

(7) It was assumed that state agencies are of central importance to the emergence of lead markets. This assumption can be fully supported since it was reflected in all cases.

(8) It was assumed that NGOs can play an important role and that the role of multinational companies was less clear. While the first assumption can be supported since NGOs played an important role in some of the cases, especially in the

case of the particulate filter, international companies did play a significant role in all cases which tends to underline their general importance.

(9) It was assumed that the underlying environmental problems were local or global. If they were local, similar problems would be occurring locally in other regions of the world. Also, the environmental problems were part of an international agenda. This assumption was confirmed in the case studies: The environmental problems at stake were classified as part of an international agenda in all of the cases.

(1) It was observed that in most cases subsidies paid by the state helped either to directly reduce the cost of innovation or its complementary goods or helped indirectly by increasing the benefit of the innovation. For the in-depth case studies however policy measures affecting prices were only found to be relevant in half of the cases. The assumption that the policy style is flexible and innovation oriented can be fully supported.

The rather rare relevancy of network externalities observed during the first round of case studies is not fully confirmed in the in-depth case studies since they were found to be relevant in half of the cases.

13.5 Conclusions

A number of conclusions may be drawn from the comparison of the in-depth case studies. The overall selection of factors considered to be relevant for lead market creation seems to be adequate. While there are few constant factors in lead market creation, most factors play a role in only a number of cases. This underlines the assumption that lead market emergence depends more on the market's specific circumstances than on a fixed number of key elements. It is however notable that policy measures relating to a flexible and innovation friendly policy style represent the most frequent type of lead market factors.

As the most important subgroup, determinants of the international market could be singled out (relevancy average 6.5). Regarding policy advice this means that putting the determinants of internationalisation in place or screening for them deserves high priority.

The conclusions and assumptions of the first part of the book were confirmed for the most part by the results of the in-depths case studies. Only NGOs and state subsidies affecting prices were found to be of a little lesser importance. The findings of the comparison underline that monitoring is vital to the political support of lead markets. The factors determining a lead market differ from case to case and only close monitoring will reveal the relevant factors of a specific case.

14 Policy Patterns to Develop International Markets of Innovations for Sustainability

While in the previous chapter we draw some conclusions on a comparison of the type of technologies, the actors involved and the economic capabilities as factors to explain the emergence of lead markets. Public policies and the related actors were found to have a crucial role in every case we studied so far. Therefore, in the following we zoom into this group of factors. What types of strategies and instruments have been actually successful? Both the theoretical considerations and the close analysis of the case studies form the basis for the formulation of policy recommendation in the last chapter.
Many of the case studies on which the following observations are based describe innovations in a very early phase. This may be crucial for the conclusions presented here; in particular, R&D-policy may be more important in this early stages than in later ones.

Almost always R&D-policy plays an essential role in the case studies (exception: particulate filters), up to and including the market introduction phase. If a national pioneering policy is present at all, it can be identified in this particular policy area. Support of basic research plays a comparatively moderate role, although its importance for generating a multitude of solutions is recognised. Quite frequently pilot- and demonstration projects have been funded. Subsidisation of the market introduction of new technologies (push-off financing) has been used as an instrument only in a few cases; this may be due to the high costs of such policy. When this instrument was applied it was quite effective. A limited application of this instrument may make sense if – immediately after the market introduction – considerable cost decreases can be realised, e.g. though learning.

Only rarely is the development or market introduction of new solutions enforced by setting – or announcing – standards. Such technology forcing causes considerable resistance in the affected sector which frequently is capable of mobilising political actors to support its interests. Therefore distributive policy instruments such as subsidies which are easier to implement are preferred.

To increase the cost of using the environment by means of taxes or other economic instruments creates in some cases a favourable background for R&D efforts. However, in the case studies, these signals by themselves seem not to have been sufficient to stimulate R&D towards sustainability.

In some cases (wind energy, green dot, SRI) R&D support has also led to the emergence of new actors such as producers and producer associations which subsequently have played an important role for promoting the innovation in the policy process; likewise it is expected that economic sectors will originate in the fields of photovoltaics and fuel cells. An orientation of policies towards a systematic promotion of such political capacities has not been observed, however.

Policies which aim at increasing the number of competitors or reducing existing limitations of competition can secure an efficient use of research resources and contribute to an accelerated diffusion of innovations. Although observable in some cases (phosphates, stationary fuel cells), such policies have not been systematically pursued. Thus, the potential of policies creating a variety of solutions by promoting competition remains largely unexploited.

Patents allow companies to refinance their R&D expenditures and thus create an incentive for such activities. This objective conflicts with the aim of a swift and broad diffusion of sustainability innovations which may be impeded by patent protection. Promoting licence agreements can mitigate this conflict. In one of the cases (stationary fuel cells) an incentive is created to exchange research results by allowing for the utilisation of patents within a research network. In the case of phosphate substitutes the economic ministry, before setting standards on admissible levels of phosphates, demanded from the then only producer of the substitute to licence the process to competitors at mutually acceptable conditions. In both cases a compromise was found between the protection of R&D investments and a rapid diffusion of an environmental innovation.

Public procurement could play an important role in creating cost reductions through scale and learning effects. Efforts to set up e-government, for example, could be directed towards a promotion of paper saving technologies. Similarly, policies could be designed to promote the application of environmentally friendly solutions in areas where some private actors have a higher willingness to pay because of the particular advantages these solutions offer. An example are fuel cells as an emergency power source in hospitals or computer departments; in the case studies such policies were an exception, however.

Almost always environmental policy measures play an important role in the case studies as well (except for the paper substitution case). Environmental policies affect the demand as well as the supply of innovations for sustainability. A very broad scale of instruments is applied, ranging from command-and-control to economic incentives. Never one single instrument is used alone. The instruments frequently aim at reducing the cost of an innovation. Rarely instruments are applied to raise the costs of – or to ban – alternative less environmentally friendly technologies. Potentials which could be created by the credible announcement of measures to limit the applicability of old technologies remain unutilised. Sometimes limitations on the use of more harmful technologies are raised gradually in line with the development of the innovation. An acceleration of the mutual adjustment of technological development and regulatory support seems to be desirable. For the development on the supply side the formulation of environmental goals which reduce uncertainty is of importance. On the demand side instruments for moral suasion or to provide information are used. Flexible instruments which do not restrict the decisions of actors and avoid lock-ins are particularly successful.

Hints to a strategic orientation of regulation – trying to create advantages for domestic enterprises – are obvious in few cases only. In Japan, the programs to develop photovoltaic and mobile fuel cells seem to be designed as industrial policy. It is intended to make Japan a lead market for "Clean High Tech" while "Clean Low Tech" potentials like wind and biomass energy are deliberately neglected. No evidence is found that *environmental* regulation in a country is set stricter than in other countries for strategic reasons. On the contrary, frequently environmental policy is restrained in order to facilitate its embedding into international processes. A possible exemption is the ordinance limiting maximum energy consumption for refrigerators in Denmark (Jänicke et al., 1999).

The formulation of environmental objectives is of great importance. This provides a great deal of flexibility because the objectives can be met through a variety of instruments. The objective of doubling the share of renewable energies within a 10-year period in Europe, for example, is promoted through a variety of programs including feed-in tariffs, subsidies and quota systems. The dynamic development of mobile fuel cells has primarily been created through setting objectives in the US (California Zero Emission Vehicles Initiative) besides the announcement of an early market introduction (by Daimler-Chrysler).

Cooperation between government and industry in environmental policy plays an important role in the promotion of the emergence of lead markets. Such cooperation includes the negotiation of framework conditions between government and industry, the moderation by governments of the development of technical standards or informational obligations, public financial support of industry initiatives, and voluntary agreements. Usually these activities do not have an international perspective, though.

An international diffusion of environmental innovations is promoted through firms and industry associations, e.g. by promoting international standard setting, in such cases where profitable solutions have been developed.

Some lead markets emerged through environmental standards which were strict in comparison to other countries although the national market was not able to offer the technologies needed to comply with these standards (substitutes for cadmium in Sweden; catalytic converters and mobile fuel cells for cars in California). In most cases, however, a lead market originated from the support of the supply of environmental innovations (wind energy in Denmark and Germany, phosphate substitutes etc.). These – supply oriented – lead markets emerge in countries where the supply sectors have high technological competence. It may be inferred that it is a promising strategy to focus lead market policies on sectors with high technological competence.

Policies to promote lead markets are not integrated into trade policies. It seems conceivable to compensate initially higher costs of environmental innovations for domestic companies by border adjustments. Although such a policy seems difficult to implement within the legal system of international trade it is not totally excluded (Biermann and Brohm, 2003).

An enlargement of markets through the removal of trade barriers could create opportunities for additional economies of scale. So far, such policies are not systematically pursued to promote environmental innovations.

For many environmental innovations it is necessary to overcome lock-ins of traditional technologies by creating a suitable physical, human and institutional infrastructure. This need is generally acknowledged by policy. However, actual measures are generally limited to pilot and demonstration applications because of the high cost involved. Notable exceptions are a) the installation of heat distribution networks in Denmark and Sweden which allowed for the diffusion of combined cycle power stations based on biomass, and b) the obligation of industry in Germany to set up an appropriate infrastructure for the separate collection of packaging wastes which was a prerequisite for developing innovative recycling technologies. In both cases the international diffusion of these technologies is impeded by the fact that in foreign countries such infrastructure is missing.

The case studies gave evidence of the importance for the successful international diffusion of environmental innovations of taking into account preferences for environmental quality abroad. Scandinavian suppliers were stimulated to switch to environmentally more benign chlorine reduced paper bleaching processes by preferences in Germany revealed by a Greenpeace campaign. In the case of phosphate substitutes the early regulation in the US favoured the success of innovation activities in Germany.

In several cases an international diffusion of discussions on environmental and health risks was observed. This happened, for example, with some phosphate substitutes; as a consequence their large scale application turned out to be unlikely. This influenced the direction of innovation activities in Germany.

However, no evidence was found of systematic policies to avoid idiosyncratic solutions; in particular, environmental policies are not designed in a way which assures that preferences abroad are taken into account in an early stage. If international preferences are communicated in international negotiations on environmental standards, the dominant concern is about negative impacts of cost increases on competitiveness.

The variety of markets within the European Union offers a market structure advantage which is not taken advantage of yet, however. Similarly the potentials of designing institutions and programs of basic research in a way which favour sustainability and thus create a market structure advantage for lead markets have not yet been observed.

European environmental regulation is frequently oriented towards demanding objectives and has high binding force. Therefore, the institutions of the European Union offer an arena for smaller member countries to promote the diffusion of their environmental standards – and thus of their environmental technologies – to other members.

Because of the size of the European market environmental standard setting in the European Union influences policies outside the Union. As for product regulation European law in effect forces other countries to follow. Sometimes expected regulation in Europe is even anticipated in other countries (for example in Korea: Jänicke, 1998).

Policies to generate external scale effects by promoting the formation of technological clusters do not play a large role in the cases studies. An exception is the case of fuel cells. In the USA networks of public and private actors were initiated and financially supported to cooperate on the development and market introduction of fuel cells. The European Commission meanwhile recommends this approach.

Technology specific measures of export promotion are uncommon; this seems appropriate as based on the case studies we expect such measures as well as strategies for "exporting" regulation to be of supplementary relevance for the emergence of lead markets only.

In several cases the demonstration of the economic, technological and political feasibility of the innovation (including the corresponding regulation) was decisive for the international success. In these cases, export promotion may use comparatively soft measures and be restricted to inform about innovations. Far reaching, risky and expensive policies of export promotion are needed only if new technologies are little developed.

Government policies to utilise transfer advantages by systematically involving multinational companies or other internationally oriented actors into the process of developing lead markets were rarely observed in the case studies.

Non-governmental actors took the role of developing ambitious environmental policy goals in some cases (chlorine reduced paper bleaching).

The role of a country as an example is also dependent on the specific issue. In areas where a country moved ahead in the past, a leading role can be expected again (for example: exhaust standards in California). A pioneering position in a field of environmental policy improves the chances for the respective country to emerge as a lead market.

A swift international diffusion of sustainability innovations among industrialised countries is favoured if such innovations display lower cost or – at least equally important – functional advantages. Frequently this is not the case, however; then the international diffusion of the innovation depends on the diffusion of the regulation. Systematic attempts to "export" regulation have not been observed in the case studies. A role of a country as an example seems to come about rather incidentally, for example if regulation in a country corresponds to an international regulatory trend. Efforts to diffuse regulation internationally have rather been observed for non-governmental actors such as industry associations.

15 Policies for Lead Markets

Both the empirical and the theoretical studies have revealed a wide range of possible points of governmental intervention for the establishment of lead markets for environmental innovations. They have to be distinguished regarding the phase of development of a technology as depicted in the following graph. Policies in support of lead markets can be distinguished more generally in two phases: Firstly in a phase of stimulating environmental innovations and secondly a phase of the international diffusion of environmental innovations.

Fig. 52. Recommendations for the development of lead markets

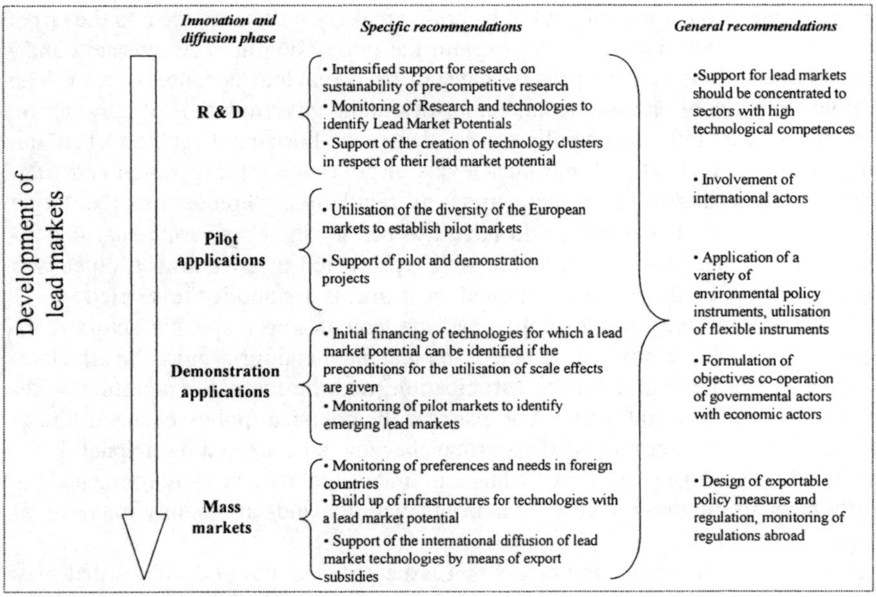

15.1 Policies to Stimulate the Emergence of Environmental Innovations

Policies that are likely to promote the emergence of environmental innovations have been described and analysed by several authors. Their contributions encompass the "multi-impulse hypotheses" (Blazejczak et al., 1999), "design criteria" for environmental policies (Norberg-Bohm, 1999) or „strategic niche management" (Kemp et al., 1998). Our case studies confirm the findings of this literature. The innovation effects of regulations cannot be assigned to single policy instruments only. Policy instruments are a necessary condition for innovation, but on their own, they are not sufficient. Regulatory measures have to be evaluated in a specific context that can, however, be analysed systematically and hence inferences for policy advice can be drawn. According to this literature innovation effects of policies can be ascribed to (1) the configuration of actors, (2) the policy style and (3) the instrumentation.

Actors and Their Configuration

Policymakers aim at restricting, determining or broadening the set of feasible alternatives for (groups of) actors or to influence the consequences or the evaluation of their action. Target groups can be firms (both polluting sectors as well as 'helping' industries, i.e. producers of environmental technologies, insurance companies, environmental consultants, etc.), private households, but also NGOs, governmental departments or other governments.

The selection of a policy instrument and its specific design is a complex process. A simple two actor model with the policy maker on the one side and the target group on the other side could not explain the policy output. The internal conditions of the policy making process have to be taken into account as well: The relative strengths of environmental authorities in the government is of importance, their abilities to implement policies, the degree of horizontal (among other departments) and vertical (among other levels of government) integration and fragmentation determines the effectiveness of regulations. Frequently, the target groups of environmental policy do have trustees in 'their' governmental departments and by them their interests are well represented in government, objectives of environmental policies are questioned, instruments are applied less strictly.

Policy programmes are developed and implemented in a specific actors' configuration: Whether a policy is adopted, implemented and turns out to be effective, depends to a large degree on the participation (and the mutual recognition of legitimacy) of the relevant actors. For example the chemical policy changed fundamentally after the environmentalists groups became an accepted participant in the policy networks during the 1980s while e.g. in the steel industry environmentalists hardly have an important role and environmental demands are mainly imposed by the public authorities.

It is not only governmental actors that issue policies, but also NGOs that may take an equivalent role. Many policy instruments, in particular persuasive instruments are available to private actors as well. Furthermore, NGOs play a vital role in the development of objectives, communicating problems, monitoring the achievement of targets, all of them are important parts of the policy making process. Increasingly, there are private-private alliances between NGOs and firms that have the potential to influence environmental policy making to a large degree (Jacob and Jörgens, 2001). However, these resources are hardly utilised strategically in the policy process.

Policies aiming at stimulating innovations have to take into account the capacity of the target group to innovate.

Policy Style

The effects of policies, in particular those policies that don't imply a complete determination for the target group, largely depend on the policy style. Policy style describes the manner how a policy is formulated and implemented. Policy makers may seek a consensus with the target group or prefer a strategy of conflict. Their behaviour may be calculable or erratic. In particular the effectiveness and the scope of voluntary approaches depend on the (perceived) readiness to implement regulatory measures in case of failure. Innovation effects of other instruments rely on credible long-term commitments: For example the innovation effects of an eco-tax will be higher, if a rise in rates is announced for several years in advance, compared to the same tax that is raised on an ad hoc basis.

Policy analysts as well as policy makers have stressed the importance of long-term objectives in particular to stimulate innovations. However, objectives cannot be chosen freely, they are subject to dispute and change in a bargaining process inside government and with the target group. Therefore, policy objectives are frequently based on a minimal consensus between departments, hence unclear, short termed and not operationalised for target groups.

Instruments

The number of possible instruments is limited only by the creativeness of policy actors. There are many typologies in the literature, mostly based on the degree of determination for the target group. They range from voluntary/persuasive instruments over economic instruments (subsidies, taxes, certificates, etc.), to so-called „command and control" measures. Furthermore, instruments can be distinguished regarding direct or indirect effects: Direct instruments aim at influencing the behaviour of the target group, while indirect instruments stimulate other actors to enforce environmental friendly behaviour. For example liability rules may induce insurance companies to become actors that influence the environmental performance of a firm. More generally, indirect instruments generate interests helping to solve environmental problems.

Policy instruments may be demanding, ranging from technology forcing, support for diffusion of improved technologies, to fixing the current technological standards only. Empirically, environmental policy measures frequently support the diffusion of technologies only, rather than their generation (Conrad, 1998, Jacob, 1999).

Policies often aim at stimulating competition, and search processes inside the target group. In order to be successful in this direction it is necessary that regulation does not determine the target groups' behaviour completely (in this case, innovation is not necessary), but to remain flexible. That is in particular a goal of the so-called 2nd and 3rd generation of environmental policies that aim to change the framework conditions for companies and trigger search processes for the most efficient solution.

Different policy instruments are needed for each stage of the development of innovations (Jacob and Jänicke, 1998). In early stages, supportive measures are required, and it is necessary to protect innovations from sometimes overwhelming market forces, until learning costs have been refinanced. In later stages of development, it is more important to support the diffusion of environmental technologies by discriminating the competing old technology, by giving recommendation to adapt to the new technology or by making the new technology even obligatory.

It is crucial, however, for policies to avoid favouring a specific single technology in an early stage of the policy process. Policy makers should define problems to be solved and assess technological pathways. An assessment of technologies and their likelihood to become successful should focus on possible pathways allowing different competing technologies, rather than single technologies to avoid (possibly expensive) mistakes. Furthermore, by stimulating competition among different technologies it is possible to probably identify the most suitable solutions that are also more likely to be successful abroad.

Firms or other target groups are rarely influenced by a single policy measure only, but they are very often subject to a complex and hybrid regulatory framework. Thereby, the effectiveness of policy measures depends to a large degree on the institutional context. For example a label is effective only if the environmental awareness is high, regulation depend on the capacity for monitoring and enforcement, etc.

The aspect of institutional fit is in particular crucial regarding the adoption of European policies in the member states. When European policy innovations are implemented by the Member States, the wide range of different regulatory traditions has an impact on the effects of a policy. For example the effects of right to know acts vary considerable among the Member States.

Any blueprinting of regulation to stimulate environmental innovation, has to consider these factors, briefly discussed above, that influence the effectiveness (regarding competitiveness, innovation, and environmental effects) and efficiency (or cost effectiveness) of a planned policy.

For the emergence of lead markets for environmental innovations it is important that supporting policies diffuse as well as the supported technologies. The diffusion of policies – either from country to country, or promoted by international organisations – also cannot be explained by analysing the instruments only. Policy diffusion depends on the capacity to adopt the innovation, the type of the underlying problem, the type of the policy instruments and finally the promotion by international organisations (Kern et al., 2000).

Hence, for regulations that are likely to generate lead markets for environmental innovations two conditions must be fulfilled:

- The regulation should be innovation friendly, that is, consider the main actors, involve environmental actors, set long-term, ambitious targets, ensure good institutional fit and avoid of contradictions, and apply flexible, however, demanding instrumentation, and
- the regulation should be easily transferable to other countries.

The second point is less important, since (1) the adopting countries may choose different policies that are a functional equivalent but with a better institutional fit,

(2) the leading country has demonstrated the feasibility of a technology (and the supporting policy) already, and (3) eventually the technology may already be on a stage of development which allows a diffusion even without supporting measures.

15.2 R&D Policies

Our empirical studies as well as theoretical reasoning reveal that the support for environmental innovations should begin as early as possible. There is a need of "greening the innovation system" at early stages of the development of technologies. Thereby, already the development of technologies should be directed towards sustainability. Market forces alone are not sufficient for directing the Innovation System towards an incorporation of sustainability goals at an early stage of development. Policies for this transformation may utilise traditional instruments of R&D policy, that is the funding for research institutes, universities, etc., as well as project based funding. Furthermore, the incorporation of environmental actors such as the environmental ministry, agencies or NGOs at an early stage of the development of R&D funding programs may contribute to the safeguarding of the consideration of environmental objectives. Environmental actors may also become e.g. board members of state financed research institutes. The environmental effects of R&D policies should be regularly assessed and evaluated, by this a learning process can be achieved and funding policies may be permanently improved.

Research activities and the technologies under development should be monitored regarding possible lead market chances. As part of this assessment the needs and preferences of foreign countries should be assessed as well. Technologies that are successful according to this assessment should be selected for funding of pilot and demonstration projects.

The structure of the European market(s) has on the one hand the advantage of its huge size and hence market power. For many technologies that are traded internationally non-European countries already today adopt to European environmental standards because otherwise there would be major trade barriers. On the other hand the European market is diversified and new technologies may be tested under many different market conditions. Policies that aim at stimulating technologies that become adopted should therefore be coordinated in the European Union, without however giving up the advantages of diversity.

Regulators should routinely observe not only technologies, but also pilot markets in order to identify their lead market potentials at an early stage and to set up policies accordingly. We expect from our case studies those countries to become leading where sectors have a relatively high technological competence. Supporting policies should concentrate on these sectors. However, often these sectors are also well established and hence protected in the political system and ambitious policies are more difficult to become adopted. There are also examples of countries that became leading in the development of environmental friendly technologies without hosting the affected sector at all. The development of ambitious policy objectives may be easier in this case, however, it remains uncertain if these countries are actually successful in enforcing their standards on foreign industries.

For those technologies that bear the potential to become adopted by other countries, a support by public funding is often necessary in order to utilise learning and scale effects. Even more expensive and hence risky is the build-up of a potentially necessary infrastructure. If a technology requires an infrastructure, the costs for adoption in other countries are higher as well.

15.3 Environmental Policies for the International Diffusion of Environmental Innovations

Environmental policies should use flexible instruments that allow the target group to adjust to the requirements differentially. By this, several technological options can be tested and the most efficient solution can evolve. These technologies are more likely to diffuse into other countries.

Rather than adopting one single instrument policy makers should use many different policy instruments. By this, the shortcomings of single measures can be levelled out. A broad policy mix is also likely to be more supportive for a diversity in the development of innovations. Furthermore, the adoption of a policy mix rather than the focus on a single instrument is likely to respond to the different conditions of the various target groups.

From a lead market perspective it is sensible to adopt medium- or long-term environmental policies that credibly set up requirements for future technological standards that are beyond feasibility in the present. This "technology forcing" has up to now little tradition in Europe, while it is more common in the US, in particular in California. The considerable potentials that are related to this type of policy should lead to a reconsideration of this tradition. In those cases where technology forcing has been successful and other countries have taken over the regulation and the technology, there have been once again also economic advantages for the leading country.

Environmental policies are still, to a large degree, focused on end-of-pipe (EOP) technologies. This is because policies and regulations are easier adopted and implemented since these requirements do not question the major processes of an industry. The international diffusion of end-of-pipe (EOP) technologies often requires also the diffusion of supporting policies, while in case of integrated technologies that bear additional improvements in efficiency a diffusion may occur even without a parallel diffusion of regulatory measures. Furthermore, our case studies once again reveal that investments in EOP technologies represent a barrier to more advanced measures of ecological modernisation. Therefore, environmental policy should remain flexible regarding the development of technological responses to environmental problems.

It is an important function of environmental policy to support the agenda setting in favour of environmental objectives. This agenda setting may take place in the target group, in the innovation system and among the various branches of government. The setting up of environmental objectives and the monitoring to what extent these objectives are achieved frequently triggers innovation processes. However, the development of objectives is not an easy process. The different branches of government have often conflicting interests and therefore avoid the selection of common objectives or even interfere in the sphere of environmental policy.

A lead market policy is more likely to be successful in policy fields where national actors are perceived as a front runner in environmental policy making. For example Denmark or Germany are perceived as pioneers in energy policy, Sweden in chemical policy, California in terms of air pollution control. These countries have built up comparatively high administrative and political capacities for environmental policy making, they often serve as an example for other countries. By this it is possible to stimulate innovations even abroad.

For the stimulation of environmental innovations and for the safeguarding of their diffusion it is important that the policies of the different branches of government are integrated. The policies of other branches of government than the environment should reflect their potential effects on the environment in general and on the innovation effects in particular and should take these considerations as premises in the formulation of their policies. A range of different strategies and instruments have been developed in the past that aim to bring forward the case of policy integration (Jacob and Volkery, 2003). However, evaluation studies on the application of these measures reveal that political leadership is required for their success. Environmental departments often have not sufficient influence, therefore a high level support for the case of environmental policy integration (EPI) from e.g. the cabinet, the prime ministry or the parliament is required at least for an initial stage.

15.4 Economic Policies

Industrial policies do have an important role to play in the diffusion phase of environmental innovations. Furthermore, the departments on industry and economics often represent the interests of possibly competing industries in the policy process. In order to avoid contradicting policies joint strategies and action plans should be formulated. An assessment of the lead market potential of selected technologies and sectors should be the basis for such a policy planning. It can be useful to incorporate economic actors in this policy development, thereby developing public-private cooperations. Private actors should bear a part of the economic risks by means of a cost sharing regarding the support for technologies. From a lead market perspective it is useful to include international organisations in the process of policy planning. Supporting policies should provide incentives for cooperation among the various companies, e.g. by privileged patent licensing or by offering joint research projects. Thereby, a critical size of technological clusters may be achieved.

Policy measures that support the technology adoption should stimulate in the first phase of market introduction a competition on quality rather than on prices. That contributes to the safeguarding of the technological development and to the development of production capacities. The example of feed-in tariffs in support of technologies for renewable energies may serve as an example. These subsidies proved to be more successful than quotas or auctions for energy from renewable sources as they were introduced in Britain.

A lead market policy should focus on the proof of technological and economic feasibility on the home market rather than on the transfer activities. However, to utilise the potentials of international diffusion, policy may contribute by a monitoring of foreign markets regarding environmental needs. Beyond this, it is also useful to monitor the policy development in other countries and to select policy measures that are likely to be adopted in other countries as well. Technologies with a high lead market potential, however, might be subject to measures of export support. By this scale and learning effects might be achieved more rapidly.

To conclude, a lead market policy is long-term in its character, it encompasses both an innovation friendly policy as well as the support and demand for the diffusion of environmental innovations. To be successful, many different actors have to be engaged. Policies of different branches of government have to be integrated. Lead market policies should be strategically based on a comprehensive policy planning. The starting point is a careful assessment of the technologies and policies regarding their lead market potential. The successful implementation bears considerable economic as well as environmental potentials.

List of Figures

List of Tables

References

Abdul-Khalek I. et al. (1998), *Diesel Trap Performance: Particle Size Measurements and Trends*, SAE Technical Paper Series. 982599, Warrendale.

ACEA (2002), *ACEA Programme on Emissions of Fine Particles from Passenger Cars*, Brussels.

Åhman, M. (2003), *Government Policy and the Development of Electric Vehicles in Japan*, MS.

Ahrens, R. (2002), *Dokumentation des Workshops „Wirtschaftliche Auswirkungen der neuen EU-Chemikalienpolitik", Workshop VI der Reihe „Gesprächsstoffe – Dialog zu Chemikalien, Mensch und Umwelt. Eine gemeinsame Initiative von VCI und IG BCE"* www.vci.de.

Alliance for Environmental Innovation (1999), *Leading by Example. How Businesses Are Expanding the Markets for Environmentally Preferable Paper*, Boston and Washington D.C., MS.

Altemöller, F. (1998), *Handel und Umwelt im Recht der Welthandelsorganisation WTO. Umweltrelevante Streitfälle in der Spruchpraxis zu Artikel III und XX GATT*, Frankfurt a.M.

Altnau, G. (2001), *Safer Solvents for Safer Products*. http://www.coatings.de/articles/ altnau.pdf.

Anderson, J. (2000), *Keeping Cool Without Warming the Planet: Cutting HFCs, PFCs, and SF6 in Europe* http://www.climnet.org/pubs/PIGGfinal.pdf.

Anderson, M. S. and D. Liefferink (1997), *European Environmental Policy. The Pionieers.*, Manchester.

Arp, H. (2002), Technical Regulation and Politics: The Interplay Between Economic Interests and Environmental Policy Goals in EC Car Emission Legislation, in: A. Jordan, *Environmental Policy in the European Union. Actors, Institutions and Processes,* London.

Arthur D. Little (2002a), *Global Comparative Analysis of HFC and Alternative Technologies for Refrigeration, Air Conditioning, Foam, Solvent, Aerosol Propellant, and Fire Protection Applications. Final Report to the Alliance for Responsible Atmospheric Policy* http://www.arap.org/adlittle/HFCstudy3-22JD.pdf.

Arthur D. Little (2002b), *Wirtschaftliche Auswirkungen der EU-Stoffpolitik. Bericht zum BDI-Forschungsprojekt*, Wiesbaden.

ASUE (2000), *Stationäre Brennstoffzellen. Grundlagen, Einsatzmöglichkeiten, Stand der Technik, Perspektiven*, Kaiserslautern.

ATLAS (2003), *Fuel Cells for Transport Applications*. http://europa.eu.int/comm/energy_transport/atlas.

Auer, M. (2000), Who Participates in International Environmental Governance? Partial Answers from International Relations Theory, *Policy Sciences* 33 (2), 155-180.

Bahbout, A., G.P. Tartaglia, and U. Bünger (2000), *Hydrogen Activities in the European Union Work-Programme*, 21th World Gas Conference, June 6-9, 2000, Nice.

Barde, J.-P. (2000), *Green Tax Reforms in OECD Countries: An Overview*, Supporting A Sustainable Future: Making Dollar and Sense, Vancouver.

Barrett, S. (1994), Strategic Environmental Policy and International Trade, *Journal of Public Economics* 54 (3), 325-338.

Barrett, S. (2002), Fuel Cells R&D and Intellectual Property, *Fuel Cells Bulletin* (August), 10-12.

Bass, F. (1969), A New Product Growth Model for Consumer Durables, *Management Science* 15, 215-227.

Beise, M. (1999), *Lead Markets and the International Allocation of R&D*, 5. ASEAT Conference "Demand, Markets, Users and Innovation: Sociological and Economic Approaches", Manchester.

Beise, M. (2001), *Lead Markets. Country-Specific Success Factors of the Global Diffusion of Innovations*, Heidelberg.

Beise, M., J. Blazejczak, D. Edler, K. Jacob, M. Jänicke, T. Loew, U. Petschow, and K. Rennings (2003), *The Emergence of Lead Markets for Environmental Innovations*, FFU rep 03-02, Berlin.

Beise, M. and K. Rennings (2003), *Lead Markets for Environmental Innovations: A Framework for Innovation and Environmental Economics*, ZEW Discussion Paper 03-01, Mannheim.

Bergius (2002), *Nachhaltig anlegen heißt an Wert gewinnen,* Handelsblatt online, 11.7.2002.

Berner, P., A. Obermeier, R. Friedrich, D. Ondratschek, and K. Schaber (1996), *Strategien zur Minderung der VOC-Emissionen ausgewählter Emittentengruppen in Baden-Württemberg*, Forschungsbericht FZKA-PEF 147, Karlsruhe.

Berth, P. (1984), Der Einsatz von NTA in Ländern außerhalb der Bundesrepublik Deutschland, in: NTA-Koordinierungsgruppe, *NTA Studie über die aquatische Umweltverträglichkeit von Nitrilotriacetat (NTA),* St. Augustin

Biermann, F. and R. Brohm (2003), *Implementing the Kyoto Protocol of Energy Tax Adjustments at the Border*, Global Governance Working Paper No 5, Potsdam.

Binder, M. (2002), *Umweltpolitische Basisinnovationen im Industrieländervergleich*, FFU-Report 02-06, Berlin.

BINE (2000), *Kraft-Wärme-Kopplung mit Bennstoffzellen. Projektinfo 5/00.* http://bine.fiz-karlsruhe.de/pdf/publikation/bi0500.pdf.

Birnbaum, U., H. Dienhart, J. Nitsch, F. Staiß and M. Walbeck (1999), *Die Marktsituation von Brennstoffzellen*, Jahrestagung Forschungsverbund Sonnenenergie – Zukunftstechnologie Brennstoffzelle. 15.-16.9.1999

Bizer, K. and M. Führ (2000), *Emissionsminderung durch Produktpolitik. Das Beispiel organischer Lösemittel in Farben und Lacken*, Sofia-Diskussionsbeiträge zur Institutionenanalyse Nr. 00-3, Darmstadt.

Blazejczak, J. and D. Edler (1998), *Elemente innovationsfreundlicher Politikmuster – ein internationaler Vergleich am Beispiel der Papierindustrie. Untersuchung im Auftrag des BMBF*, Berlin, MS.

Blazejczak, J. and D. Edler (2003), *Fallstudie Technologien mit Potentialen zur Substitution von Papier*, Berlin, MS.

Blazejczak, J., D. Edler, J. Hemmelskamp and M. Jänicke (1999), Umweltpolitik und Innovation: Politikmuster und Innovationswirkungen im internationalen Vergleich, *Zeitschrift für Umweltpolitik und Umweltrecht* 22 (1), 1-32.

BMBF (1996), *BMBF-Förderschwerpunkt Wasserstofftechnologie und Brennstoffzelle.* www.hydrogen.org/Politik/bmbf.html.

BMU and VCI (1997), Gemeinsamer Abschlussbericht zum Dialog des BMU und des VCI zu Umweltzielen am Beispiel VOC,

BMWi (2001a), *Nachhaltige Energiepolitik für eine zukunftsfähige Energieversorgung. Energiebericht.* http://www.bmwi.de/textonly/Homepage/download/energie/Energiebericht9MB.pdf.

BMWi (2001b), *Projekte mit Perspektiven. Energieforschung.* http://www.bmwi.de/ textonly/ Homepage/ download/energie/Energieforschung1.pdf.

Bommer, R. (1996), Das Drei-Liter-Auto: Ein sinnvoller Lösungsansatz?, *Wirtschaftsdienst* (5/1996), 256-260.

Bonifant, B. (1994), *Competitive Implications of Environmental Regulation in the Paint and Coatings Industry.* http://yosemite.epa.gov/ee/epa/eermfile.nsf/vwAN/EE-0045-03.pdf/$File/EE-0045-03.pdf.

Brown, D. R. and R. Jones (1999), *An Overview of Stationary Fuel Cell Technology. Research Report prepared for the U.S. Army Forces Command.*

Brueckner, S. (2002), *European Diesel Engine Technology: an overview. Presentation given at the Diesel Engine Emissions Reduction Conference, San Diego 25-29 August.*

BTM Consult (2002), *BTM statistics* http://www.btm.dk.

Bünger, U. (2000), *Einsatzbedingungen und Marktchancen von Brennstoffzellen als Klein-BHKW.*, Effiziente und umweltfreundliche Strom- und Wärmeerzeugung mit Brennstoffzellen. 20.-21. Juli 2000, Friedrichshafen.

Busch, P.-O. (2003), *Die Diffusion von Einspeisevergütungen und Quotenmodellen: Konkurrenz der Modelle in Europa*, FFU-Report 03-03, Berlin.

Busch, P.-O. and H. Jörgens (2003), *The Diffusion of Environmental Policy Innovations*, ffu-rep, Berlin.

Butz, C. (2002), *PV 2002: Markt Akteure und Prognosen*, Sarasin Studie, Basel.

California EPA Air Resources Board (2003), *Federal, State and Local Incentives for Cleaner Vehicles Including Electric, Hybrid Electric and Alternative Fuel Vehicles*, Sacramento. http://www.arb.ca.gov/msprog/zevprog/zip/incentiv.htm.

Californian Environmental Protection Agency (1999), *Air Resource Board. 1998 Architectural Coatings Survey, Final Report.* http://www.arb.ca.gov/coatings/arch/Survey/ results/FReport.PDF.

Cardiff (2002), *Cardiff Software Corporate Overview* www.cardiff.com.

Carraro, C. and D. Siniscalco (1992), Environmental Innovation Policy and International Competiton, *Environmental and Resources Economics* 2, 183-200.

Carstens, S., C. Baerts and E. Knaus (2001), Anspruchsvolle Temperatursensorik zum Einhalten der Abgasnorm Euro IV, *Motortechnische Zeitschrift* 6/2001, 464-473.

CEFIC (2002), *Business Impact Study. Sectoral Fact Sheets* www.chemicalspolicy-review.org.

CEN (2000), *Market, Environment and Objectives of CEN/TC 139 – Paints and Varnishes, as Approved by Resolution BTC 103/2000.* http://www.cenorm.be/standardization/ tech_bodies/ cen_bp/resources/a139.pdf.

Cerny, P. (1999), Globalization and the Erosion of Democracy, *European Journal of Political Research* 36 (1), 1-26.

Cirkel, H.-J. (2000), *SOFC Fuel Cells for Stationary Power Generation*, Hyforum 2000 – The International Hydrogen Energy Forum, 11-15 September 2000, Munich.

Concord Equity Research (2002), *DMS Deutschland – Sektor Report 19/04/02* www.concord-equity.de.

Conrad, J. (Ed.) (1998), *Environmental Management in European Companies. Success Stories and Evaluation*, Amsterdam.

Cooper, R. G. and E. J. Kleinschmidt (1987), Success Factors in Product Innovation, *Industrial Marketing Management* 16, 215-223.

Cowan, R. (1990), Nuclear Power Reactors: A Study in Technological Lock-in, *Journal of Economic History* 50 (3), 541-567.

Cropper, M. (2002), *Fuel Cell Market Survey: Stationary Applications* www.fuelcelltoday.com/FuelCellToday/FCTFiles/FCTArticleFiles/Article_467_MarketSurveyStationaryApplications.pdf.

Cropper, M. (2003), *Fuel Cell Market Survey – Large Stationary Applications* http://www.fuelcelltoday.com/FuelCellToday/FCTFiles/FCTArticleFiles/Article_667_LgeStatSurvey0903.pdf.

Cropper, M., S. Geiger, and D. Jollie (2003), *Fuel Cell Systems: A survey of worldwide activity* http://www.fuelcelltoday.com/ FuelCellToday/FCTFiles/FCTArticleFiles/ Article_ 696 _ WorldWideSurvey1103.pdf.

Danish Wind Industry Association (2002), *Wind Power Information* http://www.windpower.dk.

Decopaint (2000), *Decopaint. Study on the Potential for Reducing Emissions of Volatile Organic Compounds (VOC) Due to The Use Of Decorative Paints and Varnishes for Professional and Non-Professional Use. Final Report* http://europa.eu.int/comm/environment/ air/decopaint.pdf.

Dekimpe, M. G., P. M. Parker, and M. Sarvary (1998), "Globalisation": Modelling Technology Adoption Timing Across Countries, INSEAD working paper No. 98/69/MKT

Department of Defense (1998), *Report to the Congressional Defense Committee on the Utilization and Demonstration of Fuel Cells. August 1998*

Department of Energy (2002), *SECA Program Plan. Making Fuel Cells Available to America.*

Department of Energy (2003), *Fuel Cell Report to Congress* http://www.eere.energy.gov/hydrogenandfuelcells/pdfs/fc_report_congress_feb2003.pdf.

Desai, U. (Ed.) (2002), *Environmental Politics and Policy in Industrialized Countries*, Cambridge, MA.

deVries, M. S. (2001), The Attack on the State: a Comparison of the Arguments, *International Review of Administrative Sciences* 67 (3), 389-414.

Diabaté, S. (2003), Toxikologie von Nanopartikeln, in: M. Steinfeldt, *Mit Nanotechnologie zur Nachaltigkeit? Prospektive Technologiebewertung einer zukünftigen Schlüsseltechnologie,* Berlin

Dienhart, H., J. Nitsch, and M. Pehnt (1998), *Oekologische und oekonomische Bewertung der PEFC-Brennstoffzelle am Beispiel der Nahwaermeversorgung.* http://www.dlr.de/TT/system/ projects/BZellen/pefcbhkw.pdf.

Dienhart, H., M. Pehnt, and J. Nitsch (2000), *Analyse von Einsatzmöglichkeiten und Rahmenbedingungen von Brennstoffzellen in industrieller Kraft-Wärme-Kopplung und zentraler Stromversorgung (Zusammenfassung)* http://www.dlr.de/TT/system/ publications/BZanalyse.

Dolowitz, D. and D. March (1996), Who Learns from Whom? A Review of the Policy Transfer Literature, *Political Studies* 44, 343-357.

Dorenkamp, R. and H. Stehr (2001), Potenzial der Hochdruckeinspritzung, *Motortechnische Zeitschrift* special edition: 25 Jahre VW-Dieselmotoren, 50-54.

Dosi, G., K. Pavitt, and L. Soete (1990), *The Economics of Technical Change and International Trade*, New York.

Ecchia, G. and Mariotti (1994), *A Survey on Environmental Policy, Technological Innovation and Strategic Issus*, 44.94, Milano.

Eckart, M. (1999), *Financing Solar Energy in the U.S.*, MS.

ECMT (2002), *Vehicle Emission Trends*, Paris.

Economic Commission for Europe/VOC Task Force (1990), *Emissions of Volatile Organic Compounds (VOC) from Stationary Sources and Possibilities of their Control. Final Report*, Berlin.

Elsener, M., M. Koebel, and G. Madia (2001), NOx-Verminderung in Dieselabgasen mit Harnstoff-SCR bei tiefen Temperaturen, *Motortechnische Zeitschrift* 2/2001, 166-175.

Entec/PRA (2000), *Reducing VOC Emissions from the Vehicle Refinishing Sector. Study for the European Commission.* http://europa.eu.int/comm/environment/air/ vehrefinish.pdf.

Environmental Defence Fund (1995), *Paper Task Force Recommendations for Purchasing and Using Environmentally Preferable Paper. Project Synopsis*, New York, MS.

Esty, D. C. (1999), Economic Integration and the Environment, in: N. J. Vig and R. Axelrod, *The Global Environment. Institutions, Law, and Policy,* Washington DC, 190-209.

Esty, D. C. and M. E. Porter (2000), Measuring National Environmental Performance and Its Determinants, in: Harvard University and World Economic Forum, *The Global Competitiveness Report 2000,* New York/Oxford, 60-75.

Europäische Umweltagentur (2001), *Environmental Signals. Environmental assessment report No 8*, Copenhagen.

European Commission (2001), *Whitebook "Strategy for a future chemicals policy"*, COM(2001)88 final, Bruxelles.

European Commission (2002a), *2001 – Annual Energy Review January 2002*, Luxemburg.

European Commission (2002b), *eEurope 2005: An Information Society for All*

European Commission DG XIII/E (1996), *Strategic Developments for the European Publishing Industry towards the Year 2000*, Brussels, Luxembourg.

European Commission Enterprise Directorate General (2002), *ICT and e-Business in the Media and Printing Industries. The European e-Business Market Watch*, Sector Report No. 8, October 2002

European Conference of Ministers of Transport (2000), *Vehicle Emission Trends*, Paris. http://www.oecd.otg/cem.

Faiz, A., C. S. Weaver, and M. P. Walsh (1996), *Air Pollution from Motor Vehicles, Standards and Technologies for Controlling Emissions*, Washington, D.C.

Federal Highway Administration (2000), *Highway Statistics 2000*, Washington, D.C.

Feess, E. (1998), *Umweltökonomie und Umweltpolitik*, München.

Feess, E. and G. Muehlheusser (2002), Strategic Environmental Policy, Clean Technologies and the Learning Curve, *Environmental and Resource Economics* 23 (2), 149-166.

Feess, E. and G. Taistra (2001), Strategische Umweltpolitik – Überblick und weiterer Forschungsbedarf, *Zeitschrift für Umweltpolitik und Umweltrecht* (1/2001), 1-19.

FhG-ISI (1998), *DELPHI '98 Umfrage. Studie zur globalen Entwicklung von Wissenschaft und Technik. Zusammenfassung der Ergebnisse; Methoden- und Datenband*, Karlsruhe. http://www.isi.fhg.de/publ/downloads/isi98b07/.

Fisher, J. C. (1973), *Energy Crises in Perspective*, New York.

Flaig, B. and F. Zimmermann (2000), Elektrisch betätigtes AGR-Ventil, *Motortechnische Zeitschrift* 9/2000, 572-579.

Fleischer, M., S. Kelm, and D. Palm (2000), *Regulation and Innovation in the Chemical Industry*, Sevillia.

Franke, A. (1998), Auf dem Weg zum 3-Liter-Auto – Minderung der verkehrsbedingten CO2-Emissionen, in: I. Institut, *Abschätzung der innovativen Wirkungen umweltpolitischer Instrumente – dargestellt am Beispiel des Systems Straßenverkehr*, München, 146-179.

Friedrich, A., M. Tappe, and R. K. W. Wurzel (2000), A New Approach to EU Environmental Policy Making? The Auto-Oil I Programme, *Journal of European Public Policy* 7 (4), 593-612.

Fritsche, U. R. (1999), *Umweltaspekte von Brennstoffzellen*, Workshop Status der Entwicklung und Anwendung der Brennstoffzellentechnik. 11. November 1999, Bremen.

Fröhlich-Merz, G. (2001), Umwelt: Partikelfilter macht Diesel-Pkw zum Saubermann, *VDI Nachrichten* (7.9.2001), 25.

FTD (2003), *VW verzichtet wegen hoher Kosten auf Rußfilter*. Financial Times Deutschland, 19.2.2003.

Fuhs, W. (2000), Photovoltaic – Stand und Perspektiven, *FVS DGS Themen,*

Gates, B. (1999), *Business @ the Speed of Thought*, New York.

Geiger, S. (2003), *Brennstoffzellen in Deutschland – Marktanalyse relevanter Tätigkeiten* http://www.fuelcelltoday.com/FuelCellToday/FCTFiles/FCTArticleFiles/Article_621_GermanySurvey0603de.pdf.

Gemünden, H. G. (1981), *Innovationsmarketing: Interaktionsbeziehungen zwischen Hersteller und Verwender innovativer Investitionsgüter*, Tübingen.

German Advisory Council on the Environment (2003), *On the Economic Impact of the planned Reform of European Chemicals Policy*, Berlin. http://www.umweltrat.de/03stellung/ downlo03/stellung/ Stellung_Reach_Juli2003_ eng.pdf.

Goldstein, L., J. Mortensen, and D. Trickett (1999), *Grid Connected Renewable Electric Policies in the European Union*, Washington, D.C.

Goodwin, F. (1999), *Controlling Traffic Pollution and the Auto Oil Programme*, Brussels.

Green, D. and M. Griffith (2002), Globalization and Its Discontents, *International Affairs* 78 (1), 49-68.

Grundmann, R. (1999), *Transnationale Umweltpolitik zum Schutz der Ozonschicht*, Frankfurt.

Haas, P. M. (2002), UN Conferences and Constructivist Governance of the Environment, *Global Governance* 8 (1)

Haas, P. M. and et al. (1993), *Institutions for the Earth. Sources of Effecitve International Environmental Protection*, Cambridge, MA.

Haas, R. (Ed.) (2001), *Promotion Strategies for Electricity from Renewable Energy Sources*, Vienna.

Handelsblatt (2003a), *Benzinschlucker kommen unter die Räder*. Handelsblatt online, 12.2.2003.

Handelsblatt (2003b), *Bosch glaubt an Diesel-Durchbruch in den USA*. Handelsblatt online, 7.5.2003.

Handelsblatt (2003c), *Neue Dieselfilter bescheren Auto-Zulieferern Umatzschub*. Handelsblatt online, 6.8.2003.

Hardt, M. and A. Negri (2000), *Empire*, Cambridge, M.A.

Harmon, C. (2000), *Experience Curves of Photovoltaic Technology*, IIASA Interim Report 00-014, Laxenburg.

Hartje, V. J. (1985), *Environmental Product Regulation and Innovation: Limiting Phosphates in Detergents in Germany*, Berlin.

Hay, C. and B. Rosamond (2002), Globalization, European Integration and the Discursive Construction of Economic Imperatives, *Journal of European Policy* 9 (2), 147-167.

Hekkert, M. and R. van den Hoed (2003), *Competing Technologies and the Struggle Towards a New Dominant Design: The Emergence of the Hybrid Vehicle at the Expense of the Fuel Cell Vehicle? Paper presented at the International Conference of the Greening of Industry Network "Innovating for Sustainability", October 12 to 15 2003, San Francisco*, MS.

Held, D. and et al. (1999), *Global Transformations: Politics, Economics and Culture*, Cambridge.

Héritier, A., S. Mingers, C. Knill, and M. Becka (1994), *Die Veränderung von Staatlichkeit in Europa – Ein regulativer Wettbewerb: Deutschland, Großbritannien, Frankreich*, Opladen.

Herrmann, H. O., O. Lang, I. Mikulic, and V. Scholz (2001), Partikelfiltersysteme für Diesel-Pkw, *Motortechnische Zeitschrift* 9/2001, 652-660.

Heymann, M. (1995), *Die Geschichte der Windenergienutzung 1890-1990*, Frankfurt a.M.

Hirschenhofer, J. H., D. B. Stauffer, R. R. Engleman, and M. G. Klett (1998), *Fuel Cell Handbook 1998*

Hoberg, G. (2001), Trade, Harmonization, and Domestic Autonomy in Environmental Policy, *Journal of Comparative Policy Analysis: Research and Practice* 3, 191-217.

Hoffmann, J. (2002), *Automobilmarketing im Spannungsfeld von gesellschaftlichen Umweltzielen und Kundennutzen*, Frankfurt a.M.

Holihan, P. (2000), *Technology Manufacturing and Market Trends in the U.S. and International Photovoltaics Industry* www.eia.doe.gov.

Holmström, B. R. and J. Tirole (1987), The Theory of the Firm, in: R. Schmalensee and R. Willig, *Handbook of Industrial Organization,* Amsterdam, 61-133.

Homma, T. (2000), Present Status of Fuel Cells RD&D in Japan, *U.S. Eco-Energy* February 27-28, Tokyo.

Homma, T. (2001), *Oral Presentation*, Properties and Phase Equilibria for Product and Process Design, Kurashiki, Japan.

Ifeu (2001), *Vergleichende Analyse von Energieverbrauch und CO -Emissionen im Straßengüterverkehr und Kombinierten Verkehr Straße/Schiene*, Heidelberg.

Industry Canada, PriceWaterhouseCooper and Fuel Cells Canada (2003), *Canadian Fuel Cell. Commercialization Roadmap.* http://strategis.ic.gc.ca/epic/internet/inmse-epe.nsf/vwapj/FuelCellsTRM_e.pdf/$FILE/FuelCellsTRM_e.pdf.

Institute for Health and Environment (2001), *Testing Requirements for Proposals Under the EC White Paper "Strategy for a Future EU Chemicals Policy"*, IHE Web Report W6.

Institute for Solar Energy Technology (2002), *Renewable Energy Information System on Internet – REISI* http://reisi.iset.uni-kassel.de.

International Energy Agency (1998), *Advanced Fuel Cell Program. Strategy for the Period 1999 to 2003*

International Energy Agency (1999), *Energy Policies of IEA Countries. Japan 1999 Review*, Paris.

International Energy Agency (2000a), *Experience Curves in Environmental Technology Policies*, Paris.

International Energy Agency (2000b), *Experience Curves in Environmental Technology Policies*, Paris.

International Energy Agency (2000c), *Final Report of the IEA Advanced Fuel Cells Implementing Agreement (1996 – 1999)*.

International Energy Agency (2002), *Trends in Photovoltaic Applications in selected IEA countries between 1992 and 2001*, Paris.

International Energy Agency (2003a), *Saving Oil and Reducing CO2 Emissions in Transport*, Paris.

International Energy Agency (2003b), *Trends in Photovoltaic Applications: Survey report of selected IEA countries between 1992 and 2002*, Paris.

International Energy Agency and OECD (2002), *Energy Balances of OECD Countries 1960 – 2000*, Paris.

ISSA (1999), *ISSA State Phosphate Survey. December 1999* http://www.issa.com/legislative/pdfs/phosphate.pdf.

Jacob, K. (1999), *Innovationsorientierte Chemikalienpolitik. Politische, soziale und ökonomische Faktoren des verminderten Gebrauchs gefährlicher Stoffe*, München.

Jacob, K. and M. Jänicke (1998), Ökologische Innovationen in der chemischen Industrie: Umweltentlastung ohne Staat? Eine Untersuchung und Kommentierung zu 182 Gefahrstoffen, *Zeitschrift für Umweltpolitik & Umweltrecht* 21 (4/98), 519-547.

Jacob, K. and H. Jörgens (2001), *Gefährliche Liebschaften? Kommentierte Bibliografie zu Kooperationen von Umweltverbänden und Unternehmen*, FS II 01- 304, Berlin.

Jacob, K. and A. Volkery (2003), *Instruments for Policy Integration. Intermediate Report of the Project POINT*, FFU rep 03-06, Berlin. http://www.fu-berlin.de/ ffu/download/ rep_2003-06.pdf.

Jacobson, M. Z. (2002), Control of Fossil-Fuel Particulate Black Carbon and Organic Matter, Possibly the Most Effective Method of Slowing Global Warming, *Journal of Geophysical Research* 107 (D19).

Jacobson-Brown, H. and C. Weiss (Eds.) (1998), *Engaging Countries. Strengthening Compliance with International Environmental Accords*, Cambridge, MA.

Jaffe, A., R. Newell, and R. Stavins (2002), Environmental Policy and Technological Change, *Environmental and Resources Economics* 22 (1-2), 41-70.

Jänicke, M. (1998), Umweltpolitik: Global am Ende oder am Ende global?, in: U. Beck, *Perspektiven der Weltgesellschaft,* Frankfurt/M., 332-344.

Jänicke, M. (2000), *Ecological Modernization. Innovation and Diffusion of Policy and Technology*, FFU-Report 00-8, Berlin.

Jänicke, M., J. Blazejczak, D. Edler, and J. Hemmelskamp (2000), Environmental Policy and Innovation: an International Comparison of Policy Frameworks and Innovation Effects, in: J. Hemmelskamp, K. Rennings and F. Leone, *Innovation-oriented Environmental Regulation. Theoretical Approaches and Empirical Analysis,* Heidelberg, New York, 125-152.

Jänicke, M. and K. Jacob (2002), *Ecological Modernization and the Creation of Lead Markets*, FFU rep 02-03, Berlin.

Jänicke, M., L. Mez, P. Bechsgaard, and B. Klemmensen (1999), Innovative Effects of Sector Specific Regulation Patterns. The Example of Energy Efficient Refrigerators in

Denmark, in: P. Klemmer, *Innovation and the Environment. Case Studies on the Adaptive Behavior in Society and the Economy,* Berlin, 49-69.

Jänicke, M. and H. Weidner (Eds.) (1997), *National Environmental Policies: A Comparative Study of Capacity-Building*, Berlin.

Johnstone, B. (1999), *We were Burning: Japanese Entrepreneurs and the Forging of the Electronic Age*, New York.

Jörgens, H. (1996), Die Institutionalisierung von Umweltpolitik im internationalen Vergleich, in: M. Jänicke, *Umweltpolitik der Industrieländer. Entwicklung – Bilanz – Erfolgsbedingungen,* Berlin, 59-111.

Jung, A. (2002), *Rahmenbedingungen für die Nutzung erneuerbarer Energien. Paper presented on the Conference "Renewable Energies" in Wiesbaden, August 28 and 29 2002*, MS.

Kahrstedt, J. and R. Buchwald (2001), *Vorteile eines hybriden Brennverfahrens auf der Basis eines aufgeladenen DI-Dieselmotors. 8th conference: Der Arbeitsprozess des Verbrennungsmotors*, Graz.

Kalish, S., V. Mahajan, and E. Muller (1995), Waterfall and Sprinkler New-Product Strategies in Competitive Global Markets, *International Journal of Research in Marketing* 12 (2), 105-119.

Kampffmeyer, U. (2002), *Dokumenten-Management den Kinderschuhen entwachsen* www.PROJECT-CONSULT.com.

Keck, O. (1980), Government Policy and Technical Choice in the West German Reactor Programme, *Research Policy* 9, 302-356.

Kelemen, R. D. (2001), The Limits of Judicial Power. Trade-Environment Disputes in the GATT/WTO and the EU, *Comparative Political Studies,* 34 (6), 622-650.

Kemp, R. (2000), *Technology and Environmental Policy: Innovation Effects of Past Policies and Suggestions for Improvement*, Paper for OECD workshop on Innovation and Environment, Paris.

Kemp, R., X. Olsthoorn, F. Oosterhuis, and H. Verbruggen (1994), Policy Instruments of Stimulate Cleaner Technologies, in: H. Opschoor and K. Turner, *Economic Incentives and Environmental Policies. Principles and Practice,* Dordrecht, Boston, London, 275-300.

Kemp, R., J. Schot, and R. Hoogma (1998), Regime Shifts to Sustainability through processes of Niche Formation. The Approach of Strategic Niche Management, *Technology Analysis and Strategic Management* 10 (2), 175-195.

Keohane, R. O. and L. L. Martin (1995), The Promise of Institutionalist Theory, *International Security* 20 (1), 39-51.

Kern, K. (2000), *Die Diffusion von Politikinnovationen*, Opladen.

Kern, K., H. Jörgens, and M. Jänicke (2000), Die Diffusion umweltpolitischer Innovationen. Ein Beitrag zur Globalisierung von Umweltpolitik, *Zeitschrift für Umweltpolitik & Umweltrecht* (4), 507-546.

Klemmer, P., U. Lehr, and K. Löbbe (1999), *Umweltinnovationen. Anreize und Hemmnisse*, Berlin.

Knill, C. and D. Lehmkuhl (2002), Private Actors and the State. Internationalization and Changing Patterns of Governance, *Governance* 15 (1), 41-63.

Koehn, P. H. and J. Rosenau (2002), Transnational Competence in an Emergent Epoch, *International Studies Perspectives* 3 (2), 105-127.

Kolke, R. (1998), *Technische Optionen zur Verminderung der Verkehrsbelastung, Brennstoffzellenfahrzeuge*, Berlin.

Köllinger, P. (2003), Internetnutzung in Deutschland: Nach Boom nur langsamerer Anstieg erwartet, *DIW Wochenbericht* (30/2003), 477-483.

Krebs, R. and J. Theobald (2001), *Die Thermodynamik der FSI-Motoren von Volkswagen. 22nd International Vienna Engine Symposium*, Vienna, MS.

Lääne et al. (2002), *Evaluation of the implementation of the 1988 Ministerial Declaration regarding nutrient load reductions in the Baltic Sea catchment area*, Helsinki. http://www.vyh.fi/eng/orginfo/publica/electro/fe524/fe524.pdf.

Lafferty, W. B. and J. Meadowcraft (Eds.) (2000), *Implementing Sustainable Development: Strategies and Initiatives in High-Consumption Societies*, Oxford.

Lange, B. (1997), *BERICHT über den Vorschlag und den geänderten Vorschlag für eine Richtlinie des Europäischen Parlaments und des Rates über Maßnahmen gegen die Verunreinigung der Luft durch Emissionen von Kraftfahrzeugen und zur Änderung der Richtlinien 70/156/EWG und 70/220/EWG des Rates*, Brussels.

Langenbach, C. J. and O. Ulrich (Eds.) (2002), *Elektronische Signaturen. Kulturelle Rahmenbedingungen einer technischen Entwicklung*, Berlin.

Langraf, B. and T. Kellner (2000), *Windenergie in Europa: Was bringen Gesetzgebung und Fördermaßnahmen. Interwind AG, im Auftrag des Bundesamtes für Energie (Ch)*, Zürich.

Lehmann, H. and T. Reetz (1995), *Zukunftsenergien – Strategien einer neuen Energiepolitik*, Basel.

Levitt, T. (1983), The Globalisation of Markets, *Harvard Business Review* 61 (3), 92-102.

Liefferink, D. and M. S. Andersen (1998), *Strategies of the 'green' member states in EU environmental policy-making. Journal of European Public Policy*: 254-270.

Lievonen, J., J. C. Císcar, D. Kyriakou, A. Eerola (Eds.) (2000), *IPTS-ESTO Techno-Economic Analysis Report 1999-2000* ftp://ftp.jrc.es/pub/EURdoc/eur19626en.pdf.

Linder, S. B. (1961), *An Essay on Trade and Transformation*, Uppsala.

Loew, T. (2002), *Internationale Entwicklung der Regulierungen zur Förderung ökologisch-ethischer Finanzdienstleistungen*, Diskussionspapier des IÖW 56/20, Berlin.

Lohbeck, W. (1999), *The Greenfreeze Wave Keeps on Rolling. In: Development and Trends in ODS Phase Out*, Yearbook 1997-1999 http://www.gtz.de/proklima.

Lorentzen, G. (1995), *The Use of Natural Refrigerants. A Complete Solution to the CFC/HCFC-Predicament*, GTZ Yearbook 1995 http://www.gtz.de/proklima.

Löschel, A. (2002), *Technological Change in Energy – Economy – Environmental Models*, Risk and Uncertainty in Environmental and Resource Economic, Wageningen.

Lundvall, B.-A. (1988), Innovation as an Interactive Process – from User-Producer Interaction to the National System of Innovation, in: G. Dosi et al. (Eds.), *Technical Change and Economic Theory*, London, 349-369.

Mansfield, E. (1968), *Industrial Research and Technological Innovation: An Econometric Analysis*, New York.

Masaaki, T., Z. Nobuyuki, M. Toshiya, S. Shogo, and Y. Yoshi (2003), Development of Molten Carbonate Fuel Cell, *IHI ENGINEERING REVIEW* February 2003

Maté, J. (n.d.), *A Non-Governmental Organization's Campaign to Save the Ozone Layer. Case Study of the Greenpeace Ozone Campaign* http://a1216.g.akamai.net /7/1216/ 1532/cf99977c7ebe16/archive.greenpeace.org/~climate/climatecountdown/documents/ makingadiff.pdf.

Maty, J. (2000), *Special Report: Regulations* http://www.pcimag.com/ CDA/ ArticleInformation/ features/ BNP__Features__Item/0,1846,7273,00.html.

McKinney, R. W. J. (1995a), Wastepaper Preparation and Contaminant Removal, in: R. W. J. McKinney, *Technology of Paper Recycling,* London, 48-129.

McKinney, R. W. J. (1995b), Wastepaper Recovery and Collection, in: R. W. J. McKinney, *Technology of Paper Recycling,* London, 1-27.

Menzel, S. (2002), *Filtersysteme säubern Diesel-Abgase*. Handelsblatt, 21.5.2002.

Meyer-Krahmer, F. (1999), Was bedeutet Globalisierung für Aufgaben und Handlungsspielräume nationaler Innovationspolitiken?, in: K. Grimmer, S. Kuhlmann, and F. Meyer-Krahmer (Eds.), *Innovationspolitik in globalisierten Arenen,* Opladen, 43-74.

Michelin, J., F. Terres, and H. Weltens (2002), Partikelfilter für Diesel-Pkw. Beladungs- und Regenerationsverhalten, *Motortechnische Zeitschrift* 7-8/2002, 568-577.

Miles B. et al. (Eds.) (2000), *International Regime Effectiveness. Global Environmental Accord*, Cambridge, M.A.

Mistra (2001), *Screening of Screening Companies. Socially Responsible Investment, SRI. An Assessment of existing Products*, Stockholm.

Mitchell, B. (1980), *European Historical Statistics 1750-1975*, London.

Mitchell, R. (1994), *Intentional Oil Pollution at Sea: Environmental Policy and Treaty Compliance*, Cambridge, M.A.

Mol, A. P. J. (1995), *The Refinement of Production. Ecological Modernization Theory and the Chemical Industry*, Utrecht.

Mol, A. P. J. and D. A. Sonnenfeld (Eds.) (2000), *Ecological Modernization Around the World. Perspectives and Critical Debates*, London/Portland (Or.).

Nakicenovic, N. (1986), The automobile Road to Technological Change: Diffusion of the Automobile as a Process of Technological Substitution, *Technological Forecasting & Social Change,* 29 (4), 309-340.

Neunzig, D. and H. Wallentowitz (1998), *Neue technische Entwicklungen und deren Potentiale zur Verringerung der Emissionen von Landverkehrsmitteln*, Aachen.

Nitsch, J. and H. Dienhart (1998), *Wirtschaftlichkeit und Marktperspektiven der Energiewandlung mit Brennstoffzellen* http://www2.dlr.de/ TT/system/ projects/ BZellen/ wrtstkt.pdf.

Norberg-Bohm (1999), Stimulating 'Green' Technological Innovation: An Analysis of Alternative Policy Mechanisms, *Policy Sciences* 32, 13-38.

Nordbeck, R. and M. Faust (2002), *European Chemicals Regulation and its Effect on Innovation: An Assessment of the EU's White Paper on the Strategy for a Future Chemicals Policy*, UFZ-Discussion Papers 4/2002, Halle.

Nork, M. E. (1992), *Umweltschutz in unternehmerischen Entscheidungen. Eine theoretische und empirische Analyse*, Wiesbaden.

Nösler, H. G. (1974), Zum Stand der internationalen Gesetzgebung: Noch keine Harmonie, *Umwelt* (1), 39-41.

NTA-Koordinierungsgruppe (1984), *NTA Studie über die aquatische Umweltverträglichkeit von Nitrilotriacetat (NTA)*, St. Augustin.

Nye, J. and J. Donahue (Eds.) (2000), *Governance in a Globalizing World*, Cambridge, MA.

Oberthür, S. (1997), *Umweltschutz durch internationale Regime. Interessen, Verhandlungsprozesse, Wirkungen*, Opladen.

OECD (1994), *Capacity Development in Environment*, Paris.

OECD (2002a), *Energy Balances of OECD Countries 1960 – 2000*, Paris.

OECD (2002b), *OECD Information Technology Outlook*, Paris.

Oertel, D. and T. Fleischer (2000), *TA-Projekt "Brennstoffzellen-Technologie". Endbericht*, TAB-Arbeitsbericht Nr. 67

Padró, C. E. G. and V. Putsche (1999), *Survey of the Economics of Hydrogen Technologies*

Palmer, K., W. E. Oates, and P. R. Portney (1995), Tightening Environmental Standards: The Benefit-Cost or the No-Cost Paradigm?, *Journal of Economics Perspectives* 2, 119-132.

Paquet, T. (2001), *A new Diesel Aftertreatment System for Simultaneous Reduction of NOx and Particulate Emissions. Hart 6th Annual World Fuels Conference*, Brussels, MS.

Park, J. (2002), Unbundling Globalization: Agent of Policy Convergence?, *International Studies Review* 4 (1), 230-233.

Pavitt, C. and L. Soete (1997), *The Economics of Industrial Innovation*, Cambridge.

Pearce, D. and P. Koundouri (2003), *The Social Costs of Chemicals. The Costs and Benefits of Future Chemicals Policy in the European Union*, WWF Chemicals and Health Campaign Report, London.

Pehnt, M. and J. Nitsch (2000), *Einsatzfelder und Marktchancen von Brennstoffzellen in der industriellen und öffentlichen Kraft-Wärme-Kopplung*, Conference "Brennstoffzellen...effiziente Energietechnik der Zukunft", 21/22 July, Friedrichshafen.

Pehnt, M. and S. Ramesohl (2003), *Fuel Cells for Distributed Power: Benefits, Barriers and Perspectives*, Heidelberg and Wuppertal.

Petersen, R. and H. Diaz-Bone (1998), *Das Drei-Liter-Auto*, Berlin.

Pischinger, S., J. Schnitzler, V. Scholz, and A. Wiartalla (2003), Untersuchungen zum Einsatz eines NOx-Speicherkatalysators im Pkw-Dieselmotor, *Motortechnische Zeitschrift* 3/2003, 214-221.

Pokojski, M. (2000), *The First Demonstration of a 250 kW Polymer Electrolyte Membrane (PEM) Fuel Cell for Stationary Application*, Hyforum 2000, 11-15 Sep., Munich.

Pollano, G., J. P. Sperelakis, and R. J. Seidewand (2000), *Gaining Sustainable Advantage in the Coatings and Resins Industries* http://www.pcimag.com/ CDA/Article Information/features/ BNP__Features__Item/0,1846,17202,00.html.

Porter, M. E. (1990a), *The Competitive Advantage of Nations*, New York.

Porter, M. E. (1990b), The Competitive Advantage of Nations, *Harvard Business Review* March-April, 1990, 74-87.

Porter, M. E. and C. van der Linde (1995a), *Green and Competitive: Ending the Stalemate. Harvard Business Review*: 120-134.

Porter, M. E. and C. van der Linde (1995b), Toward a New Conception of the Environment-Competitiveness Relationship, *Journal of Economic Perspectives* 9, 97-118.

Posner, M. V. (1961), International Trade and Technical Change, *Oxford Economic Papers* 13 (3)

Pucher, H. (2002), *Grundlagen der Verbrennungskraftmaschinen*, Berlin.

Reinking, G. (2003), *Im VDA bröckelt Allianz gegen Dieselfilter*. Financial Times Deutschland, 3.3.2003.

Renault (2003), *Renault Presents New Generation Particulate Filter*. Renault press release: 73rd International Geneva Motor Show 2003, 4.3.2003.

Rennings, K. (2000), *Redefining Innovation – Eco-Innovation Research and the Contribution from Ecological Economics. Ecological Economics*: 319-332.

Rentz, O., C. Röll, D. Oertel, T. Holtmann, J. Hein, and U. Karl (1993), *Minderung der VOC Emissionen in der Bundesrepublik Deutschland*, UBA Texte 11/1994, Berlin.

Resch, J. (2002), *Grundsatzpapier: Initiative "Kein Diesel ohne Filter"*, Radolfzell.

Risk and Policy Analysis (2003), *Assessment of the Impact of the New Chemicals Policy on Occupational Health. Final Report prepared for the European Commission Enterprise Directorate General*, London.

Risk and Policy Analysis and Statistics Sweden (2002), *Assessment of the Business Impact of New Regulations in the Chemicals Sector. Final Report Prepared for the European Commission Enterprise Directorate*, London.

Rohe, D. (1988), Waschmittel-Zeolith. Phosphataustausch setzt sich durch, *Chem. Ind.* (4/88), 28 ff.

Rose, R. (1993), *Lesson-Drawing in Public Policy. A Guide to Learning across Time and Space*, Chatham/NJ.

Rugman, A. M. and A. Verbeke (1998), Corporate Strategy and International Environmental Policy, *Journal of International Business Studies* 29 (4), 819-833.

Sakakibara, M. and M. Porter (2001), Competing at Home to Win Abroad: Evidence From Japanese Industry, *Review of Economics and Statistics* 83 (2), 310-322.

Scharpf, F. W. (1999), *Regieren in Europa. Effektiv und demokratisch?*, Frankfurt/New York.

Schindler, K. P. (2002), *Advances in Diesel Engine Technologies for European Passenger Vehicles. 8th Diesel Engine Emissions Reduction Conference, San Diego*, MS.

Scholz, C. M. and F. Stähler (1999), *Unilateral Environmental Policy and International Competitiveness*, 299, Tübingen.

Schwab et al. (Eds.) (2003), *The World Competitiveness Report 2002-2003*, Oxford.

Shaker Verlag (2002), *Entwicklung des wissenschaftlichen Publizierens*

Sicars, S. (1995), *Natural Fluid Based Refrigeration*, gtz Yearbook 1995 http://www.gtz.de/ proklima.

Sicars, S. (1999), *The ECOFRIG Project Support of Hydrocarbon Technology Developments in India*, Development and Trends in ODS Phase Out. Yearbook 1997-1999 http://www.gtz.de/proklima.

Siemens (2002), *Environmental Report 2002*. http://www.siemens.com/ Daten/ siecom/ HQ/ CC/ Internet/ Siemens_Corporate/ WORKAREA/ cseditor/ templatedata/ Deutsch/ file/binary/umweltbericht2002_en.pdf.

Simader, G. and T. Heissenberger (1999), *Brennstoffzellen-Systeme – Energietechnik der Zukunft? Entwicklungsstand und Perspektiven der stationären Brennstoffzellen-Technologie* http://www.eva.wsr.ac.at/publ/pdf/fuelcell.pdf.

SIRI Group (2002), *Green, social and ethical funds in Europe 2002* www.sricompass.org.

Social Investment Forum (2001), *Trends Report, After South Africa*. www.socialinvest.org/areas/resarch/trends/1995-Trends.htm.

Spanos, Y. E. and L. Spyros (2001), An Examination Into the Causal Logic of Rent Generation: Contrasting Porter's Competitive Strategy Framework and the Resource Based Perspective, *Strategic Management Journal* 22 (10), 907-934.

Sparkes (2003), *Socially Responsible Investment: a Global Revolution*, Chichester.

SRU (2002), *Umweltgutachten 2002. Für eine neue Vorreiterrolle*, Stuttgart.

Stähler, F. (1998), *Competitiveness and Environmental Policies in Strategic Environmental Policy Models*, 858, Kiel.

Stevens, C. (2000), OECD Programme on Technology and Sustainable Development, in: J. Hemmelskamp, K. Rennings and F. Leone, *Innovation-Oriented Environmental Regulation. Theoretical Approaches and Empirical Analysis,* Heidelberg and New York

Stimmig, U., M. Rzepka, and F. Ziegler (2000), *Primärenergie für die Brennstoffzelle: Quellen, Umweltbelastung und Energieverbrauch*, Die Brennstoffzelle. Zukünftige

Querschnitttechnologie für den Industriestandort Deutschland? Konferenz der Friedrich Ebert Stiftung 6.12.2000, Berlin.

Stockholm Environment Institute (1999), *Costs and Strategies Presented by Industry During the Negotiation of Environmental Regulations.* Study prepared for the Swedish Ministry of the Environment, Stockholm.

Stolten, D. and B. Höhlein (2000), *Die Brennstoffzelle. Querschnittstechnologie für den Industriestandort Deutschland,* Konferenz Die Brennstoffzelle. Zukünftige Querschnitttechnologie für den Industriestandort Deutschland? 6.12.2000, Berlin.

Strange, S. (1998), *Mad Money. When Markets Outgrew Governments*, Ann Arbor.

Sturm, A., M. Wackernagel, and K. Müller (2000), *The Winners and Losers in Global Competition. Why Eco-Efficiency Reinforces Competitiveness: A Study of 44 Nations*, Chur/Zürich.

Suranovic, S. (2002), International Labour and Environment Standards Agreements: Is this Fair Trade?, *The World Economy* 25 (2), 231-245.

Sustainable asset management (SAM) (Ed.) (2003), *Newsflash – Shell vergibt ein Mandat für die Verwaltung von Euro 100 Mio. an SAM*, Zollikon.

Taistra, G. (2000), *Die Porter-Hypothese zur Umweltpolitik*, Wiesbaden.

Takada, H. and D. Jain (1991), Cross-National Analysis of Diffusion of Consumer Durable Goods in Pacific Rim Countries, *Journal of Marketing* 55 (April), 48-54.

Takase, C. (2002), *Selected Approaches to Sustainable Public Procurement Policies,* Paper presented at an Expert Meeting on Sustainable Public Procurement in Copenhagen, www.un.org/esa/sustdev/sdissues/ consumption/spp_copenhagen.pdf MS.

Taminiau, Y. (2001), *Room for Manoeuvre. 25 Years of European Emission Regulations Culminating in the Auto-Oil-Programme Analysed from aTtechnology and Policy Perspective*, Amsterdam.

Tews, K. (2002), *Die Ausbreitung von Energie/CO2-Steuern. Internationale Stimuli und nationale Restriktionen*, FFU rep 02-08, Berlin.

Tews, K., P.-O. Busch, and H. Jörgens (2003), The Diffusion of New Policy Instruments, *European Journal of Political Research* 42 (4), 569-600.

The Boston Consulting Group (1999), *Paper and the Electronic Media: Creating Value from Uncertainty*

Theenhaus, R. and K. Bonhoff (1999), *Brennstoffzellensysteme – Ein Überblick*, Forschungsverbund Sonnenenergie – Zukunftstechnologie Brennstoffzelle. Jahrestagung vom 15-16.9.1999

UK Social Investment Forum (without year), *What Is SRI?* www.uksif.org.

Ulph, A. (1996), Strategic Environmental Policy and International Trade – The Role of Market Conduct, in: C. Carraro, Y. Katasoulacos and A. Xepapadeas, *Environmental Policy and Market Structure,* Dordrecht, 99-127.

Ulph, A. and D. Ulph (1996), Trade, Strategic Innovation and Environmental Policy and Market Structure, in: C. Carraro, Y. Katasoulacos and A. Xepapadeas, *Environmental Policy and Market Structure,* Dordrecht, 181-208.

Umweltbundesamt (1995), *Passenger Cars 2000*, Berlin.

Umweltbundesamt (1999), *Umweltfreundliche Beschaffung. 4. Auflage*, Berlin.

Umweltbundesamt (Ed.) (2000), *Ökobilanzen für graphische Papiere*, Berlin.

Umweltbundesamt (2001), *Presse-Information no. 31/01: Der Partikelfilter für Diesel-Pkw besteht den Langzeittest*, Berlin.

Umweltbundesamt (2002), *Die Lösemittelverordnung. Einführung und Vorschläge zur Umsetzung in der Praxis*, UBA Forschungsbericht 500 44 301, Berlin. www.umweltbundesamt.de.

Underdal, A. (1998), *The Politics of International Environmental Management*, Dortrecht.

Underdal, A. (2001), *International Institutions and Transnational Policy Diffusion*, Berlin Conference on the Human Dimension of Global Change: Global Environmental Change and the Nationstate. 7-8 December 2001, Berlin.

UNEP (1998), *1998 Report of the Refrigeration, Air Conditioning and Heat Pumps Technical Options Committee* http://TEAP:PUBLIC@teap.org/RTOC1998.pdf.

Union of Concerned Scientists (2002), *Clean Vehicles: Battery Electric Vehicles*, Cambridge. http://www.ucsusa.org/ clean_vehicles/ advanced_vehicles/ page.cfm?pageID=211.

United Nations (several years), *UN Statistical Yearbook*, Geneva.

Utterback, J. M. (1994), *Mastering the Dynamics of Innovation*, Boston.

van den Reek, J. A. (1999), *Reduction of CO2 Emissions by Reduction of Paper Use for Publication Applications*, Utrecht.

Vandenberg, M. (2002), *Link Between Firms and Civil Society Supporting Ethical Investment*, MS.

VCI (2003), *Ausführungen von Herrn Professor Dr. Wilhelm Simson, Präsident des Verbandes der Chemischen Industrie, am 3.7.2003 vor der Presse in Frankfurt* www.vci.de.

VDA (1998), *Annual report by Verband der Automobilindustrie e.V.*, Frankfurt a.M.

VDA (2000), *Annual report by Verband der Automobilindustrie e.V.*, Frankfurt a.M.

VDI (2001), Diesel: Auf Dauer rußfrei, *VDI Nachrichten*

Vernon, R. (1966), International Investment and International Trade in the Product Cycle, *Quarterly Review of Economics* 88 (May), 190-207.

Vernon, R. (1979), The Product Cycle Hypothesis in a New International Environment, *Oxford Bulletin of Economics and Statistics* 41 (4), 255-267.

Virta, R. L. (1995), Zeolites, *U.S. Geological Survey Minerals Yearbook – 1995,*

Virta, R. L. (2000), Zeolites, *U.S. Geological Survey Minerals Yearbook – 2000,*

Vitovec, W., H. Puxbaum, and R. Knienider (1998), *Die ökologischen Auswirkungen der Lösemittelverordnungen 1991 und 1995. Studie im Auftrag des Fachverbandes der Chemischen Industrie Österreichs*, Vienna. http://fcio.at/home/publikationen/voc2.pdf.

Vogel, D. (1995), *Trading Up. Consumer and Environmental Regulation in a Global Economy*, Cambridge, London.

Vogel, D. (1999), *Environmental Regulation and Economic Integration. Workshop on Regulatory Competition and Economic Integration: Comparative Perspectives*

Volkery, A. and K. Jacob (2003), *Pioneers in Environmental Policy Making. Konferenzbericht*, FFU rep 03-04, Berlin.

Von der Weiden, S. (2002), Automobil: Ford und PSA-Konzern entwickeln gemeinsam neues Verfahren zur Schadstoffreduktion von Pkw-Motoren, *VDI Nachrichten* (12.4.2002), 16.

Vratsanos, L. A. (2001), *Meeting the Challenge of Formulating for the Future. Paper, presented at the International Coatings Exposition, Nov. 5, 2001*, Atlanta, http://www.airproducts.com/polymers/PDF2/TP_151-0262.pdf MS.

Wachter, W. (2002), *Die Umweltrelevanz des Dieselmotors*, Graz.

Walsh, M. P. (2000), *Overview of Worldwide Regulation of Diesel Vehicle and Engine Emissions. Corning Diesel Symposium, Germany*

Watanabe, C., K. Wakabayashi, and T. Miyazawa (2000), Industrial Dynamism and the Creation of a Virtuous Cycle Between R&D, Market Growth and Price Reduction – The Case of Photovoltaic Power Generation (PV) Development in Japan, *Technovation* 20, 299-312.

Weidner, H. and M. Jänicke (Eds.) (2002), *Capacity Building in National Environmental Policy. A Comparative Study of 17 Countries*, Berlin.

Wengel, J., E. Schirrmeister, and F. Marscheider-Weidemann (2000), *Industrielle Kernkompetenzen und Beschäftigung: Brauchen wir die Brennstoffzelle für die Wettbewerbsfähigkeit des Industriestandorts Deutschland?*, Die Brennstoffzelle. Zukünftige Querschnitttechnologie für den Industriestandort Deutschland? Konferenz der Friedrich Ebert Stiftung 6.12.2000, Berlin.

Westfalenpost (2003), *HJS verkaufte Rechte für Diesel-Partikelfilter*. Westfalenpost, 21.5.2003.

Wheeler, D. (2001), Racing to the Bottom? Foreign Investment and Air Pollution in Developing Countries, *Journal of Environment and Development* 10 (3), 225-245.

Wichmann, E. (2003), *Abschätzung positiver gesundheitlicher Wirkungen durch den Einsatz des Partikelfilters bei Dieselfahrzeugen in Deutschland. Gutachten im Auftrag des UBA*, Berlin.

World Bank, GTZ and Swiss Agency for Development and Cupertino SDC (1996), *Assessment of the Prospects for Hydrocarbon Technology in the global Domestic Refrigeration Market* http://www.hychill.com/pdf/worldbnk.pdf.

World Economic Forum (2003), *The Global Information Technology Report 2002-2003: Readiness for the Networked World*, Geneva.

World Trade Organisation (1999), *Trade and Environment*, Special Studies 4, Geneva.

Wurzel, R. (2002), *Environmental Policy-Making in Britain, Germany and the European Union. The Europeanisation of Air and Water Pollution Control*, Manchester, New York.

Wüst, C. (2000), Selbstmord geht nicht mehr. Peugeot führt Partikelfilter ein und bringt die Branche in Argumentationsnot, *Der Spiegel* 44/2000

Young, O. (2002), *The Institutional Dimension of Environmental Change: Fit, Interplay and Scale*, Cambridge, MA.

Zeodet – Association of Detergent Zeolites Producers (2000), *Zeolites for Detergents – as Nature Intended*, Brussels. http://www.zeodet.org/downloads/Zeolites.pdf.

Zürn, M. (1998), *Regieren jenseits des Nationalstaats. Globalisierung und Denationalisierung als Chance*, Frankfurt a.M.

Interviews

Interviews were conducted with the following individuals and ACEA in connection with this case study:

ACEA	Association des Constructeurs Européens d'Automobiles
Ambrosi, Nikolaus	Renault
Demmel, Anton	ADAC
Glück, Karl-Heinz	OMG
Feth, Gerd Gregor	Frankfurter Allgemeine Zeitung

Giesen, Norbert	DaimlerChrysler
Greening, Paul	DG Industry, European Commission
Hennen, Isfried	Ford
Hohenthal, Moritz von	Motortechnische Zeitschrift
Lange, Bernhard	Member of the EU Parliament
Metz, Norbert	BMW Group
Mönch, Lars	German Federal Environmental Agency
Naschke, Wolfgang	Rhodia
Resch, Jürgen	Deutsche Umwelthilfe
Mr Rippe	Corning
Rodt, Stefan	German Federal Environmental Agency
Schalberger, Thomas	Peugeot
Skibbe, Alexander	Volkswagen
Dr Scherm	Engelhard
Dr Stöpler	Faurecia
Mr Stüttem	Zeuna Stärker
Taschner, Carola	European Environmental Bureau
Teubner, Klaus	Eberspächer
Tölkes, Elvira	Opel
Treiber, Peter	Emitec
Vogt, Claus Dieter	NGK

Inquiries were also made with the press offices at the following automobile companies and with representatives from these companies (who requested to remain unnamed):
Audi, BMW, DaimlerChrysler, Ford, Opel, Toyota

Druck: betz-druck GmbH, D-64291 Darmstadt
Verarbeitung: Buchbinderei Schäffer, D-67269 Grünstadt